pv

NAPOLEON
ON NAPOLEON

Napoleon in 1799, wearing the uniform of the Institute, the year he was appointed a consul following the coup of Brumaire, from the engraving of the portrait by Jean Baptiste Guerin.

NAPOLEON ON NAPOLEON

AN AUTOBIOGRAPHY OF THE EMPEROR

EDITED BY
SOMERSET DE CHAIR

The English in general know nothing of the affairs of the Continent, particularly those of France.

All my laws were liberal, even those concerning conscription and the state prisons: the people were never my enemies, in any country.

The favourable opportunity must be seized, for fortune is female – if you balk her today, you must not expect to meet with her again tomorrow.

Napoleon

BROCKHAMPTON PRESS
LONDON

FROM THE ORIGINAL EDITION

For my late son Peter Dudley Somerset de Chair
1939–1962

Somerset de Chair and the publisher would like to thank
Roy Gasson for his invaluable help with the text.

Cassell
Wellington House, 125 Strand, London, WC2R 0BB

First published 1992

This edition published 1998 by Brockhampton Press,
a member of Hodder Headline PLC Group

ISBN 1 86019 8767

Distributed in Australia

British Library Cataloguing-in-Publication Data
Napoleon 1 *Emperor of the French 1769–1821*
Napoleon on Napoleon: An autobiography of an Emperor.
1. France. Napoleon 1, Emperor of the French, 1769–1821
I. Title II. De Chair, Somerset 1911–
944.05092

Typeset by Litho Link Ltd, Welshpool, Powys, Wales

Printed at Oriental Press, Dubai, U.A.E.

CONTENTS

NAPOLEONIC TITLES   *Page 8*
redividing Europe

THE BONAPARTE MARRIAGES   *Page 10*
the new alliances

CHRONOLOGY OF EVENTS   *Page 12*

EDITOR'S FOREWORD   *Page 17*

NAPOLEON'S INTRODUCTION   *Page 20*
the nature of history, conquest, and empire

I   CORSICA   *Page 47*
family history, childhood, and the English occupation of Corsica

II   SUPPER AT BEAUCAIRE, 1793   *Page 59*
the revolt of Marseilles

III   TOULON   *Page 71*
defeating the English fleet

IV   13 VENDÉMIAIRE   *Page 84*
the whiff of grapeshot: General of the Army of the Interior

CONTENTS

V   THE BATTLE OF ARCOLE   *Page 94*
defeat of the Austrian Army

VI   INTO EGYPT   *Page 107*
capture of Alexandria: conversion to Islam

VII   THE BATTLE OF ABOUKIR   *Page 113*
the loss of the French fleet

VIII   SYRIA   *Page 126*
the seige of Acre: negotiations with Constantinople

IX   18 BRUMAIRE   *Page 135*
rise of the first consul: end of the revolution

X   THE ARREST AND EXECUTION OF THE DUKE
D'ENGHIEN   *Page 157*
Bonaparte's orders: the arrest

XI   POLITICAL CRIMES   *Page 165*
'My hands . . . were never stained with guilt.'

XII   BERNADOTTE   *Page 168*
from general to King of Sweden

XIII   OVERTURES FOR PEACE IN 1800   *Page 172*
rejection by England: why the war had to continue

XIV   THE REBELLION OF TOUSSAINT-LOUVERTURE   *Page 175*
'Brave Blacks, remember that France alone acknowledges your liberty!'

XV   RELATIONS WITH THE POPE   *Page 185*
Concordat 1801: annexation of papal land 1808: annexation of the states of Rome 1810

XVI   THE NOBILITY   *Page 196*
not contrary to equality: the legion of honour

XVII   PRISON REFORM   *Page 200*
changing the criminal law: the need for civil liberty

XVIII   AUSTERLITZ   *Page 204*
the Russians defeated

CONTENTS

XIX   WAYS OF WAR   *Page 207*
inspiring troops: different types of campaign

XX DIVORCE FROM JOSEPHINE   *Page 210*
a painful sacrifice: negotiating a new marriage

XXI   WAR IN SPAIN AND RUSSIA   *Page 216*
tactical failures: the courage of the enemy

XXII   THE RETURN FROM MOSCOW   *Page 223*
changes in the weather: return to Paris

XXIII   THE BATTLE OF LEIPZIG   *Page 228*
Saxon treachery: Allied demands

XXIV   ABDICATION 1814   *Page 237*
'I voluntarily yielded myself up . . . .'

XXV   THE RETURN FROM ELBA   *Page 240*
1 100 men become 40 000: the Congress in discord: war resumes

XXVI   THE BATTLE OF MONT-ST-JEAN (WATERLOO)   *Page 254*
orders are given: the arrival of Blücher: defeat

XXVII   FINAL OBSERVATIONS   *Page 278*

INDEX   *Page 286*

Napoleonic Titles

Redividing Europe

Joseph Bonaparte *King of Naples and King of Spain*
Louis Bonaparte *King of Holland*
Jérôme Bonaparte *King of Westphalia*
Caroline Bonaparte *Queen of Naples*
Eugène de Beauharnais *Viceroy of Italy*
Hortense de Beauharnais *Queen of Holland*
Joachim Murat *King of Naples*

Augereau, Pierre François Charles *Duke of Castiglione*
Bernadotte, Jean Baptiste Jules *Prince of Pontecorvo and Crown Prince (later King) of Sweden*
Berthier, Louis Alexandre *Prince of Neuchâtel and Prince of Wagram*
Bessières, Jean Baptiste *Duke of Istria*
Caulaincourt, Armand Augustin Louis de *Duke of Vicenza*
Champagny, Jean Baptiste Nompère de *Duke of Cadore*
Clarke, Henri Jacques Guillaume *Duke of Feltre*
Davout, Louis Nicolas *Duke of Auerstädt and Prince of Eckmühl*
Drouet, Jean Baptiste *Count of Erlon*
Duroc, Géraud Christophe Michel *Duke of Friuli*
Fouché, Joseph *Duke of Otrante*
Junot, Andoche *Duke of Abrantes*
Kellerman, François Christophe *Duke of Valmy*
Lannes, Jean *Duke of Montebello*

Lefebvre, Pierre François Joseph *Duke of Danzig*
Macdonald, Jacques Etienne Joseph Alexandre *Duke of Taranto*
Maret, Hugues Bernard *Duke of Bassano*
Marmont, Auguste Frédéric Louis Viesse de *Duke of Ragusa*
Masséna, André *Duke of Rivoli and Prince of Essling*
Moncey, Bon Adrien Jeannot de *Duke of Conegliano*
Mortier, Edouard Adolphe Gasimir Joseph *Duke of Treviso*
Mouton *Count of Lobau*
Ney, Michel *Duke of Elchingen and Prince of the Moskowa*
Oudinot, Nicolas Charles *Duke of Reggio*
Savary, Anne Jean Marie René *Duke of Rovigo*
Soult, Nicolas Jean de Dieu *Duke of Dalmatia*
Suchet, Louis Gabriel *Duke of Albufera*
Talleyrand-Périgord, Charles Maurice de *Prince of Benevento*
Victor, Claud Perrin *Duke of Belluno*

THE BONAPARTE MARRIAGES

THE NEW ALLIANCES

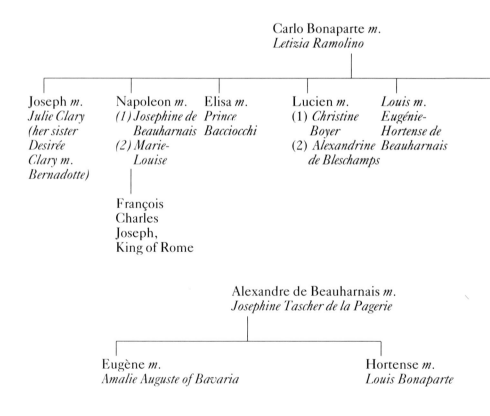

Carlo Bonaparte *m.*
Letizia Ramolino

Joseph *m.*
Julie Clary
(her sister
Desirée
Clary m.
Bernadotte)

Napoleon *m.*
(1) Josephine de
Beauharnais
(2) Marie-
Louise

Elisa *m.*
Prince
Bacciocchi

Lucien *m.*
(1) Christine
Boyer
(2) Alexandrine
de Bleschamps

Louis *m.*
Eugénie-
Hortense de
Beauharnais

François
Charles
Joseph,
King of Rome

Alexandre de Beauharnais *m.*
Josephine Tascher de la Pagerie

Eugène *m.*
Amalie Auguste of Bavaria

Hortense *m.*
Louis Bonaparte

Pauline *m.*   Caroline *m.*   Jérôme *m.*
(1) Charles   Joachim Murat   (1) Elizabeth
Leclerc   Patterson
(2) Prince   (2) Catherine of
Camillo   Württemberg
Borghese

LEFT *Louis Bonaparte, King of Holland, in 1806. He abdicated in 1810
rather than comply with his brother's demands. His son later became
Napoleon III.*

RIGHT *Eugénie-Hortense de Beauharnais, wife of Louis Bonaparte,
King of Holland.*

CHRONOLOGY OF EVENTS

1768
Corsica reunited with France.

1769
15 August: Napoleon, second son of Carlo Bonaparte and Letizia Ramolino, born at Ajaccio, Corsica.

1774
10 May: Louis XVI ascends throne of France.

1779
Napoleon admitted to the *Ecole Militaire* in Brienne.

1784
Napoleon chosen for the *Ecole Militaire* in Paris.

1785
Death of Carlo Bonaparte.
Napoleon receives his first posting, to Valence, as a second-lieutenant in a regiment of artillery.

1789
Start of the French Revolution.
5 May: Estates-General assembles at Versailles.
14 July: Fall of the Bastille.

26 August: Declaration of the Rights of Man.
September: Napoleon returns to Corsica on leave.

1790

Napoleon active in the political life of Corsica.

1791

January: Napoleon joins the Jacobins.
February: He rejoins his regiment.
20 June: Flight of the French royal family to Varennes.
October: Napoleon returns to Corsica.

1792

Napoleon active as a Jacobin politician in Corsica, except during the period May to August, when he was in Paris.
10 August: Napoleon witnesses the storming of the Tuileries.

1793

21 January: Louis XVI guillotined.
11 June: Having lost the political struggle against Paoli, the Corsican separatist, the Bonaparte family takes refuge in mainland France.
September–December: Napoleon distinguishes himself at the siege of Toulon.
22 December: He is appointed general of brigade by Robespierre.

1794

February: Napoleon appointed commander of artillery in the Army of Italy.
27 July: The fall of Robespierre.
8 August: Napoleon arrested, but released through the intervention of his patron, Saliceti.

1795

5 October: Napoleon turns his cannon on insurgents besieging the National Convention in Paris.

1796

8 March: Napoleon marries Barras' ex-mistress, Josephine, widow of the Viscount de Beauharnais.
11 March: He is appointed Commander-in-Chief of the Army of Italy.

1797

4 September: Coup d'état of 18 Fructidor.
17 October: Treaty of Campo Formio with Austria ends the first Italian campaign. France obtains Belgium, the Ionian Islands, and Lombardy.

1798
19 May: Napoleon sails from Toulon to invade Egypt.
1 August: French fleet defeated by Nelson at battle of the Nile.

1799
10 May: Napoleon's final assault on Acre is repulsed.
25 July: He defeats Turkish army at Aboukir.
22 August: He sets sail back to France, landing 9 October.
9 November: Napoleon's *coup d'état* of 18 Brumaire establishes the Consulate.

1800
19 February: Napoleon installs himself at the Tuileries.
May–June: His second Italian campaign.
14 June: Austrians routed at Marengo.

1801
9 February: Napoleon signs the Treaty of Luneville with Austria.
10 September: He concludes Concordat with the Pope.

1802
25 March: Treaty of Amiens signed with Great Britain.
2 August: Napoleon made Consul for life and given right to choose his successor.

1803
18 May: The British break the Treaty of Amiens and declare war.
Napoleon plans the invasion of Britain.

1804
20–21 March: Kidnap and execution of the Duc d'Enghien.
21 March: Promulgation of the Civil Code.
18 May: The Senate confers upon Napoleon the title of Emperor.
2 December: Napoleon's coronation at Notre Dame by Pope Pius VII.

1805
July–August: European coalition formed between Great Britain, Russia, Sweden, and Austria.
20 October: Austria surrenders at Ulm.
21 October: The French fleet under Villeneuve is defeated by Nelson at Trafalgar.
13 November: Napoleon enters Vienna.
2 December: He defeats the Austro-Russian armies at Austerlitz.
26 December: Treaty of Pressburg with Austria.

1806
12 July: Napoleon forms the states of southern Germany into the Confederation of the Rhine under French protection.
September: New alliance between Russia, Prussia, Great Britain, and Sweden.
14 October: Napoleon defeats the Prussians at Jena and at Auerstadt.
27 October: He enters Berlin.
21 November: The Berlin Decree closes continental ports against British imports (the Continental System).
16 December: The French make their entry into Warsaw.

1807
8 February: Battle of Eylau.
24 May: Taking of Danzig.
14 June: Russians defeated at Friedland.
7 July: Peace of Tilsit with Tsar Alexander.
27 October: By the Treaty of Fontainebleu France and Spain agree on a joint invasion of Portugal.

1808
March: Occupation of Spain. Joseph, Napoleon's brother, placed on the throne.
2 May: Insurrection in Madrid against the French occupation.
22 July: General Dupont surrenders at Bailén to the Spanish.
21 August: Wellesley defeats the French at Vimeiro.
27 September–14 October: Congress of Erfurt between Russia and France.
4 December: Napoleon enters Madrid to re-establish Joseph on the Spanish throne.

1809
9 April: The Austrians invade Bavaria.
22 April: Napoleon defeats the Austrians at Eckmühl.
6 July: He defeats the Austrians at Wagram.
14 October: Treaty of Schonbrünn between Austria and France.
15 December: Napoleon divorces Josephine.

1810
22 April: Napoleon marries the Archduchess Marie-Louise of Austria.
27 September: Wellington defeats the French at Bussaco.

1811
20 March: Birth of Napoleon's son, who is given the title of King of Rome.

1812
May: Napoleon invades Russia.
23 October: General Malet's abortive *coup d'état* in Paris.

1813

Coalition between Russia, Prussia, Great Britain, Sweden, and Austria.
2 May: Napoleon defeats the Russo-Prussian army at Lützen.
20–21 May: . . . and at Bautzen.
16–18 October: Napoleon defeated at Leipzig.

1814

1 January: The Allies cross the Rhine and invade France.
31 March: The Allies march into Paris.
11 April: Napoleon abdicates at Fontainebleu.
20 April: He bids farewell to the Guard and departs for Elba.
5 May: Louis XVIII arrives in Paris.
1 November: Congress of Vienna opens.

1815

26 February: Napoleon escapes from Elba.
1 March: He lands at Golfe Juan.
20 March: . . . and is back in Paris. Louix XVIII having fled to Ghent.
18 June: He is defeated at Waterloo.
22 June: He abdicated for the second time, intending to leave for America.
15 July: Having surrendered to the British, he boards the *Bellerophon* and is taken to Plymouth Sound.
7 August: Leaves on the *Northumberland* for exile on St Helena.

1821

5 May: Napoleon dies on St Helena.

EDITOR'S FOREWORD

HISTORY and literature alike are indebted to Napoleon's exile on St Helena.

Without the leisure (if such it may be called) that he enjoyed on the island – which he would never have enjoyed had he remained Emperor of France – he would have had neither the opportunity nor the desire to give us his own account of his own era. Thus the British, by tying him, like Prometheus, to his rock in the South Atlantic, gave a powerful impetus to the Napoleonic legend that inspired the Second Empire of his nephew Napoleon III.

The entourage that accompanied Napoleon to St Helena consisted of General Henri-Gratien Bertrand and his wife (who, according to Napoleon, provided him with small favours); General Charles-Tristan de Montholon and his wife; the former naval captain Emmanuel de Las Cases and his twelve-year-old son Emmanuel; and General Gaspard Gourgaud.

Madame Bertrand, who was half-English, half creole (and related on the creole side to the Empress Josephine), was described by an English lady on the island as 'a most engaging, fascinating woman' of 'interesting appearance; her eyes black, sparkling, soft, and animated'. When she had heard that Napoleon was to be exiled to St Helena, Madame Bertrand had flung herself into his cabin on the *Northumberland* and tried to drown herself by throwing herself through the cabin window. She was restrained by her husband, who grabbed her by the ankles, while General Savary (who wanted to accompany Napoleon but was forbidden to go), between fits of laughter, shouted unsympathetically, 'Let her go!'. While on St Helena Madame Bertrand presented her husband with a baby, whom she introduced to Napoleon as the first visitor to arrive on the island without the permission of Lord Bathurst, the British secretary of state for war! The quiet, unassuming Madame de Montholon, who entertained Napoleon by playing the piano and singing to him, says that she lived through their long captivity in complete harmony with this tall, spirited, seductive creature.

Four of these companions became the amanuenses to whom Napoleon dictated his memoirs and commentaries. They were Las Cases, who left early, expelled from St Helena in 1816; Gourgaud, who left later, in 1818; and Montholon and Bertrand, who both stayed to the end, until Napoleon's death in 1821. Napoleon never edited his own words or put them in any sort of order. Instead, Montholon and Gourgaud, on their return to Europe, published whatever they had happened to take down from Napoleon's dictation. This absolutely chaotic production, published in 1823 in London and Paris, was never resurrected in Britain until my own edition appeared well over a century later.

Napoleon's residence on St Helena was Longwood – a long, low, white house built of wood, which had formerly been a row of cattle stalls. Here he was attended by his own valet, Constant, and by other servants – he had what would seem by modern standards to be a comfortably large domestic staff, for there were fifty-one persons on the ration strength at Longwood. Among them were Chinese gardeners and a Corsican general factotum, Santini, who acted as Napoleon's tailor, barber, and gamekeeper, but who failed totally to control the plague of rats at Longwood. There was also an Irish doctor, Barry O'Meara, who was later replaced by a useless Corsican doctor, Francesco Antommarchi.

O'Meara published, in 1822, his own book, *A Voice from St Helena*, and Antommarchi followed, in 1825, with his *Les derniers moments de Napoléon*. Both Gourgaud and Montholon published, as well as the *Memoires*, their own journals. Bertrand's memoirs have recently been discovered and throw a vivid light on the agonizing symptoms of Napoleon's last illness, the stomach cancer that killed him.

In this book, though, it is only Napoleon himself who speaks, through the words he dictated to members of his entourage.

I have visited all the principal battlefields that Napoleon describes, from Toulon to Acre. I have seen Lobau (that flat island in the Danube, swept by Austrian gunfire, where Marshal Lannes was wounded and died in Napoleon's arms), Wagram, Bailén (the turning point in Napoleon's fortunes, where General Dupont surrendered to the Spaniards in 1808), the Somosierra pass, north of Madrid (where Napoleon launched a Polish squadron uphill to capture the Spanish guns), and, of course, the Château of Hougoumont and the field of Waterloo.

In the high summer of 1933 I climbed through the Ligurian foothills to that ridge commanding the valleys of the Bormida where, between Montenotte and Millesimo, Napoleon won his first and perhaps most brilliant battles. I drifted lazily across the plain of Lombardy – visiting Marengo, Lodi, Rivoli, and Castiglione. I went to Arcole, a little village drowsing in the hot Lombardy sunshine, where a narrow, rusted iron bridge spans a dyke with precipitous grass sides. On the farther bank is a square grey house, from the windows of which, in 1796, Austrian guns swept a little stone bridge with grapeshot, as Napoleon fought shoulder to shoulder with the bravest in the Army of Italy to get across it. Standing there, I could picture him, only twenty-seven years old, a tiny figure in general's uniform, his skin still pale and taut from his poverty and illness in Paris before 13 Vendémiaire, his brown hair hanging down to his shoulders, the hard glitter of ambition in his eyes. He himself has described what happened:

> I determined to try a last effort in person. I seized a flag, rushed on the bridge, and planted it there. The column I commanded reached the middle of the bridge, but then flanking fire and the arrival of a division of the enemy frustrated the attack. The grenadiers at the head of the column, finding themselves abandoned by the rear, hesitated, but were swept away in the flight. They persisted, though, in holding on to their general; they seized me by my arms and by my clothes and dragged me along with them amidst the dead, the dying, and the smoke. I was precipitated into a morass, in which I sunk up to the waist, surrounded by the enemy. The grenadiers saw that I was in danger; the cry went up, 'Forward, soldiers, to save the general!' These brave men immediately turned back, ran upon the enemy, drove him beyond the bridge, and saved me. This was a day of devoted military service. Lannes had hastened from Milan; he had been wounded at Governolo and was still suffering, but he threw himself between me and the enemy, covering me with his body, and received three wounds, determined never to abandon me.

As I stood on the bridge, looking down into the dyke into which Napoleon had been swept, some urchins of Fascist Italy gathered around me, pointing to the small obelisk that commemorated the battle. And one of them said, proudly, of his village, *Piccola, ma grande* – 'Little, but great' – for at Arcole the Napoleonic legend was born.

Somerset de Chair

St Osyth Priory
Essex

Author's Note on the Dedication

When the Folio Societ wanted to publish a new edition of my translation of the latter part of *Napoleon's Memoirs* under the title of *The Waterloo Campaign*, I asked Peter, who was studying the Napoleonic period at school, to prepare the maps for it. I handed over the royalties from the Folio Society to him, and was amused to learn that he had transferred the task to his history tutor, and half the money.

Owing to the low-lying conditions near the river at Eton, my son contracted rheumatic fever and two valves of his heart were burnt out. This was before the breakthrough in heart surgery by Dr Barnard. He never fully recovered, as his brain was starved of blood. In the gathering darkness of his mind he faced death face to face, and shot himself on the night of December 9th, 1962.

Had he been allowed to live, he would have relished the completed autobiography of the emperor, presented in these pages, and I have therefore dedicated them to his memory.

Napoleon's Introduction

THE NATURE OF HISTORY, CONQUEST, AND EMPIRE

NATIONS, like individuals, have their different ages – infancy, strength and decay. A national government is one that arises and maintains itself independently of foreign force. Property, municipal laws, the love of country, and religion are the bonds of every species of government. Should a victorious army ever enter London, the world would be astonished at the trifling resistance that would be offered by the English.

When the Russians gain possession of Constantinople, they will retain there as many Muslims as they think fit, by securing them their property and tolerating their religion. The Moors of Spain submitted to everything, even to the Inquisition. All indirect means to expel them failed; in the end Ferdinand and Isabella[1] had to order them out.

A modern Turkish army is a thing of very little importance; the Ottomans will not be able to hold their ground in Asia Minor, Syria, or Egypt, when once the Russians have taken possession of Constantinople as well as the Crimea, the Rioni, and the shores of the Caspian Sea. Neither the patriotism of the people nor the policy of the courts of Europe prevented the partition of Poland or the despoilment of several other nations, and they will not prevent the fall of the Ottoman empire. Maria Theresa[2] entered into the conspiracy against Poland, a nation placed at the entrance of Europe, only unwillingly, to defend it from the northern nations. Vienna feared the consequent aggrandisement of Russia, but

---

[1] Ferdinand II (1452–1516) and Isabella I (1474–1504), joint rulers of Castile and Aragon, spent most of their reign fighting the Moors in Spain.

[2] Maria Theresa (1717–80), Archduchess of Austria and Queen of Hungary and Bohemia, joined with Russia and Prussia in dividing up Poland in 1772.

---

felt great satisfaction, nevertheless, at acquiring several million souls and enriching its treasury by many millions. Austria would in the same manner feel averse, at the present day, to the partition of Turkey, but would nevertheless consent to it – it would increase her vast dominions by adding to them Serbia, Bosnia, and the ancient Illyrian provinces, of which Vienna was formerly the capital. What will England and France do then? One of them will take Egypt – a poor compensation! A statesman of the first order used to say, 'Whenever I hear of fleets sailing under the Greek cross, casting anchor under the walls of the Seraglio, I seem to hear a cry prophetic of the fall of the empire of the Crescent.'

Asia and Europe differ greatly in their territorial circumstances. The deserts that rim Asia are inhabited by populous nations of barbarians, who breed a great quantity of horses and camels. The Scythians, the Arabs, the Tartars, under the caliphs, the Genghis Khans, Tamerlanes, and others, emerged from those immense wildernesses and swamped the plains of Persia, the Euphrates, Asia Minor, Syria, and Egypt with millions of cavalry. These conquests were rapid, because they were undertaken by whole populations inured to war and

Bust of Napoleon, modelled in Egypt and later cut in marble in France.

accustomed to the hard, frugal life of the desert. But Europe, inhabited from north to south and from east to west by civilized nations, is not exposed to similar revolutions.

Every offensive war is a war of invasion; every well-conducted war is methodical. Defensive war does not preclude attack, any more than offensive war is necessarily exclusive of defence, although its object is to force the frontier and invade the territory of the enemy. The principles of war are those that have ruled the great captains whose deeds have been handed down to us by history: Alexander, Hannibal, Caesar, Gustavus Adolphus, Turenne, Prince Eugène, Frederick the Great,[1] and others.

Alexander conducted eight campaigns, during which he conquered Asia and part of India; Hannibal, seventeen, one in Spain, fifteen in Italy, and one in Africa; Caesar, thirteen, eight against the Gauls and five against Pompey's legions; Gustavus Adolphus, three, one in Livonia against the Russians, and two in Germany against Austria; Turenne commanded in eighteen, nine in France and nine in Germany; Prince Eugène in thirteen, two against the Turks, five in Italy against France, and six on the Rhine or in Flanders; Frederick conducted eleven, in Silesia, in Bohemia, and on the banks of the Elbe. A meticulously written history of these eighty-eight[2] campaigns would be a complete treatise on the art of war from which would flow spontaneously the principles that should be followed in both offensive and defensive war.

ALEXANDER

Alexander crossed the Dardanelles in 334 BC with an army of about 40,000 men, of which an eighth part was cavalry. He forced the passage of the Granicus, which was defended by an army under Memnon, a Greek, who commanded on the coasts of Asia for Darius, and then spent the whole of the year 333 in establishing his power in Asia Minor. He was supported by Sardis, Ephesus, Tarsus, Miletus, and other Greek colonies on the shores of the Black Sea and Mediterranean. His conquest of the Persian Empire was made easier because it was not one nation but a confederation of states in which the provinces and cities governed

[1] Napoleon discusses the careers of three of his seven 'great captains' in some detail (pp. 22–29) and, of the others, Frederick the Great of Prussia (1712–86) is a household name who needs no footnote. The remaining three are: Gustavus Adolphus (1594–1632), King of Sweden, who fought against Denmark and Russia and supported the Protestant cause in the Thirty Years War against the Catholic armies of the Holy Roman Empire, the Vicomte de Turenne (1611–75), French marshal, who also fought against the Empire during the Thirty Years War and afterwards commanded Louis XIV's armies against the Spanish Netherlands, the Palatinate, and Alsace; and Prince Eugène of Savoy (1663–1736), French-born soldier and statesman in the service of Austria, who fought against the Turks and in the War of the Spanish Succession and was largely responsible for making Austria a power in Europe.

[2] Napoleon's arithmetic is at fault; the total is eighty-three.

themselves by their own peculiar laws. Alexander, who wanted only the Persian throne, easily appropriated the rights of sovereignty to himself, because he respected the usages, manners, and laws of the people, who suffered no change of condition.

In the year 332 he encountered Darius,[1] at the head of 600,000 men, occupying a position at Issus, near Tarsus. He defeated him, entered Syria, and took Damascus, where the Great King's treasures were deposited. Then he laid siege to Tyre, but that proud metropolis of world trade held out against him for nine months.

He took Gaza, after a two-month siege, crossed the desert in seven days, entered Pelusium and Memphis, and founded Alexandria. He met with no obstacle, because Syria and Egypt were always linked by common interest with the Greeks; because the Arab nations, for religious reasons, hated the Persians; and finally because the Greek troops of the satraps joined the Macedonians. In less than two years, after two battles and four or five sieges, he conquered the coasts of the Black Sea, from the Phasis to Byzantium, and of the Mediterranean as far as Alexandria, as well as all Asia Minor, Syria, and Egypt.

In 331 he retraced his steps across the desert, encamped at Tyre, passed through Syria, entered Damascus, crossed the Euphrates and Tigris, and on the plains of Arbela defeated Darius, who was advancing against him at the head of an army even more numerous than that of Issus. Babylon opened its gates to him. In 330 he forced the pass of Susa and took that town, Persepolis, and Pasargadae, where the tomb of Cyrus was.[2] In 329 he turned northward, entered Ecbatana, and extended his conquests to the Caspian Sea; punished Bessus,[3] the vile assassin of Darius; and penetrated into Scythia and defeated the Scythians. It was in this campaign that he brought shame upon his many trophies by having Parmenio[4] murdered. In 328 he forced the passage of the Oxus, received 16,000 recruits from Macedon, and subdued the neighbouring nations; in this year, too, killed Cleitus[5] with his own hand and required the Macedonians to worship him, which they refused to do. In 327 he crossed the Indus, defeated Porus[6] in a

---

[1] Darius III, 'Great King' of Persia, 336–330 BC.

[2] Cyrus the Great (c.585–c.529 BC), creator of a Persian Empire stretching from the Aegean to the Indus.

[3] Bessus was one of Darius's satraps; after murdering Darius he usurped the Persian throne as Artaxerxes IV.

[4] Parmenio had been Alexander's second-in-command in the conquest of Persia. Alexander had him assassinated because his son, Philotas, another of Alexander's generals, had been executed for treason.

[5] Cleitus, another of Alexander's generals, was murdered by Alexander after he had, at a banquet, criticized Alexander for adopting eastern manners and morals.

[6] Porus ruled over lands in the Indus valley; after Alexander reinstated him in his kingdom, he remained a supporter until his death in c. 315 BC.

MEMOIRS

OF THE

HISTORY OF FRANCE

DURING THE REIGN OF

NAPOLEON,

DICTATED BY THE EMPEROR

AT SAINT HELENA

TO THE GENERALS WHO SHARED HIS CAPTIVITY;

AND PUBLISHED

FROM THE ORIGINAL MANUSCRIPTS

CORRECTED BY HIMSELF.

HISTORICAL MISCELLANIES.

VOL. I.

DICTATED TO THE COUNT DE MONTHOLON.

LONDON:

PRINTED FOR HENRY COLBURN AND CO.

AND MARTIN BOSSANGE AND CO.

1823.

MEMOIRS

OF THE

HISTORY OF FRANCE

DURING THE REIGN OF

NAPOLEON,

DICTATED BY THE EMPEROR

AT SAINT HELENA

TO THE GENERALS WHO SHARED HIS CAPTIVITY;

AND PUBLISHED

FROM THE ORIGINAL MANUSCRIPTS

CORRECTED BY HIMSELF.

VOL. I.

DICTATED TO GENERAL GOURGAUD,

HIS AIDE-DE-CAMP.

LONDON.

PRINTED FOR HENRY COLBURN AND CO.

AND MARTIN BOSSANGE AND CO.

1823.

Title page to Napoleon's Memoirs, *1823, dictated to Montholon*
(3 volumes of notes and miscellany).

Title page to the Memoirs, 1823, dictated to General Gourgaud (4 volumes of memoirs).

pitched battle and took him prisoner, but treated him as a king. He intended to cross the Ganges, but his army mutinied. In 326 he sailed down the Indus with 800 ships; on reaching the sea he sent Nearchus,[1] with a fleet, to explore the coast as far as the mouth of the Euphrates. In 325 he spent sixty days crossing the desert of Gedrosia, entered Kerman, returned to Pasargadae, Persepolis, and Susa, and married Stateira,[2] one of Darius's daughters. In 324 he marched northward again and returned to Ecbatana; he died, poisoned, at Babylon.

Alexander made war methodically, in a way that deserves the highest praise. None of his convoys were ever intercepted. His armies constantly kept increasing – at their weakest when he commenced operations at the Granicus, by the time he arrived at the Indus their numbers had tripled (and this leaves out of the reckoning the corps commanded by the governors of the conquered provinces, which were composed of invalid or wearied Macedonians, recruits sent from Greece or drawn from the Greek troops in the service of the satraps, or native levies from conquered lands). Alexander merits the glory he has enjoyed for so many ages among all nations. But suppose he had been defeated at Issus, where the army of Darius was drawn up across his line of retreat, with its left to the mountains and its right to the sea; while the Macedonians had their right toward the mountains, their left toward the sea, and the pass called the Cilician Gates behind them! Or suppose he had been beaten at Arbela, when he had the Tigris, the Euphrates, and the deserts in his rear, no fortresses within reach, and was nine hundred leagues from Macedon! Or suppose he had been driven back to the Indus and vanquished by Porus!

HANNIBAL

In 218 BC Hannibal left Cartagena, crossed the Ebro, the Pyrenees (mountains previously unknown to the Carthaginian arms), the Rhône, and the farther Alps, and in his first campaign established himself in the midst of the Cisalpine Gauls, a people who had been constantly hostile to the Romans – sometimes defeating them, more often defeated by them – but had never been subjected to their sway. This march of four hundred leagues took Hannibal five months; he left no garrison nor depot in his rear and lost all contact with Spain and with Carthage – with Carthage he had no communication until after the battle of Trasimeno. A vaster, more comprehensive scheme was never executed by man – Alexander's expedition was much less daring and difficult and had a much greater chance of success. Nonetheless, Hannibal's offensive war, which made the Cisalpine people of Milan and Bologna Carthaginians under him, was methodically executed. Had he left fortresses or depots in his rear he must have weakened his army, and hazarded the success of his operations; he would have been vulnerable

---

[1] Satrap of Lycia and Pamphylia (d. *c.* 312 BC).

[2] His second wife. His first wife, Roxana, had her killed as soon as Alexander died.

at all points. In 217 he crossed the Apennines, defeated the Roman army in the plains of Trasimeno, marched toward Rome, and occupied the lower coasts of the Adriatic, whence he communicated with Carthage.

In 216, 80,000 Romans attacked him and he defeated them at the field of Cannae. Had he marched, six days afterward, he would have entered Rome and Carthage would have been the mistress of the world! But even without this, the effect of the great victory at Cannae was immense. Capua opened its gates; all the Greek colonies, and a great number of the towns of lower Italy, abandoned the cause of Rome and espoused the victorious side. Hannibal's principles were: to keep all his troops together; to garrison only a single depot, under his own control, to hold his hostages, his great war machines, his important prisoners, and his sick; and to rely for his communications on the loyalty of his allies. He maintained himself for sixteen years in Italy, with no support from Carthage, and he left the country only, at the orders of his government, to fly to the defence of his homeland. Fortune betrayed him at Zama, and Carthage ceased to exist. But had he been vanquished at Trebbia, Trasimeno, or Cannae, could any greater disasters have befallen than those that followed the battle of Zama? Defeated at the gates of his capital, he could not save his army from utter destruction.

CAESAR

Caesar was forty-one years of age when he commanded in his first campaign, in 58 BC, 140 years after Hannibal. Some 300,000 people of Helvetia had left their country to settle on the coast. With 90,000 men in arms they were passing through Burgundy. The people of Autun called upon Caesar to come to their aid. He left Vienne, a fortress of the Roman province, marched up the Rhône, crossed the Saône at Chalons, came up with the army of the Helvetians a day's march from Autun, and defeated them in a long-fought battle. After driving them back to their mountains, he crossed back over the Saône, occuped Besançon, and crossed the Jura to fight the army of Ariovistus.[1] He met that army a few marches from the Rhine, defeated it, and drove it back into Germany. At this battle he was ninety leagues from Vienne, at the battle with the Helvetians seventy leagues. In this campaign he always kept the six legions that composed his army united into a single corps. He left the care of his communications to his allies, having always a month's provisions in his camp, and a month's provisions in a fortress, where, like Hannibal, he kept his hostages, magazines, and hospitals. On the same principles he conducted his seven other campaigns in Gaul.

During the winter of 57 the Belgians raised an army of 300,000 men, which they placed under the command of Galba, King of Soissons. Caesar, having learned of this from his allies, the Rhemi, hastened to encamp on the Aisne. Galba, having no hopes of forcing his camp, crossed the Aisne to advance on Rheims, but Caesar frustrated this manoeuvre, and the Belgians disbanded; all

[1] A Germanic tribal chief, leader of the Suebi.

their towns submitted in succession. The people of Hainaut, though, surprised him on the Sambre, near Maubeuge, giving him no time to draw up a line – of his eight legions six were still raising the fortifications of the camp and two were still in the rear with the baggage. Fortune was so adverse to him on this day that a body of cavalry from Treves deserted him and spread the story, wherever they went, that the Roman army had been destroyed. Caesar was, however, in the end victorious.

In the year 56, he advanced at one push on Nantes and Vannes, detaching corps of considerable strength into Normandy and Aquitaine. His nearest depot at that time was Toulouse, 130 leagues away, and separated from him by mountains, great rivers, and forests.

In 55, he carried the war to Zutphen, in the interior of Holland, where 400,000 barbarians were crossing the Rhine to invade Gaul. He defeated them, killing most of them, driving back the survivors to a considerable distance. He then crossed back over the Rhine at Cologne, marched through Gaul, embarked at Boulogne, and made a raid upon England.

In 54, he again crossed the Channel, with five legions, conquered the banks of the Thames, took hostages, and returned into Gaul before the equinox. In the autumn, having received intelligence that his lieutenant, Sabinus, with fifteen cohorts, had been slaughtered near Treves, and that Quintus Cicero[1] was besieged in his camp at Tongres, he assembled 8,000 or 9,000 men, marched against Ambiorix,[2] who advanced to meet him, defeated him, and relieved Cicero.

In 53, he suppressed the revolt of the people of Sens, Chartres, Treves and Liège, and crossed the Rhine a second time.

The Gauls were in revolt; insurrection burst forth on every side. During the winter of 52, the whole population – even the loyal people of Autun – rose in rebellion. The Roman yoke was odious to the people of Gaul. Caesar was advised to go back into Gaul across the Alps but, rejecting advice, he took his ten legions across the Loire and, in the depth of winter, besieged Bourges. He took the city in the sight of the army of Vercingetorix.[3] He then laid siege to Clermont, but here he failed. He also lost his hostages, magazines, and horses, which were at his depot at Nevers, which fell to the people of Autun. Nothing could have appeared more critical than his situation. Labienus, his lieutenant, was kept on the alert by the people of Paris; Caesar ordered him to join him, and with the combined armies laid siege to Alesia, where the Gallic army was bottled up. He spent fifty days fortifying his lines of countervallation and circumvallation. Gaul raised a new army more numerous than that which she had just lost; only the people of

---

[1] Brother of the great Cicero, the orator, politician, and philosopher.

[2] Leader of the Belgian Gauls; he was chief of the Eburones tribe.

[3] Chief of the Arveni and leader of the revolt of the Gauls against Rome. He was, after Alesia, taken to Rome, exhibited in a triumph, and executed.

Rheims remained loyal to Rome. This Gallic army arrived to relieve Alesia and, together with the garrison, tried for three days to destroy the Romans in their lines. But Caesar triumphed over all obstacles; Alesia fell, and the Gauls were subdued.

During this great contest, the whole of Caesar's army was in his camp; he left no point vulnerable. He availed himself of his victory to regain the affection of the people of Autun, among whom he passed the winter, although he made successive expeditions, at a hundred leagues distance from each other, with different troops. At length, in 51, he laid siege to Cathors, where the last of the Gallic army perished. Gaul became a Roman province, the tribute from which added to the wealth of Rome eight millions of money annually.

In Caesar's campaigns of the civil war, he conquered by following the same method and the same principles, but he ran much greater risks. He crossed the Rubicon with a single legion; at Corfinium he took thirty cohorts, and in three months drove Pompey out of Italy. What speed! What despatch! What boldness! While his fleet was gathering to cross the Adriatic and pursue his rival to Greece, he crossed the Alps and the Pyrenees, traversed Catalonia at the head of 900 horses (a force scarcely sufficient for his escort), arrived before Lerida, and, in forty days, subdued Pompey's legions under the command of Afranius.[1] He then rapidly covered the distance between the Ebro and the Sierra Morena, pacified Andalusia, and returned to make his triumphant entry into Marseilles, which his troops had just taken. He then went to Rome, exercised the dictatorship there for ten days, and departed once more to put himself at the head of twelve legions that Antony[2] had assembled at Brindisi.

In the year 48 he sailed across the Adriatic with 25,000 men and contained all Pompey's forces for several months, until he was joined by Antony, who had defied the enemy fleet to cross the sea to join him. Together they marched on and invested Dyrrachium, Pompey's base. Pompey was encamped a few miles away, near the sea and Caesar, not content with having invested Dyrrachium, also invested the camp. On the summits of the surrounding hills he raised twenty-four forts, thus establishing a countervallation six leagues long. Pompey, hemmed in on the shore, was provisioned and reinforced by sea – his fleet commanded the Adriatic. Taking advantage of his central position, he attacked and defeated Caesar, who lost thirty standards and several thousand soldiers, the best of his veteran troops. His luck seemed to have faltered – he could expect no reinforcements; the sea was closed against him; Pompey had every advantage. But Caesar made a march of fifty leagues, carried the war into Thessaly, and defeated Pompey's army on the plains of Pharsalia. Pompey, now almost alone, although still master of the sea, fled, and presented himself as a suppliant on the coast of Egypt, where he fell by the hand of a base assassin.

[1] Roman consul and general. He joined Pompey in Greece after this battle and was finally captured at the battle of Thapsus and executed in 46 BC.

[2] Mark Antony (82–31 BC), later to become Cleopatra's lover.

A few days after, Caesar went in pursuit of him to Alexandria, where the citizens and the army of Achillas[1] besieged him in the palace and amphitheatre. At length, after nine months of danger and continual battles, the loss of any one of which would have been fatal to him, he triumphed over the Egyptians.

In the meanwhile the remnants of Pompey's party, Scipio,[2] Labienus,[3] and King Juba,[4] ruled in Africa with fourteen legions and, with their numerous squadrons, scoured the sea. At Utica, Cato[5] breathed the hatred he felt into every bosom. Caesar embarked with a few troops, reached Adrumetum, and sustained reverses in several engagements. At length, though, he was joined by his whole army and defeated Scipio, Labienus, and King Juba on the plains of Thapsus. Cato, Scipio, and Juba killed themselves. Neither fortresses, numerous squadrons, nor the oaths and duties of states, could save the vanquished from the ascendancy and activity of the victor.

In the year 45, the sons of Pompey, having assembled in Spain the remnants of the armies of Pharsalia and Thapsus, found themselves at the head of a more numerous force than that of their father. Caesar set out from Rome, reached the Guadalquivir in twenty-three days, and defeated Sextus Pompey[6] at Munda. It is said that at Munda, in danger of losing the battle and seeing that even his old legions seemed shaken, he had thoughts of killing himself. Labienus fell in the battle; the head of Sextus Pompey was laid at the victor's feet. Six months later, on the ides of March, Caesar was assassinated in the midst of the Roman senate. Had he been defeated at Pharsalia, Thapsus, or Munda he would have suffered the fate of Pompey the Great, of Metellus, Scipio, and Sextus Pompey. Pompey, surnamed the Great when he was only twenty-four years old, who, after conquering in eighteen campaigns, triumphed over three parts of the world and carried the name of Rome to such heights of glory, was defeated at Pharsalia and there closed his career. Yet he was master of the sea, while his rival had no fleet.

Caesar's principles were the same as those of Alexander and Hannibal – to keep his forces united; to be secure from all sides; to advance rapidly on important points; to bank on moral means, the reputation of his arms, and the fear he inspired; and to bank also on political means, to keep his allies loyal and conquered nations obedient.

[1] Guardian and army commander of Ptolemy, brother, co-ruler, and rival of Cleopatra, who had allied himself with Pompey.

[2] Metellus Pius Scipio had been co-consul with Pompey in 52 BC.

[3] Labienus had been Caesar's legate in Gaul (*see* p.27), but had joined Pompey at the beginning of the Civil War.

[4] King of Numidia.

[5] Cato the Younger (95–46 BC), Roman politician and supporter of Pompey.

[6] Pompey the Younger (75–35 BC), Pompey the Great's second son.

GUSTAVUS ADOLPHUS

Gustavus Adolphus crossed the Baltic, took possession of the isle of Rügen and Pomerania, and led his forces to the Vistula, the Rhine, and the Danube. He fought two battles; was victorious both at Leipzig and at Lützen, but met his death in the latter field. In this short career, however, he established a great reputation, by his bravery, the speed of his movements, and the discipline and boldness of his troops. Gustavus Adolphus was inspired by the principles of Alexander, Hannibal, and Caesar.

TURENNE[1]

Turenne conducted five campaigns before the Treaty of Westphalia,[2] eight between that treaty and the Treaty of the Pyrenees,[3] and five more between that treaty and his death, in 1675. His manoeuvres and marches during the campaigns of 1646, 1648, 1672, and 1673 were conducted on the same principles as those of Alexander, Hannibal, Caesar, and Gustavus Adolphus.

PRINCE EUGÈNE

Prince Eugène of Savoy vanquished the Turks in the campaign of 1697, when the battle of Zenta produced peace. In 1701 he entered Italy by Trento, at the head of 30,000 men, crossed the Adige at Carpi, penetrated into Brescia, and compelled Catinat[4] to fall back behind the Oglio. He defeated Villeroi[5] at Chiari. In 1702 he surprised Cremona and lost the battle of Luzara to Villeroi. In 1704 he commanded in Flanders and won the battle of Höchstädt.[6] In 1705 he fought the Italian campaign against Vendôme,[7] sustaining a check at Cassano. In 1706 he marched from Trento along the left bank of the Adige, crossed that river in the face of a French army, reascended the left bank of the Po, and exposing his flank to the enemy, crossed the Tanaro in the face of the Duc d'Orléans.[8] He

---

[1] Napoleon devotes an entire volume of the *Notes and Miscellanies* dictated at St Helena to the wars of Turenne.

[2] 1648.

[3] 1609.

[4] Nicolas Catinat (1637–1712), the French general in command of the Italian army.

[5] François, Duc de Villeroi (1644–1730), Marshal of France and favourite of Louis XIV.

[6] Better known as the battle of Blenheim.

[7] Louis Joseph, Duc de Vendôme (1654–1712), the French commander in northern Italy.

[8] Philippe, Duc d'Orléans (1674–1723), had taken command of the French army in Italy only in this year.

---

joined the Duke of Savoy[1] beneath Turin, where he turned all the French lines, attacking their right between the Sesia and the Doria, and broke them. This march is a masterpiece of daring enterprise.

In 1707 he penetrated into Provence and besieged Toulon. In 1708 he commanded on the Rhine, fought the action of Oudenaarde, and besieged Lille for four months. In 1709 he won the battle of Malplaquet.[2] In 1712 he took Le Quesnoy, and besieged Landrecy. Marshal Villars saved France at Denain.[3] The peace of 1704 put an end to this war. In the campaign of 1716 against the Turks, Prince Eugène conquered at Temesvar, besieged and took Belgrade, and forced the Porte to make peace. In 1733 he fought his last campaign, but his great age had rendered him timid – he was unwilling to risk his fame in an eighteenth battle and he allowed Marshal Berwick[4] to outface him at Philippsburg and take the town.

FREDERICK THE GREAT

Frederick, in his invasions of Bohemia and Moravia, in his marches on the Oder, and to the banks of the Elbe and Saale, frequently put in practice the principles of those great captains; he placed his especial confidence in the discipline, bravery, and tactics of his army.

NAPOLEON

I fought fourteen campaigns: two in Italy, five in Germany, two in Africa and Asia, two in Poland and Russia, one in Spain, and two in France.

In the first campaign of Italy, in 1796, I set out from Savona, crossed the mountains at the weak point where the Alps end and the Apennines begin, separated the Austrian army from that of Sardinia, took possession of Cherasco, a fortress at the confluence of the Tanaro and Stura, twenty leagues[5] from Savona, and established my magazines there. I compelled the King of Sardinia to

[1] Victor Amadeus II (1666–1732), Eugène's cousin, had been on the opposite side at Chiari but had now joined the alliance against France. He later, in 1713, became King of Sicily.

[2] It is interesting that in all this Napoleon makes no mention of the Duke of Marlborough, Eugène's great friend and ally, who fought alongside him not only at Malplaquet but also at Höchstädt (Blenheim) and Oudenaarde.

[3] Claude, Duc de Villars (1653–74), Marshal of France, had already fought against Eugène at Malplaquet. He 'saved France' here by inflicting a decisive defeat on Eugène.

[4] James Fitzjames, Duke of Berwick (1670–1734), an illegitimate son of James II of England, was made Marshal of France in 1706, after serving with the French army in Spain. He was killed at the siege of Philippsburg.

[5] A league equals about three miles.

surrender to me the fortress of Tortona, situated twenty leagues east of Cherasco in the direction of Milan, and established myself there. I crossed the Po at Piacenza and seized Pizzighettone, a fortress on the Adda, twenty-five leagues from Tortona. Then I advanced on the Mincio, took Peschiera, thirty leagues from Pizzighettone on the line of the Adige, seized the wall and forts of Verona on the left bank, which secured me the three stone bridges of that city, and occupied Porto Legnano, which gave me another bridge over that river. I remained in this position until I besieged and took Mantua. Between my camp beneath Verona and Chambéry, my first base on the frontier of France, I had four fortified places in echelon. These contained my hospitals and magazines, and needed only garrisons of 4,000 men, for which convalescents and conscripts were adequate. Thus I had, on this line of a hundred leagues, a base at every four marches. After the taking of Mantua, when I pushed on into the Papal States, Ferrara was my first base on the Po and Ancona, seven or eight marches farther on at the foot of the Apennines, my second.

In the campaign of 1797, I crossed the Piave and the Tagliamento, fortifying Palma-nuova and Osopo, situated eight marches from Mantua, then crossed the Julian Alps, repaired the old fortifications of Clagenfurth, five marches from Osopo, and took up a position on the Simmering. There I was eighty leagues from Mantua, but on my line of operations I held three places in echelon and had a base at every five or six marches.

In 1798 I began my operations in the East by taking Alexandria, then I fortified that great city and made it my base and depot. When I marched on Cairo, I established a fort at Rehmaniah, on the Nile, twenty leagues from Alexandria,

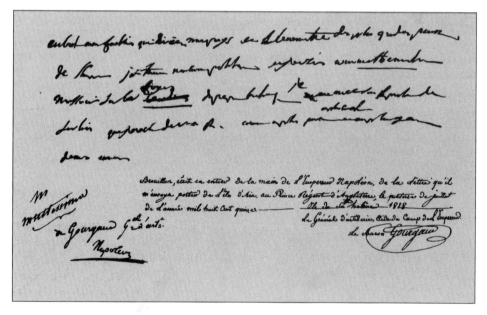

Napoleon's handwriting and signature on a page dictated by Gourgaud.

and had the citadel and several forts at Cairo put in a state of defence. I had a fort built thirty leagues from Cairo, at Salahia, a gateway to the desert on the road to Gaza. Encamped at this village, the army was fifteen days' march from Alexandria, but it had three fortified bases on its line of operations.

During the campaign of 1799, I covered a distance of eighty leagues in the desert, laid siege to Acre, and pushed my reconnaissance corps to the Jordan, two hundred and fifty leagues from Alexandria, where my main base was. I had forts built at Quatieh, in the desert twenty leagues from Salahia, at El-Arich, thirty leagues from Quatieh, and at Gaza, thirty leagues from Salahia. On this line of operations of two hundred and fifty leagues, I had eight places strong enough to resist any attack I could envisage. In fact, in these four campaigns I never had a convoy or a courier intercepted – in 1796 a few stragglers were massacred near Tortona and in Egypt a few *djermes* were stopped on the Nile, between Rosetta and Cairo, but this was at the very beginning of operations. The dromedary regiments that I organized in Egypt were so completely accustomed to the desert that they always kept communications open between Cairo and Acre and in Upper and Lower Egypt. With an army of 25,000 men, I then occupied Egypt, Palestine, and Galilee – an area of nearly 30,000 square leagues, enclosed in a triangle. It was three hundred leagues from my headquarters before Acre to Desaix's[1] headquarters in Upper Egypt.

The campaign of 1800 was conducted on the same principles. When the Army of Germany reached the Inn, it secured the fortresses of Ulm and Ingolstadt and so gained two important depots. The armistice of Pfullendorf omitted to require the surrender of these places, but I considered them so crucial to the success of my operation in Germany that their surrender was made the *sine qua non* of the extension of the armistice.

The Gallo-Batavian army at Nuremberg secured the left wing, on the Danube, and the army of the Grisons the right wing, in the valley of the Inn. When the Army of Reserve came down from the St Bernard Pass its first depot was established at Ivrea. Even after the battle of Marengo, I did not consider the whole of Italy reconquered, until after the fortified places between me and the Mincio had been occupied by my troops. I gave Melas[2] permission to retire on to Mantua only on condition that all those fortresses were surrendered.

In 1805, having carried the Ulm against the Austrian army, 80,000 strong, I advanced on the Lech, had the ancient ramparts of Augsburg repaired, lined them, and made this town, which offered me so many resources, my depot. I would have restored Ulm, but the fortifications had been razed, and the local circumstances were too unfavourable. From Augsburg I marched on Braunau

[1] General Louis Desaix (1768–1800) had commanded the advance guard of the Army of Egypt and now commanded in Upper Egypt. He was killed at Marengo.

[2] Michael von Melas (1729–1806), the general in command of the Austrian army in Italy.

and, by taking this important position, secured myself a bridge over the Inn. Braunau was my second depot; possession of it enabled me to proceed as far as the capital, Vienna, which was fortified against any sudden assault. I afterwards crossed into Moravia and seized the citadel of Brünn, forty leagues from Vienna, which was immediately armed and provisioned and became my base of operations in Moravia. A day's march away, I fought the battle of Austerlitz. From that field of battle I could retreat on Vienna and recross the Danube there, or march by the left bank to Linz and cross the river by its bridge, covered by strong works on the hills above the town.

In 1806 I established my headquarters at Bamberg and effected the junction of the different corps of my army on the Rednitz. The King of Prussia[1] thought, by advancing to the Maine, to bring me to a halt by cutting off my line of operations on Mentz and he sent there Blücher's[2] corps and that of the Duke of Weimar.[3] The French army's line of communication, though, was no longer on Mentz, but ran from the fort of Cronach, at the foot of a pass over the mountains of Saxony, to Forsheim, a fortified place on the Rednitz, and thence to Strasbourg. Having now nothing to fear from the offensive march of the Prussians, I made my dispositions. My left, in three columns, marched out by Coburg, under the command of the Dukes of Montebello[4] and Castiglione;[5] it was composed of the fifth and seventh army corps. My centre, with which I marched, moved out by Cronach and Schejlitz; it was formed of the first and third corps, commanded by Marshal Bernadotte[6] and the Prince of Eckmühl,[7] the guard, and reserves of cavalry. The right marched via Bayreuth and went on to Hof, it was composed of the fourth and sixth corps, commanded by the Duke of Dalmatia[8] and the

---

[1] Frederick William III (1770–1840).

[2] Gebhard von Blücher (1742–1819), the Prussian general who was later to play a key role at Waterloo.

[3] Charles Augustus (1757–1828), later rewarded for fighting with Prussia against Napoleon at the Congress of Vienna, which turned him into a Grand Duke.

[4] Jean Lannes, Duc de Montebello (1769–1809). The son of a stable hand, he had been with Napoleon since the beginning – he took part in the *coup d'état* of 18 Brumaire and had fought in Italy and Egypt.

[5] Pierre Augerau, Duc de Castiglione (1757–1816), was a Directorate general who had initially opposed Napoleon.

[6] Jean Bernadotte (1763–1844), who at this time had already been French Minister of War and had commanded the Army of the West. In 1804 he had been created Marshal of Empire. Later, in 1818, he became King of Sweden and Norway.

[7] Louis Davout (1770–1823) was, strictly, not at this time a prince – Napoleon gave him that title only in 1809. He was, though, already a Marshal of France.

[8] Better known as Marshal Soult (1769–1851).

Prince of the Moskowa.[1] The Prussian army, between Weimar and Neudstadt, which had already set off to support its vanguard, halted. Cut off from the Elbe and Berlin, and with all its magazines taken, it realized its danger, but not before its posititon was quite desperate. It was beaten and, although so near Magdeburg, in the heart of its country, and two marches only from the Elbe, it was cut off and could effect no retreat. Not a man of this old army of Frederick escaped, except the king and a few squadrons, who with difficulty gained the right bank of the Oder. More than 100,000 men, and hundreds of cannon and colours, were the trophies of this day.

In 1807, being master of Cüstrin, Glogau, and Stettin, I crossed the Vistula at Warsaw. I had Praga fortified, to serve me at once as my bridgehead and depot, built a fort at Modlin, and fortified Thorn. The army took up a position on the Passarge, to cover the siege of Danzig, which became its base and depot for the operations that preceded the battle of Friedland, which decided the war. Had hostilities continued, I would have been able to shorten the war by taking the fortress of Pilau before the army passed the Niemen.

In 1808 most of the fortresses of the north of Spain – San Sebastian, Pamplona, Figueras, and Barcelona – were in the power of the French army when it marched on Burgos.

In 1809 the first guns were fired near Ratisbon; Augsburg was my centre of operations. The Austrians having razed Braunau, I fortified instead the citadel of Passau, which, because it was situated at the confluence of the Inn and the Danube, gave me the much greater advantage of securing me straightway a bridge over each river. I also secured the bridge of Linz by works of the first strength. My army, on arriving at Vienna, had, as well as its communications with Bavaria, a secure line of communication with Italy, by the castle of Gratz and the fortified place of Clagenfurth.

In 1812 Danzig, Thorn, Modlin, and Praga were my places on the Vistula; Veilau, Kowno, Grodno, Wilno, and Minsk my magazines near the Niemen; and Smolensk my main depot for my movement on Moscow. In this operation I had a fortified base at every eight days' march. All these stations were fortified and entrenched and, although they were occupied only by one company and one piece of cannon, they were so effective that during the whole campaign not a single courier or convoy was intercepted – even during the retreat (except for the four days when Admiral Chicago[2] was driven back beyond the Beresina) the army's lines of communications with its depots were always open.

In 1813 Königstein, Dresden, Torgau, Wittenberg, Magdeburg, and Hamburg were my bases on the Elbe; Merseburg, Erfurt, and Würtzburg my echelons for reaching the Rhine.

In the campaign of 1814 I had fortresses in all directions. The full importance

[1] Better known as Marshal Ney (1769–1815).

[2] Pavel Chichagov, one of the three Russian army commanders attempting to prevent the retreating French army from crossing the Beresina.

Jérôme Bonaparte, youngest of the Bonaparte brothers, was created King of Westphalia in 1807 where his extravagance ruined an already poor country.

of those of Flanders would have been seen if Paris had not been treacherously surrendered or even if, after its fall, the defection of the sixth army corps to the enemy had not prevented me from marching on the city. Had I been able to do so, the Allies would have been forced to abandon the capital, for surely their generals would never have risked a battle on the left bank of the Seine, with that great city in their rear, which they had occupied for only three days. The treachery of several ministers and civil agents facilitated the entrance of the enemy into Paris, but it was that of a marshal[1] that prevented the momentary occupation of the capital from becoming fatal to the Allies.

TOULON

At the end of August, 1793, when the Allied troops entered Toulon, Lyons had displayed the white flag and civil war in Languedoc and Provence was only half extinguished. The victorious Spanish army had crossed the Pyrenees and poured

[1] Auguste Marmont (1774–1852), created Marshal of France, in 1809, who surrendered Paris and deserted to the Allies.

into Roussillon; the Piedmontese army had cleared the Alps and was at the gates of Chambéry and Antibes. The Allies were not fully sensible of the importance of the conquest they had made. Had 6,000 Sardinians, 12,000 Neapolitans, 6,000 Spaniards, and 6,000 English joined the 12,000 federalists in Toulon, this army of 40,000 might have reached Lyons and combined, on its right, with the Piedmontese, and, on its left, with the Spanish army.

I, then twenty-four years of age, was chief of a battalion of artillery; the Committee of Public Safety selected me to be second-in-command of the artillery train. I arrived at the beginning of September. On 15 October, a council of war, presided over by member of the Convention Gasparin, met at Ollioules. A memorial was read on the conduct of the siege of Toulon. The celebrated D'Arcon had drawn it up and it had been approved by the committee of fortifications. I opposed its adoption and proposed a simpler plan. I said that a battery of sixty guns placed at the extremities of the promontories of Eguillette and Balagnier would fire shot and bombs on every point of the roadstead, which would oblige the English and Spanish squadrons to evacuate and to stand out to sea. Toulon would then be blockaded both by land and sea and the enemy would undoubtedly evacuate it rather than leave a garrison which could, at best, defend itself there for thirty days and then be obliged, in order to obtain an honourable capitulation, to relinquish all the advantages it might derive from a voluntary evacuation. However, the capes of Eguillette and Balagnier were commanded by the heights of Le Caire, so it would be necessary to gain possession of these heights in the first instance. I pointed out that a month before the enemy had established themselves on the heights I had proposed to the general-in-chief that I should occupy them myself with 3,000 men, in order, under their protection, to establish batteries to fire red-hot shot at the extremities of the two capes; this would have enabled me to enter Toulon in a few days. The general, though, had thought proper to send only 400 men under the command of General Laborde. Forty-eight hours afterwards the English had landed 4,000 men and taken possession up to the outskirts of the village of Seine. They had now constructed their fort Mulgrave, armed with forty pieces of cannon in battery. So it would now be necessary to establish strong batteries to batter the fort, and then to carry it by assault. Seventy-two hours later, Toulon would be taken. This scheme was adopted.

My predictions were exactly fulfilled. Such is the history of this event, which so greatly astonished Europe and has never been well understood.

I, who was a chief of battalion of artillery and second-in-command in that branch of the service at the siege of Toulon, had nothing whatever to do with Barras,[1] who, at that period was on a mission to Marseilles and Nice. The representative of the people who first singled me out and supported, by his authority, the plans that produced the fall of Toulon, was Gasparin, deputy for Orange, a keen member of the Convention and formerly a captain of dragoons, an

---

[1] Paul Barras (1755–1829), then just a member of the National Convention.

enlightened and well-educated man. It was this deputy who guessed the military talents of the commandant of artillery. I formed no connection with Barras until 13 Vendémiaire.

I was never unemployed. After the siege of Toulon I was appointed general commandant-in-chief of the artillery of the Army of Italy and joined that army, which was commanded by the brave veteran General Dumerbion. I laid down the plan which caused Saorgio, the Col di Tende, Oneglia, and the sources of the Tanaro, to fall into the power of France. In October of the same year, I directed the army in its movement on the Bormida, at the action of Dego, and at the taking of Savona. In February 1785, I commanded the artillery of the naval expedition prepared at Toulon, destined at first for Corsica and afterwards for Rome. I was of the opinion that the squadron ought first to sail from the port without the convoy and drive off the English Mediterranean squadron. This plan was adopted. It led to the naval action of Noli, where the *Ça Ira* was taken.[1] The French squadron returned and the expedition was countermanded. The same year I quelled an insurrection at the arsenal, by my influence over the gunners of the land and sea services, and saved the lives of the representatives Mariette and Chambon.[2]

In May 1795 I was, on the recommendation of Aubry, placed on the list as a general of infantry to serve in the Army of the Vendée until there should be vacancies in the artillery. I went to Paris and refused the posting to the Army of the Vendée. In the mean time, Kellermann[3] having been defeated on the coast of Genoa and the Army of Italy forced to retreat, I was required by the Committee of Public Safety, then composed of Sieyès, Le-Tourneur, and Pontecoulant, to draw up instructions for that army. A short time afterwards I obtained, through the affair of 13 Vendémiaire, the chief command of the Army of the Interior at Paris, which I held until March 1796.

On 13 Vendémiaire, the Convention was defended by 6,000 men, troops of the line, and thirty pieces of cannon. It did not sit at the Manège, but at the Tuileries, in the theatre there.

I was called to the chief command of the Army of Italy by the wishes of the officers and soldiers who had won their laurels at Toulon in 1793 and in the countship of Nice and on the coast of Genoa in 1794 and 1795. This army was proving very expensive at a time when the treasury was empty.

---

[1] By Nelson, who reduced this French 80-gun ship to, in his own words, 'a perfect wreck'.

[2] Aubin Chambon had been Mayor of Paris during the trial and execution of Louis XVI.

[3] François Kellermann (1735–1820) commanded the Army of the Alps. He was later created Marshal of France. His son, another François, became one of Napoleon's generals and fought at Waterloo.

ITALY

It was my desire to raise the Italian nation from its ruins – to reunite the Venetians, Milanese, Piedmontese, Genoese, Tuscans, Parmesans, Modenese, Romans, Neapolitans, Sicilians, and Sardinians in one independent nation bounded by the Alps and the Adriatic, Ionian, and Mediterranean Seas. This was the immortal trophy I was raising to my glory. This great and powerful kingdom would have been, by land, a check to the House of Austria while by sea it fleets, combined with those of Toulon, would have ruled the Mediterranean and protected the ancient route of Indian commerce, by the Red Sea and Suez. Rome, the capital, was the eternal city. But I had many obstacles to surmount. I said at the Council of Lyons that it would take me twenty years to re-establish the Italian nation.

The geographical configuration of Italy has greatly influenced its fate. If the Ionian Sea had washed the foot of Monte Velino, if all the countries that form the Kingdom of Naples, Sicily, and Sardinia had been placed between Corsica, Leghorn, and Genoa, then how materially would events have been affected! Before the Romans, the Gauls took possession of all the north of Italy, from the Alps to the Magra westward and the Rubicon eastward, while the nations of Greece occupied Tartentum, Reggio, and all the south of the peninsula: the Italians were confined within the limits of Tuscany and Latium.

All the organizations of Italy were provisional. I wanted to make a single power of that great peninsula and for that reason I reserved the iron crown to myself, in order to keep in my own hands the guidance of the different people of Italy. I preferred to unite Rome, Genoa, Tuscany, and Piedmont to the Empire rather than to the Kingdom of Italy because the people of those countries preferred it, because the Imperial influence would be the more powerful, because it was a means of calling a great number of the inhabitants of those countries into France and of sending a number of French to Italy in exchange and because it would bring the conscripts and sailors in those provinces to strengthen the French regiments and the crews of Toulon. With regard to Naples alone it was necessary to pursue a different course, and to give a definite appearance to the provisional arrangements made there. That powerful city was accustomed to great independence. Ferdinand[1] was in Sicily, and an English squadron was on the coast of Naples, but had all Italy been proclaimed a single kingdom, and a second son of mine, by my marriage with the Archduchess Marie Louise, been crowned King of Italy, the Italians of Sicily, Sardinia, Naples, Venice, Genoa, Piedmont, Tuscany, and Milan would have eagerly and immediately thronged around the throne of the ancient and noble land of Italy. I had not disposed of the Grand Duchy of Berg. It was my intention to reinstate Joachim[2] when he left Naples.

[1] Ferdinand I (1751–1825), King of Naples. He twice fled from the French and was restored permanently to his throne only after Napoleon's fall.

[2] Joachim Murat (1767–1815), cavalry commander and Marshal of France, married Napoleon's sister Maria and became King of Naples in 1808.

The plans of all my fourteen campaigns are conformable to true principles of war; my wars were bold, but methodical; nothing can be more satisfactorily proved than this is by the defence of the Adige in 1796.

THE CAMPAIGN OF 1796 IN GERMANY

But if an instance of an offensive war conducted on false principles be looked for, we shall find it in that of 1796 in Germany. The 50,000-strong French Army of the Sambre and Meuse took possession of the citadel of Würtzburg and established itself on the Rednitz. At the same time that the left and centre of the Army of the Rhine and Moselle crossed the Necker and advanced with 50,000 men on Neresheim, its right, 20,000 strong, marched, under the command of Ferino, on the Voralberg, at the foot of the mountains of the Tyrol. These three army corps, separated from each other by mountains and great rivers, each had its own line of communication with France, so that the defeat of any one of them would endanger the other two. The flanks are the weak part of an invading army – you should try to support them both, or at least one of them, on a neutral country or some great natural obstacle. In contempt of this first principle of war, the French army, by dividing into three separate corps, created six flanks, although by skilful manoeuvring it would have been easy to support both its wings very strongly. The column of the centre fought at Neresheim with its left uncovered and its right not even supported on the Danube, because it neglected to seize the fortress of Ulm, which the enemy had abandoned. The capture of Ulm could alone have turned this into an orthodox campaign. As it was, the column found itself wholly isolated, eighty leagues from the Rhine, with no base of operations to use as an immediate depot. The Archduke,[1] having lost the principal part of the forces with which he had opposed the Army of the Sambre and Meuse and the corps of the right commanded by Ferino, advanced to Neresheim. Having failed there because of the courage of the French, he crossed back over the Danube and the Lech, weakened himself by leaving 25,000 men before the left and centre of the Army of the Rhine and Moselle, which had just defeated him at Neresheim, and went on to overwhelm the Army of the Sambre and Meuse and drive it beyond the Rhine.

In this campaign the general of the Army of the Rhine[2] also committed a great error – he left two great fortified places, Philippsburg and Mannheim, in his rear, without blockading them, merely causing them to be kept under surveillance by a corps of 4,000 men. He ought to have invested them strictly, and deprived them of all communication with the Archduke, all knowledge of the events of the war, and all intelligence from the country. Such a blockade would have made a

[1] Charles, Archduke of Austria (1771–1847), brother of the Emperor Francis II, commanded the Austrian Army of the Rhine.

[2] General Victor Moreau (1763–1813), who was later (1804) exiled for plotting against Napoleon.

considerable contribution toward the fall of the two towns. He was severely punished for this imprudence. The garrisons of the two towns, as soon as they heard of the Archduke's successes, drove the corps he had left on watch beyond the Rhine, excited the peasants to insurrection, and intercepted his communications – they even came very close to taking by surprise Kehl and the bridge of Strasbourg. The principles of war and prudence were never more grossly violated than in this campaign. The plan of the Cabinet was defective, the execution still more so. What, then, should have been done? First, the three armies should have been under one general-in-chief; secondly, the forces should have marched as a combined force, having only two wings, and one of them should have been constantly supported on the Danube; thirdly, the French should in the first instance have possessed themselves of four of the enemy's fortresses on the Rhine, or at least have opened trenches before two, and secured Ulm, so that they had their main depot on the Danube, at the debouch of the Black Mountains.

THE PENINSULAR WAR

Another offensive campaign, which was equally contrary to the most important rules of the art of war, was that of Portugal. The Anglo-Portuguese army consisted of 80,000 men, 15,000 of whom were militia, who were in observation at Coimbra, and supported on Oporto. The French army, after taking Cuidad-Rodrigo and Almeida, entered Portugal, 72,000 strong: it attacked the enemy in position on the heights of Busaco. The two armies were of equal force, but the position at Busaco was very strong: the attack failed, and the next morning the army turned the lines by proceding on Coimbra. The enemy then effected his retreat on Lisbon, burning and laying waste the country.

The French general[1] pursued him closely, left no corps of observation to restrain the division of 15,000 Portuguese militia at Oporto, abandoned his rear and Coimbra, his depot where he left 5,000 sick and wounded. Before he arrived opposite Lisbon, the Portuguese division had already occupied Coimbra and cut him off from all means of retreat. He ought to have left a corps of 6,000 men to defend and fortify Coimbra and deter the Oporto division.

It is true that he would, in that case, have arrived at Lisbon with only 60,000 men, but that number would have been sufficient if it was the English general's[2] intention to embark. If, though he intended to maintain himself in Portugal, as there was every reason to believe, the French ought not to have passed Coimbra, but to have taken up a good position before that city, even at several marches distance, fortified themselves there, sent a detachment to subdue Oporto, organized their rear and their communications with Almeida, and then waited

[1] André Massena (1757–1817), Prince of Essling, was in command at Busaco (1810).

[2] Wellington.

until Badajoz had been taken and the Army of Andalusia arrived on the Tagus.

When he arrived at the foot of the entrenchments of Lisbon, the French general failed in resolution, yet he was aware of the existence of these lines, since the enemy had been working on them for three months. The general opinion is that, had he attacked them on the day of his arrival, he would have carried them, but two days later it was no longer possible. The Anglo-Portuguese army was reinforced by a great number of battalions of militia. Thus, without gaining any advantage, the French general lost 5,000 sick and wounded and his communications with his rear. When he arrived before Lisbon, he discovered that he had not enough ammunition – before the operation he had made no calculation of what he would need.

CHARLES XII

Another offensive campaign, which was likewise conducted contrary to all the principles of war, was that of Charles XII[1] in 1708 and 1709. That prince set out from his camp at Allstadt, near Leipzig, in September 1707, at the head of 45,000 men, and crossed Poland. Another 20,000 men, under the command of Count Levenhaupt, landed at Riga. There were 15,000 men in Finland, so Charles was able to assemble a force of 80,000 of the best troops in the world. He left 10,000 at Warsaw to guard King Stanislaus[2] and in January 1708, arrived at Grodno, where he wintered. In June he crossed the forest of Minsk, and appeared before Borisov, overcame the Russian army, which occupied the left bank of the Berezina, beat 20,000 Russians who were entrenched behind some morasses, crossed the Dnieper at Mogilev and, on 22 September, defeated a corps of 16,000 Muscovites near Smolensk. He was near the boundary of Lithuania and about to enter Russia proper. The Tsar,[3] alarmed, made him proposals of peace. Up to that time Charles's march had been conducted according to rule – his communications were secure, he was master of Poland and Riga, and he was only ten days' march from Moscow. It is probable that he could have entered that capital, but he quitted the high road leading to it, and directed his march on the Ukraine, to join up with Mazepa,[4] who brought him only 6,000 men. By this movement he exposed the flank of his line of operations, which ran for four hundred leagues from Sweden to Russia. He could not preserve his communications and it became impossible for him to receive any assistance. General Levenhaupt, with 16,000 men and 8,000 wagons, crossed the Dnieper at Mogilev twelve days after him. He had scarcely made four marches in the direction of the Ukraine, when he was attacked by the Tsar, at the head of 40,000 men. He

[1] King of Sweden, 1697–1718.

[2] Stanislaus I of Poland (1677–1766), a puppet king created by Charles XII.

[3] Peter the Great (1672–1725).

[4] Ivan Mazepa (c. 1644–1709), a Cossack who had turned against Peter the Great.

fought valiantly, on the 7, 8, 9, and 10 October, but he lost his whole convoy and 11,000 men, and when he joined his master in the Ukraine he had only 5,000 men and was in want of everything. In May 1709, the Tsar having formed great magazines at Poltava, Charles XII laid seige to that place, but in June the Tsar appeared with 60,000 men to compel him to raise the siege. The king, who now had only 30,000 men, some of whom were Cossacks of the Ukraine, attacked the Russian army and was defeated. His army was completely destroyed and it was only with great difficulty that he, with 1,000 men, reached Turkey by crossing the Dnieper.

If Charles XII wished to reach Moscow, he ordered his march correctly until he arrived near Smolensk – his line of operations with Sweden and Riga was protected by the Dvina as far as the Dnieper at Mogilev. But, if his plan was to winter in the Ukraine, in order to raise the Cossacks there, he ought not to have crossed the Niemen at Grodno and traversed Lithuania. He should have set out from Cracow, proceeded to the lower Dnieper, and brought his convoys from Sweden, behind the Oder and the Vistula, by the Cracow road. It was impossible for him to maintain his communications with his states by a line which ran along the Russian frontier for four hundred leagues, exposing the flank, but it would have been easy for him to have preserved them by Cracow, covered by Lithuania, the Niemen, and the Vistula. Yet he did not follow Hannibal's example and dispense with all communications with Sweden. General Levenhaupt, who commanded so considerable a detachment and a convoy of such importance, followed him twelve days' march behind. Charles therefore banked on Levenhaupt's arrival.

To this primary error, which was likely to produce his ruin, he added another – that of attacking the Russian army at Poltava. He was only twelve leagues from the Dnieper and he might, therefore, in two marches have placed that river between the Tsar and himself and established himself in Volhynia and Podolia. For what was there to induce him to give battle? If he had conquered at Poltava, what could he have expected to do with an army in which there were not above 18,000 Swedes, and at forty days' march from Moscow! He could no longer entertain the hope of striking a decisive blow against the enemy. He had, therefore, every inducement to avail himself of the fine weather, and of the fear that he still inspired in the Moscovites, and to cross the Dnieper in May and re-enter Poland. He should have given battle in such a manner as to secure his retreat, and to have had boats and a fort twelve leagues from Poltava, on the Dnieper. But he did not make war methodically. He did not understand war – he was only a brave and intrepid soldier. As soon as he quitted the high road to Moscow, he lost his line of communications and received no more news from Sweden – he heard of the disaster that General Levenhaupt had sustained only from that general himself. Certainly the mistakes he made did not escape the observation of many of the officers of his staff, who, despairing of persuading him to give up his plan to march on the Ukraine, long urged him to wait at Smolensk for the arrival of General Levenhaupt and his valuable convoy.

After this summary notice of the campaigns of the greatest captains, I think it unnecessary to make any observations on so-called 'systems' of the art of war. In the war of Hanover a great number of fortresses were constructed to serve as bases of operations for the French armies, but the French forces were so weakened by having to garrison these places that the successes of Prince Ferdinand of Brunswick were only rendered the more easy and brilliant. By fortifying capital cities, generals have all their resources, riches, and influence, at command.

These afford cellars and public buildings which serve to contain the magazines of the army. As almost all these towns have anciently had fortifications, they still retain ramparts of masonry, sluices, etc. which are useful, whilst places fortified with works of earth only are not entirely secure from a sudden attack, unless guarded by a garrison as numerous as that of an intrenched camp. What immense labour would it not require to raise blockhouses sufficient to secure the magazines from the injuries of the air and of bombs and howitzers! If the army of reserve be composed of raw recruits, it will be of no use, either to rally the army and stop it in a defeat, or to keep the country in awe. This system creates vulnerable points, of which the enemy may avail themselves, who being in their own country, have an opportunity of changing their line of operations at pleasure.

The conquered provinces ought to be kept in obedience to the victor by moral means, the responsibility of the communes, and the mode of organizing the administration: hostages are one of the most powerful restraints; but to be so they must be numerous, and chosen from among persons of the greatest influence; and the people must be persuaded that the death of the hostages would be the immediate consequence of a breach of faith on their part.

Unity of command is of the utmost importance in war. Two armies ought never to be placed on the same scene of action. Modern troops have no more occasion for bread and cake than the Romans had – give them flour, rice, or pulses on their marches and they will take no harm.

It is an error to suppose that the generals of antiquity did not pay great attention to their magazines – it may be seen in Caesar's *Commentaries* how much he was occupied by this care in several campaigns – but they had discovered the art of not being slaves to their supplies and of not being obliged to depend on their purveyors, and this art has been understood by all our great captains. The system followed by the French in the war of Hanover was the art of getting great armies beaten by small ones and of doing nothing with immense means.

Generals-in-chief are guided by their own experience or their genius. Tactics, evolutions, and the sciences of the engineer and the artillery officer may be learned from treatises, much in the same way as geometry, but knowledge of the higher branches of the art of war is only to be gained by experience and by studying the history of the wars and battles of great leaders. Can one learn in a grammar to compose a book of the *Illiad*, or one of Corneille's tragedies?

THE NAPOLEONIC WAR COMPARED WITH THOSE OF LOUIS XIV

The largest number of troops I ever had ready for action was 600,000 men. The population of my empire was above forty million souls, double the population of France under Louis XIV, who long kept 400,000 soldiers in pay. It would be an extraordinary mistake to imagine that all the conscriptions decreed were actually levied. These decrees were stratagems of war employed to deceive foreigners; they were used as a source of power, and it was the constant adherence to this system that always made people think the French armies more numerous than they actually were.

In Egypt all the corps commanders in their orders of the day exaggerated by a third the actual quantity of provisions, arms, clothing, and other articles distributed. Hence the author of the Military Summary of the campaign of 1799 is surprised that according to the orders of the day issued in that army it amounted to 40,000 men, whilst all the other authentic information he could procure went to prove that its effective force was considerably below that number. In the reports of the campaigns of Italy in 1796, 1797, and subsequent years the same means were used for conveying exaggerated ideas of the strength of the French.

No conscription was ever raised during the Imperial reign, without a law drawn up in privy council, presented to the senate by the speakers of the council of state, referred to a committee, and voted for by ballot. These deliberations were perfectly free – the voting was by white and black balls and there were often seven or eight black balls. Nearly all the senators, therefore, considered these operations useful. In this opinion they were supported by the whole nation, which was convinced that in its political circumstances it ought to be ready to make any sacrifices – as long as England should refuse to acknowledge its rights and the freedom of the seas – to restore its colonies and to put an end to the war.

It would be easy to prove that, of all the powers in Europe, France has suffered the fewest losses since 1800. Spain, which sustained so many defeats, has sustained a greater loss in proportion to her population – consider what Aragon alone sacrificed at Sargossa. The levies of Austria destroyed in 1800 at Hohenlinden and Marengo, in 1805 at Ulm and Austerlitz, and in 1809 at Eckmühl and Wagram were all disproportionate to her population. In these campaigns the French armies had with them a number of foreign troops – Bavarians, Württemburgers, Saxons, Poles, Italians, and Russians – who composed one half of the grand army; one third of the other half, under the Imperial eagle, was composed of Dutch, Belgians, inhabitants of the four departments of the Rhine, Piedmontese, Genoese, Tuscans, Romans, and Swiss. Prussia lost her whole army, of between 250,000 and 300,000 men, in her first campaign of 1806.

Our losses in Russia were considerable, but not so great as people have imagined. Four hundred thousand men crossed the Vistula, but only 160,000 went beyond Smolensk to march on Moscow – 240,000 remained in reserve between the Vistula, the Dnieper, and the Dvina. The force consisted of the corps of Marshals, the Dukes of Taranto, Reggio, and Belluno and of Count Saint-Cyr, Count Reynier, and Prince Schwarzenburg and the divisions of Loison at Wilno, Dabrowski at Borisov, and Durutte at Warsaw. Of these 400,000 men, one half were Austrians, Prussians, Saxons, Poles, Bavarians, Württemburgers, people of Berg and Baden, Hessians, Westphalians, Mecklenburgers, Spaniards, Italians, and Neapolitans. One third of the Imperial army, properly so called, was composed of Dutchmen, Belgians, inhabitants of the banks of the Rhine, Piedmontese, Swiss, Genoese, Tuscans, Romans, inhabitants of the 32nd military division, Bremen, Hamburg, &c. It contained scarcely 140,000 men who spoke the French language. The campaign of 1812 in Russia did not cost the present Kingdom of France 50,000 men. The Russian army, in its retreat from Wilno to Moscow, and in the different battles, lost four times more than the French. The burning of Moscow cost the lives of 100,000 Russians, who perished in the woods, of cold and want. Finally, the Russian army, in its march from Moscow to the Oder, was affected by the inclemency of the weather. It amounted to only 50,000 men on its return from Wilno and to fewer than 18,000 by the time it reached Kalitsch. It may be asserted, taking everything into consideration, that the losses of Russia in this campaign were six times greater than those of modern France.

The losses that England suffered in India and the West Indies, and those she sustained in her expeditions to Holland, Buenos Aires, San Domingo, Egypt, Flushing, and America, exceed all that can be imagined. The generally received opinion that the English are sparing of their soldiers is absolutely false – on the contrary, they are very prodigal of their lives, constantly exposing them in hazardous expeditions, in assaults contrary to all the rules of the art, and in most unhealthy colonies. It may be said that this nation pays its purest blood for the trade of the Indies. This may suffice to explain how the population of France has increased considerably since 1800. Empty rhetoric born of malice or ignorance made Europe believe in 1814 that there were neither men, cattle, agriculture, nor money left in France; that the people of that country were reduced to the last degree of misery; that nobody was to be seen in the fields but old men, women and children. Yet France was at that time the richest country in the universe, and possessed more species than all the rest of Europe together.

I

CORSICA

I BEGAN by memoirs with the siege of Toulon, because I did not think of my actions before then as belonging to history. But public curiosity seeks information about the origins and rise of a man who has played so large a part on the theatre of life, and it therefore seems that some notice of his family, his early years, and the beginnings of his distinguished career would not be misplaced here.

The Bonapartes are of Tuscan origin. In the Middle Ages they figured as senators of the republics of Florence, San Miniato, Bologna, Sarzana, and Treviso and as prelates attached to the court of Rome. They were allied to the Medici, the Orsini, and Lomellini families. Several of them were engaged in the public affairs of their native states; others employed themselves in literary pursuits at the period of the renaissance of literature in Italy. Guiseppe Bonaparte published *The Widow*, one of the first regular comedies of that age. Copies exist in Italian libraries and in the Royal Library at Paris, where is also preserved the *History of the Siege of Rome* by the Constable de Bourbon, of which Niccolò Bonaparte, a Roman prelate, is the author. This narrative is highly esteemed. In 1797, literary men, whom no coincidence escapes, remarked the circumstance that since the time of Charlemagne Rome had been twice menaced by great foreign armies and that at the head of one was the Constable de Bourbon and of the other one of that historian's remote descendants.

When the French army entered Bologna,[1] the Senate made sure that their *Libro d'Oro* was presented to me, by Counts Marescalchi and Caprara, so that I could see the names of several of my ancestors inscribed among those of the senators who had contributed to the honour of their city.

[1] In 1796.

In the 15th century a younger brother of the Bonaparte family settled in Corsica. At the time of the campaign of Italy, the Abbé Gregorio Bonaparte, Knight of Saint Stephen and Canon of San Miniato, was the only survivor from all the Italian branches of the family. He was an old man of great respectability and wealth. In my march on Leghorn, I stopped at San Miniato and was received with my whole staff at the house of my relation. During supper, the conversation turned entirely on a Capuchin member of the family who had been beatified a century before. The Abbé solicited my interest to procure his canonization. The same proposal was several times made to me as Emperor after the Concordat – but less importance was attached to these pious honours at Paris than at Rome.

Those who are well acquainted with the Italian language know that it is permissible to write either *buona* or *bona*. The members of the Bonaparte family have used both these spellings indiscriminately – it has happened that of two brothers one has written his name with the *u*, and the other without it. It seems that the suppression of this letter was common in very ancient times – in the town of San Miniato, in the church of Saint Francis, which belongs to the Minor Friars, on the right of the principal altar, is a tomb with this inscription:

> CLARISSIMO SUAE AETATIS ET PATRIAE VIRO
> JOANNI JACOBI MOCCII DE BONAPARTE
> QUI OBIIT ANNO M. CCCCXXXXI. DIE XXV.
> SEPTEMBRIS NICOLAUS DE BONAPARTE
> APOSTOLICAE CAMERAE CLERICUS FECIT
> GENITORI BENEMERENTI ET POSTERIS.

The Christian name Napoleon has also been the subject of much discussion. It was common in the Orsini and Lomellini families, from whom it was adopted by the Bonaparte family. The manner of writing it has been disputed in Italy. Some maintained that it was derived from the Greek (and meant 'Lion of the Desert'), others that it was derived from the Latin. The correct way of writing it is Napoleone. This name is not found in the Roman calendar, but from searches made in the martyrologies at Rome at the time of the Concordat it appears that Saint Napoleone was a Greek martyr.

My great grandfather had three sons – Joseph, Napoleon, and Lucien. The first of these left only one son, whose name was Carlo. The second left only a daughter, named Elizabeth, who was married to the head of the Ornano family. The third was a priest; he was archdeacon of the chapter of Ajaccio and died in 1791, aged eighty. Carlo, who was thus his father's sole heir, was my father. He was educated at Rome and Pisa, where he took his degree of Doctor of Laws. At a very early age he married Letizia Ramolino, an Italian lady of a very good family descended from that of Colalto of Naples. By her he had five sons and three daughters.

Carlo Bonaparte was twenty years old when war broke out in 1768.[1] He was a

---

[1] i.e. Corsica's war of independence from France.

Carlo Bonaparte, father of Napoleon. He had no fortune and only minor aristocratic connections.

warm friend to Paoli[1] and a most zealous defender of the independence of his country. Because the town of Ajaccio was, at the beginning of the war occupied by French troops, he removed with his family to Corte in the centre of the island. His young wife, then pregnant with me, followed Paoli's headquarters and the army of the Corsican patriots across the mountains in the campaign of 1769 and resided for a long time on the summit of Monte Rotondo, in the parish of Niolo. But, her pregnancy advancing, she obtained from Marshal Devaux a safe conduct to return to her house at Ajaccio. I was born on 15 August, the Feast of Assumption.

When Paoli withdrew from the island, Carlo Bonaparte followed him as far as Porto Vecchio. Carlo wanted to embark with Paoli, but the entreaties of his family, his attachment to his children, and his affection for his young wife held him back.

---

[1] Pasquale Paoli (1725–1807), Corsican patriot, national hero, and war leader.

Marie-Laetitia Ramolino Bonaparte, mother of Napoleon. 'Madame Mère.'
Napoleon said, 'As a mother she was without equal.' But he also described her
as 'more masculine than feminine in nature.'

Corsica lies twenty leagues from the coast of Tuscany, forty from that of
Provence, and sixty from that of Spain. It belongs, geographically, to the Italian
peninsula, but as Italy is not a nation, Corsica naturally forms an integral part of
France. The island is five hundred square leagues in area. It contains four coastal
towns – Bastia, Ajaccio, Calvi, and Bonifacio; sixty three *pieves*[1] or valleys; four
hundred and fifty villages or hamlets; and three great roadsteads – Saint-Florent,
Ajaccio, and Porto Vecchio – capable of sheltering the largest fleets. The island is
mountainous – a chain of lofty granite mountains runs through it from the north-
west to the south-east, dividing it into two parts. The highest peaks of this range
are permanently covered with snow. The three principal rivers are the Golo, the
Liamone, and the Tavignano. Rivers and torrents gush from the high mountains
and flow to the sea in all directions; toward their mouths there are little plains a
league or two in circumference. The coast facing Italy, from Bastia to Aleria, is a

---

[1] These were the districts – rather more than parishes, rather less than
cantons – into which the island was divided.

50

plain twenty leagues long and three to four leagues wide.

The isle is woody. The plains and hills are, or may be, covered with olives, mulberry, orange, lemon, and other fruit trees. The mountainsides are clothed with chestnut trees, among which are villages naturally fortified by their position, and on the mountain-tops are forests of pines, firs, and evergreen oaks. The olive trees are as large as those of the Levant. The chestnut trees are enormous, and of the largest species. The pines and firs are not inferior to those of Russia in height and bulk but as topmasts they will not last more than three or four years, becoming dry and brittle after that time, whereas the Russian pine always retains its elasticity and pliancy. Oil, wine, silk, and timber are the four major exports that enrich the island. The population is less than one hundred and eighty thousand souls; it might be five hundred thousand. The country provides the corn, chestnuts, and sheep necessary to feed them. Before the invasion of the Saracens, the whole of the coast was populated – Aleria and Mariana, two Roman colonies, were great cities of sixty thousand souls. However, the Muslim incursions in the 7th and 8th centuries, and those of the Barbary powers later, drove the whole population into the mountains. The plains thus became uninhabited and, of course, unhealthy.

Corsica is a beautiful country in the months of January and February. In the

Marie-Anne-Elisa Bonaparte, sister of Napoleon, was created Grand Duchess of Tuscany in 1809.

dog-days, though, it becomes dry and water grows scarce, especially in the plains. The inhabitants then like to take up their residences on the sides of the hills, whence they descend into the low grounds in winter, either to graze their flocks or to cultivate the plains.

The French government gave provincial status to Corsica and continued the magistracy of the twelve nobles, who, like the Burgundian deputies, governed the country. Carlo Bonaparte, who was very popular in the island, was a member of this magistracy; he was counsellor to the tribunal of Ajaccio. This post was an intermediate stage toward membership of the supreme council of the nation, which he achieved in 1779, when the Corsican estates appointed him as deputy in Paris. He represented the nobles; the clergy chose the Bishop of Nebbio and the third estate a Casabianca. Carlo Bonaparte took with him his two sons, Joseph and myself, the one aged eleven years, the other ten. He placed the former in the boarding school of Autun and I entered the military school at Brienne as a pupil.

I remained six years at that school. In 1783, Field Marshal the Chevalier Kergariou, inspector of the military schools, chose me to pass the following year to the military school at Paris, to which three of the best scholars, chosen by the inspector, were annually sent from each of the twelve provincial schools. I remained only eight months at Paris. In August 1785, when I was sixteen, I was examined by the Academician Laplace[1] and received the brevet of a second-lieutenant of artillery in the regiment of La Fère. Phelippeaux, Pecaduc, and Demasis passed at the same examination. All three emigrated at the beginning of the Revolution. The first defended Acre, where he demonstrated much talent

Napoleon in 1785, aged 16, the second son of a provincial lawyer.

Napoleon as a lieutenant in the artillery. He chose the artillery because the cavalry, and to some extent the infantry, were the preserves of the rich and aristocratic.

and where he died; the second, a Breton, attained the rank of major in the Austrian army; the third, who returned to France during the Consulate, was appointed chamberlain and administrator of the crown moveables.

My first posting was to the regiment of La Fère at Valence in Dauphiné. There had been some unrest in the town of Lyons and I was sent there with my battalion. The regiment afterwards went to Douai in Flanders and to Auxonne in Burgundy. I went back to Valence in 1791, when I was made a captain in the regiment of artillery of Grenoble, which was stationed there. Revolutionary ideas began to prevail. Some officers emigrated. Four captains – Gouvion, Vaubois, Galbo Dufour, and I – having preserved the good opinion of the soldiers, kept them under control.

I was in Corsica for six months in 1792. I took the earliest opportunity of waiting on Paoli, with whom my father had been very friendly. Paoli received me

[1] Pierre de Laplace (1749–1827) was at this time professor of mathematics at the military school. A considerable scholar, he made several mathematical and astronomical discoveries of great importance.

very amicably and did all in his power to retain me, to keep me out of the way of the disturbances that threatened the mother country.

In January and February 1793 I was entrusted with a counter-attack on the north of Sardinia while Admiral Truguet was attacking Cagliari. When the expedition failed, I brought my troops safely back to Bonifacio. This was my first military achievement; it won me a local reputation and, from my soldiers, testimonials of their affection for me.

A few months later, Paoli,[1] against whom charges had been laid by the Convention, threw off the mask and rebelled. Before declaring himself he communicated his scheme to me, the young artillery officer of whom he used frequently to say, 'You see that youth; he is a man for a Plutarch's biography.' But all the persuasions and influence of this vulnerable old man were unavailing. I agreed with him that France was in a frightful state, but reminded him that *nothing that is violent can last long.* I told him that, because he had an immense influence over the inhabitants and controlled the strongholds and the troops, he should maintain peace in Corsica and let the fury of the moment pass away in France. The island ought not to be torn from its natural connection on account of a momentary disorder – it had everything to lose in such a convulsion. It could never be English – it belonged geographically either to France or to Italy and, as Italy was not a single undivided power, it ought always to remain French. The old general could not controvert all this, but he persisted in his plans. I left the convent of Rostino, where this conference was held, two hours afterwards. Affairs grew worse – Corte openly rebelled and bodies of insurgents from all quarters advanced on Ajaccio, where there were no regular troops or adequate means of resistance.

In the course of twenty years, from 1769 to 1789, the island of Corsica was greatly improved. But all those benefits had no effect on the hearts of the inhabitants, who were anything but French at the time of the revolution. A lieutenant-general of infantry, who was crossing the mountains, once talked with a shepherd about the ingratitude of his fellow-Corsicans. Enumerating the benefits of the French administration, he said 'In your Paoli's time you paid double what you pay now.' 'That is true, Signor,' the shepherd replied, 'but then we gave it, and now you take it.'

The native wit of the islanders is always apparent. Thousands of examples might be given of their gift for repartee. To take one at random: several titled officers were travelling in Niolo, and one evening they said to their host, one of the poorest inhabitants of the *pieve,* 'What a difference there is between us Frenchmen and you Corsicans; see how we are clothed and maintained!' The peasant stood up, carefully looked them over, and asked each in turn his name. One was a marquis, another a baron, and the third a chevalier. 'Pooh!' said the peasant, 'I should like to be dressed as you are, I own; but, pray, are all Frenchmen marquises, barons, or chevaliers?'

[1] By now back in Corsica as French military governor.

The Revolution changed the status of the islanders – they became French in 1790. Paoli then left England,[1] abandoning a pension allowed him by Parliament. He was well received by the Constituent Assembly, by the National Guard of Paris, and even by Louis XVI. His arrival in the island produced a general rejoicing – the whole population flocked to Bastia to see him. His memory was wonderful – he knew the names of all the families, having been acquainted with their former heads. Within a few days he gained a greater influence over the people than he had ever had before. The Executive Council appointed him a general of division, and gave him command of the regular troops in the island. The National Guards chose him to command them. The Electoral Assembly nominated him as president. He thus combined in himself every kind of power. The conduct of the Executive Council was perhaps not so much political as ascribable to the spirit of the period. But, however, that may be, Paoli faithfully served the Revolution until 10 August. The death of Louis XVI completed his disillusionment. Then he was denounced by the popular societies of Provence and the Convention,[2] which never hesitated for any consideration whatsoever, summoned him to its bar. He was nearly eighty years of age and this was simply an invitation for him to lay his head on the scaffold. He had no alternative but to appeal to his countrymen and he prevailed on the whole island to revolt against the Convention. When the Convention's commissioners arrived on the island to enforce its decree, they could only hold on to the fortified places of Bastia and Calvi, with the aid of a few battalions.

Paoli would never have succeeded, though, had the decision to revolt depended on an assembly of the principal families. Although these families generally deplored the excesses that had been committed in France they thought they would prove transient. They argued that it would not be expedient, simply to avoid temporary inconvenience, to separate from the country that alone could secure the welfare and tranquillity of the island. Paoli was astonished at the little attention he obtained in private conferences – many of the very individuals who had followed him to England, where they had spent twenty years in cursing France, were now the most stubbornly opposed to him. But among the mass of the people there was only one answer when their old leader called upon them. The banner of the death's head was instantly hoisted on every steeple and Corsica ceased to be French.

A few months afterwards the English occupied Toulon. When they were forced to evacuate the town, Admiral Hood[3] anchored off San Fiorenzo. He

---

[1] To which he had fled, in 1769, after the failure of his rebellion.

[2] i.e., the National Convention in Paris.

[3] Rear-Admiral Samuel Hood (1724–1816), commander of the British Mediterranean fleet. Paoli had agreed to cede Corsica to Great Britain if the British would help him to expel the French from the island.

Pascal Paoli, Corsican nationalist. 'The history of Corsica,' wrote Napoleon,
'is nothing but the history of a perpetual struggle between the small people who
wish to live in freedom and their neighbours who wish to oppress them.'

landed 12,000 men, whom he placed under the command of Nelson. Paoli joined them with 6,000 men. They surrounded Bastia. La Combe, Saint-Michel, and Gentili[1] defended the town with the greatest courage and it capitulated only after a siege of four months. Calvi resisted for forty days after the opening of the trenches. General Dundas,[2] who commanded an English corps of 4,000 men and was encamped at San Fiorenzo, refused to take part in the siege of Bastia, not choosing to compromise his troops without the special orders of his government.

An extraordinary event now took place. The King of England placed the crown of Corsica upon his head, where it was strangely associated with the crown of Fingal. In June 1794 the Council of Corsica, of which Paoli was president, proclaimed that the island's political connection with France was for ever broken off and that the crown of Corsica should be offered to the King of England. A deputation, consisting of Filippo of Vescovato, Negroni of Bastia, and Cesari Rocca of La Rocca, under the presidency of Galeazzi, proceeded to London and

[1] The three National Convention commissioners.

[2] Sir David Dundas (1735–1820). He was to command the military contingent at Nelson's funeral.

the king accepted the crown. He appointed Sir Gilbert Elliot viceroy. The Council at the same time decreed a constitution, modelled on that of England, to secure the liberties and privileges of the country. Elliot was a man of merit – he was appointed Governor-General of India in 1806[1] – but he soon quarrelled with Paoli, who had retired to the mountains. Paoli disapproved of the conduct of the viceroy, who was influenced by two young men, Pozzo di Borgo and Colonna, his secretary and his aide-de-camp. Paoli in his turn was accused of being a restless character, of not being able to make up his mind to live as a private individual, and of always wanting to act the part of master of the island. Nonetheless, the influence he possessed there, which was undisputed, the services he had rendered to England, and the respectability of his character and conduct induced English ministers to treat him with great indulgence and he had several conferences with the viceroy and the secretary of state. In one of these, piqued by several observations that had been made, he said, 'This is my kingdom, I carried on war against the King of France for two years; I expelled the republicans. If you violate the privileges and rights of the country, I can still more easily expel your troops.' A few months afterwards the King of England, out of the interest he felt for Paoli's tranquillity and happiness, wrote to him urging him to come and end his days in a country in which he was respected and had been happy. The secretary of state took this letter to him at Ponte-Lechio. Paoli felt it was an order. He hesitated, but there were then no signs of the ending of the Reign of Terror in France and the Army of Italy was still in the county of Nice. In declaring war against the English, Paoli would have exposed himself to the hostility of two great belligerent powers. He submitted to fate and went to London, where he died in 1807. I owe it to his memory to state that, in all his letters from England during the last eight years of his life, he constantly advised his countrymen never to separate from France but to share the fortune, good or bad, of that great nation. He left by his will considerable sums to establish a university at Corte.

Had the English wished to preserve their influence in Corsica,[2] they should have acknowledged the independence of the country, established Paoli's power, and granted a few trifling subsidies. Then they could have preserved a kind of supremacy and retained privileges of anchorage for their squadrons in the principal roadsteads, especially that of San Fiorenzo. They would have then possessed a bridgehead in the Mediterranean; they might, in case of need, have raised an auxiliary corps of five or six thousand brave men for service in this sea; and the ports of Corsica would have been at their command. The numerous refugees who were in France would gradually have rallied to a national government and France herself, at the peace, would readily have sanctioned a

[1] In fact in 1807, by which time Elliot (1751–1814) had been created Baron Minto.

[2] France regained the island in 1796.

state of affairs that public opinion had suggested to Choiseul.[1]

The Corsicans were extremely dissatisfied with the English governors – they understood neither their language, their habitual gloom, nor their manner of living. Men who were continually at table, almost always intoxicated, and of uncommunicative dispositions exhibited a remarkable contrast to their own manners. The difference of religion was also a cause of dislike. This was the first time since the origin of Christianity that their territory had been profaned by an heretical worship and everything they saw confirmed them in their prejudices against the Protestant religion. The lack of ritual and ceremony in its worship and its unadorned, dismal temples disappointed the southern imaginations which find so agreeable the pomp and splendour of the Catholic religion, its beautiful churches adorned with pictures and frescoes, and its imposing ceremonies. The English scattered gold profusely; the inhabitants accepted it, but felt no gratitude toward the givers.

The Bonaparte family retired to Nice and afterward into Provence. Our property in Corsica was devastated – our house, after being pillaged, was long used as barracks by an English battalion. On reaching Nice, I was preparing to join my regiment, when General Dugear, who commanded the artillery of the Army of Italy, required my services and employed me in the most delicate operations. The general-in-chief[2] was greatly embarrassed by a whole series of circumstances – a few months after I arrived in Nice Marseilles had revolted and the Marseillese army had now taken possession of Avignon, the communications of the Army of Italy were cut off, there was a lack of ammunition, and a powerful convoy had been intercepted. General Dugear sent me to the Marseillese insurgents, to try to induce them to let convoys pass and to take all necessary measures to secure and accelerate their passage. I went to Marseilles and Avignon, had interviews with the leaders of the insurgents, convinced them that in their own interests they should not antagonize the Army of Italy, and got the convoys through. Meanwhile, Toulon had surrendered to the English. I, now a major (*chef de bataillon*), was ordered to serve at the siege of Toulon, on the proposal of the committee of artillery. I joined the besieging army on 12 September 1793.[3]

While I was staying at Marseilles I had the opportunity to observe all the insurgents' weaknesses and the gaps in their defences and I drew up a little pamphlet, which I published before I left. I tried to open the eyes of these desperate people and predicted that the only result of their revolt would be to give the men of blood of the day an excuse to send the ringleaders of the revolt to the scaffold. This pamphlet, which had a powerful effect, played a part in calming the prevailing unrest.

[1] Etienne, Duc de Choiseul (1719–85), the French politician who had bought Corsica for France in 1768.

[2] General Jean Carteaux.

[3] For Napoleon's part in the siege of Toulon *see* pp. 36–7 and 71–83.

II

SUPPER AT
BEAUCAIRE, 1793

I WAS in Beaucaire on the last day of its fair. Chance gave me for companions at supper two businessmen from Marseilles,[1] a man from Nîmes, and a manufacturer from Montpellier.

After several minutes taken up with introducing ourselves, it transpired that I was from Avignon[2] and was a soldier. My companions' attention, which had all the week been concentrated on business matters and money-making, was now turned to current affairs and the immediate future, as was the conversation. They were anxious to hear my opinion, so that they could compare it with their own and revise or add to their assumptions about the future, which would affect each of them in a different way.

The two Marseillais seemed especially subdued. The evacuation of Avignon had led them to have misgivings about everything. Nothing was left to them but a considerable anxiety as to the lot in store for them. Mutual confidence, however, soon rendered all members of the party talkative, and they began a discussion, more or less in the following terms:

[1] Marseilles had risen against its Jacobin municipal authorities in June 1793 – part of a counter-revolutionary movement in many French provincial towns. The rebels, who called themselves Federalists, by and large supported the Girondists who had been overturned in Paris. They were mostly middle-class citizens who had lost local power after the fall of the French monarchy and who had been subjected to minor Reigns of Terror and some oppression by the Jacobin authorities.

[2] There had been a Federalist revolt in Avignon, too, which had received support from Marseilles.

THE NÎMOIS: Is the army of Carteaux[1] strong? I am told that it suffered considerable loss in the attack, but if it is true that it was repulsed, why have the Marseillais evacuated Avignon?

NAPOLEON: The army was four thousand strong when it attacked Avignon. It is six thousand strong today. Within four days' time it will be ten thousand strong. It has lost five men killed and four wounded. It has not in any way been repulsed, for it has not made a single attack in battle formation. It cantered around the place, made some attempts to force the gates by setting mines up against them and fired a few cannon balls to test the strength of the garrison. It then retired within its quarters to concert its plan of attack for the following night. The Marseillais were three thousand six hundred strong. They had more artillery and their guns were of larger calibre. Yet they have been obliged to recross the Durance. That astonishes you, does it? The reason is that only veteran troops can stand up to the uncertainties of a siege. As it was, we were masters of the Rhône, of Villeneuve, and of the surrounding country. We would have been able to cut all their communications. Therefore they had to evacuate the town. The cavalry pursued their retreat, and have taken many prisoners, while losing only two guns.

THE MARSEILLAIS: That is not the account I heard. I do not wish to question the truth of your statements, seeing that you were present, but you must admit that what you have just told us is nonsense. Our army is at Aix. Three good generals have arrived to replace the former ones. Fresh battalions are being raised at Marseilles. We have a new train of artillery, including several 24-pounders. In no time we will be in a position to retake Avignon, or at the very worst we shall remain masters of the Durance.

NAPOLEON: There you are! That is precisely what they tell you to drag you into a precipice that deepens at every instant and which perhaps will swallow up the most beautiful town in France, the town that has deserved more than any other the praise of patriots. They told you that you would sweep across France and call the tune for the Republic to dance to. Yet your first stages have been reverses. They told you that Avignon could hold out a long time against twenty thousand men, yet a single column of the army, without siege artillery, was master of the place within twenty-four hours. They told you that the South had risen to a man, and yet you stand alone. They told you that the Nîmois cavalry would crush the Allobroges,[2] when these were already at Saint-Esprit and Villeneuve. They told you that four thousand Lyons[3] men were on the march to reinforce you. At that moment the Lyonnais were negotiating their terms for peace.

Admit then that you are being deceived. Consider the incompetence of your leaders and mistrust their calculations. *The most dangerous counsellor is self-*

---

[1] *See* p.58, note 2.

[2] A light cavalry force that formed part of Carteaux's army.

[3] Another city in revolt. The rebellion there was finally put down, bloodily, in October 1793.

---

esteem. You are by nature of quick intelligence. You are being led to your destruction by the same process which has ruined so many peoples – your vanity is being flattered. You have riches and a considerable population, but you are told that they are greater than they are. You have rendered striking services to the cause of Liberty. They remind you of them without drawing attention to the fact that the Genius of the Republic was then on your side, whereas it abandons you today.

Your army, you say, is at Aix with a great train of artillery and good generals. Well, I can only tell you that whatever it does it will be beaten. You had three thousand six hundred men; a good half have slunk away. Marseilles and a few refugees of the department can furnish you with four thousand men. That is a lot. You will therefore have five to six thousand men, lacking cohesion, lacking unity, without war experience.

You have good generals. I have never heard of them. I am not in a position to contest their ability, but their whole attention will be taken up with details. They will not be backed up by their subordinates. Whatever reputation they may have acquired, they will be able to do nothing to maintain it, because they would need two months to organize their army decently, and within four days Carteaux[1] will be over the Durance – and with what soldiers! He will have the excellent light troop of the Allobroges, the veteran regiment of Burgundy, a good regiment of cavalry, the fine battalion of the Côte-d'Or, which has a hundred times seen victory go before it into battle, and six or seven other corps, all of veteran soldiers, fortified by their successes on the frontiers and over your army.

You have some 24- and 18-pounders and you believe it impossible that you should be dislodged. Your authority is popular opinion, but the trained soldier will tell you, and a disastrous experience is going to show you, that good 4- and 8-pounder cannon are as effective for field work as pieces of larger calibre, and are in many respects preferable to them. You have gunners freshly recruited; your antagonists have artillerymen, from regular regiments, who are the masters of Europe in their profession.

What will your army do if it concentrates on Aix? It will be beaten. It is an axiom in the military art that to remain in one's entrenchments is to be defeated – practice and theory are in agreement on this point. The walls of Aix are more worthless than the worst trench in open country if you consider their great length and the houses that cluster around them within pistol range. Rest assured then that this course of action, which seems to you to be the best, is the worst. Besides, how will you be able, in so short a time, to provision the town with all that it will need?

Will your army advance to attack the enemy? It is fewer in numbers, its artillery is less adapted for open country – it will be broken in pieces. After that, complete rout – for the cavalry will prevent it from rallying.

[1] General Jean Carteaux defeated the Marseillais army on 25 August 1793 and entered the city.

Suppose, then, that you wait to fight it out in the Marseilles territory. One party of considerable strength there is in favour of the Republic. It will be just the opportunity they want. They will effect a junction and this city, the centre of the commerce of the Levant, the trading centre for the south of Europe, will be overthrown.

Remember the recent example of Lille and consider the barbarous rules of war. Why, what madness has all of a sudden taken possession of your people? What fatal blindness is it that leads them on to ruin? How can you hope to hold out against the entire Republic? Even if you should force this army to fall back before Avignon, can you doubt that within a few days new combatants will come to replace the first? Do you suppose that the Republic, which gives the law to Europe, is going to take it from Marseilles?

In conjunction with Bordeaux, Lyons, Montpellier, Nîmes, Grenoble, the Jura, the Eure, and the Calvados, you undertook a revolution. You had a fair chance of success. The people who started it may have been wrongly motivated, but at least you had an imposing array. Today, on the other hand, when Lyons, Nîmes, Montpellier, Bordeaux, the Jura, the Eure, Grenoble, and Caen have adopted the Constitution, when Avignon, Tarascon, and Arles have given way, admit that your obstinacy in holding out is folly. The reason for it is that you are under the influence of men who, no longer having anything to lose, are dragging you down with them to ruin.

Your army will be composed of the most comfortably off elements of the wealthy of your city, because the Sans-Culottes are only too likely to turn against you. You are, therefore, going to endanger the flower of your youth, who are accustomed to sway the commercial balance of the Mediterranean and enrich you by their business methods and their speculations. You are going to pit them against veteran soldiers who have been spattered a hundred times with the blood of aristocrats mad with rage or of ferocious Prussians.

Leave it to poor countries to fight to the bitter end. The inhabitant of the Vivarais, the Cévennes, or Corsica need not fear the result of a fight. If he wins, he has fulfilled his aim. If he loses, he finds himself where he was before, in a position to make peace. He is no worse off.

But you! Lose one battle, and happiness and the fruit of a thousand years of effort, pain, and sacrifice become the prey of the soldier.

Those are the risks that you are being made to run with so little heed.

THE MARSEILLAIS: You move quickly and you alarm me. I agree with you that the situation is critical. It may even be true that not enough heed is being paid to the position we are in.

But admit that we still have immense resources with which to oppose you.

You have persuaded me that we cannot hold at Aix. Your remark that we cannot sustain a long siege is perhaps unanswerable, but do you really believe that the whole of Provence will for long stand impassively while Aix is blockaded? The South will rise spontaneously and your army, shut in on all sides, will be lucky if it can get back over the Durance.

NAPOLEON: That shows how little you understand the temper of men or of the moment. Everywhere there are two parties. From the moment you are besieged, the secession party will be worsted in all the provinces. The example of Tarascon, Orgon, and Arles ought to convince you of that. Twenty dragoons were enough to restore the former administrators and put the others to rout. From now on any great movement in your favour is impossible in your department. There might have been a chance when the army was beyond the Durance and you were united. At Toulon, now, feelings are very divided, and the separatists have not the same ascendancy as at Marseilles. They will therefore have to remain inside the town in order to hold their enemies.

As for the department of the Lower Alps, you know that the Constitution has been accepted there almost unanimously.

THE MARSEILLAIS: We will attack Carteaux in our mountainous country, where his cavalry will not be able to help him.

NAPOLEON: As if an army guarding a town were master of the point of attack! In any case, it is not true that there are mountains near Marseilles sufficiently precipitous to allow you to discount the cavalry. On the other hand, your olive groves are steep enough to make the attack from artillery more formidable and to give your enemies a great advantage, because in this cut-up country the good artillerymen's speed and certainty of movement and accuracy of range-finding give him the superiority.

THE MARSEILLAIS: You consider us stripped of all resources, then! Can it be possible that it was written in the destiny of this town – which resisted the Romans, and maintained some of its own laws under the despots who succeeded them – that it should become the prey of a few brigands? Is the Allobroges, loaded with the spoils of Lille, to rule in Marseilles! Are Dubois de Crancé and Albitte[1] to go unchallenged! Are these men, athirst for blood, whom chance misfortunes of circumstance have placed at the helm of affairs, to be the absolute masters? What a melancholy prospect you offer! Our properties, on one pretext or another, would be invaded. Hourly, we should be the victims of brutal troopers drawn together under the colours only by the hope of pillage. Our best citizens would be imprisoned and criminally put to death. The Club[2] would raise its monstrous head again to carry out its infamous projects! Nothing can be worse than so horrible a picture. Better to risk oneself with the possibility of victory than to become a victim without hope.

NAPOLEON: That is just the trouble with civil war. We tear each other to pieces, we hate each other, and we kill each other without knowing what our opponents are like. What do you suppose the Allobroges are? Africans? Or the inhabitants of Siberia? Well, they are not! They are your compatriots, men of Provence, of

[1] Edmond Dubois de Crancé and Antoine Albitte were the National Convention's representatives in the area. They had tried, unsuccessfully, to disarm the rebellious National Guard in Lyons.

[2] i.e., of Jacobins.

63

Dauphiné, of Savoy. They are considered barbarians because their name is foreign. If your phalanx happened to be called the Phocian phalanx, the most fabulous reports would be believed on the strength of it.

Admittedly you have reminded me of one instance of barbarity, that of Lille. I am not trying to justify it, but I will explain it. The people of Lille killed the negotiator who had been sent to them under a flag of truce. They resisted, although with no hope of success. They were taken by assault. The victorious soldiers entered the city, under fire, in the midst of dead and dying. Exasperation did the rest. It was not possible to restrain them. But these soldiers, whom you call brigands, are our best troops, our most disciplined battalions, their reputation above calumny.

Dubois de Crancé and Albitte, long-standing friends of the people, have never deviated from the straight path. They are criminals in the eyes of the wicked. But Condorcet, Brissot, and Barbaroux[1] were also regarded as criminals when they were pure. It is the prerogative of good people to have evil thought of them by the bad. You seem to think that they are ruthless with you, whereas in point of fact they treat you as erring children. Do you suppose that, if they had wished to prevent it, Marseilles would have been allowed to withdraw the goods which it had at Beaucaire? They could have confiscated them until the issue of war was decided! They did not choose to do it, and thanks to them you can return in peace to your homes.

You call Carteaux an assassin. Indeed! Perhaps you do not know that this general worries himself to death over order and discipline. Witness his conduct at Saint-Esprit and at Avignon. Not a pin was plundered. He had a sergeant imprisoned for violating the sanctuary of a citizen's home without a specific order. The sergeant's only crime was that he had arrested one Marseillais of your army who had stayed behind in the house. Some people in Avignon were penalized for going so far as to point out a house as that of an aristocrat. I could cite the case of a writ issued against a common soldier on the accusation of theft. Your army, on the other hand, has killed or murdered more than thirty people, has broken into the sanctuary of families, and has filled the prisons with citizens on the vague pretext that they were brigands. Do not get alarmed about the army. It respects Marseilles, because it knows that no city has done as much for the public weal. You have eighteen thousand men away at the front, and you have not spared yourselves in any circumstances. Shake off the yoke of the small number of aristocrats who are leading you, adopt once again more reasonable counsels, and you will have no truer friend than the soldier.

[1] These were three of the early Revolutionaries. The Marquis de Condorcet became a member of the National Convention in 1792; a victim of the Girondists, he was arrested and died in prison in 1794. Jacques Brissot had been one of the mob that stormed the Bastille; he became a leader of the Girondins in the Convention and was guillotined in 1793. Charles Barbaroux, a deputy for Marseilles in the Convention and a follower of Brissot, was one of the leaders of the Federalist revolt in Caen.

THE MARSEILLAIS: Oh! but your soldiers have degenerated far below what they were in the army of 1789. That army would not take arms against the nation. Your soldiers ought to emulate so fine an example and not turn their weapons against their fellow-citizens.

NAPOLEON: By that thinking, the Vendée would by now have planted the Bourbon flag above the walls of a rebuilt Bastille, and the camp of Jalès would rule over Marseilles!

THE MARSEILLAIS: The Vendée wants a king, wants a counter-revolution. The war of the Vendée[1] and of the camp of Jalès is a war of fanaticism. Ours, on the contrary, is one of true republicans, enemies of anarchy and scoundrels. Do we not fly the tricolour flag? And why should we want slavery?

NAPOLEON: I know well that the people of Marseilles are poles apart from those of the Vendée in the matter of a counter-revolution. The people of Vendée are robust and healthy, those of Marseilles are weak and ill. The pill has to be sugared, and to establish the new doctrine they have to be deceived. But after four years of revolution, after so many plots, plans, and conspiracies, human perversity has been stretched to its utmost limits in all directions. Men have sharpened their natural faculties to perfection.

This is so true that, in spite of the departmental coalition, despite the skill of the leaders, and the great variety of tricks to which the enemies of the revolution have resorted, the common people have everywhere woken up, just when they were believed to be completely bewitched.

You have the tricolour flag, you say?

Paoli flew it on Corsica, too, in order to gain time to deceive the people, to crush the true friends of liberty, and to drag his countrymen into his ambitions and criminal projects. He flew the tricolour flag and he had buildings belonging to the Republic fired upon. He had our troops driven out of the fortresses, and he disarmed those who were in them. He mobilized in order to drive out the Republicans in the island, and he pillaged the magazines, selling everything they contained, at any price he could get, to fund his rebellion. He violated and confiscated the properties of the most well-to-do families simply because they supported the unity of the Republic. He had himself appointed generalissimo so as to declare all who remained in our armies enemies of the country. He had already made the expedition (to the Maddalena Islands) against Sardinia fail, yet he had the impudence to call himself the friend of France[2] and a good Republican and he tricked the Convention which decreed his dismissal. Finally he behaved so cleverly that, even when he had been found out through his own letters found at Calvi, it was too late. The enemy fleets were able to intercept all

[1] The Vendeé rose in revolt in spring 1793. Beginning with riots against army recruitment levies operating in the area, the revolt turned into a full-scale civil war.

[2] Paoli led an expedition to capture Sardinia in 1793. The French suspected that he deliberately brought about its failure because he was conspiring with the British.

communications and stop any information reaching the mainland.

It is no use playing with words. It is necessary to analyse actions – and you must admit that, if your actions are examined, it is easy to prove you counter-revolutionaries.

What effect has the movement you set on foot produced in the Republic? You have led her to the brink of ruin. You have delayed the operations of our armies. I do not know if you are in the pay of the Spaniard and the Austrian, but certainly they could not wish for a better diversion of our strength. What more could you do if you were in their pay?

Your success is day and night the object of the greatest concern of the best-known aristocrats. You have placed at the head of your organizations and your armies avowed artistocrats such as Latourette, an ex-colonel, and Soumise, an ex-lieutenant-colonel of engineers, men who deserted their regiments in the hour of war so as not to have to fight for the liberty of peoples. Your battalions are full of such men and your cause would not be theirs if it were that of the Republic.

THE MARSEILLAIS: But are Brissot, Barbaroux, Condorcet, Buzot, Vergniaud also aristocrats?[1] Who then established the Republic? Who overthrew the tyrant? Who, finally, kept up the fighting during the most critical phase of the last campaign?

NAPOLEON: I am not concerned with whether these men, who have done such wonderful services for the people on so many occasions, have conspired against the people. It is enough for me to know that, after the Mountain,[2] either from public spirit or party spirit, took extreme measures against them, carried hostility to them to the last extreme and decreed them prisoners, and (I will even allow you this) falsely accused them, the Brissot party would have been finished had there been no civil war to give them the opportunity to lay down the law to their enemies.

Thus your war was especially wasted on them. Had they been worthy of their former reputation, they would have upheld the Constitution by throwing down their arms – they would have sacrificed their own interests to the public good. But it is easier to quote Decius[3] than to imitate him, and today they stand

---

[1] The answer is no. For Brissot, Barbaroux, and Condorcet *see* p. 64, note 1. François Buzot and Pierre Vergniaud were both Girondist members of the National Convention. Vergniaud became a victim of the anti-Girondist purge of 1793; Buzot left Paris to take part in the Federalist uprising in Caen. Their arch-enemy Jean-Paul Marat once characterized them as 'Buzot the hypocrite' and 'Vergniaud the stool-pigeon'.

[2] The Mountain was the name given to the Jacobin deputation from Paris in the National Convention. Led by Robespierre, it took its name from the seats, high up in the back of the hall, it had taken in the old Legislative Assembly.

[3] Decius, Emperor of Rome from 249 to 251 was said to have been unwilling to become emperor but did so, at the army's insistence, with the words quoted by Napoleon.

convicted of the worst of all crimes. By their own actions they have justified the decree of execution against them. The blood they have spilled has cancelled out the services they once rendered.

THE MANUFACTURER OF MONTPELLIER: Even though you have looked at this matter from the point of view most favourable to the Brissot party, you have most convincingly proved that they were really guilty. But, guilty or not, we no longer live in times when we go to war over the life of a few individuals.

England spilt torrents of blood for the families of Lancaster and York, and France for the Lorraines and the Bourbons. Are we still in those barbarous times?

THE NÎMOIS: Yes, that is why we abandoned the people of Marseilles as soon as we realized that they wanted a counter-revolution, and that they were fighting over private quarrels. They were unmasked from the moment they refused to publish the Constitution. Then we forgave the Mountain a few irregularities. We forgot Rabaud[1] and his Jeremiads and saw only the new-born Republic, surrounded by the most terrible of coalitions, threatening to stifle it in its cradle; we saw only the joy with which the aristocrats and all Europe wished to conquer it.

THE MARSEILLAIS: You deserted us in cowardly fashion, after having encouraged us with short-lived deputations.

THE NÎMOIS: We acted in good faith, while you had the fox under your cloak all the time. We wanted the Republic, and so we accepted a republican constitution. You were dissatisfied with the Mountain and the events of 31 May.[2] You ought therefore to have accepted the constitution to overthrow the Mountain legally and put an end to its mission.

THE MARSEILLAIS: We want the Republic too, but we want our constitution to be framed by representatives who are free in their actions. We want liberty, but we want to be given it by representatives whom we respect. We do not want our constitution to uphold pillage and anarchy. Our first conditions are: no Club,[3] none of these interminable primary assemblies, and lastly, respect of private property.

THE MANUFACTURER OF MONTPELLIER: It is clear to anyone who cares to think about it that a part of Marseilles wants the counter-revolution. They pretend to want the Republic, but that is a veil which would become more transparent every day. You would soon see the counter-revolution in all its nakedness and would take it for granted. For a long time the veil which covered it was only made of

[1] Does Napoleon mean Jean Rabaut Saint-Etienne? A Protestant pastor, he was one of the earliest Revolutionaries and became a member of the Convention, but he became sickened by the excessss of the Revolution and ended up a victim of the guillotine.

[2] On 31 May 1793 the Paris mob surrounded the Convention. Three days later the Girondists were purged and the Reign of Terror may be said to have begun.

[3] i.e. the Jacobins of the Mountain.

gauze. Your people were good, but, if it were not for the Genius of the Revolution which watches over them, they would have been perverted.

Our troops have done a great service to the country in fighting you so energetically. There was no reason for them to imitate the army of 1789, for you are not the nation. The centre of unity is the Convention, which is the true sovereign, above all when the people are divided.

You have overthrown all the laws and all the conventions. By what right did you strip your department of its constitutional authority? As if Marseilles had created it in the first place! By what right does the battalion of your city over-run the surrounding districts? By what right did your National Guards presume to enter Avignon? The department as such being dissolved, the district of this town was of greater antiquity than yours. By what right did you presume to trespass on the territory of Drôme? And why should you imagine that this department has not the right to call the public arm to its defence? Thus you have cut across every established right. You have set up anarchy, and since you choose to justify your actions by the right of force, I presume you must be brigands and anarchists.

You have set up a popular government. Marseilles alone has elected it. It is in defiance of all the laws and can only be a tribunal of blood, because it is the tribunal of a single faction. You have subjected the whole of your department to this tribunal, by force. By what right? Are you not therefore usurping the very authority which you censure in Paris? Your sectional committee has acknowledged that it has affiliations. There, then, you have an amalgamation comparable to that of the Clubs against which you protest. Your committee has executed administrative acts among the communes of Var. There, then, is an instance of the abuse of territorial divisions.

At Avignon you have imprisoned whole administrative bodies without authority, without decree, without warrant. You have violated the sanctuary of families, and abused the liberty of the individuals. You have assassinated in cold blood in the public squares. You have renewed the very scenes which sullied the origin of the revolution, and whose horror you exaggerated, without information, without legal procedure, without even knowing the victims, merely on the accusation of their enemies. You have seized them, snatched them from beside their children, dragged them through the streets, and sabred them to death.

The number you have sacrificed in this manner is reckoned as high as thirty. You have dragged the Statue of Liberty in the mud. You have given her a public execution. Unbridled youth subjected her to every degree of violence. You have slashed at her with swords. You cannot deny that. It was in broad daylight, and more than two hundred of your people witnessed this criminal outrage. The procession passed through several streets and arrived at the Clock Square.

I will check my reminiscences and my indignation.

Is this, however, what you want the Republic to be? You have slowed up the progress of our armies at the front by stopping the convoys. How can you deny the evidence of so many facts, and escape the title of 'enemies of the country'?

NAPOLEON: There is no doubt about the Marseillais having hindered the operations of our armies and having wished to destroy liberty. That is not the point at this moment. The question is whether they have any hope and what course of action remains for them to adopt?

THE MARSEILLAIS: We certainly seem to be worse off than I thought, but *one is very strong when one is resolved to die*, and we are prepared to die rather than assume once more the yoke of the men governing the state.

You know that a drowning man will clutch at any straw, and so will we, rather than let ourselves be murdered.

Yes, we have all taken a hand in this new revolution; we shall be sacrificed as the victims of revenge. Two months ago there was a conspiracy to slaughter four thousand of our best citizens. Imagine to what excesses they would go today. One can never forget that monster, who, nevertheless, was one of the leading men of the Club. He had a citizen hanged, plundered his house, and raped his wife, after making her drink a glass of her husband's blood.[1]

NAPOLEON: How horrible! But is it true? I doubt it, because you know that no one believes in rape now.

THE MARSEILLAIS: Anyway, rather than submit to such men, we will go to any length. We will hand ourselves over to the nation's enemies. We will call in the Spaniards, then whom no-one could be more unlike us and no-one more hateful to us. By the sacrifice that we are prepared to make, judge for yourself the dastardliness of the men whom we fear.

NAPOLEON: Surrender to the Spaniards! We will not give you the time.

THE MARSEILLAIS: They are reported every day to be outside our harbours.

THE NÎMOIS: That threat alone would be enough for me to judge whether the Confederates[2] or the Mountain were the real republicans. The Mountain was at one moment in the weakest possible position. The disorder appeared to be universal. But did it ever speak of calling in the enemy? Don't you realize that the struggle between the patriots and the despots of Europe is a fight to the death?

If therefore you expect help from them, it means that your leaders have good reasons for being accepted by them. But I still have too high an opinion of your people to believe that you, at Marseilles, would be the foremost in so cowardly a project.

NAPOLEON: Do you even think that you would be inflicting any damage on the Republic, and that your threat is at all alarming? Consider it.

The Spaniards have no troops to disembark. Their ships cannot enter your harbour. If you called in the Spaniards, that would be a useful ruse for your leaders to get away with some part of their fortune. But indignation would be general throughout the Republic. You would have sixty thousand men on top of you within a week. The Spaniards would carry off what they could from Marseilles and there would still be enough left to enrich the victors.

---

[1] Presumably Robespierre is meant. The accusation is pure canard.

[2] Of Marseilles.

If the Spaniards had thirty or forty thousand men in their fleet ready to disembark, your threat would be frightening. As it is, it is only silly and it will simply hasten your end.

THE MANUFACTURER OF MONTPELLIER: If you were really capable of such a vile action, not a single stone ought to be left standing in your superb city. It should be dealt with in such a way that a traveller passing through the ruins a month from now would believe that you had been destroyed a hundred years ago.

NAPOLEON: Listen to me, my friends from Marseilles, shake off the yoke of the few criminals who are leading you into the counter-revolution. Re-establish your constitutional authorities. Accept the Constitution. Restore to the deputies their liberty. Let them go to Paris to plead for you. You have been led astray. It is nothing new for the people to be so led by a small number of conspirators and intriguers. In all ages the gullibility and ignorance of the mob have been the cause of most civil wars.

THE MARSEILLAIS: Ah, sir! Who can do any good in Marseilles? Is it to be the refugees who arrive among us from all sides of the department? Their only interest is to act like desperadoes. Is it to be those who govern us? Are they not in the same predicament? Is it to be the people? One half does not know its own plight, being blinded and fanatic. The other half is disarmed, suspected, trampled down. In direst sorrow, then, I see only misfortunes without remedy.

NAPOLEON: There, you see reason at last. Why should not a similar change of heart be accomplished among a large number of your fellow citizens who have been deceived and who are still of good intentions? Then Albitte, who can only want to spare French blood, will send you some man who is loyal and capable. Our disputes will be at an end, and without halting for another instant, the army will march to the walls of Perpignan and make the Spaniard, who is puffed up with some slight success, dance the Carmagnole. Marseilles will continue to be the centre of gravity for liberty. It will only be necessary for her to tear a few pages out of her history.

This happy forecast put the company in good humour once more. The Marseillais willingly paid for several bottles of champagne, which entirely dissipated cares and anxieties alike. We went to bed at two o'clock in the morning, arranging to meet again at breakfast the next day, when the Marseillais had several more doubts to put forward, and I plenty of interesting truths to bring home to him.

III

TOULON

THE Constituent Assembly went in some respects too far and in others not far enough. It was composed of men endowed with distinguished talents, but devoid of experience. It committed two errors, which might have produced the total ruin of the nation. The first was to establish a Constitution,[1] at odds with the experience of all ages and states, whose mechanism was contrived not to strengthen social order and promote national prosperity but to restrict and annul the public power, which is that of government. Great as this error was, it was less flagrant and had less deplorable consequences than the second – that of persisting in re-establishing Louis XVI on the throne after the affair of Varennes. What then ought the Assembly to have done? It ought to have sent commissioners extraordinary to Varenness, not to bring the king back to Paris, but to clear the way for him, and to conduct him safely beyond the frontiers; to have decreed, by virtue of the Constitution, that he had abdicated; to have proclaimed Louis XVII king; and to have created a regency, confiding the care of the king, during his minority, to a princess of the House of Condé and a council of regency made up of the principal members of the Constituent Assembly. A government so conformable to principle, and so national, would have found means to remedy the disadvantages of the Constitution – the force of events would soon have led to the adoption of the necessary modifications. It is probable that France would then have triumphed over all her enemies, domestic and foreign, and experienced neither anarchy nor revolutionary government. By the time the king reached his majority the Revolution would have been so well

---

[1] That of 1791. Signed by the king on 14 September, it dissolved the Constituent Assembly and replaced it with a new Legislative Assembly.

---

rooted that it might have defied every attack. But to act otherwise was to entrust the navigation of the vessel, during a most tremendous storm, to a pilot no longer capable of steering her, to call the crew to insurrection and revolt in the name of public safety and to invoke anarchy.

In the Constituent Assembly the Royalists sat on the right and the Constitutionalists on the left, placing themselves at the head of the people. But in the Legislative Assembly the Constitutionalists took the right side, and the Girondins the left. In the Convention,[1] the Girondins in their turn formed the right side, and the faction called the Mountain formed the left side, directing the popular party. In the Constituent Assembly the Constitutionalists proclaimed the principle that the Assembly should be protected by the National Guard and called for the expulsion of the regular troops. In the Legislative Assembly they maintained a contrary opinion and clamoured to be guarded by regular troops, but the Girondins indignantly rejected the use of a hired army against the majority of the people. Then the Gironde party, in its turn, claimed the protection of a regular army against the popular party. Thus did the different parties alternately change their opinions according to circumstances.

The factions of the Gironde and the Mountain were too violent in their mutual animosity. Had they both continued to exist, there would have been so many impediments to the administration of the government that the Republic could not have maintained the contest against the combination of all Europe. The good of the country required the triumph of one of these parties. On 31 May [1793], the Gironde fell, and the Mountain thenceforth governed without opposition. The consequence is known – the campaigns of 1793 and 1794 delivered France from foreign invasion.

Would the result have been the same had it been the Gironde party that gained the day and the Mountain that had been sacrificed on 31 May? I think not. The Mountain party, although checked, would always have possessed great influence in France, in the popular societies and armies, and this would have diminished the energies of the nation, the whole of which were necessary at that crisis. There was undoubtedly more talent in the Gironde than in the Mountain, but the Gironde was composed of more speculative men, less resolute and less decisive, who would have governed more mildly – probably under their rule only a few of the excesses that the revolutionary government of the Mountain committed would have taken place. The Gironde prevailed in the towns of Lyons, Marseilles, Toulon, Montpellier, Nîmes, Bordeaux, and Brest and in several provinces. The Mountain had its base in the capital and it was supported by all the Jacobins in France. On 31 May it triumphed; twenty-two deputies, the leaders of the Gironde, were proscribed.

At the beginning of the winter of 1793, the Army of Italy had experienced a check – the first maritime expedition attempted by the Republic, the attack on

[1] The National Convention succeeded the Legislative Assembly in September 1792.

[2] *See* p.66, note 2.

Sardinia, covered us with shame. Never, indeed, was an expedition planned with such want of forethought and so little talent.

Admiral Truguet, who commanded the squadron, was master of the sea. He had attacked and burnt the little town of Oneglia, which belonged to the King of Sardinia, and the outrages committed on that occasion by his men had filled all Italy with horror.

Some people thought that the expedition against Sardinia had been proposed by Truguet, not, as others held, by the Executive Council, but in either case it was Truguet who was responsible for its management and direction.

The General of the Army of Italy, who was to furnish Truguet with troops, chose not to give him those who had crossed the Var and placed at his disposal 4,000 or 5,000 men from the Marseillese phalanx, who were still at Marseilles. General Paoli, who commanded in Corsica, furnished three battalions of regular troops from that island. The Marseillese phalanx was as undisciplined as it was cowardly, the officers being no better than the men, and it was riddled with all sorts of revolutionary disorder and excess. Nothing could be expected from such a rabble. The three Corsican battalions drawn from the 23rd Division, on the other hand, were picked troops.

In February 1793 the French troops landed, in the face of fire from the batteries defending the shores of Cagliari. Next morning, at daybreak, a regiment of Sardinian dragoons charged the Marseillese advanced posts, which, instead of resisting, took to flight, crying 'Treason'. These Marseillese massacred the excellent regular officer who had been chosen to lead them. The Sardinian dragoon regiment would have cut off the whole of the Marseillese phalanx had not the three regular battalions from Corsica stopped the charge and given Admiral Truguet time to re-embark his troops without further loss. The admiral then returned to Toulon, after having lost many ships – burnt by his own orders on the shores of Cagliari.

There was, in fact, no real purpose to this expedition, although its pretended aim was to make it easier for Provence to obtain much-needed corn from Africa and from the grain-rich island of Corsica. But then the Executive Council should have chosen a general officer fitted for the command and have given him artillery officers and engineers of sufficient ability, with several troops of cavalry and horse artillery. The force should have consisted of 15,000 effective men, not mere revolutionary levies. The blame was afterwards laid upon the general who commanded the Army of Italy, but that was unjust – he disapproved of the expedition and, in reserving his regular troops to defend the frontier and the county of Nice, he studied the interest of the Republic. He was tried and perished on the scaffold, under the pretext that he had committed treason in Sardinia and Toulon, but in fact he was guiltless in both places.

The squadron was composed of good vessels, which were manned without exception by able seamen. But the crews were, like the Marseillese troops, undisciplined and mutinous – they formed themselves into clubs and popular assemblies and debated the affairs of the nation. When they arrived in any port they would falsely accuse some of the citizens of being nobles or priests and try to hang them and, generally, they spread terror wherever they went.

In consequence of the events of 31 May in Paris, Marseilles revolted, raised several battalions, and sent them to the assistance of Lyons. General Carteaux, who was detached from the Army of the Alps with 2,000 men, defeated the Marseillese at Orange, drove them out of Avignon, and entered Marseilles on 24 August 1793. Toulon, which had joined Marseilles in the insurrection, received the principal Marseillese insurgents within its walls and in concert with them its inhabitants summoned the English and gave up the place to them. Toulon was a place of the utmost importance to us – we had there from twenty to twenty-five ships of the line, as well as grand buildings and vast stores. On hearing the news, General Lapoype, accompanied by representatives of the people Freron and Barras, set out from Nice with 4,000 men. He advanced on Saulnier, observing the redoubts of Cape Brun (which the enemy occupied with a part of the garrison of Fort la Malgue), the screen formed by the forts of Pharaon, and the line between Cape Brun and Fort Pharaon.

Approaching from the opposite direction, General Carteaux, with representatives of the people Albitte, Gasparin, and Salicetti, advanced on Beausset and observed the passes of Ollioules, which were in possession of the enemy. The combined troops – English, Spanish, Neapolitans, Sardinians, etc., collected from all quarters – were in possession not only of Toulon itself but also of all the defiles and avenues for six miles around the town.

On 10 September, General Carteaux made an attack upon the passes of Ollioules, and gained possession of them. His advanced posts arrived within sight of Toulon and of the sea.

Twelve or fifteen days after the taking of the passes of Ollioules, I, at that time chief of a battalion of artillery, arrived from Paris, having been sent by the Committee of Public Safety to command the besieging artillery. Throughout the Revolution, non-commissioned officers and ensigns had been promoted to the higher ranks of the artillery. Many of them were capable of making good artillery generals, but many had neither the ability nor the knowledge necessary for the high rank to which their seniority and the spirit of the times had promoted them.

On my arrival, I found the headquarters at Beausset. The troops were busy making preparations to burn the Allied squadrons in the roadstead of Toulon. Next day I went with the General-in-Chief to visit the batteries. I was greatly surprised to find a battery of six 24-pounders positioned a quarter of a league from the passes of Ollioules, three gunshots away from the English vessels and two from the shore, and all the volunteers of the Côte-d'Or and the soldiers of the regiment of Burgundy busy in all the local country houses heating cannon balls. I did not conceal my astonishment.

My first care as commandant of artillery was to gather together a great number of artillery officers who had been dispersed by the circumstances of the Revolution. At the end of six weeks, I was able to assemble, organize, and supply a park of two hundred pieces of artillery. Colonel Gassendi was placed at the head of the constructions depot at Marseilles. The batteries were advanced and sited on the most advantageous points of the shore from where their effect was such that some large vessels were dismasted and several smaller ones sunk, and the enemy was forced to abandon that part of the roadstead.

While preparations for the siege were still being made, the army was considerably reinforced. The Committee of Public Safety sent plans and instructions for the conduct of the siege. They had been drawn up in the committee of fortifications by General D'Arçon of the engineers, an officer of great merit. The chief of battalion, Marescot, and many brigades of engineer officers arrived. Everything seemed to be ready. A council was called under the presidency of representative Gasparin, a sensible and well-informed man who had himself been in the service. The instructions from Paris were read – they detailed at great length the operations necessary to recover Toulon by a regular siege.

For a month I had been carefully reconnoitring the ground and I had made myself perfectly acquainted with the whole terrain. It was I who proposed the plan of attack that resulted in the reduction of Toulon. I regarded all the proposals of the committee of fortifications as totally useless and was of the opinion that a regular siege was simply not necessary. If from fifteen to twenty mortars, thirty or forty pieces of cannon, and furnaces for red-hot balls could be positioned where they could maintain fire upon every point of the great and lesser roadsteads, then it was evident that the combined squadron would be obliged to withdraw. The garrison would then be placed in a state of blockade, being unable to communicate with the squadron, which would be forced to stand out to sea. That being so, I was convinced that the combined forces would prefer to withdraw the garrison, and burn the French vessels and magazines, rather than leave in the fortress 15,000 or 20,000 men who sooner or later would be obliged to surrender, but who would then have no bargaining power to ensure terms of capitulation for themselves.

In short, I said that there was no need to march against the town at all, but only to occupy the position I proposed. This at the extreme point of the promontory of Balagnier and l'Eguillette: I had discovered this position a month before, and had pointed it out to the General-in-Chief, assuring him that if he would occupy it with three battalions he would take Toulon in four days. But the English had become, since I first observed it, so sensible of its importance, that they had disembarked 4,000 men there, had cut down all the wood that covered the promontory of Le Caire, which commanded the whole position, and had employed all the resources of Toulon, even the galley-slaves, to entrench themselves there, making of it, in their words, 'a little Gibraltar'. Now, therefore, the point, which a month ago might have been seized and occupied without opposition, required a serious attack. It would not be advisable to risk a direct assault. Instead, batteries of 24-pounders and mortars should destroy the breastworks, which were built of wood, break down the palisades, and throw a shower of shells into the interior of the fort. Then, after forty-eight hours of vigorous fire, the fort should be stormed by picked troops. Two days after the fort had been taken, I judged, Toulon would belong to the Republic. This plan of attack was much discussed and the engineer officers who were present at the council were of the opinion that my project was a necessary preliminary to a regular siege, the first principle of all sieges being the establishment of a strict blockade. From this time on there was unanimity of opinions.

The enemy constructed two redoubts under the two hillocks, one of which immediately commanded l'Eguillette and the other Balagnier. These redoubts flanked Little Gibraltar and covered the two sides of the promontory.

In accordance with their plan, the French raised five or six batteries against Little Gibraltar and constructed platforms for fifteen mortars. A battery had also been raised of eight 24-pounders and four mortars against Fort Malbosquet, the construction of which was a profound secret to the enemy, as the men who were employed on the work were entirely concealed from observation by a plantation of olives. It was intended that this battery should not be unmasked until the moment came to march against Little Gibraltar.[1] On 20 November, however, the representatives of the people went to inspect it and were told by the cannoneers that, although it had been ready for eight days and although its effect was expected to be great, no use had yet been made of it. Thereupon, without further explanation, the representatives ordered the cannoneers to open fire. With great joy, the cannoneers obeyed, opening alternating[2] fire from the battery.

General O'Hara, who commanded the Allied army at Toulon, was greatly surprised that so considerable a battery had been sited close to a fort of such importance as Malbosquet and he gave orders that a sortie should be made against it at daybreak. The battery was situated in the centre of the left of the army, where about 6,000 troops, occupying the line from Fort Rouge to Malbosquet, were so disposed as to prevent all individual communication, though too much scattered to make an effectual resistance at any given point.

An hour before dawn, General O'Hara sallied out of the garrison with 6,000 men and, meeting with no obstacle, his skirmishers only being engaged, spiked the guns of the battery.

In the meanwhile, the drums beat the call to arms at headquarters, and Dugommier with all haste rallied his troops. I posted myself behind the battery, on a little hillock where I had previously established an arms depot. A communication trench led from this point to the battery. Seeing from this point that the enemy had formed to the right and left of the battery, I conceived the idea of leading a battalion stationed near me through the communication trench. By this plan I succeeded in coming out unperceived among the brambles close to the battery and immediately commenced a brisk fire upon the English, whose

---

[1] Known to British military historians as Fort Mulgrave.

[2] As opposed to firing volleys.

surprise was such that they imagined it was their own troops on the right who, through some mistake, were firing on those on the left. General O'Hara hastened towards the French to rectify the supposed mistake, when he was wounded in the hand by a musket-ball, and a sergeant seized and dragged him prisoner into the communication trench. His disappearance was so sudden that his own troops did not know what had become of him.

In the mean time, Dugommier, with the troops he had rallied, placed himself between the town and the battery. This movement disconcerted the enemy, who forthwith commenced their retreat. They were hotly pursued as far as the gates of the fortress, which they entered in the greatest disorder and without being able to ascertain the fate of their general. Dugommier was slightly wounded in this affair. A battalion of volunteers from the Isère distinguished itself during the day.

General Carteaux had conducted the siege at its commencement, but the Committee of Public Safety had found it necessary to relieve him of the command. This man, originally a painter, had become an adjutant in the Parisian corps. He was afterwards employed in the army and, having been successful against the Marseillese, had been appointed by the deputies of the Mountain, on the same day, both brigadier-general and general of division. He was extremely ignorant and had nothing military about him, but he was not ill-disposed and committed no excesses at Marseilles when the city was taken.

General Doppet succeeded Carteaux. A Savoyard physician, he was an unprincipled man, entirely governed by interested motives. He was a decided enemy to all who possessed talent. He had no idea of war, and was anything but brave. This Doppet nevertheless, by a singular chance, in forty-eight hours after his arrival very nearly took Toulon. A battalion of the Côte-d'Or and a battalion of the regiment of Burgundy, on duty in the trenches before Little Gibraltar, had one of their men taken by a Spanish company on guard at the redoubt. They saw their companion ill-treated and beaten, and at the same time the Spaniards offered them every insult by shouts and indecent gestures. The French, enraged, ran to their arms, commenced a brisk fire, and marched against the redoubt.

I immediately hastened to the General-in-Chief, who was ignorant of what was going on. We galloped to the scene of action and there, seeing how matters stood, I persuaded him to support the attack, assuring him that to advance would incur no greater loss than to retire. Doppet, therefore, ordered the different corps of reserve to advance. All were quickly on the alert, and I marched at their head. Unfortunately, an aide-de-camp was killed by Doppet's side. Panic-stricken, he ordered the drums to beat a general retreat, recalling his soldiers at the very moment when the grenadiers, having repulsed the enemy skirmishers, had reached the gorge of the redoubt and were about to take it. The troops were highly indignant, and complained that painters and physicians were sent to command them. The Committee of Public Safety recalled Doppet and, perceiving at last the necessity of employing a real military man, they sent Dugommier, an officer who had seen fifty years of service, who was covered with scars, and who was as dauntless as the weapon he wore.

The enemy was every day receiving reinforcements. There was much public anxiety about the direction of the siege operations. People could not conceive why every effort should be directed against Little Gibraltar, quite in an opposite direction to the town. 'Nothing has been done yet,' it was said all over the country, 'except to lay siege to a fort which has no connection at all with the permanent fortifications of the town. They will afterwards have to take Malbosquet and open trenches against the town.' All the popular societies made denunciation after denunciation on this subject. Provence complained of the long duration of the siege. Shortages became so great that Fréron and Barras, losing all hope of the prompt reduction of Toulon, wrote in great alarm from Marseilles to the Convention, to persuade it to consider whether it might not be better that the army should raise the siege and recross the Durance. (This manoeuvre had been planned by Francis I at the time of the invasion of Charles V. He retired behind the Durance while the enemy troops laid Provence waste and then, when famine compelled them to retreat, he attacked them with fresh vigour.[1]) The representatives argued that, if our troops were to evacuate Provence, the English would have to find provisions for its support. Then, after the harvest, offensive operations might be renewed with considerable advantage by an army complete in itself and invigorated by rest. This measure was, they said, absolutely necessary; after four months' operations, Toulon had not as yet even been attacked and, as the enemy was continually being reinforced, we should in the end be obliged to do precipitately and in confusion what at the present moment might be effected with regularity and order. However, a few days after the letter had been received by the Convention, Toulon was taken. The letter was now disowned by the representatives as a forgery. This was ill-judged – the letter was genuine and it gave a true picture of the opinions held, at the time it was written, about the outcome of the siege and the difficulties prevailing in Provence.

Dugommier determined that a decisive attack should be made upon Little Gibraltar. I accordingly threw 7,000 or 8,000 shells into the fort, while thirty 24-pounders battered the works.

On 18 December, at four in the afternoon, the troops left their camps and marched towards the village of Seine. The plan was to attack at midnight, in order to avoid the fire of the fort and the intermediate redoubts. Then, at the moment when everything was ready, the representatives of the people held a council to deliberate whether the attack should be carried out or not. Probably they feared failure and wanted to throw all the responsibility for the affair upon General Dugommier, or perhaps they were influenced by the opinion, held by many officers, that success was impossible, chiefly on account of the dreadful weather – the rain was falling in torrents.

Dugommier and I ridiculed these fears. Two columns were formed, and marched against the enemy.

[1] This was during the war between Charles V (1500–1558), Holy Roman Emperor, and Francis I (1494–1547), King of France. The Imperial army invaded Provence in 1524.

The Allied troops, to avoid the barrage of shells and balls that fell upon the fort, occupied a station a small distance to its rear. The French had great hopes of getting to the fort before its defenders could reach it, but the Allies had placed a line of skirmishers in front of the fort and, as the musketry commenced firing at the very foot of the hill, their troops hastened to the defence of the fort, whence a very brisk fire was immediately opened. Case-shot showered all around. At length, after a most furious attack, Dugommier, who was in his customary place at the head of the leading column, was obliged to give way. In the utmost despair he cried out 'I am a lost man!' Success was in every way important in those days, for the want of it usually led the unfortunate general to the scaffold.

Cannon- and musket-fire continued. I detached my second-in-command, Captain Muiron of the artillery, a young man full of bravery and resource, with a battalion of light infantry, which moved forward, supported by the second column a musket-shot behind. Muiron had a perfect knowledge of the terrain and he made such good use of the windings of the ascent that he led his troops up the mountain without sustaining any loss. He emerged at the foot of the fort and rushed through an embrasure. His soldiers followed him – and the fort was taken. The English and Spanish cannoneers were all killed at their guns. Muiron himself was dangerously wounded by a thrust from the pike of an English soldier.

As soon as they were masters of the fort, the French turned the cannon against the enemy.

Dugommier had been in the redoubt for three hours when the representatives of the people came, with their drawn swords in their hands, to load the occupying troops with eulogies. (This contradicts the accounts of that time, which incorrectly state that the representatives marched at the head of the columns.)

At break of day the French marched on Balagnier and l'Eguillette, which the enemy had already evacuated. The 24-pounders and the mortars were brought up to these emplacements, in the hope of firing from there upon the combined fleets before noon, but I considered it impossible to station the guns there. The emplacements were of stone, and the engineers who had constructed them had made a mistake by placing a large tower of masonry just at their entrance, so near the platforms that any balls that struck them, as well as splinters and debris, would have rebounded on the gunners. The French cannon were therefore positioned on the heights behind the batteries. They could not have opened fire until next day, but no sooner did Lord Hood, the English admiral, see that the French had occupied these positions, than he made signal to weigh anchor.

He then went to Toulon to let it be known that there was not a moment to be lost in getting the fleet to sea. The weather was dark and cloudy and everything pointed to the approach of the Libeccio (or Lebèche), the south-west wind so terrible at this season. The council of the combined forces immediately met and, after mature deliberation, agreed unanimously that Toulon was no longer tenable. They accordingly proceeded to make arrangements to embark the troops, to set fire to the marine establishments, and to burn and scuttle such French vessels as they could not carry away with them. They also gave notice to all the inhabitants that any who wished to leave might embark on board the English and Spanish fleets.

These disastrous tidings caused scenes of such confusion that they would be difficult to describe. So, too, would the disarray and shock of the garrison and the unfortunate inhabitants, who only a few hours before – reckoning on the great distance of the besiegers from the town, the slow progress of the siege during four months, and the expected arrival of reinforcements – had hoped not only to effect the raising of the siege but even to become masters of Provence.

In the night, Fort Poné was blown up by the English, and an hour afterwards a part of the French squadron was set on fire. Nine 74-gun ships and four frigates or corvettes became a prey to the flames.

The fire and smoke from the arsenal resembled the eruption of a volcano and the thirteen vessels burning in the road were like so many magnificent displays of fireworks. The masts and shapes of the vessels were silhouetted against the blaze, which lasted many hours and formed an unparalleled spectacle. It was a heart-rending sight to the French to see such great resources and so much wealth consumed within so short a period. They feared, at first, that the English would blow up Fort La Malgue, but it seemed that they had not time to do so.

I then went to Malbosquet. The fort was already evacuated. I ordered the field-pieces to sweep the ramparts of the town. The howitzers heightened the confusion by throwing shells into the port until the mortars, which, with their carriages, were on the road, could be positioned in the batteries and also shell the port.

General Lapoype took possession of Fort Pharaon, which was evacuated by the enemy. During all this time the batteries of l'Eguillette and Balagnier kept up an incessant fire on the vessels in the roadstead. Many of the English ships were much damaged and a great number of transports with troops on board were sunk. The batteries continued their fire all night. At daybreak the English fleet was seen out at sea. By 9 o'clock in the morning a high Libeccio wind got up and the English ships were forced to put into the Hyères.

Many thousands of the families of Toulon had followed the English, so that the revolutionary tribunals found only a few of the guilty in the town – all the parties most deeply implicated had left. Nevertheless, more than a hundred unfortunate wretches were shot within the first fortnight.

Orders afterwards arrived from the Convention to demolish the houses of Toulon. The absurdity of this measure did not impede the execution of it, and many houses were pulled down, which had subsequently to be rebuilt.

On 18 December, at 10 o'clock at night, Colonel Cervoni broke down a gate and entered the city at the head of a patrol of 200 men. He traversed the whole town. The deepest silence prevailed. The port was cluttered with baggage that the inhabitants had not had time to put on board. A rumour spread that matches had been lit to blow up the powder magazines and squads of cannoneers were accordingly sent to secure the magazines. Immediately after, the troops intended to guard the city entered. All was confusion at the naval arsenal, where eight or nine hundred galley slaves were making the most strenuous exertions to extinguish the fire. These convicts had rendered the greatest services, having intimidated the English officer, Sir Sidney Smith,[1] who had been ordered to burn the ships and the arsenal. He had performed his task very ill and the Republic was indebted to him for all the valuable treasures recovered. I went to the spot with all available cannoneers and workmen and succeeded, in the course of a few days, in extinguishing the fire and preserving the arsenal. The loss the navy had suffered was considerable, but it still retained immense resources – all the magazines were saved except the general one. There were thirty-one ships of war at Toulon at the time of its treacherous surrender. Four sail had been employed in carrying 5,000 soldiers to Brest and Rochefort. The combined troops burned nine in the roads, left thirteen dismantled in the basins, and carried off four, one of which was burnt at Leghorn.[2] Fears had been entertained that they would blow up the basin and several of the jetties, but they had not had enough time. The wrecks of the thirteen ships and frigates burnt and sunk in the roads constricted the channel and many attempts were made to remove them in the course of the ten following years; in the end, some Neopolitan divers succeeded in getting them all out, bit by bit, by sawing up the hulls. The army entered Toulon on the 19th. The troops had been seventy-two hours under arms amid mud and rain; they abandoned themselves, on entering the town, to some excesses, which seemed authorized by the promises made to the soldiers during the siege.

The General-in-Chief restored order by declaring that all effects in Toulon were the property of the army. He had the contents of the private warehouses and the furniture of the deserted houses collected in central magazines. The Republic afterwards seized everything, allowing only the bonus of a year's pay to every officer and soldier. The emigration from Toulon was very considerable – refugees crowded the English, Neapolitan, and Spanish ships, which were consequently obliged to anchor in the roads of Hyères and to make the refugees encamp in the isles of Porquerolles and the Levant. It is said that the number of these emigrants amounted to 14,000. Dugommier gave orders to leave the white flag flying on all the forts and bastions of the roadsteads and in this way a large number of ships of war and merchantmen bringing men or supplies intended for the enemy were deceived – in the first thirty days after the taking of the city, richly laden vessels were captured daily. On one occasion an English frigate carrying supplies to the amount of several millions cast anchor beneath the great tower. She was considered to be taken and accordingly two naval officers in a

[1] Six years later, in 1799, Sidney Smith (1764–1840) crossed Napoleon's path again; he led the seamen and marines who reinforced Acre against Napoleon's siege. *See* p.130.

[2] All this adds up to thirty ships. Napoleon seems to have omitted one from his reckoning.

small boat boarded her and informed the captain that they took possession of the frigate as their prize. The captain clapped them into the hold, cut his cables, and was lucky enough to escape without further loss. One evening towards the end of December I was on the quay at about 8 o'clock when I saw an English skiff draw alongside. An officer landed from it and asked me for directions to Lord Hood's lodgings. He was the captain of a fine brig which brought despatches and announced the approach of reinforcements. The brig was taken and the despatches read.

The representatives established a revolutionary tribunal, according to the laws of the time. In general, though, all the guilty had escaped and fled with the enemy and all those who had decided to stay were conscious of their innocence. Nevertheless, the tribunal had several people arrested who had been prevented by various accidents from following the enemy and caused them to be punished in expiation of their guilt. But eight or ten victims were too few and recourse was had to a dreadful measure, characteristic of the spirit of that time. It was proclaimed that everyone who had been employed in the arsenal while the English were in possession of the town must attend a roll call in the Champ de Mars. These people were led to believe that this was so that they might be re-employed and so, confidently, nearly two hundred head workmen, inferior clerks, and other junior employees attended and had their names registered. Thus it was proved by their own confession that they had retained their posts under the English government, and the revolutionary tribunal, in the open field, immediately sentenced them to death. A battalion of Sans-Culottes and Marseillese, brought expressly for the purpose, shot them. This deed requires no comment. It was, though, the only execution that took place at Toulon. That any persons whatever were killed by grapeshot is untrue – neither I nor the regular cannoneers would have lent themselves to such an action. It was the cannoneers of the Revolutionary Army who committed atrocities at Lyons.

By a decree of the Convention, the Port of Toulon was renamed Port de la Montagne, and all its public buildings except those deemed necessary for the navy and the public service, were ordered to be demolished. This extravagant decree was put into execution, but very tardily – only five or six houses were demolished, and these were rebuilt shortly after. The English squadron remained for a month or six weeks in Hyères roadstead, which created some anxiety – there were no mortars in Toulon capable of throwing projectiles farther than 1,500 *toises*[1] and the squadron was anchored 2,400 *toises* from the shore. Had we then had some of the Villantroys mortars that we later used, the squadron would not have been able to anchor in the roadsteads. At length, after blowing up the forts of Porquerolles and Porteros, the enemy sailed to the roadsteads of Porto-Ferrajo, where they landed a great number of the emigrants from Toulon.

The news of the taking of Toulon, at the moment when it was least expected, produced a wonderful effect in France and throughout Europe. On 25 December

[1] A *toise* equals 6ft 6in (1.98 metres).

the Convention ordered a national festival. The taking of Toulon was the signal for the successes that attended the campaign of 1794. Shortly afterwards the Army of the Rhine retook the Weissenburg Lines[1] and raised the blockade of Landau. Dugommier, with part of the army, marched for the eastern Pyrenees, where Doppet was only making blunders. Another part of this army was sent into the Vendée, and many battalions returned to the Army of Italy. Dugommier ordered me to follow him, but other orders arrived from Paris, directing me first to secure the defences of the Mediterranean coasts, and especially of Toulon, and then to join the Army of Italy in command of the artillery.

It was at Toulon that my reputation began. All the generals, representatives, and soldiers who had heard me give my opinions in the different councils, three months before the taking of the town, anticipated my future military career. From that moment I won the confidence of all the soldiers of the Army of Italy. Dugommier wrote to the Committee of Public Safety soliciting the rank of brigadier-general for me, and using these words, 'Reward this young man and promote him, for if he is ungratefully treated he will promote himself.' In the Army of the Pyrenees, Dugommier was always talking about his commandant of the artillery at Toulon, and his high opinion was impressed on the minds of all the generals and officers who afterwards went from the Army of Spain to the Army of Italy. Whenever Dugommier gained victories he would send couriers from Perpignan to me at Nice.

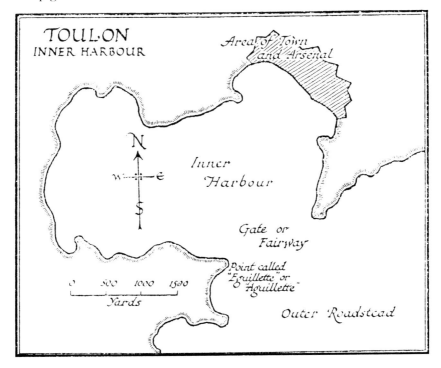

[1] Actually taken in October 1793.

IV

13 VENDÉMIAIRE[1]

THE fall of Danton and Robespierre's municipality of 31 May[2] led to the overthrow of the Revolutionary government. The Convention was afterwards governed by a succession of factions none of which ever succeeded in gaining supremacy and as a result its principles varied every month. A dreadful system of reaction afflicted the interior of the Republic, properties ceased to be saleable, and the *assignats*[3] were depreciating daily. The armies were unpaid – the soldier was no longer certain even of his bread and only requisitions and the *maximum*[4] supplied him with the means of subsistence. Troop recruitment, the laws about which had been applied with the greatest rigour under the Revolutionary government, ceased. The armies still continued to gain brilliant successes, because they were more numerous than ever, but they suffered daily losses which there were now no means of repairing.

The foreigners' party, ostensibly aiming at the restoration of the Bourbons, increased daily in strength; communications with foreign countries had become easier; and the destruction of the Republic was openly being contrived. The

---

[1] 5 October 1795.

[2] Danton was executed on 5 April 1794. Robespierre's fall came a little later – he was guillotined on 28 July 1794.

[3] *Assignats* were originally notes given to creditors of the government; they were made legal tender in August 1790 and so became the paper currency of Revolutionary France.

[4] The *maximum*, setting a ceiling on the prices of grain and some groceries and household goods, was imposed in September 1793.

Revolution had lost its novelty. It had alienated many people by adversely affecting their interests. All this was now recalled and it excited popular opposition, growing daily more violent, against those who had governed, held administrative posts, or in any manner participated in the success of the Revolution. Pichegru had sold himself, yet the enemies of the Republic had few converts in the army, which remained faithful to the principles for which it had shed so much of its blood and gained so many victories. All parties were tired of the Convention – it was even tired of its own existence. At length it saw that its own safety, and that of the nation, required that it should fulfil its commission without delay. On 21 June 1795 it decreed the constitution known as the Constitution of the year III, which confided the government to five persons called the Directory, and the legislature to two councils called those of the Five Hundred and of the Ancients. This constitution was submitted to the acceptance of the people convoked in primary assemblies.

It was the general opinion that the short duration of the Constitution of 1791 was to be attributed to the law by which the Constituent Assembly excluded its members from the legislature. The Convention did not fall into the same error,

Louis-Marie de Laraveillière-Lepeaux, a member of the Directory.

but annexed to the constitution two additional laws, by which it prescribed that two thirds of the new legislature should be composed of members of the Convention, and that the electoral assemblies of the departments should on this occasion only have to nominate one third of the two councils. These two additional laws were submitted to the acceptance of the people. They excited general dissatisfaction. The partisans of the foreigners saw all their schemes frustrated: they had flattered themselves that the majority of the two councils would be composed of men inimical to the Revolution, or even of those who had suffered by it, and had hoped to accomplish a counter-revolution by means of the legislature itself. This party found many excellent reasons with which it disguised the true motives of its discontent. It alleged that the rights of the people were disregarded by the Convention, which, having been empowered only to propose a constitution, was usurping the functions of an electoral body. As to the constitution itself, it was, undoubtedly, preferable to what then existed. On this point all parties were unanimous. Some, indeed, would have preferred a president to the five directors and others would have desired a more popular council, but in general this new constitution was favourably received. The secret committees which directed the foreign party were by no means anxious about forms of government which they did not mean to maintain. They studied nothing in the constitution but the means of availing themselves of it to operate the counter-revolution – and whatever tended to wrest authority out of the hands of the Convention and of the conventionals was conducive to that end.

The forty-eight Sections of Paris assembled, forming forty-eight tribunes, which were immediately occupied by the most violent orators – La Harpe, Serizi, Lacretelle the younger, Vaublanc, and Regnault de Saint Jean d'Angely. It required little talent to excite people against the Convention, but several of these orators displayed much.

After 9 Thermidor, the city of Paris had organized its National Guard. Its object had been to get rid of the Jacobins, but it had fallen into the contrary extreme, and the counter-revolutionists formed a considerable number of its members. This National Guard, which consisted of 40,000 armed and uniformed men, shared the exasperation that all the Sections felt against the Convention. The Sections rejected the additional laws and succeeded each other at the bar of the Convention, loudly declaring their opinions. The Convention, however, imagined that all this agitation would subside as soon as the provinces had declared their opinions by accepting the constitution and the additional laws; it mistakenly compared this agitation in the capital to the commotions so common in London, or those that so often occurred in Rome at the time of the Comitia. On 23 September, the Convention proclaimed the acceptance of the constitution and additional laws by the majority of the primary assemblies of the Republic, but on the following day the Sections of Paris, taking no notice of this acceptance, appointed deputies to form a central assembly of electors, which met at the Odéon.

The Sections of Paris had measured their strength; they despised the weakness of the Convention. This assembly at the Odéon was a committee of insurrection. The Convention awoke from its lethargy, annulled the meeting at the Odéon, declared it illegal, and ordered its committees to dissolve it by force. On 10 Vendémiaire the armed power proceeded to the Odéon and executed this order. A few men collected on the square of the Odéon and indulged in some murmuring and abuse, but offered no resistance. But the decree for closing the Odéon excited the indignation of the Sections. The Lepelletier Section, whose district house was the Convent of the Filles Saint-Thomas, was the most angered. The Convention decreed that the place of its sitting should be closed, the meeting dissolved, and the Section disarmed. On 12 Vendémiaire, at 7 or 8 o'clock in the evening, General Menou, accompanied by the representatives of the people, Commissioners to the Army of the Interior, proceeded with a numerous body of troops to the Lepelletier Section's meeting place to execute the decree of the Convention. The infantry, cavalry, and artillery were all crowded together in the Rue Vivienne, at the end of which is the Convent of the Filles Saint-Thomas. The Sectionaries occupied the windows of the houses in this street. Several of their battalions drew up in line in the courtyard of the convent, and the military force under General Menou found itself compromised. The Committee of the Section had declared themselves representatives of the sovereign people and refused to obey the orders of the Convention. After spending an hour in useless conferences, General Menou and the Commissioners of the Convention withdrew by a sort of capitulation, without having dissolved or disarmed the meeting. The Section, thus victorious, declared itself to be permanent, sent deputations to all the other Sections, boasted of its triumph, and urged the measures calculated to ensure the success of its resistance. In this manner it prepared for the action of 13 Vendémiaire.

I had been for some months attached to the Committee directing the movements of the armies of the Republic and was at the Feydeau theatre when I heard of the extraordinary scenes that were happening so near me. I was curious to see all that was occurring. I saw the conventional troops repulsed and hastened to the tribunes of the Convention to witness the effect of this news and see what character and colouring would be given it. The Convention was in the greatest agitation. The representatives deputed to the army, wishing to exculpate themselves, eagerly accused Menou, attributing to treachery what arose from unskilfulness alone. Menou was put under arrest. Different representatives then appeared at the tribune, stating the extent of the danger, the magnitude of which was only too clearly shown by the news arriving every moment from the Sections. Everyone proposed his own choice for the general to succeed Menou. The Thermidorians proposed Barras, but he was by no means agreeable to the other parties. Those who had been at Toulon with the Army of Italy, and the members of the Committee of Public Safety, who were in daily communication with me, proposed me as the person most capable of extricating them from their present danger, because of my quick eye and the energy and moderation of my character. Mariette, who belonged to the party of the Moderates, and was one of the leading members of the Committee of Forty, approved this choice. I, who was in the crowd and heard all that passed, deliberated for about half an hour on the course I was to adopt. At length I made up my mind, and repaired to the Committee, where I represented in the most forcible manner the impossibilitty of directing so important an operation while clogged by three representatives, who in fact would exercise all power, and impede all the operations of the general. I added that I had witnessed the events in the Rue Vivienne; that the commissioners had been most to blame, and had nevertheless appeared in the Assembly as triumphant accusers. Struck with the truth of this reasoning, but unable to remove the commissioners without a long discussion in the Assembly, the Committee, to conciliate all parties (for it had no time to lose), determined to propose Barras as general-in-chief, appointing me second-in-command. Thus they got rid of the three commissioners without giving them any cause of complaint. Barras was of tall stature; he sometimes spoke in moments of violent contention, and his voice would then fill the hall. His moral faculties, however, did not allow him to go beyond a few phrases; the passionate manner in which he spoke might have made him pass for a man of resolution. He did not possess habits of application, yet he succeeded better than was expected. He was censured for his extravagance, his connections with contractors, and the fortune he made during the four years he was in office, which he took no pains to conceal, and which greatly contributed to the corruption of the administration at that period. As soon as I found myself invested with the command of the forces that were to protect the Assembly, I went to the room in the Tuileries where Menou was held, to obtain from him the necessary information about the strength and disposition of the troops and the artillery. The army consisted of only 5,000 soldiers of all arms; the artillery park was composed of forty pieces of cannon, at the Sablons, guarded by twenty-five men. It was 1 o'clock in the morning. I immediately despatched a major of the 21st Chasseurs,[1] with 300 horse, to the Sablons, to bring off all the artillery to the garden of the Tuileries. Had another moment been lost, he would have been too late. Reaching the Sablons at 3 o'clock in the morning, he fell in with the head of a column from the Section Lepelletier which was coming to seize the park. His troops being cavalry, and the ground a plain, the Sectionaries judged, however, that all resistance was useless and accordingly retreated. At 5 o'clock in the morning the forty pieces of cannon entered the Tuileries.

Between 6 o'clock and 9 o'clock, I placed my artillery pieces at the head of the Pont Louis XVI, the Pont Royal, and the Rue de Rohan, at the Cul de Sac Dauphin, in the Rue Saint-Honoré, at the Pont Tournant, etc., entrusting the guarding of them to officers of known loyalty. The matches were lighted, and the little army was distributed at the different posts or in reserve in the garden and at the Carrousel. The drums beat to arms in every quarter. During this time the

---

[1] This was Murat. Napoleon is surprisingly casual about this first appearance on the scene of the man who was to become one of his most distinguished generals and loyal followers and his brother-in-law.

---

battalions of the National Guard were stationing themselves at the outlets of the streets surrounding the palace and the garden of the Tuileries – their drums had the audacity to come and beat the call to arms at the Carrousel and the Place Louis XV. The danger was imminent – 40,000 well-armed and well-organized National Guards were in the field and enraged against the Convention. The regular troops entrusted with the Convention's defence were few in number, and might easily be led away by the feelings of the people surrounding them. In order to increase its forces, the Convention distributed arms to 1,500 men called the Patriots of 1789; these were men who, after 9 Thermidor, had lost their jobs and been driven from their departments by public opinion. They were formed into three battalions and placed under the command of General Berruyer. These men fought with the most determined valour – they were an example to the regular troops and the success of the day was mainly due to them.

While the urgency of the danger increased every moment, a committee of forty members, consisting of the Committees of Public Safety and General Security, directed all the affairs, discussed much, but resolved on nothing. Some proposed that the Convention should lay down arms and receive the Sectionaries as the Roman senators received the Gauls. Others wished the members to withdraw to Caesar's camp on the heights of Saint Cloud, there to be joined by the Army of the Coasts; and others proposed that deputations should be sent to the forty-eight Sections, to make them various proposals.

During these vain discussions, at about 2 o'clock in the afternoon, a man named Lafond, at the head of three columns from the Section Lepelletier, descended on the Pont Neuf, while another column of the same force advanced from the Odéon to meet them. They joined in the Place Dauphine. General Carteaux, who was stationed on the Pont Neuf with 400 men and four pieces of cannon, with orders to defend the two sides of the bridge, quitted his post and fell back under the wickets of the Louvre. At the same time a battalion of National Guards occupied the Infant's Garden. They declared themselves loyal to the Convention, but nevertheless seized this post without orders. On another side, Saint Roche, the Théâtre Français, and the Hôtel de Noailles were occupied in force by the National Guard. The Conventional posts were not more than twelve or fifteen paces from them. The Sectionaries sent women to corrupt the soldiers; even the leaders presented themselves several times, unarmed, and waving their hats, to fraternize!

The danger rapidly increased. Danican, the general of the Sections, under a flag of truce, summoned the Convention to withdraw the troops who were threatening the people and to disarm the Terrorists. The bearer of the message passed through the posts, with his eyes bandaged and all the formalities of war, at about 3 o'clock. He was introduced into the midst of the Committee of the Forty, amongst whom his threats caused much alarm, but he obtained nothing. Night was coming on; the Sectionaries could have availed themselves of the darkness to climb from house to house to the Tuileries itself, which was closely blockaded. I had 800 muskets, belts, and cartridge boxes brought into the hall of the

Convention, to arm the members themselves and the clerks, as a corps of reserve. This measure alarmed several of them, who only then began to understand the extent of the danger. At length, at 4 o'clock, some muskets were discharged from the Hôtel de Noailles. Some balls fell on the steps of the Tuileries and a woman who was going into the garden was wounded. At the same time Lafond's column debouched by the Quay Voltaire, marching on the Pont Royal and beating the charge. The batteries then fired – a shot from an 8-pounder at the Cul de Sac Dauphin was the signal to open fire. After several discharges Saint-Roche was carried. Lafond's column, taken in front and flank by the artillery placed on the quay within the wickets of the Louvre and at the head of the Pont Royal, was routed. The Rue Saint-Honoré, the Rue Saint-Florentin, and the places adjacent, were swept by the guns. About a hundred men attempted to make a stand at the Théâtre de la République, but were dislodged by a few shells. At 6 o'clock in the evening all was over. A few distant cannon shots were heard during the night, but these were fired only to prevent the setting-up of barricades, which come of the inhabitants attempted to form with casks. Nearly two hundred Sectionaries were killed or wounded. Almost as many fell on the side of the Convention – most of them at the gates of Saint-Roche. Three representatives, Freron, Louvet, and Sieyès, showed resolution. So completely had the political oscillations of the Convention alienated the goodwill of the people that only one Section, that of the Quinze-Vingts in the Faubourg Saint-Antoine, which sent 250 men, came to its aid. The Faubourgs, however, although they did not rise in favour of the Convention, did not act against it. The strength of the army of the Convention was 8,500 men, including the representatives themselves.

Assemblies still continued to form in the Section Lepelletier. On the morning of the 14th some columns debouched against them by the Boulevards, the Rue de Richelieu, and the Palais Royal. Cannon had been positioned at the principal avenues and the Sectionaries were speedily dislodged. The rest of the day was occupied in travelling about the city, visiting the rendezvous of the Sections, collecting arms, and reading proclamations. By evening order was everywhere restored and Paris was completely quiet. After this great happening the officers of the Army of the Interior were presented in a body to the Convention and I was appointed, by acclamation, Commander-in-Chief of the Army of the Interior. Barras was no longer allowed to combine the title of Representative with any military functions. General Menou was delivered up to a council of war. The Committees wanted his death. I saved him by telling the members that, if he merited death, so did the three Representatives who had directed operations and parleyed with the Sectionaries. The Convention had, therefore, only to pass sentence on the three Deputies, and then Menou also might be condemned. Esprit de corps prevailed over the voices of the General's enemies and he was acquitted.[1] The Commission condemned several persons – Vaublanc among

[1] Jacques François de Menou (1750–1810) went on to command the French army in Egypt and to capitulate to the English in 1801.

them – to dishonourable death but Lafond was the only person executed. This young man had displayed great courage in the action – the head of his column, on the Pont Royal, reformed three times, under grapeshot, before it entirely dispersed. He was an emigrant and it was impossible to save him, although the officers were very desirous to do so – the imprudence of his answers constantly frustrated their good intentions.

It is not true that at the beginning of the action the troops were ordered to fire with powder only – that would only have served to embolden the Sectionaries and endanger the troops. It is true, though, that during the latter part of the action, when success was no longer doubtful, they fired with blank cartridges.

After 13 Vendémiaire, I had to reform the National Guard, which was an object of the greatest importance, as it amounted to no less than 104 battalions. At the same time I organized the guards of the Directory, and reformed those of the Legislative body. These very circumstances were afterwards among the principal causes of my success on the famous 18 Brumaire. I left such impressions on those corps that on my return from Egypt the soldiers disregarded the Directory's recommendation that I should not be rendered any military honours and could not be prevented from beating the Advance the moment I appeared. The interval of a few months during which I commanded the Army of the Interior was replete with difficulties and trouble, arising from the installation of a new government, the members of which were divided amongst themselves and often opposed to the councils; the silent ferment that existed among the old Sectionaries, who were still powerful in Paris; the active turbulence of the Jacobins, who used to meet in a patriotic assembly, under the name of the Society of the Pantheon; the agents of the foreigners who fomented discord in all quarters; and above all, from the terrible famine which at that time desolated the capital. Ten or twelve times the scanty distributions of bread that the government usually made every day failed entirely. An uncommon degree of activity and dexterity was needed to surmount so many obstacles and to maintain tranquillity in the capital under such unfavourable and afflicting circumstances. The Society of the Pantheon daily caused the government more anxiety, but the police were afraid to attack it openly. I caused the doors of their assembly rooms to be sealed up and the members stirred no more, as long as I was present. (After my departure, they appeared once more, under the influence of Baboeuf, Antonelle, and others, and occasioned the affair of the camp of Grenelle.) I frequently had occasion to harangue the people in the markets and streets, in the sections and in the faubourgs, and it is worthy of remark that, of all parts of the capital, the Faubourg Saint-Antoine was that which I always found the readiest to listen to reason and to yield to a generous impulse.

It was while I commanded at Paris that I became acquainted with Madame de Beauharnais. After the disarming of the Sections, a youth ten or twelve years old presented himself to the staff, soliciting the return of a sword which had belonged to his father, formerly a general in the service of the Republic. This youth was Eugène de Beauharnais, afterwards Viceroy of Italy. Affected by the nature of his petition, and by his juvenile grace, I granted his request. Eugène burst into tears when he beheld his father's sword. Touched at his sensibility, I behaved so kindly to him that Madame de Beauharnais thought herself obliged to wait on me the next day, to thank me for my attention. Everyone knows the extreme grace of the Empress Josephine and her sweet and attractive manners. The acquaintance soon became intimate and tender, and it was not long before we married.

Scherer, who commanded the Army of Italy, was reproached with not having profited by his victory at Loano; his conduct had not given satisfaction. There were many more agents than officers at his headquarters. He was constantly applying for money to pay his troops, and refit different branches of the service, and for horses to replace those that had died for want of forage. The government, being unable to supply him with either, gave him dilatory answers and misled him with vain promises. Scherer saw through this and gave notice that if there

Josephine de Beauharnais, whose first husband Alexandre was executed in the Terror. She was the mistress of Barras before she became the wife of Napoleon.

*Napoleon's stepson, Prince Eugène de Beauharnais, Prince of Eichstadt, was
a brilliant general and a 'genuinely good man.' He threatened to resign as
Viceroy of Italy when Napoleon's divorce from Josephine was first suggested,
but finally accepted that it was politically necessary and that Napoleon was
entering into it against his personal wishes.*

were any further delays he would be obliged to evacuate the Genoese Riviera, to
withdraw to the Roya, and perhaps to recross the Var. The Directory consulted
the General of the Army of the Interior, who presented a memorial on this
subject.

A young man of twenty-five could no longer remain at the head of the army of
Paris. His reputation, and the confidence reposed in him by the Army of Italy,
pointed to him as the only person capable of extricating that army from its
embarrassing situation. These considerations determined the government to
appoint me General-in-Chief of the Army of Italy and I left Paris on 4 March
1796. General Hatry, a veteran of sixty, succeeded me in the command of the
army of Paris, which had become less important now that the scarcity crisis had
been overcome and the government was established.

V

THE BATTLE
OF ARCOLE

T HE couriers who reached Vienna with news of Prince Charles's successes
were followed by couriers from Wurmser[1] bringing accounts of his disasters. The
court passed the whole month of September in these alternations of joy and
sorrow. The satisfaction derived from the triumphs did not compensate for the
consternation excited by the defeats. Germany was saved, but Italy was lost – the
army guarding that frontier had disappeared. Its numerous staff, its old Marshal,
and a remnant of troops had been able to find temporary safety only by shutting
themselves up in Mantua, and that city, reduced to the last extremity, in want of
everything, and ravaged by autumnal fevers, would soon be compelled to open
its gates to the conqueror. The Aulic Council felt the need to make extraordinary
efforts. It assembled two armies – one in the Friuli, the other in the Tyrol –
appointed Marshal Alvinzi to command them, and ordered him to march to
relieve Mantua and rescue Wurmser.

The influence of the Armies of the Sambre and Meuse and of the Rhine was
calculated to be speedily felt in Italy. If those two armies could not maintain
themselves on the right bank of the Rhine, it was of the utmost importance that
they should send strong detachments to reinforce the Army of Italy. The
Directory promised much, but performed little. It did, however, send twelve
battalions, drafted from the Army of la Vendée, who reached Milan in the course
of September and October. They marched in twelve columns and the notion was
spread abroad that each of these columns was a regiment with its full complement
of men – which would have been a very considerable reinforcement. It is true

---

[1] Marshall Dagobert Siegmond von Würmser (1724–97), commander in
Italy against Napoleon, had defeated the French and taken Mantua in 1795.

---

that the French soldiers did not need encouragement – they were full of confidence in their chief and in their own superiority; they were well paid, clothed and fed; their artillery was fine and numerous; and their cavalry was well mounted. The Italians of every state had allied themselves with the interests of the army on which their liberty and independence depended. They were as convinced of the superiority of the French over the German soldiers, as they were of that of the general who had vanquished Beaulieu and Wurmser over Marshal Alvinzi. Public opinion had undergone a great change since the preceding month of July. At that time, when Wurmser's approach was announced, all Italy expected his triumph. Now no-one doubted the triumph of the French army. The public spirit of the Transpadane States of Bologna, Modena, and Reggio was such that they might be depended on to repulse the Pope's army themselves, if it should carry out its threat to enter their territories.

At the beginning of October Marshal Alvinzi was still with his army before the Isonzo, but at the end of the month he removed his headquarters to Conegliano, behind the Piave. Massena, stationed at Bassano, was watching his movements.

André Masséna, created Prince of Essling in 1810, was the son of a wine merchant. He went to sea as a cabin boy, and was a fruit seller and smuggler before being elected colonel in a volunteer regiment. He died in disgrace in 1817.

Davidowich had assembled an army corps of 18,000 men in the Tyrol, surrounding the Tyrolese militia. General-of-division Vaubois covered Trent, occupying the Avisio with a corps of 12,000 men. Augereau's division, the reserve of cavalry, and the headquarters of the French army were at Verona. Alvinzi's plan was to join up with Davidowich in Verona and to march from there on to Mantua. On 1 November he threw two bridges across the Piave, and marched in three columns towards the Brenta. Because Massena threatened to attack him, he was forced to deploy his whole army. Massena, with upwards of 40,000 men, raised his camp at Bassano, recrossed the Brenta, and approached Vicenza, where I joined him with Augereau's division and my reserve. At daybreak on 6 November I advanced to give battle to Alvinzi, who had followed Massena's movement. He had made his headquarters at Fonte Niva. His van, under General Liptay, was at Carmignano, on the right bank of the Brenta in advance of his left, commanded by General Provero. His right, under the command of Quasdanowich, was in position between Bassano and Vicenza. General Metrouski commanded a reconnaissance corps in the gorges of the Brenta and General Hohenzollern commanded the reserve. Massena attacked at dawn and, after an action of several hours, drove Quasdanowich, Liptay, and Provero back to the left bank of the river, killing a great number of men and taking many prisoners. I advanced against Quasdanowich at the head of Augereau's division, and drove him from Lenova back upon Bassano. It was four o'clock in the afternoon. I thought it of the greatest importance that we should cross the bridge and take the town on this day. But Hohenzollern had come up, so I ordered my reserve brigade to advance to support the attack on the bridge. A battalion of 900 Croats, which had been cut off, had occupied a village on the high road. These Croats met the head of the reserve with a very brisk fire when it tried to enter the village and it became necessary to bring up howitzers. The village was taken and the Croats shot, but they had caused a delay of two hours. The troops did not reach the bridge until night and were obliged to postpone the forcing of this passage until the following day.

Vaubois had received orders to attack the enemy's position on the right bank of the Avisio. On 1 November, he attacked those of Saint-Michael and Segonzano. The enemy were in considerable force and defended themselves with the greatest courage. Vaubois was not altogether successful, nor was the attempt he made the following day more fortunate. At length he was himself attacked in turn, his position on the Avisio was forced, and he was obliged to abandon Trent. Having rallied his troops, he took up a position at Calliano; but Landon, manoeuvring by the right bank of the Adige with his Tyrolese, had outflanked him, and gained possession of Nomi and Torbole. It appeared to be his intention to advance on Montebaldo and Rivoli. Vaubois had no longer any troops on the right bank, or any means of opposing this manoeuvre, which, had it been executed by the enemy, would have endangered not only his corps but the whole of the French army. This news reached the French headquarters at 2 o'clock in the morning. There was now no room for hesitation – it was essential to hasten to

Bonaparte on the Bridge of Arcole, 1776. Painting by Baron Gros.
Hermitage, Leningrad (Bridgeman Art Library).

OPPOSITE ABOVE *The battle of the Nile, where Nelson defeated the forces of Napoleon, 31 July 1798. Painting by William Anderson. Leger Gallery, London.*

OPPOSITE BELOW *Napoleon visiting the plague victims of Jaffa, 1798. Painting by Baron Gros. Louvre, Paris (Bridgeman Art Library).*

ABOVE *Napoleon inspecting the fountains at Moise, 1798. Painting by Jean-Simon Barthelemy. Château de Versailles, France (Bridgeman Art Library).*

ABOVE *Louis David's famous painting of Bonaparte crossing the Alps.*
Château de Malmaison, Paris (Bridgeman Art Library).

OPPOSITE ABOVE *The surrender of the French army in Egypt to the*
British, 1798. Painting by Appiani the Elder.
Musée des Beaux-Arts, Nantes (Bridgeman Art Library).

OPPOSITE BELOW *Bonaparte as First Consul, 1799. Painting by Ingres.*
Musée des Beaux-Arts, Liège (Bridgeman Art Library).

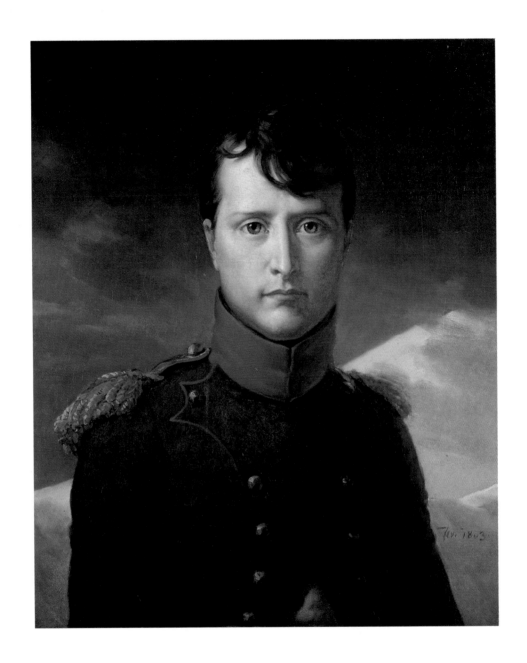

First Consul, 1803. Painting by François Gerard.
Musée Condé, Chantilly (Bridgeman Art Library).

July 1804, Napoleon visits the French camp at Boulogne.
The invasion of England was planned and ready.
Painting by François Gerard. Château de Versailles, France
(Bridgeman Art Library).

DRAWN BY AUGUST WILL.

KEY TO DAVID'S PAINTING OF THE CORONATION.

1. Napoleon ; 2. Josephine ; 3. Pope Pius VII. ; 4. Arch-Treasurer (Lebrun) ; 5. Arch-Chancellor (Cambacérès) ; 6. Marshal Berthier ; 7. Talleyrand ; 8. Eugène Beauharnais ; 9. Master of the Horse (Caulaincourt) ; 10. Marshal Bernadotte ; 11. Cardinal Fesch ; 12. Italian Priests ; 13. Cardinal-legate Caprara ; 14. Cardinal Braschi ; 15. Greek Bishop ; 16. Marshal Murat ; 17. Marshal Sérurier ; 18. Marshal Moncey ; 19. Marshal Bessières ; 20. Master of Ceremonies (Ségur) ; 21. General d'Harville, Senator ; 22. Treasurer-General of the Household of the Emperor (Estève) ; 23. Mme. de la Rochefoucauld ; 24. Mme. de la Valette ; 25. Archbishop of Paris and his two Vicar-Generals ; 26. Madame Mère (Napoleon's mother) ; 27. Mme. de Fontanges ; 28. M. de Cossé-Brissac (Chamberlain) ; 29. M. de la Ville ; 30. Mme. Soult ; 31. Master of the Horse (M. de Beaumont) ; 32. Joseph Bonaparte ; 33. Louis Bonaparte ; 34. Caroline Bonaparte Murat ; 35. Pauline Bonaparte Borghese ; 36. Élise Bonaparte Bacciocchi ; 37. Mme. Joseph Bonaparte ; 38. Prince Napoleon ; 39. Hortense Beauharnais (Mme. Louis Bonaparte) ; 40. General Junot ; 41. M. de Remusat, Prefect of the Palace ; 42. Chamberlains ; 43. Grand Marshal of the Palace (Duroc) ; 44. Marshals Lefebvre, Kellerman, and Pérignon ; 45. Admiral Gravina ; 46. Count Cobenzl ; 47. M. de Marescalchi ; 48. United States Minister ; 49. Turkish Ambassador ; 50. Various celebrated men, Painters, Sculptors, Antiquaries, Poets, etc. (This picture was painted by order of Napoleon, and is not historically accurate in all respects ; for instance, Madame Mère was not present.)

Louis David's famous painting of the coronation in 1804 of Napoleon by Pope Pius VII. Louvre, Paris (Giraudon/Bridgeman Art Library).

Verona, now so imminently threatened, to abandon the former plan, and to create a diversion. My original scheme was, after driving Alvinzi beyond the Piave, to proceed up the defiles of the Brenta and to cut off Davidowich. Colonel Vignolles of the staff, a trusted officer, was sent to collect all the troops he could muster at Verona and to march with them on La Corona and Rivoli. He found there a battalion of the 40th, just arrived from la Vendée, and overawed the first enemy skirmishers to reach La Corona. On the following day, Joubert reached that important position, with the 4th light demi-brigade, brought from the blockade of Mantua. After this there was nothing to fear. At the same time Vaubois threw bridges over the Adige, crossed back to the right bank, and occupied La Corona and Rivoli in force.

Throughout the day of 7 November the French army, back from the Brenta, filed through the city of Vicenza. The inhabitants, who had witnessed its victory, could not understand this movement in retreat. Alvinzi had also begun his retreat, at 3 o'clock in the morning, intending to cross the Piave. But his light cavalry informed him of the French army's withdrawal and returned to the Brenta and next day crossed that river to follow his enemy's movement.

I had Vaubois's division assembled on the plain of Rivoli, and addressed them thus: 'Soldiers, I am not satisfied with you. You have shown neither discipline, perseverance, nor bravery. Nothing could rally you. You abandoned yourselves to a panic terror. You suffered yourselves to be driven from positions in which a handful of brave men might have stopped an army. Soldiers of the 39th and 85th, you are not French soldiers. Quarter-master-general, let it be inscribed on their colours, "They no longer form part of the Army of Italy!" This harangue, delivered with severity, drew tears from these old soldiers – discipline could not suppress their grief. Several grenadiers cried out, 'General, we have been slandered; place us in the van and you shall see whether the 39th and 85th belong to the Army of Italy.' Having produced the effect I wished, I addressed a few words of consolation to them. A few days later these two regiments covered themselves with glory.

Notwithstanding the reverses that Alvinzi had sustained on the Brenta, his operations were crowned with the most brilliant success. He was master of the whole of the Tyrol and of all the country between the Brenta and the Adige. But the most difficult task still remained, namely, to force the passage of the Adige in the face of the French army, and to effect his junction with Davidowich by marching over the bodies of the brave soldiers posted before Verona. The road from Verona to Vicenza runs along the Adige for three leagues, as far as Villa-Nuova, where it turns to the left at right angles and runs straight to Vicenza. At Villa-Nuova the little River Alpon cuts it and, after running through Arcole, falls into the Adige near Albaredo. To the left of Villa-Nuova are some heights known as the Caldiero, by occupying which Verona is covered and it becomes easy to fall on the rear of an enemy manoeuvring on the lower Adige. As soon as the defence of Montebaldo was provided for, and Vaubois's troops had regained their confidence, I determined to occupy Caldiero. On the 11th, at 2 o'clock in the

General Barthélmy-Catherine Joubert, defeated and killed in 1799 at Novi
by the Austro-Russian army under the Russian General Alexander Suvarov.

afternoon, the army crossed the bridges of Verona. Verdier's brigade, which was in the van, overthrew the enemy's vanguard, took several hundred prisoners, and took up a position, at night, at the foot of Caldiero. The fires of the bivouacs and the reports of spies and prisoners left no doubt respecting Alvinzi's intentions – he was ready to receive battle. He had established himself in a fine position, resting his left on the marsh of Arcole and his right on Mount Olivetto and the village of Colognola. This position is good in both directions. He had protected himself with some redoubts and formidable batteries. At daybreak the enemy's line became clear. His left was impregnable, but his right seemed ill supported. Massena received orders to march with his division to take advantage of this defeat by occuping a hill which outflanked the enemy's right, and which he had neglected to occupy. Brigadier-General Launay bravely climbed the slope at the head of a corps of skirmishers, but the division which was to support him had advanced too far and could not come up with him in time, being stopped up a ravine, and he was taken prisoner. The enemy, now apprised of their error, immediately rectified their position, and it was no longer possible to attack them with any hope of success. In the mean time the whole line engaged, and fire was maintained throughout the day. The rain fell in torrents – the ground was so thoroughly soaked that the French artillery could not move, while the Austrian guns, being in fixed positions and advantageously placed, produced their full effect. The enemy made several attempts to attack in his turn, but was repulsed with loss. The two armies bivouacked in their respective positions. It continued to rain all night so heavily that I judged it expedient to return to my camp before Verona. The losses in this affair were equal on both sides, but the enemy, with reason, claimed the victory. His advanced posts approached Saint-Michael, and the French situation became truly hazardous.

Vaubois had suffered considerable losses – he had not now more than 8,000 men left. The other two divisions, after having fought valiantly on the Brenta, and failed in their operation on Caldiero, did not now amount to more than 13,000 men under arms. The idea of the superior strength of the enemy pervaded every mind. Vaubois's soldiers, in excuse for their retreat, declared that the enemy were three to one against them. The enemy had also suffered loss, no doubt, but he had gained great advantages. He knew how small were the numbers of French opposing him and accordingly he had no longer any doubt of his ability to deliver Mantua and conquer Italy. In a delirium of confidence, he had a great number of scaling-ladders made and loudly threatened to take Verona by storm. The garrison of Mantua had awakened from its lethargy, and made frequent sorties, incessantly harassing the besiegers, who amounted only to 8,000 or 9,000 men, ranged against a garrison of 25,000 – of which, however, 10,000 or 12,000 were sick. The French were no longer in a situation to carry on offensive operations in any directions; they were checked on one side by the position of Caldiero, and on the other by the defiles of the Tyrol. But even if the enemy's position had allowed of any enterprise against him, his numerical superiority was too well known. It was therefore necessary to let him make the first move and to wait patiently until he should make some attempt. The weather was extremely bad; every movement was made in the mud. The affairs of Caldiero and the Tyrol had evidently damped the confidence of the French soldier; he was, indeed, still persuaded of his superiority on equal terms, but did not now feel capable of resisting such superior numbers. A great number of the bravest men had been wounded two or three times in different battles since the army entered Italy. Discontent began to show itself. 'We cannot,' said the men, 'do everybody's duty. Alvinzi's army, now present, is the same that the Armies of the Rhine, the Sambre and Meuse retreated before, and they are now idle; why are we to perform their work? If we are beaten, we must make for the Alps as fugitives and without honour; if, on the contrary, we conquer, what will be the result of our new victory? We shall be opposed by another army like that of Alvinzi, as Alvinzi himself succeeded Wurmser, and as Wurmser succeeded Beaulieu; and in this unequal contest we must be annihilated at last.'

To these remarks I caused the following answer to be made. 'We have but one more effort to make, and Italy is our own. The enemy is, no doubt, more numerous than we are, but half his troops are recruits; when he is beaten, Mantua must fall, and we shall remain masters of all; our labours will be at an end; for not only Italy, but a general peace is in Mantua. You talk of returning to the Alps, but you are no longer capable of doing so: from the dry and frozen bivouacs of those sterile rocks, you could very well conquer the delicious plains of Lombardy; but from the smiling flowering bivouacs of Italy, you cannot return to the Alpine snows. Reinforcements have reached us; there are more on the road; let not those who are unwilling to fight seek vain pretences; for only beat Alvinzi and I will answer for your future welfare.' These words, repeated by all those of generous heart in the army, raised the spirits of the troops and brought them by degrees to an opposite way of thinking. Thus the army was at one moment, in its dejection, desirous of retreating; at the next it was filled with enthusiasm and talked of advancing. 'Shall the soldiers of Italy patiently endure the insults and provocations of these slaves?'

When it became known at Brescia, Bergamo, Milan, Cremona, Lodi, Pavia, and Bologna that the army had sustained a check, the wounded and sick left the hospitals, before they had properly recovered, to resume their stations in the ranks – the wounds of many of these brave men were still bleeding. This affecting sight filled the mind with the most lively emotion.

At length, on 14 November, at nightfall, the camp of Verona got under arms. Three columns began their march in the deepest silence, passed through the city, crossed the Adige by three bridges, and formed up on the right bank. The hour of departure, the direction taken, the silence observed in the Order of the Day (contrary to the invariable custom of announcing that an engagement is to take place) – all these things indicated that the army was retreating. The first step in retreat would necessarily be followed by the raising of the siege of Mantua and foreboded the loss of Italy. Those of the inhabitants who placed their future hopes in the victories of the French followed with anxious and aching hearts the movements of this army, which was depriving them of every hope. But the army, instead of keeping the Peschiera road, suddenly turned to the left, marched along the Adige, and arrived before daylight at Ronco, where Andreossy was completing a bridge. By the first rays of the sun, the troops were astonished to find themselves, by merely facing to the left, on the opposite shore. The officers and soldiers who had traversed this country before, when in pursuit of Wurmser, now began to guess their general's intention. I intended to turn Caldiero, which I had not been able to carry by frontal attack. With only 13,000 men I could not take on 40,000 in the plain, so I was removing my field of battle to roads surrounded by vast marshes, where numbers would be unavailing, but where the courage of the heads of the columns would decide everything. Hopes of victory now animated every heart, and every man vowed to outdo himself to support so fine and daring a plan. Kilmaine had remained in Verona with 1,500 men of all arms, with the gates closed, and all communications strictly prohibited; the enemy was therefore completely ignorant of this movement. The bridge of Ronco was constructed on the right of the Alpon, about a quarter of a league from its mouth. This positioning has been criticized by ill-informed military men. In fact, if the bridge had been carried to the left bank opposite Alberedo: first, the army would have had to debouch on a vast plain, the very thing I wished to avoid; secondly, Alvinzi, who occupied the heights of Caldiero, might have covered the march of a column which he would have directed on Verona, by stationing troops on the right bank of the Alpon: he would have forced Verona, feebly guarded as it was, and would have effected his junction with the Army of the Tyrol; the division of Rivoli, caught between two fires, would have been obliged to retreat on Peschiera, and the whole army would have been compromised. But, by constructing the bridge to the right of the Alpon, the invaluable advantages were secured: first, of drawing the enemy into three roads crossing an immense marsh; secondly, of being in communication with Verona, by the dyke which runs up the Adige and passes by the villages of Porcil and Gambione, where Alvinzi's headquarters were, without leaving any position for the enemy to take, or any natural obstacle to cover the movement of any troops he might detach to attack Verona. Such an attack was, indeed, now impossible, for the whole French army would have taken such troops in the rear, whilst the walls of the city would have stopped them in front. Three roads branch out from the bridge of Ronco – the first, on the left, goes up the Adige towards Verona and passes the village of Bionde and Porcil, where it debouches in a plain; the second, centre one, leads to Villa-Nuova and runs through the village of Arcole, crossing the Alpon by a little stone bridge; the third, on the right, runs down the Adige and leads to Albaredo. It is 3,600 toises from Ronco to Porcil, 2,000 from Porcil to Caldiero, and three leagues from Caldiero to Verona. It is 2,200 toises from Ronco to Arcole, 3,000 from the bridge of Arcole to Villa-Nuova, 100 from Ronco to the mouth of the Alpon, and 500 thence to Albaredo.

Three columns entered upon these three roads; the left one marched up the Adige to the edge of the marshes, at the village of Porcil, whence the soldiers perceived the steeples of Verona – it was thenceforth impossible for the enemy to march upon that city. The centre column marched on Arcole, where the French skirmishers got as far as the bridge unperceived. Two battalions of Croats, with two pieces of cannon, had bivouacs there for the purpose of guarding the rear of the army and watching any sorties that the garrison of Legnano might make into the country, for that place was only three leagues off, on the right. The ground between Arcole and the Adige was not guarded – Alvinzi had contented himself with ordering patrols of hussars, who three times every day visited the dykes of the marshes on the side of the Adige. The road from Ronco to Arcole meets the Alpon 1,200 toises from Ronco; it then runs along the right bank of that little rivulet for 10,000 toises, as far as the stone bridge which turns to the right, at right angles, and leads into the village of Arcole. The Croats were bivouacked with their right supported on the village and their left towards the mouth of the rivulet, with the dyke in their front, separated from them by the stream; by firing in front, they took the column, the head of which was near Arcole, in flank; the soldiers fell back precipitately as far as the point where the road ceases to expose the flank to the left bank. Augereau, angry at this retreat, rushed upon the bridge at the head of two battalions of grenadiers, but, being received by a brisk flank-fire, he was driven back on his division. Alvinzi, being informed of this attack, could not at first comprehend, but at daybreak he was able to observe the movement of the French from the neighbouring steeples. His reconnoitring parties of hussars were received with discharges of musketry on all the dykes and pursued by the cavalry. He then realized that the French had crossed the Adige and were in his rear. It seemed to him absurd to suppose that a whole army could thus have been thrown into impassable marshes – he thought some light troops had moved in this direction to alarm him and to mask the real attack, which would be by the Verona road. But his reconnoitring parties brought him intelligence that all was quiet towards Verona and he thought it important to drive these light troops from the marshes. He therefore directed a division, commanded by Metrouski, on the dyke of Arcole, and another on the left dyke, commanded by Provera. Towards 9 o'clock in the morning they attacked with impetuosity. Massena, who was entrusted with the left dyke, having allowed the enemy to get fairly upon the dyke, charged, broke the enemy's column, repulsed him with great loss, and took a number of prisoners. The same thing happened on the dyke of Arcole. As soon as the enemy had passed the elbow of the road, he was charged and routed by Augereau, leaving prisoners and cannon in the victor's hands; the marsh was covered with dead. It became of the utmost importance to gain possession of Arcole, for, by debouching thence on the enemy's rear, we should have seized the bridge of Villa-Nuova over the Alpon, which was his only retreat, and established ourselves there before it could be occupied against us; but Arcole withstood several attacks. I determined to try a last effort in person; I seized a flag, rushed on the bridge, and there planted it; the column I commanded had reached the middle of the bridge, when the flanking fire and the arrival of a division of the enemy frustrated the attack; the grenadiers at the head of the column, finding themselves abandoned by the rear, hesitated, but being hurried away in the flight, they persisted in keeping possession of their general; they seized me by the arms and by my clothes, and dragged me along with them amidst the dead, the dying, and the smoke; I was precipitated in a morass, in which I sunk up to the middle, surrounded by the enemy. The grenadiers perceived that their general was in danger; a cry was heard of 'Forward, soldiers, to save the general!' These brave men immediately turned back, ran upon the enemy, drove him beyond the bridge, and I was saved. This was the day of military devotedness. Lannes, who had been wounded at Governolo, had hurried from Milan. He was still suffering but he threw himself between the enemy and me, covering me with his body, and receiving three wounds, determined never to abandon me. Muiron, my aide-de-camp, was killed in covering his general with his own body. Heroic and affecting death! Belliard and Vignolles were wounded in rallying the troops forward. The brave General Robert was killed – he was a soldier who never shrank from the enemy's fire.

General Guieux crossed the Adige at the ferry of Albaredo with a brigade. Arcole was taken in the rear. In the mean time Alvinzi, having learned the real state of affairs, had become fully sensible of the danger of his position. He had abandoned Caldiero precipitately, destroyed his batteries, and made all his parks and reserves cross back over the bridge – from the steeples of Ronco the French had the mortification of seeing this booty escape them. It was only when the precipitate movements of the enemy were seen that the whole extent and consequences of my plan could be comprehended. Everyone then saw what might be the results of so profound and daring a combination. The enemy's army was escaping from destruction by a hasty retreat; General Guieux was not able to march on Arcole by the left bank of the Alpon until near four o'clock; the village was carried without striking a blow; but it was now unimportant, being six hours too late; the enemy had resumed his natural position. Arcole was now only an intermediate post between the fronts of the two armies, whereas in the morning

Marshal Jean Lannes, created Duke of Montebello in 1808, was the son of a stable keeper. A close friend of Napoleon, the Emperor wept at his death in 1809.

103

it had been in the rear of the enemy. The day was, however, crowned with important results. Caldiero was evacuated; Verona was no longer in danger; two divisions of Alvinzi's army had been defeated with considerable loss; numerous columns of prisoners, and a great number of trophies, filed off through the camp, and filled the officers and soldiers with enthusiasm; the troops regained their spirits, and the confidence of victory.

In the mean time Davidowich with the corps of the Tyrol had attacked and taken La Corona; he occupied Rivoli. Vaubouis occupied the heights of Bussolengo. Kilmaine, relieved from all apprehensions for the left bank by the evacuation of Caldiero, had directed his attention to the walls of Verona and the right bank. But if Davidowich should march on Vaubois, and force him to throw himself on Mantua, he would oblige the French to raise the blockade of that city, and cut off the retreat of the headquarters and the army at Ronco. It is thirteen leagues from Rivoli to Mantua, and ten from Ronco to that city, by very bad roads. It was therefore necessary to be ready, by daylight, to support Vaubois, protect the blockade of Mantua and the communications of the army, and beat Davidowich, who had advanced in the course of the day. In order to succeed in this plan, it was necessary to calculate the timing. Uncertain what might have passed during the day, I thought it best to suppose that everything had been unfortunate on Vaubois's side; that he had been forced, and had taken up a position between Roverbella and Castel-Nuovo. I caused Arcole, which had cost so much blood, to be evacuated; made the army fall back on the right bank of the Adige, leaving on the left bank only one brigade and a few pieces of cannon, and ordered the soldiers to prepare their mess in this position. If the enemy had marched on Rivoli, the bridge over the Adige must have been raised, and the army must have disappeared before Alvinzi, and reached Vaubois in time to assist him. I left bivouacs at Arcole with lighted fires kept up by piquets of the grand guard, in order that Alvinzi should perceive nothing. At four in the morning the army got under arms; but at the same time one of Vaubois's officers brought word that he was at 6 o'clock the preceding evening still at Bussolengo and that Davidowich had not moved. That general had commanded one of Wurmser's corps – he remembered the lesson he had received, and was not eager to compromise himself. Alvinzi, however, being informed of the French retreat at about 3 o'clock in the morning, had Arcole and Porcil occupied, and at daylight directed two columns on the two dykes. The firing began about 200 toises from the bridge of Ronco. The French charged over the bridge, fell on the enemy, broke them, and pursued them as far as the outlets of the morasses, which they filled with Austrian dead. Several standards, a cannon, and a number of prisoners were the trophies of this day, on which two more Austrian divisions were defeated. In the evening I, from the same motives and calculations as the preceding day, made the same movements as before, concentrating all my troops on the right bank of the Adige and leaving only a vanguard on the left bank.

Alvinzi, deceived by a spy who assured him that the French were marching on Mantua and had left only a vanguard at Ronco, debouched from his camp before dawn. At 5 o'clock in the morning, it was known at the French headquarters that Davidowich had made no movement and that Vaubois was still in the same positions. The army again crossed the bridge and the heads of the columns of the two armies met half-way up the dykes. The action was obstinate, and for a time doubtful. The 75th were broken and shots reached the bridge. I placed the 32nd in ambush, lying on their faces, in a little wood of willows, along the dyke, near the head of the bridge. They rose at the proper moment, fired a volley, bayonet-charged and overthrew into the morass a close column of 3,000 Croats, who all perished there. Massena, on the left, experienced some vicissitudes; but he marched at the head of his troops, with his hat at the end of his sword by way of a standard, and made a horrible carnage of the division opposed to him. In the afternoon I conceived the decisive moment had at length arrived, for if Vaubois had been defeated this day by Davidowich, I would have been obliged to proceed the next night to his aid and to that of Mantua. Alvinzi would then advance on Verona, and would carry off the honour and benefit of victory. All the advantages gained during these last three days would then be lost. But by driving Alvinzi back beyond Villa-Nuova, I would be able to march to the assistance of Vaubois, by Verona. I had the prisoners carefully counted, and recapitulated the losses of the enemy, by which means I convinced myself that the Austrian force had been diminished by upwards of 25,000 men, in the course of these three days – henceforth his numbers in the field would not exceed those of the French by much more than a third. I ordered the army to march out of the morasses and to attack the enemy in the plain. The events of these three days had so materially altered the characters of the two armies that victory was certain. The army passed the bridge constructed at the mouth of the Alpon. Elliot, my aide-de-camp, had been ordered to construct a second; he was killed there. At 2 o'clock in the afternoon the French army was formed in line, with its left on Arcole and its right in the direction of Porto Legnago. The enemy was in front, with his right resting on the Alpon and his left on some marshes; he occupied both sides of the Vicenza road. Adjutant-General Lorset had marched from Legnago with 6,000 or 7,000 men, four pieces of cannon, and 200 horse, to turn the marshes on which the enemy supported his left. Towards 3 o'clock, when this detachment was advancing, the cannonade being brisk throughout the line, and the skirmishers engaged, Major Hercule was ordered to proceed with twenty-five guides and four trumpets across the reeds, and to charge the extreme left of the enemy when the garrison of Legnago should begin to cannonade them in the rear. That officer executed the movement in an able manner and contributed greatly to the success of the day; the line was broken, the enemy commenced his retreat. The Austrian general had placed 6,000 or 7,000 men in echelon in his rear, to secure his parks and his retreat; he had not more troops than the French on the field of battle; he was closely pursued all the evening, and had a great number of men taken prisoners. The army passed the night in its position.

Notwithstanding the victories of these three days, it was a matter of speculation among the generals and superior officers as to what orders I would give for the next day. They thought that I would be content with having dispersed the enemy, and would not enter the plains of the Vicentine, but return to Verona by the left bank of the Adige, to march thence against Davidowich and occupy Caldiero, which had been the first object of my manoeuvre. But the enemy's losses had been so severe during these three days, both in men and confidence, that he was no longer formidable in the plain. At daylight it was perceived that he had retreated on Vicenza. The army pursued him, but, after reaching Villa-Nuova the cavalry alone continued the pursuit, the infantry waiting for reports of where his rearguard would make a stand.

I entered the convent of Saint Boniface, whose church had served as an hospital. Between 400 and 500 wounded had been crowded into it. Most of them were dead; a cadaverous smell issued from the place. I was retiring, struck with horror, when I heard myself called by my name. Two unfortunate soldiers had been three days amongst the dead, without having had their wounds dressed; they despaired of relief, but were recalled to life at the sight of their general. Every assistance was afforded them.

Having ascertained by the reports that the enemy was in the utmost confusion, was making no stand in any direction, and that his rearguard had already got beyond Montebello, I faced to the left, and proceeded to Verona to attack the Army of the Tyrol. The scouts captured a staff officer sent by Davidowich to Alvinzi; he came from the mountains, and supposed himself in the midst of his friends. It was found from his despatches that the enemy had had no communications for three days, and that Davidowich was ignorant of all that had taken place. In the three days' engagements at Arcole, Alvinzi had lost 18,000 men (of whom 6,000 were taken prisoners), four standards, and eighteen pieces of cannon.

The French army re-entered Verona in triumph by the Venice gate, three days after having quitted that city almost clandestinely by the Milan gate. It would be difficult to conceive the astonishment and enthusiasm of the inhabitants; the most declared enemies of the French could not suppress their admiration and added their homage to that of the patriots. The army, however, did not stay there, but passed the Adige and advanced on Davidowich, who had attacked Bussolengo on the 17th, and driven Vaubois on Castel-Nuovo. Massena marched thither, joined Vaubois, and attacked Rivoli. Augereau marched on Dolce, on the left bank of the Adige, took 1,500 men, two pontoon trains, nine pieces of cannon, and a great quantity of baggage.

But these grand results were not obtained without loss. The army stood more than ever in need of rest. It was not expedient for it to enter the Tyrol and spread itself so far as Trent. It was to be expected that Mantua would open it gates before the Austrian general could form a new army; the garrison of that place had been reduced to half rations; desertion from it had become frequent; the hospitals were crowded to excess; everything announced a speedy surrender; the mortality was dreadful, and diseases daily swept off more men than would have sufficed to win a great battle.

VI

INTO EGYPT

T HE expedition to Egypt had three aims: to establish on the Nile a French colony which would prosper without slaves and serve France in place of the republic of Santo Domingo and all the sugar islands; to open a market for our manufactures in Africa, Arabia, and Syria and supply our commerce with all the production of those vast countries, and to gain Egypt as a base from which an army of 60,000 men would set out to the Indus to excite the Mahrattas and oppressed people of those extensive regions to insurrections. These 60,000 men, half Europeans and half recruits from the burning climates of the equator and tropics, carried by 10,000 horses and 50,000 camels, with provisions for fifty or sixty days and water for five or six days, accompanied by a train of artillery of a hundred and fifty field-pieces, with double supplies of ammunition, would have reached the Indus in four months – since the invention of shipping the ocean has ceased to be an obstacle and the desert is no longer an impediment to an army possessed of camels and dromedaries in abundance.

The first two of these aims were fulfilled, and notwithstanding the loss of Admiral Brueys's squadron at Alexandria, the intrigue by which Kléber was induced to sign the Convention of El-Arisch, and the landing of from 30,000 to 35,000 English commanded by Abercrombie at Aboukir and Cosseir, the third aim also would have been attained – a French army would have reached the Indus in the winter of 1801–2 – had not the command of the army devolved in consequence of the murder of Kléber on a man who, although abounding in courage, business talent, and goodwill, was of a disposition wholly unfit for military command.[1]

[1] This was General Menou (*see* pp. 87, 88 and 90).

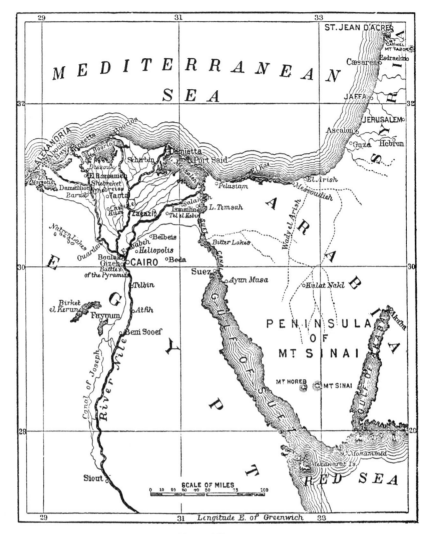

Map of Egypt.

The Koran ordains that idolators should be exterminated or made to pay to tribute; it does not permit obedience and submission to an infidel power. In this it is contrary to the spirit of our religion: 'Render unto Caesar the things that are Caesar's,' said Jesus Christ; 'My kingdom is not of this world; obey the powers that be.' In the 10th, 11th and 12th centuries, when Christians reigned in Syria, religion was the cause of war; the Crusades were a war of extermination that cost Europe several million men.

If a similar spirit had animated the Egyptians in 1798, it would have been impossible to sustain such a struggle with 25,000 or 30,000 Frenchmen, who were not impelled by fanaticism of any kind and were already disgusted with the country. After Alexandria and Cairo had been taken and the Mamelukes defeated at the Pyramids, the question of conquest was still undecided, unless the ulemas and all the ministers of the Muslim religion could be conciliated. Ever since the Revolution, the French army had exercised no worship – even in Italy it never attended church. Advantage was taken of this circumstance – the army was presented to the Muslims as an army of converts, disposed to embrace Mohammedanism. The Coptic, Greek, Latin, and Syrian Christians were numerous; they wanted to avail themselves of the presence of the French army to escape the restrictions imposed on their worship. I opposed this proceeding, and took care to keep religious affairs on the footing on which I found them. Every morning at sunrise, the sheiks of the Grand Mosque of Gemil-Azar (a sort of Sorbonne) used to come to my levee. I had all possible respectful attentions to be shown them and I discoursed with them at length on the various circumstances of the Prophet's life and on the chapters of the Koran. After my return from Salahiyeh I suggested to them that they should publish a *fetam* ordering the people to take an oath of obedience to me. This proposal startled and greatly perplexed them. After some hesitation, Sheik Cherkaoui, a respectable old man, replied: 'Why should not you and your whole army become Muslims? In that case a hundred thousand men would flock to your standard, and when they were disciplined in your manner, you would restablish the Arabian nation and subdue the East.' I said that two objections were the necessity of circumcision and the ban on wine, a beverage indispensable to the French soldier. After some

Submission of the Mamelukes.

109

discussions on this point, it was agreed that the grand sheiks of Gemil-Azar should try to find some way of removing these two obstacles. The three-week-long disputes on the subject were animated, but the report that spread through Egypt, that the grand sheiks were engaged in making the French army Mohammedans, filled all the faithful with joy. The French were already perceived in a better light – they were no longer looked upon as idolators. When the ulemas reached agreement, the four muftis published a *fetam* declaring that circumcision was only a perfection, and not an indispensable condition for being a Muslim, but that without it Paradise must not be expected in the other world. Half the difficulty was thus removed, and it was easy to make the muftis understand that the second objection was not reasonable. This became the subject of six weeks' additional debates. At length they declared that it was possible to be a Muslim and drink wine, provided that a fifth of one's income, instead of a tenth, was employed in acts of benevolence. I then had plans drawn up for a mosque larger than that of Gemil-Azar. I declared that I intended to have it built, by way of a monument, to commemorate the period of the conversion of my army. In fact, I only wished to gain time. The *fetam* of obedience was issued by the sheiks, and I was declared a close friend of the Prophet, and under his special protection. It was generally reported that before the end of a year the whole French army would wear the turban. This was the line of conduct that I constantly tried to follow, reconciling my determination to remain in the religion in which I was born with the occasions of my policy and ambition. During the whole stay of the army in Egypt, General Menou was the only person who became a Muslim, which was useful and had a good effect. When the French left Egypt only five or six hundred men who enlisted with the Mamelukes and embraced the Mohammedan religion remained behind.

After the battle of Aboukir, on 3 August 1799, the English commodore sent to Alexandria the English papers, and the French Gazette of Frankfurt of the months of April, May, and June, which communicated the news of the reverse sustained by the Armies of the Rhine and of Italy. We heard of the war of the second coalition at the camp at Acre.

I returned to France, for three reasons: first, because my instructions authorized me to do so (I had carte-blanche in all respects); secondly, because my presence was necessary to the Republic; thirdly, because the Army of the East, which was victorious and numerous, would not, for a long time, have any enemy to contend with. The first object of the Egyptian expedition had been accomplished; the second could not be attained so long as the frontiers of the Republic were menaced and anarchy prevailed in its interior. The Army of the East had been victorious over the two Turkish armies that had opposed it during the campaign. The army of Syria had been defeated at El-Arisch, Gaza, Jaffa, Acre, and Mount Tabor and had lost its park of forty field-pieces, with all its magazines; that of Rhodes had been defeated at Acre and Aboukir, where it had lost its train of thirty-four field pieces, and its general-in-chief, the vizier with three tails, Mustafa Pasha. The Army of the East was numerous; it comprised

25,000 fighting men, of whom, 3,500 were cavalry; it had a hundred field-pieces of horse artillery, and 1,400 other pieces of artillery of all calibres, well supplied. It has been said that I left my army in distress, without artillery, clothing, or bread, and reduced to 8,000 effective men. These false reports deceived the English ministry. On 17 December 1799 the English government determined to break the capitulation of El-Arisch – it ordered its admiral in the Mediterranean not to allow the Army of the East to return to France, as the capitulation provided, but to stop the ships carrying the troops and bring them to England. Kléber then understood his situation; he shook off the yoke of intrigue, and became himself again, turned on the Ottoman army, and defeated it at Heliopolis. After such a criminal violation of the law of nations, the Cabinet of Saint-James's perceived its error and sent into Egypt 34,000 English, under the command of Abercrombie, who, joining 26,000 Turks under the grand-vizier and the captain-pasha, succeeded in making themselves masters of that important colony in September 1801, twenty-seven months after my departure and after a

Gérard-Christophe-Michel Duroc, Duke of Friuli, was wounded at Acre. He became one of Napoleon's closest confidants. The Emperor was devastated by the death of his friend in 1813 at Reichenbach.

General Jean-Baptiste Kléber, appointed to command the army in Egypt following Napoleon's return to France. Kléber was murdered in 1800, shortly after he retook Cairo.

very brisk six-month-long campaign. This would have ended in the overthrow of the English had Kléber not been assassinated, and had Menou, than whom a less military man never commanded, not been at the head of the army. But after all, this campaign of 1801 cost the English government several million sterling, 10,000 picked soldiers, and the commander-in-chief of its army. General Belliard obtained at Cairo, on 27 June 1801, and General Menou at Alexandria, on 2 September in that year, the same capitulation that conspirators had made Kléber sign at El-Arisch twenty months before, on 24 January 1800. The French army was to be carried to France at the expense of the English, with its arms, cannon, baggage, and colours, and without being made prisoners of war. The reports of its state on arriving at the lazarettos of Marseilles and Toulon prove that it consisted of 24,000 French; its losses in 1800 and 1801 had amounted to 4,000 men. When, therefore, I left the command to Kléber, it must have had 28,000 men, of whom 25,000 were in a condition to take the field. It is notorious that, when I left Egypt in August 1799, I thought that country forever secured to France and hoped one day to be able to realize the second object of the expedition. As to the ideas I then entertained on the affairs of France, I communicated them to Menou, who has often repeated them; I projected the revolution of 18 Brumaire.

VII

THE BATTLE
OF ABOUKIR

INTELLIGENCE was received in England, from various quarters at the same time, that considerable armaments were preparing at Brest, Toulon, Genoa, and Civitavecchia; that the Spanish squadron of Cadiz was actively fitting out; and that numerous camps were being established on the Scheldt, on the coasts of the Pas-de-Calais, of Normandy, and of Brittany. Having been appointed General-in-Chief of the Army of England, I was inspecting all the coasts and visiting every port. I had assembled around me in Paris all who were left of the old naval officers who had acquired their reputations during the American war – those such as Buhor, Marigny, etc. – but they did not justify their celebrity. The liaison that the French maintained with the United Irishmen could not be kept so secret but that the English government should hear something of it. The English Cabinet at first thought that all these preparations were directed against England and Ireland and that France wished to take advantage of the peace that had just been re-established on the Continent, to end the long struggle by a war at close quarters. It believed that the armaments that were being assembled in Italy were merely intended to mislead and that the Toulon fleet would pass the Straits and join the Spanish fleet at Cadiz. The combined fleets would then arrive before Brest and carry one army to England and another to Ireland. In this uncertainty the English Admiralty contented itself with hastily fitting out a new squadron. As soon as it heard that I had sailed from Toulon, it despatched Admiral Rogers with ten ships of war to reinforce the English squadron before Cadiz, where Admiral Lord St Vincent commanded. This reinforcement gave him a fleet of twenty-eight or thirty ships under his command. There was another squadron of equal force before Brest.

Admiral St Vincent had in the Mediterranean a light squadron of three ships, cruising between the coasts of Spain, Provence, and Sardinia to collect information and keep watch. On 24 May he detached ten ships from before Cadiz and sent them into the Mediterranean, with orders to join those commanded by Nelson, and thus to form for that admiral a fleet of thirteen ships, to blockade Toulon, or to follow the French squadron if it had sailed from that port. Lord St Vincent remained before Cadiz with eighteen ships to watch the Spanish fleet, being chiefly apprehensive that the Toulon squadron would escape Nelson and pass the Straits.

In the instructions sent by this admiral to Nelson, which have been printed, it appears that everything had been foreseen, except an expedition against Egypt. The cases of the French expedition's proceeding to Brazil, the Black Sea, or Constantinople were provided for. More than 150,000 men were encamped on the coast, which produced agitation and continual alarm throughout England.

Nelson was cruising between Corsica, Provence, and Spain, with the three sail detached by Lord St Vincent, when, in the night of 19 May, he suffered from a gale which damaged his ships and dismasted that in which he sailed. He was obliged to be towed. It was his intention to anchor in the Gulf of Oristagni, in Sardinia; he could not succeed in this, but made for the roads of Saint Peter's Isles, where he repaired the damage.

On the same night, the 19th, the French squadron sailed from Toulon. It arrived before Malta on 10 June, after doubling Cape Corso and Cape Bonara. Malta could not withstand a bombardment of twenty-four hours; the place certainly possessed immense physical means of resistance, but no moral strength whatever. The knights did nothing shameful; nobody is obliged to perform impossibilities.

Nelson, having been joined by Lord St Vincent's ten ships and appointed to the command of this squadron was cruising off Toulon on 1 June. He did not then know that the French squadron had left that port. On the 15th he reconnoitred the roads of Tagliamone, on the coast of Tuscany, which he supposed to be the rendezvous of the French expedition. On the 20th he appeared before Naples, where he was informed by the government that the French squadron had landed its troops at Malta, and that Garat, the ambassador of the Republic, had stated that the expedition was intended for Egypt. On the 22nd Nelson arrived off Messina. The intelligence of the capture of Malta by the French expedition was confirmed to him and he also learned that it was making for Candia. Upon this he passed the Faro of Messina, and proceeded to Alexandria, where he arrived on 29 July.

The French squadron received the first intelligence of the presence of an English fleet in the Mediterranean, off Cape Bonara, from a ship that fell in with it. On the 25th, while the squadron was reconnoitring the coast of Candia, it was joined by the frigate *La Justice*, which had been cruising off Naples, and which brought positive news of the presence of an English squadron in these latitudes. I then gave orders that, instead of steering directly for Alexandria, the squadron should manoeuvre so as to make Cape Aza, in Africa, twenty-five leagues from

Alexandria; and should not appear before Alexandria until more intelligence had been obtained.

On the 29th, the coast of Africa and Cape Aza were sighted. Nelson had just arrived before Alexandria, but having no information about the French squadron, he steered for Alexandretta and thence made for Rhodes. He then scoured the Isles of the Archipelago, reconnoitred the entrance of the Adriatic, and, on the 18th, was obliged to anchor at Syracuse to take on water. Up to this time he had obtained no information respecting the course of the French squadron. He sailed from Syracuse and on 28 July anchored off Cape Coron, at the extremity of the Morea. It was there that he was first informed that the French army had landed in Egypt a month before. He supposed that the French squadron must have already returned to Toulon, but he proceeded to Alexandria so that he would able to furnish his government with positive intelligence and to leave there a blockading force.

When the French squadron left Toulon it was composed of thirteen sail of the line, six frigates, and a dozen brigs, sloops, and cutters. The English squadron consisted of thirteen sail, one of which carried 50 guns and all the others 74. They had been fitted out very hastily and were in bad condition. Nelson had no frigates. In the French squadron there was one ship of 120 guns, and three of 80. There was a fleet of several hundred sail under the convoy of this squadron, and particularly under the protection of two 64-gun ships, four Venetian-built frigates of 18 guns, and about twenty brigs and sloops. The French squadron, availing itself of its great number of light vessels, obtained intelligence from a great distance, so that the convoy had nothing to fear – if it should fall in with the enemy it could easily take up the most advantageous position to remain at a distance from the engagement. Every French ship had 500 veteran soldiers on board, with a company of land artillery among them. Twice a day, during the month they had been on board, the troops had had gunnery exercise. In every ship of war there were experienced generals, used to being under fire and accustomed to the chances of war.

The possibility of an engagement with the English was the general subject of conversation. The captains of ships had orders, in that case, to consider it as a permanent and constant signal that they must take part in the action and assist the ships near them.

Nelson's squadron was one of the worst that England had ever fitted out of late years.

The French squadron received orders to enter Alexandria; this was necessary for the army and for the success of my plans as the commander-in-chief. When the Turkish pilots declared they could not take 74-gun ships, much less those of 80 guns, into the old port, much astonishment was excited. Captain Barré, a very distinguished naval officer, being ordered to examine the surroundings, positively asserted the contrary. The 64-gun ships and frigates went in without difficulty, but the admiral and several naval officers persisted in considering it necessary to take new soundings before they would risk the whole squadron. As the ships of war had the artillery and the army's ammunition on board, and the breeze was pretty strong, the admiral proposed to land the whole at Aboukir, declaring that thirty-six hours would suffice for that purpose, whereas he would need five or six days for this operation if he remained under sail.

When I left Alexandria to advance to meet the Mamelukes, I repeated to the admiral the order to enter the port of Alexandria. If he thought that impossible he was to proceed to Corfu, where he would receive from Constantinople the orders of the French minister Talleyrand. If there should be much delay in the arrival of those orders, he was to proceed from Corfu to Toulon.

The squadron might have entered the old port of Alexandria. It was allowed that a ship drawing twenty-one feet of water might enter without danger. Seventy-fours, which draw twenty-three feet, would, therefore, only have to be lightened to the extent of two feet; 80-gun ships, drawing twenty-three feet and a half, would have been lightened by two feet and a half; and three deckers, drawing twenty-seven feet water, must have been lightened six feet. The ships might have been lightened in this manner without any inconvenience, either by throwing the water into the sea, or by taking out some of the guns. A 74 may be reduced so as to draw fewer feet of water merely by taking out her water and provisions, and to draw even fewer feet by taking out her artillery. This method was proposed by the naval officers to the admiral. He replied that if all the thirteen ships had been seventy-fours, he would have adopted this expedient, but as one of them carried 120 guns and three others 80 he would run the risk, when in the port, of not being able to get out again and of being blockaded by a squadron of eight or nine English ships. It would be impossible for him to put the *Orient* and the three 80-gun ships in a condition to fight if he reduced their draught to that necessary to pass the channel. This objection was of little weight – the winds that prevail in those latitudes render a rigorous blockade impracticable, and the squadron needed only twenty-four hours after clearing the passage to complete its armament. There was also a remedy – namely, to construct at Alexandria four floating half-butts, adapted to raise 80-gun ships two feet, and ships of 120 guns four feet; the construction of these floating butts for so trifling a rise would not have required much labour. The *Rivoli*, built at Venice, came out of the Malamoko completely armed, on a floating butt which raised her seven feet, so that she drew only sixteen feet of water. A few days after her launch, she fought extremely well against an English frigate and sloop. There were ships, frigates, and 400 transports in Alexandria, which would have furnished all the materials that could have been wanted. There was also a great number of naval engineers – among others M. Leroy, who had passed his whole life in the dockyards.

When the officers detailed to examine Captain Barré's report had completed that operation, the admiral sent their report to me, but it could not reach me in time to obtain an answer, because communications had been cut for a month before the taking of Cairo. Had I received this report, I should have repeated the order to enter the port by lightening the ships, and ordered the works necessary at Alexandria to facilitate the squadrons getting out to sea again. But after all, as the admiral had orders, in case he should be unable to enter the port, to proceed to Corfu, he was a competent judge and umpire of his own conduct. Corfu had a good French garrison, and magazines of biscuit and meat for six months; the admiral might have touched on the coast of Albania, whence he might have drawn provisions, and finally, his instructions authorized him to proceed thence to Toulon, where there were 5,000 or 6,000 men belonging to the regiments in Egypt. They were soldiers returned by permission, or from hospitals, and different detachments that had joined at Toulon after the expedition had sailed. Admiral Brueys did nothing of the kind; he moored his squadron in line in Aboukir roads and sent to Rosetta for rice and other provisions. There are many opinions with respect to the motives which induced the admiral to remain in those bad roads. Some people have thought that, after having judged it impossible to effect the entrance of his squadron into Alexandria, he wished, before quitting the Grand Army, to be assured of the taking of Cairo, and to be free from all anxiety respecting the situation of the army. Brueys was much attached to me; the communications had been intercepted, and, as is usual in such cases, the most alarming rumours prevailed in the rear of the army. The admiral, had, however, heard of the success of the battle of the Pyramids and the triumphal entrance of the French into Cairo on 29 July. It seems that, having waited a month, he still wished to wait a few days to receive direct news from me. But the orders he had were positive, and such motives were insufficient to justify his conduct. In no case ought he to have remained in a situation in which his squadron was unsafe. He might have satisfied himself with respect to the anxiety

'Forty centuries look down upon you . . .' Napoleon and the Sphinx.

he felt from the false reports which were spread relative to the army, and at the same time fulfilled his duty to the squadron, by cruising between the coasts of Egypt and Caramania, and by sending to obtain intelligence from the Damietta shore, or any other point from which news from the army and Alexandria might be obtained.

As soon as the admiral had landed the artillery and what he had on board belonging to the land forces, which was an affair of about forty-eight hours, he should have weighed anchor and got under sail, whether he waited for fresh information to enter the port of Alexandria, or whether he waited for news from the army before quitting these seas. But he entirely mistook his situation. He spent several days in rectifying his line of moorings; he supported his left behind the little Isle of Aboukir, where, thinking it unassailable, he placed his worst ships, the *Guerrier* and the *Conquérant*. This last, the oldest ship in the whole squadron, carried only 18-pounders in her lower tier. He had the little isle occupied, and a battery of two 12-pounders constructed. He placed in the centre his best ships, the *Orient*, the *Franklin*, and the *Tonnant*, and at the extremity of his left the *Généreux*, one of the best and best-commanded ships in the squadron. Being fearful for his left, he had it sustained by the *Guillaume Tell*, his third 80-gun ship.

In this position, Admiral Brueys entertained no apprehension of any attack on his left, which was supported by the isle; he was more anxious about his right. But had the enemy advanced against it, he must have lost the wind; in that case it seems to have been the intention of Brueys to make sail with his centre and left. He considered this left so completely sheltered from attack that he did not think it necessary to protect it by the fire of the isle. The feeble battery he established there was merely intended to prevent the enemy from landing. Had the admiral understood his position better, he would have placed on this isle twenty 36-pounders and eight or ten mortars; he would have moored his left near it; he would have recalled the two 64-gun ships from Alexandria, which would have made two excellent floating batteries, and which, drawing less water than the other ships, could have approached nearer the isle; and he would have brought 3,000 seamen of the convoy from Alexandria, whom he would have distributed amongst his ships to reinforce their crews. He had recourse, it is true, to this expedient, but not until the last moment, after the commencement of the action, so that it only increased the confusion. He completely deceived himself with respect to the strength of his line of moorings.

After the action of Rhamanieh, the Arabs of Bahire intercepted all the communications between Alexandria and the army; nor did they submit until the news of the battle of the Pyramids, and the taking of Cairo, alarmed them with respect to the resentment of the French. On 27 July, the second day after my entry into Cairo, I received, for the first time, despatches from Alexandria and the admiral's correspondence. I was extremely surprised to find that the squadron was not in safety, that it was neither in the port of Alexandria, in that of Corfu, nor on its voyage to Toulon but in the Aboukir roads, exposed to the attack of an

Bonaparte in Cairo.

enemy of superior strength. I despatched my aide-de-camp Julien from the army
to the admiral, to inform him of my great dissatisfaction and to order him to set
sail immediately and either to get into Alexandria or make for Corfu. I reminded
him that all naval ordinances dictate against accepting battle in an open road.
Chief-of-squadron Julien set out on the 27th at 7 o'clock in the evening; he could
not have arrived before 3 or 4 August; the battle took place on the 1st and 2nd.
He had reached Teramea when a party of Arabs surprised the *jerm* in which he
was, and the brave young man was massacred while courageously defending the

despatches he carried, whose importance he well knew.

Admiral Brueys remained inactive in the bad position he had placed himself in. An English frigate, which had been despatched twenty days before by Nelson, appeared before Alexandria and went on to Aboukir, where she examined, with complete impunity the whole line of moorings – not a ship, frigate, or brig was under sail. Yet the admiral had above thirty light ships with which he might have covered the sea; they were all at anchor. The principles of war required him to remain under sail with his whole squadron, whatever might be his ulterior plans. But he ought, at least, to have kept under sail a light squadron of two or three men-of-war, and eight or ten frigates and sloops, to prevent any light English ship from watching his movements and to obtain the earliest intelligence of the enemy's approach. But destiny impelled him.

On 31 July, Nelson detached two of his ships, which reconnoitred the French line of moorings without molestation. On 1 August, the English squadron appeared towards 3 o'clock in the afternoon with all sails set. A fresh gale of the wind usual at that season was blowing. Admiral Brueys was at dinner; some of the crews were on shore; the decks were not cleared in a single ship. The admiral immediately made the signal to prepare for action. He despatched an officer to Alexandria to demand the seamen of the convoy; shortly afterwards he made a signal to prepare to get under sail; but the enemy's squadron came up so rapidly that there was scarcely time to clear the decks, which was done with extreme negligence. Even on board the *Orient*, the admiral's ship, some cabins that had been constructed on the poop for the accommodation of the army officers during the passage were not taken down – they were left full of mattresses and buckets of paint and tar. The *Guerrier* and the *Conquérant* each cleared only one tier of guns for action; the side towards the land was encumbered with all that had been cleared out from the opposite side, so that when the ships were turned those tiers could not fire. The English were so astonished at this that they sent to reconnoitre the reason for this inconsistency; they saw the French flag wave without a gun being fired.

The men who had been detached from the different crews had scarcely time enough to return on board. The admiral, judging that the enemy would not be within gunshot before 6 o'clock, supposed that he would not attack until the following day, more particularly as he only observed eleven 74-gun ships – the two others had been detached at Alexandria and did not rejoin Nelson until 8 o'clock in the evening. Brueys did not think the admiral would attack him the same day, and with only eleven ships. It is supposed that he thought at first of getting under way, but that he deferred giving the order until the sailors whom he expected from Aboukir could be embarked. The cannonade then commenced and an English vessel struck on the isle, which gave Brueys fresh confidence. The sailors from Alexandria did not arrive until towards 8 o'clock, when the cannonade was already brisk between several ships. In the tumult and darkness, a great number of them did not embark but remained on shore. The English admiral's plan was to attack ship after ship – every English ship anchoring astern and placing herself across the bows of a French ship – but accident altered this disposition. The *Culloden*, intending to attack the *Guerrier*, and endeavouring to pass between the left of that ship and the isle, struck. Had the isle been supplied with a few pieces of cannon, this ship would have been taken. The *Goliath*, which followed her, manoeuvring to anchor across the bows of the *Guerrier*, was carried away by the wind and current, and did not anchor until she had passed and turned that ship. Perceiving then that the larboard tiers of the *Conquérant* did not fire, for the reasons explained above, she placed herself alongside that vessel and soon disabled her. The *Zealous*, the second English ship, followed the *Goliath* and, anchoring alongside the *Guerrier*, which could not return her fire, speedily dismasted her. The *Orion*, the third English ship, executed the same manoeuvre, but came under attack from a French frigate and anchored between the *Franklin* and the *Peuple Souverain*. The *Vanguard*, the English admiral's ship, cast anchor athwart the *Spartiate*, the third French ship. The *Defence*, the *Bellerophon*, the *Majestic*, and the *Minotaur*, carried out the same manoeuvre and engaged the centre of the French line as far as the *Tonnant*, the eighth ship. The French admiral and his two seconds formed a line of three ships, very superior to those of the English. The fire was terrible; the *Bellerophon* was disabled, dismasted, and compelled to strike. Several other English ships were obliged to sheer off and if, at that moment, Admiral Villeneuve, who commanded the right wing of the French, had cut his cables and fallen on the English line, with the five ships under his command, the *Heureux*, *Timoleon*, *Mercure*, *Guillaume Tell*, *Généreux*, and the *Diane* and *Justice* frigates, it would have been destroyed. The *Culloden* had struck on the Béquier bank, and the *Leander* was trying to bring her off. The *Alexander* and *Swiftsure*, two other English ships, seeing that our right did not stir, and that the centre of the English line was hard pressed, made towards it. The *Alexander* took the place of the *Bellerophon*, and the *Swiftsure* attacked the *Franklin*. The *Leander*, which until then had been fighting the *Culloden*, perceiving the danger in which the centre stood, hastened to reinforce it. The victory was still far from being decided. The *Guerrier* and *Conquérant* no longer fired, but they were the worst ships in the squadron; and, on the English side, the *Culloden* and *Bellerophon* were disabled. The centre of the French line had, by the great superiority of its fire, occasioned the ships opposed to it much more damage than it had sustained. The English had only seventy-fours, and those of a small rate. It was to be presumed that the fire being thus kept up all night, Admiral Villeneuve would at last get under way in the morning, and the greatest success might yet be expected from the attack of five good ships which, as yet, had neither fired nor sustained a single cannon shot. But, at 11 o'clock, the *Orient* took fire, and blew up. This unforeseen accident decided the victory. The dreadful explosion of this ship suspended the action for a quarter of an hour. Our line, undismayed by this shocking spectacle, recommenced firing. The *Franklin*, *Tonnant*, *Peuple Souverain*, *Spartiate*, and *Aquilon* maintained the action until 3 o'clock in the morning. From 3 o'clock to 5 o'clock the firing slackened on both sides. Between 5 o'clock and 6 o'clock it redoubled and became terrible. What would it have been if the *Orient* had not blown up? In short, the battle was raging at noon, and was not over before 2 o'clock. It was not until then that Villeneuve seemed to awaken and to perceive that the fleet had been fighting for twenty hours. He cut his cables and stood out with the *Guillaume Tell*, his flagship, the *Généreux*, and the *Diane* and *Justice* frigates. The three other ships of his wing ran ashore without fighting. Thus, notwithstanding the terrible accident to the *Orient*, and the singular inactivity of Villeneuve, which prevented five ships from firing a single gun, the loss and confusion of the English were such that twenty-four hours after the battle the French flag was still flying on board the *Tonnant* and Nelson had no ship in a condition to attack her. Not only were the *Guillaume Tell* and *Généreux* not pursued by any English ship, but the enemy, in the disabled state they were in, were glad to see them make off. Admiral Brueys obstinately defended the honour of the French flag; although he had received several wounds he would not go down to the cockpit. He died on his quarter-deck giving his orders. Casabianca, Thermard, and Du Petit-Thouard acquired glory on his unfortunate day. Rear-Admiral Villeneuve, according to Nelson and the English, might have decided the victory even after the explosion of the *Orient*. Even at midnight, had he got under way and engaged in the action with the ships of his wing, he might have annihilated the English squadron. He remained a peaceful spectator of the battle. As Rear-Admiral Villeneuve was a brave and good seamen, one has to ask what was the cause of this singular conduct? He waited for orders! It is asserted that the admiral made the signal for him to weigh anchor, but that the smoke prevented him from seeing it. But was there any need of an order to take part in the battle and assist his comrades?

The *Orient* blew up at 11 o'clock; from that time until 2 o'clock in the afternoon – that is to say, for fifteen hours – the fight continued. Villeneuve was then in command; why did he do nothing? Villeneuve was of an irresolute character, destitute of energy.

The crews of the three ships that grounded, and those of the two frigates, landed on the beach at Aboukir. A hundred men escaped from the *Orient*, and a great number of sailors from the other ships took refuge on land, at the decisive moment of the battle, taking advantage of the enemy's disorder. The army thus obtained 3,500 recruits. Some 1,800 of them were formed into a naval brigade, three battalions strong. The rest were recruited into the artillery, infantry, and cavalry. Many pieces of artillery, much ammunition, and several masts and other pieces of timber were salvaged and became useful in the arsenal of Alexandria. We still had in the port the two ships the *Causse* and the *Dubois*, four Venetian-built frigates, three French-built frigates, and all the light vessels and transports. A few days after the battle Nelson set sail and quitted the shores of Alexandria, leaving two ships of war to blockade the port. Forty Neapolitan transports sought and obtained from the commandant of Alexandria leave to return home; the commander of the English cruisers collected them around him, took out the crews, and burnt the vessels. This violation of the rights of nations proved prejudicial to the English; the crews of the Italian and French transports saw that their best hopes lay in the success of the French army and took appropriate measures. Nelson was received in triumph in the port of Naples.

The loss of the battle of Aboukir had great influence on the affairs of Egypt and even on those of the world. Had the French fleet been saved, the expedition to Syria would have met with no obstacle; the battering-train could have been safely and easily conveyed beyond the desert, and Acre would not have stopped the French army. But, the French fleet being destroyed, the Divan took courage and ventured to declare war against France. The army lost a great support; its position in Egypt was totally changed, and I was obliged to renounce the hope of using the expedition to Egypt to establish French power permanently in the East.

Since the least powerful ships of the line have been seventy-fours, the naval armaments of France, England and Spain have never been composed of more than thirty ships. There have, nevertheless, been armaments which have, for the time, been more considerable. A squadron of thirty ships of the line is equal to a land army of 120,000 men. An army of 120,000 men is a grand army, although there have sometimes been forces of still greater strength. A squadron of thirty ships contains at most a fifth of the number of men in an army 120,000 strong. It carries five times more artillery, and of a very superior calibre. The expense of the *matériel* is very nearly the same. If the *matériel* of the whole artillery of 120,000 men, of their waggons, provisions, and hospitals, be compared with that of thirty ships, the expenses of both are equal, or nearly so. If we calculate 20,000 cavalry, and 20,000 artillery and waggon-train for the land force, the support of the army is incomparably more expensive than that of the navy.

France might have three fleets of thirty sail as well as three armies of 120,000 men.

War by land generally destroys more men than maritime war, being more perilous. The sailor, in a squadron, fights only once in a campaign; the soldier fights daily. The sailor, whatever may be the fatigues and dangers attached to his element, suffers much less than the soldier; he never endures hunger or thirst, he has always with him his lodging, his kitchen, his hospital, and medical stores. The naval armies, in the service of France and England, where cleanliness is preserved by discipline, and experience has taught all the measures proper to be adopted for the preservation of health, are less subject to sickness than land armies. Besides the dangers of battle, the sailor has to encounter those of storms; but art has so materially diminished the latter, that they cannot be compared to those which occur by land, such as popular insurrections, assassinations, and surprises by the enemy's light troops.

A general who is commander-in-chief of a naval army, and a general who is commander-in-chief of a land army, are men who stand in need of different qualities. The qualities adapted to the command of a land army are born in us, while those necessary for commanding a naval army can be acquired only by experience.

Alexander and Condé were able to command at a very early age; the art of war by land is an art of genius and inspiration; but neither Alexander nor Condé, at the age of twenty-two years, could have commanded a naval army. In the latter, nothing is genius or inspiration, but all is positive and matter of experience. The marine general needs but one science, that of navigation. The commander by land requires many – or a talent equivalent to all, that of profiting by experience and knowledge of every kind. A marine general has nothing to guess; he knows where his enemy is, and knows his strength. A land general never knows anything with certainty, never sees his enemy plainly, nor knows positively where he is. When the armies are facing each other, the slightest accident of the ground, the least wood, may hide a part of the hostile army. The most experienced eye cannot be certain whether it sees the whole of the enemy's army or only three-fourths of it. It is by the eyes of the mind, by the combination of all reasoning, by a sort of inspiration, that the land general sees, commands, and judges. The marine general requires nothing but an experienced eye; nothing relating to the enemy's strength is concealed from him. What creates great difficulty in the profession of the land commander is the necessity of feeding so many men and animals; if he allows himself to be guided by the commissaries he will never stir and his expeditions will fail. The naval commander is never confined; he carries everything with him. A naval commander has no reconnoitring to perform, no ground to examine, no field of battle to study; Indian Ocean, Atlantic, or Channel, still it is a liquid plan. The most skilful can have no other advantage over the least experienced than what arises from his knowledge of the winds that prevail in particular seas, from his foresight of those which will prevail there, or from his acquaintance with the signs of atmosphere; qualities which are acquired by experience, and experience only.

The general commanding by land never knows the field of battle on which he is to operate. His eye for the country is one of inspiration, he has no positive data. The data from which a knowledge of the localities must be gained are so contingent that scarcely anything can be learnt from experience. It is a facility of instantly seizing all the relations of different grounds, according to the nature of the country; in short, it is a gift called the *coup d'oeil militaire*, which great generals have received from nature. Nevertheless, the observations that may be made on topographical maps, and the facilities arising from education and the habit of reading such maps, may afford some assistance.

A naval commander-in-chief depends more on the captains of his ships than does a military commander-in-chief on his generals. The latter has the power of taking on himself the direct command of the troops, of moving to every point, and of remedying the false movements made by others. The personal influence of the naval commander is confined to the men on board his own ship; the smoke prevents the signals from being seen. The winds change, or may not be the same throughout the space occupied by his line. Of all arts, then, this is the one in which the subalterns have the most to take upon themselves.

Our naval defeats are to be attributed to three causes: first, to irresolution and want of energy in the commanders-in-chief; secondly, to errors in tactics; thirdly, to want of experience and nautical knowledge in the captains of ships, and to the opinion these officers maintain that they ought only to act according to signals. The action off Ushant, those during the Revolution in the Ocean, and those in the Mediterranean in 1793 and 1794, were all lost through these different causes. Admiral Villaret, though personally brave, was wanting in strength of mind, and was not even attached to the cause for which he fought. Martin was a good seaman, but a man of little resolution. They were, moreover, both influenced by the Representatives of the People, who, possessing no experience, sanctioned erroneous operations.

The principle of making no movement, except according to signal from the admiral, is the more erroneous because it is always in the power of the captain of a ship to find reasons in justification of his failure to execute the signals made to him. In all the sciences necessary to war, theory is useful for giving general ideas which form the mind; but their strict execution is always dangerous; they are only the axes by which curves are to be traced. Besides rules themselves compel one to reason in order to discover whether they ought to be departed from.

Although often superior in force to the English, we never knew how to attack them, and we allowed their squadrons to escape while we were wasting time in useless manoeuvres. The first law of maritime tactics ought to be that as soon as the admiral has made the signal that he means to attack, every captain should make the necessary manoeuvres to attack one of the enemy's ships and to support his neighbours.

This was latterly the principle of English tactics. Had it been adopted in France, Admiral Villeneuve would not have thought himself blameless at Aboukir for remaining inactive with five or six ships – that is to say, with half the squadron – for twenty-four hours, while the enemy was overpowering the other wing.

The French navy is called on to acquire a superiority over the English. The French understand building better than their rivals, and French ships, the English themselves admit, are better than theirs. The guns are superior in calibre to those of the English by one-fourth. These are two great advantages.

The English are superior in discipline. The Toulon and Scheldt squadrons had adopted the same practice and customs as the English, and were attempting as severe a discipline, with the difference belonging to the character of the two nations. The English discipline is perfectly slavish; it is *patron* and serf. It is only kept up by the influence of the most dreadful terror. Such a state of things would degrade and debase the French character, which requires a paternal kind of discipline, more founded on honour and sentiment.

In most of the battles with the English that we have lost, we have either been inferior in strength, or combined with Spanish ships, which, being ill organized, and in these latter times degenerate, have weakened our line instead of strengthening it; or finally, the commanders-in-chief, who wished to fight while advancing to meet the enemy, have wavered when they fell in with him, retreated under various pretexts, and thus compromised the bravest men.

VIII

SYRIA

ARABIA is, in form, a trapezium. One of its sides, bounded by the Red Sea and the Isthmus of Suez, is 500 leagues long. Another, extending from the straits of Bab al-Mandab to Cape Hadd, is 450 leagues. A third, the longest, which extends from Cape Hadd across the Persian Gulf and the Euphrates to the mountains near Aleppo, is 600 leagues. The fourth, the shortest of 150 leagues, runs from Ratah, on the Egyptian border, to beyond Alexandretta and the mountains of Rosas; it separates Arabia from Syria. In Syria the cultivated lands run back thirty leagues from this border and then the desert extends for thirty leagues, as far as Palmyra. Syria is bounded on the north by Asia Minor, on the west by the Mediterranean, on the south by Egypt, and on the east by Arabia. It is the complement of Arabia, in conjunction with which it forms a large isle comprehended between the Mediterranean, the Red Sea, the Indian Ocean, the Persian Gulf, and the Euphrates. Syria differs totally from Egypt, in population, climate, and soil. Egypt is a single plain, formed by the valley of one of the largest rivers in the world; Syria is the assemblage of a great number of valleys. Five-sixths of the land are hills or mountains, a chain of which crosses all Syria and runs parallel with the coast of the Mediterranean for a distance of ten leagues. To the right, this chain pours its waters into two rivers, the Jordan and the Orontes, which run in the same direction as itself. These rivers rise in Mount Lebanon, the centre of Syria and the most elevated point of this chain. The Orontes runs between the mountains and Arabia, from south to north, and, after running sixty leagues, falls into the sea near the Gulf of Antioch. As it runs very near the foot of the mountains it receives only a small number of tributary streams. The Jordan, which rises twenty leagues from the Orontes in the Ante-Lebanon range, runs from north to south. It receives about ten smaller streams

126

from the chain of mountains that crosses Syria. After a course of sixty leagues, it is lost in the Dead Sea.

Near the source of the Orontes, on the Balbec side, spring two minor rivers. One, called the Barada, waters the plain of Damascus, and debouches into the lake of El-Margi; the other, which runs for thirty leagues, likewise runs in the heights of Balbec, and falls into the Mediterranean near Tyre. The country of Aleppo is washed by several rivulets, which rise in Asia Minor and run into the Orontes. The Qoweiq, on which Aleppo stands, is lost in a lake near that city.

It rains in Syria almost as much as in Europe. The country is very healthy, and affords the most agreeable spots. As it is composed of valleys and small mountains, very favourable to pasture, a great quantity of cattle is bred here. Trees of all kinds abound – particularly great numbers of olives. Syria would be very suitable for the cultivation of the vine; all the Christian villages make excellent wine.

This province is divided into twelve pashaliks – that of Jerusalem, which comprises the ancient Holy Land, and those of Acre, Tripoli, Damascus, and Aleppo. Aleppo and Damascus are, beyond comparison, the two largest cities. On the 150 leagues of the Syrian coast there are several towns. Gaza is situated a league from the sea, without a trace of roads or a port, but with a fine plain, two leagues in circumference, which marks the site of the city in the times of its prosperity (it is now of little importance). Jaffa, or Joppa, is the nearest port to Jerusalem, from which it is fifteen leagues distant. Caesarea presents only ruins. Acre has an open road, but the town is inconsiderable – it contains 10,000 or 12,000 inhabitants. Sour, or Tyre, is now a mere village. Said, Bairout, and Tripoli are small towns. The most important point of all this coast is the Gulf of Alexandretta, situated twenty leagues from Aleppo, thirty from the Euphrates, and 300 from Alexandria. It affords anchorage for the largest squadrons. Tyre, which commerce formerly advanced to so high a pitch of splendour, and which was the mother country of Carthage, seems to have been partly indebted for her prosperity to the trade of India, which was carried on by sailing up the Persian Gulf and the Euphrates, passing Palmyra and Amasia, and proceeding at one period to Tyre, at another to Antioch.

The highest point of all Syria is Mount Lebanon, which is but a mountain of the third order, and is covered with enormous pines; that of Palestine is Mount Tabor. The Orontes and Jordan, the largest streams of these countries, are both little rivers.

Syria was the cradle of the religions of Moses and Jesus; Islam arose in Arabia. Thus the same corner of the earth produced the three religions that have destroyed polytheism and carried to every part of the globe the knowledge of one only God, the Creator of the universe.

Almost all the wars of the Crusaders of the 11th, 12th and 13th centuries were fought in Syria and Acre, Ptolemais, Joppa, and Damascus were the principle scenes of action. The influence of the Crusaders' arms and of their residence, which lasted for several ages, have left traces that may still be perceived.

There are many Jews in Syria, who come from all parts of the world to die in the Holy Land of Japhet. There are also many Christians, some of whom are descended from the Crusaders; others are indigenous families, who did not embrace Mohammedanism at the time of the conquest by the Arabs. They are mixed together and it is no longer possible to distinguish them. Chefamer, Nazareth, Bethlehem, and part of Jerusalem are peopled by Christians only. In the pashaliks of Acre and Jerusalem, the Christians and Jews together are more numerous than the Muslims. Behind Mount Lebanon are the Druses, a nation whose religion approaches nearly to that of the Christians. At Damascus and Aleppo, the Mohammedans form a great majority; there exists, however, a considerable number of Syriac Christians. The Mutualis, Mohammedans of the sect of Ali, who inhabit the banks of the river that runs from Lebanon towards Tyre, were formerly numerous and powerful; but at the time of the expedition of the French into Syria they had greatly declined; the cruelty and oppression of Gezzar Pasha had destroyed a great number of them. All who remained, however, rendered us great services and distinguished themselves by extraordinary courage. All the traditions we have about ancient Egypt give it a large population. But Syria cannot, in this respect, have exceeded the proportions known in Europe; for there are in that country, as in those which we inhabit, rocks and uncultivated lands.

Syria, however, like every part of the Turkish empire, presents, on almost all sides, little but heaps of ruins.

The principal object of the French expedition to the East was to check the power of the English. The army that was to change the destiny of India was to march from the Nile. Egypt was to supply the place of Santo-Domingo and the Antilles, and to reconcile the freedom of the black with the interests of our manufacturers. The conquest of this province would have produced the ruin of all the English establishments in America and the Peninsula of the Ganges. Had the French once become masters of the ports of Italy, Corfu, Malta, and Alexandria, the Mediterranean would have become a French lake.

The revolution of India was likely to be more or less near, according as the chances of war should prove more or less fortunate, and the inhabitants of Arabia and Egypt should be more or less favourably disposed, in consequence of the policy the Porte should adopt under these new circumstances: the only object to be immediately attended to was to conquer Egypt and to form a solid establishment there; and the means of effecting this were all that had been provided. All the rest has been considered as a necessary consequence; the execution only had been anticipated. The French squadron refitted in the ports of Alexandria, victualled and manned by experienced crews, would have sufficed to keep Constantinople in awe. It could have landed a body of troops at Alexandria, if it had been thought necessary; and we should have been, in the same year, masters of Egypt and Syria, the Nile, and the Euphrates. The happy issue of the battle of the Pyramids, the conquest of Egypt, achieved without any sensible loss, the goodwill of the inhabitants, the zeal of the chiefs of the law, seemed at first to ensure the speedy execution of these grand projects. But a short time only had elapsed, when the destruction of the French squadron at Aboukir, the countermanding of the expedition to Ireland by the Directory, and the influence of the enemies of France over the Porte, rendered success much more difficult.

In the mean time two Turkish armies assembled, one at Rhodes, and the other in Syria, to attack the French in Egypt. It appears that they were to act simultaneously in the month of May, the first by landing at Aboukir, and the second by crossing the desert that divides Syria from Egypt. In the beginning of January news arrived that Gezzar Pasha had been appointed seraskier of the Army of Syria and that his vanguard, under the command of Abdalla, had already arrived at El-Arisch, had occupied that place, and was engaged in repairing the fort, which may be considered as the key to Egypt on the Syrian side. A train of artillery of forty guns, served by 1,200 cannoneers, the only troops of that kind in the empire that had been trained in the European manner, had landed at Jaffa; considerable magazines were forming in that town; and a great number of transports, part of which came from Constantinople, were employed for this purpose. At Gaza, stores of skins to hold water had been established; report said there were enough of them to enable an army of 60,000 men to cross the desert.

If the French had remained quiet in Egypt, they would certainly have been attacked by the two armies at once; it was also to be feared that the Turks would be joined by a body of European troops, and that the attack would be made at a moment of internal troubles. In this case, even if the French had been victorious, it would have been impossible for them to have profited by their conquest. By sea, they had no fleet; and by land, the desert of seventy-five leagues, which separates Syria from Egypt, was not passable by an army in the height of the hot season.

The rules of war, therefore, required me to anticipate my enemies, to cross the great desert during the winter, to possess myself of all the magazines the enemy had established on the coast of Syria, and to attack and destroy the troops in succession as fast as they collected.

According to this plan, the divisions of the Army of Rhodes were obliged to hasten to the aid of Syria, and Egypt remained quiet, which allowed us to march the greater part of our forces into Syria. The Mamelukes of Murad-Bey and Ibrahim-Bey, the Arabs of the Egyptian desert, the Druses of Mount Lebanon, the Mutualis, the Christians of Syria, and the whole party of the Sheik of Ayer, in Syria, might join the troops when masters of that country, and the commotion would communicate to every part of Asia. Those provinces of the Ottoman Empire in which Arabic is spoken heartily prayed for a change and waited for a leader. We might, if fortunate, have been on the Euphrates by the middle of the summer, with 100,000 auxiliaries, who would have had a reserve of 25,000 French veterans, some of the best troops in the world, with a numerous train of artillery. Constantinople would then have been menaced; and if an amicable connection could have been formed with the Porte, we might have crossed the desert, and marched on the Indus by the end of autumn.

Jaffa, a town containing from 7,000 to 8,000 inhabitants, which was the portion of the Sultana Valida, is situated sixteen leagues from Gaza, and one league from the little river of Maar, which, at its mouth, is not fordable. The wall, on the land side, is formed by a half hexagon; one of the sides looks towards Gaza, another towards the Jordan, a third towards Acre, and a fourth runs along the seaside in the form of a concave half-circle. There is a port of small ships, in a bad state, and tolerable open roads. On the Koich is the Convent of the Fathers of the Holy Land (the Recollets Chaussés), stewards of Nazareth, and proprietors of several other communities in Palestine. The fortifications of Jaffa consist of great walls flanked with towers, without ditches or counterscarps. These towers were lined with artillery, but the range of batteries had not been well understood, and the guns were unskilfully placed. The environs of Jaffa consist of a valley full of gardens and orchards; the ground affords many opportunities of approaching within a pistol-shot of the ramparts without being perceived. Above a cannon-shot from Jaffa is the rideau which commands the country; the line of counter-vallation was traced there. This was the proper place for the army to encamp in; but as it was far from the water, and exposed to the scorching heat of the sun, the rideau being open, the troops preferred stationing themselves in some groves of orange-trees, and having the military positions guarded by posts.

Mount Carmel is situated on a promontory of the same name, three leagues from Acre, forming the extreme left of the bay. It is steep on every side; at its summit there is a convent and fountains, and a rock on which there is the print of a man's foot, which tradition states to have been left by Elijah when he ascended into heaven.

This mount commands the whole coast, and ships steer by it when they are making for Syria. At its foot runs the River Caisrum, the mouth of which is 700 or 800 toises from Caiffa. This little town, situated on the sea-shore, contains 3,000 inhabitants; it has a small port, a wall in the ancient style, with towers, and is commanded by the heights of Carmel at a very short distance. The way to Acre from the mouth of the Caisrum runs along the sands on the sea shore for a league and a half, when it meets the mouth of the Belus, a little river which rises on the hills of Chefamer, and the waters of which scarcely flow. This river is marshy down to its mouth, and falls into the sea about 1,500 toises from Acre. It passes within a musket-shot of the height of Richard Coeur de Lion, situated on its right bank, 600 toises from Acre.

The siege of Acre may be divided into three periods.

First period. It began on 20 March, the day on which the trench was opened, and ended on 1 April. During this period our battering-train consisted of one 32-pounder carronade. Major Lambert had taken this at Caiffa by seizing the *Tiger's* longboat, but we could not use it with the carriage belonging to the boat and were were destitute of balls. These difficulties speedily vanished. In twenty-four hours the artillery park constructed a carriage. As for balls, Sir Sidney Smith took it upon himself to provide them. A few horsemen or waggons made their appearance from time to time, upon which the commodore approached and poured in an alternate fire from all his tiers. The soldiers, to whom the director of the park paid five sous per ball, then immediately ran to pick them up. They were so much accustomed to this manoeuvre that, with shouts of laughter, they would go and fetch them in the midst of the cannonade. Sometimes, also a sloop was brought forward, when we pretended to begin the construction of a battery. Thus we obtained 12- and 32-pounder balls. We had powder, for the park had brought some from Cairo, and more had been found at Jaffa and Gaza. On the whole, our total artillery, including our field-pieces, consisted of four 12-pounders, provided with 200 rounds each, eight howitzers, a 32-pounder carronade, and thirty 4-pounders.

The engineer General Samson, being ordered to reconnoitre the town, declared positively on his return that it had neither counterscarp nor ditch. He said he had reached the foot of the rampart, in the night, and received a musket-shot there by which he was severely wounded. His report was incorrect; he had in fact reached a wall, but not the rampart. Unfortunately measures were taken according to the information given. A hope was entertained of taking the town in three days. It was not so strong as Jaffa, it was said: its garrison is only between 2,000 and 3,000 men, while Jaffa, with a much more limited space to defend, had 8,000 men when it was taken.

On 25 March, the carronade and the four 12-pounders made a breach in the wall, in the course of four hours, which was deemed practicable. A young officer of engineers, with fifteen sappers and twenty-five grenadiers, was charged to mount to the assault, to clear the foot of the tower, and Adjutant-Commander Laugier, who was stationed in the place of arms, 100 toises from the spot, waited for the completion of this operation to rush upon the breach. The sappers, on coming out from behind the aqueduct, had but thirty toises to go, but they were stopped short by a counterscarp of fifteen feet, and a ditch which they estimated at several toises in width. Five or six of them were wounded, and rest, pursued by a dreadful fire of musketry, regained the trench precipitately.

A miner was immediately sent to work to blow up the counterscarp. In three days, that is to say on the 28th, the mine was ready; the miners declared that the counterscarp might be blown up. This difficult operation was performed under the fire of all the ramparts and of a great quantity of mortars, directed by excellent gunners, furnished by the English ships, which scattered shells in all directions. All our 8-inch mortars and fine pieces which the English had taken now strengthened the defence of the place. The mine was sprung on 28 March, but it did not succeed well; it had not been dug deep enough, and overthrew only half the counterscarp, more than eight feet of which remained. The sappers, however, asserted that it was entirely destroyed. The Staff-Officer Mailly was consequently sent with a detachment of twenty-five grenadiers to support an officer of engineers who advanced to the counterscarp with six sappers. They had taken the precaution of providing themselves with three ladders, with which they descended it. As they were annoyed by the musket fire, they fixed the ladders to the breach, and the sappers and grenadiers preferred mounting to the assault to clearing the foot of the breach. They gave notice to Laugier, who was ready to support them with two battalions, that they were in the ditch, that the breach was practicable, and that it was time to support them. Laugier hastened up to them at a running step; but on reaching the counterscarp he met the grenadiers returning, who said that the breach was too high by some feet, and that Mailly and several of their comrades had been killed.

When the Turks saw this young officer fastening the ladder, terror seized upon them; they fled to the port, and Gezzar himself had got on board ship. But the death of Mailly frustrated the whole operation; the two battalions dispersed themselves in order to return the enemy's musketry fire. Laugier was killed, and some loss was incurred without producing any result. This event was very unfortunate, for this was the day on which the town ought to have been taken; reinforcements arrived by sea daily from that time.

Second period. From 1 April to the 27th. A new well was now sunk for a mine, intended to blow up the whole counterscarp, in order that the ditch might no longer be any impediment. What had already been done was found useless; it was easier to make a new approach. Eight days were needed by the miners. The counterscarp was blown up, the operation succeeded perfectly. On the 10th, the mine was continued under the ditch in order to blow up the whole tower. There was now no hope of getting in at the breach, the enemy having filled it up with all sorts of combustibles. The approaches were carried on for six days more. The beseiged perceived what we were doing and made a sortie in three columns. That of the centre was headed by 200 English; they were repulsed, and a captain of marines was killed at the shaft of the mine.

It was during this period that the actions of Canaam, Nazareth, Saffet, and Mount Tabor were fought. The first took place on the 9th, the second on the 11th, and the others on the 13th and 16th. It was on the latter day, on 16th April, that the miners calculated that they were under the axis of the tower. At this period Rear-Admiral Perré had arrived at Jaffa, with three frigates, from Alexandria; he had landed two mortars and six 18-pounders at Tintura. Two were fixed to play upon the little isle that flanked the breach, and the four others were directed against the ramparts and curtains by the side of the tower. It was intended, by the overthrow of this tower, to widen the breach which it was supposed the mine would make, for it was apprehended that the enemy might have made an internal retrenchment and isolated the tower, which was salient.

On the 25th the mine was sprung, but a chamber under the tower disappointed us, and only the part on our side was blown up. The effect produced was the burying of 200 or 300 Turks and a few pieces of cannon, for they had embattled and occupied every storey of the tower. It was determined to take advantage of the first moment of surprise, and thirty men accordingly attempted to make a lodgement in the tower. Being unable to proceed, they maintained themselves in the lower storeys, while the enemy occupied the upper, until the 26th when General Devaux was wounded. It was then resolved to evacuate the place, in order to use the batteries against this tottering tower, and to destroy it altogether. On the 27th Cafarelli died.

Third period. From 27 April to 20 May. During this period the enemy felt that if they remained on the defensive they were lost. The countermines they had formed did not make them feel secure. All the battlements of the walls were destroyed, and the guns dismounted by our batteries. A reinforcement of 3,000 men, which had entered the place, had, however, compensated for all these losses.

But the Turks were terror-struck and it was no longer possible to induce them to remain upon the walls. They supposed every spot to be undermined. Phelippeaux[1] formed lines of counter-attack. He also dug two trenches, resembling two sides of a triangle, which took all our works in flank. The numerical superiority of the enemy, the great number of labourers in the city, and the quantity of bales of cotton with which they formed the breastworks, materially expedited the works. In a few days they flanked the whole tower on the right and left, after which they raised cavaliers, and lined them with 24 pounders; their counter-attack and batteries were several times carried and overthrown and their guns spiked; but we were never able to maintain these works, because they were so entirely commanded by the towers and the wall. The order was then given to proceed against them by sap, so that their workmen and ours were only separated by two or three fathoms of ground, and were marching directly against each other. Fougasses were also established, which afforded means of entering the enemy's boyau, and destroying all who were not on their guard.

It was thus that, on 1 May, two hours before daybreak, possession was obtained of the most salient part of the counter-attack without any loss. Twenty volunteers endeavoured, at the first peep of dawn, to effect a lodgement in the tower, the defence of which our battery had entirely razed. But at that moment the enemy made a sortie on their right and their balls striking behind the detachment, which was endeavouring to lodge itself under the ruins, obliged it to fall back. The sortie was briskly repulsed; 500 or 600 of the beseiged were killed, and great number driven into the sea. As the tower was totally destroyed, it was resolved to attack a portion of the rampart by mining, in order to avoid the retrenchment the enemy had constructed. The counterscarp was blown up. The mine was already carried across under the ditch, and was beginning to extend under the scarp, when, on the 6th, the enemy debouched by a sap covered by the ditch, surprised the mask of the mine, and filled up the well.

On the 7th, the enemy received a reinforcement of fresh troops, amounting to 12,000 men. As soon as their arrival was announced by signals, it was calculated that according to the state of the wind they could not land for six hours. In consequence of this a 24-pounder, which had been sent by Rear-Admiral Perré, was immediately brought into play; it battered down a piece of the wall to the

---

[1] A French emigrant, officer of engineers.

right of the tower, which was on our left. At night the troops attacked all the enemy's works, filled up the trenches, killed all they met with, spiked the guns, mounted the breach, made a lodgement in the tower, and entered the place; in short we were masters of the town, when the troops who had landed appeared in formidable numbers, to renew the battle. Rambaut was killed; 1,500 men fell with him, or were taken; Lannes was wounded. The beseiged sallied forth by every gate, and took the breach in rear; but there was an end of their success; our troops marched against them, and after driving them back into the town, and cutting off several columns, regained the breach. Seven or eight hundred prisoners were taken; they were armed with European bayonets, and came from Constantinople. The enemy's loss was enormous; all our batteries fired upon him with grape, and our success appeared so great, that on the 10th, at 2 o'clock in the morning, I ordered a new assault. General Debon was killed in this last action. There were 20,000 men in the place, and Gezzar's house and all the others were so thronged with defenders that we could not pass beyond the breach.

Under these circumstances what was I do do? On the one hand Rear-Admiral Perré, who had returned from a cruise, had for the third time landed artillery at Tintura. We were beginning to have sufficient artillery to entitle us to hope to reduce the town. But, on the other hand, the prisoners informed us that new reinforcements were leaving Rhodes when they embarked. The reinforcements received and expected by the enemy might render the success of the seige problematical; remote as we were from France and Egypt, we could not afford fresh losses: we had at Jaffa and in the camp 1,200 wounded; the plague was in our hospital. On the 20th the siege was raised.

IX

18 BRUMAIRE

WHEN lamentable weakness and endless vacillation are manifested in the councils of a government; when an administration, yielding by turns to the influence of every opposing party, and going on from day to day without any fixed plan or determined system, has shown its utter insufficiency; when the most modern citizens in the state are obliged to confess that it is without a government; and when rulers, insignificant at home, have shamefully brought upon their country the contempt of foreigners (the greatest of injuries in the eyes of a proud people) – then a general uneasiness spreads throughout society and, driven by the instinct of self-preservation, it looks into its own resources to try to find someone able to save it from destruction.

A populous nation always possesses this tutelary genius in its own bosom, though he may sometimes be tardy in appearing. But it is not enough that he exists; he must be known to others, and he must know himself. Until then all endeavours are vain, all schemes ineffectual. The so-called government is protected by the inertness of the multitude and, in spite of its inexperience and weakness, the efforts of its enemies cannot prevail against it. But let this deliverer, so impatiently expected, suddenly give a proof of his existence, and the nation instinctively acknowledges and calls on him. All obstacles vanish at his approach and a great people, thronging around him, seems exultingly to proclaim, 'This is the man'.

Such was the state of the public mind in France in the year 1799, when, on 9 October (16 Vendémiaire, year VIII), the frigates *La Muiron* and *La Carrère* and the xebecs *La Revanche* and *La Fortune* cast anchor, at the break of day, in the gulf of Fréjus.

No sooner were the French frigates recognized than it was conjectured they came from Egypt. The people ran in crowds to the shore, eager for news from the army. It was soon understood that I was on board; and such was the enthusiasm among the people, that even the wounded soldiers got out of the hospitals, in spite of the guards, and went to the shore. The spectators wept with joy. In a moment the sea was covered with boats. The officers belonging to the fortifications and the customs, the crews of the ships that were anchored in the road – in short everybody – thronged about the frigates. General Pereymont, who commanded on the coast, was the first to go on board. Thus we were enabled to enter, without waiting for the officers of quarantine; for the communication with the shore had been general.

Italy had just been lost; war was about to the recommenced on the Var, and Fréjus dreaded an invasion as soon as hostilities should begin. The necessity of having a leader at the head of affairs was too imperious; everyone was too much agitated by my sudden appearance at this juncture, for ordinary considerations to have any weight. The officers of quarantine declared that there was no occasion for subjecting these vessels to it, basing their report on the circumstance that communication had taken place at Ajaccio. This argument, however, far from being tenable, only went to prove that Corsica itself ought to have been put under quarantine. The administration at Marsilles made this observation a fortnight afterwards, and with reason. It is true, that during the fifty days that had elapsed from the vessels leaving Egypt, there had been no sickness on board any of them, and indeed the plague had ceased three months before their departure. At 6 o'clock that evening, accompanied by Berthier, I set off in a coach for Paris.

The fatigue of my passage, and the effect of the transition from a dry climate to a moist one, determined me to stop six hours at Aix. The inhabitants of the city and of the neighbouring villages came in crowds to testify their happiness at seeing me again. The joy was universal. Those who lived too far in the country to present themselves on the road in time rang the bells and hoisted flags upon the steeples, which at night blazed with illuminations.

It was not like the return of a citizen to his country, or a general at the head of a victorious army, but like the triumph of a sovereign restored to his people. The enthusiasm of Avignon, Montelimart, Valence, and Vienne, was surpassed only by the rapture of Lyons. That city, in which I rested for twelve hours, was in an universal delirium. The Lyonnese had at all times shown great attachment to me, either because of the natural generosity of character by which they are distinguished; or because, considering their city as the capital of the south, they felt peculiarly interested in all that concerned the security of the frontiers on the Italian side; or because, the population of Lyons being composed chiefly of natives of Burgundy and Dauphiné, they shared the sentiments most prevalent in these provinces. Their imaginations were, moreover, still in a state of exultation at that time, from the accounts that had been spread eight days before of the battle of Aboukir and of the brilliant success of the French arms in Egypt, which formed such a striking contrast to the defeat of their armies in Germany and Italy. 'We are numerous, we are brave,' the people everywhere seemed to say, 'and yet we are conquered. We want a leader to direct us: we now behold him, and our glory will once more shine forth.' In the mean time the news of my return had reached Paris. It was announced at the theatres, and caused a universal sensation – a general delirium, which the members of the Directory shared. Some of the Société du Manège trembled, but they dissembled their real feelings so well as to seem to share the general rejoicing. Baudin, the deputy from Ardennes, who was really a worthy man, and sincerely grieved at the unfortunate turn that the affairs of the Republic had taken, died of joy when he heard of my return.

I had already quitted Lyons, when my landing was announced in Paris. With a precaution which was very advisable in my situation, I expressed to my couriers my intention of taking a different road from that which I actually took; so that my wife, my family, and particular friends went in a wrong direction to meet me and because of that some days passed before I was able to see them. Having thus arrived in Paris quite unexpectedly, I was in my own house in the Rue Chantereine, before anyone knew I was in the capital. Two hours afterwards I presented myself to the Directory, and, being recognized by the soldiers on guard, was announced by shouts of gladness. All the members of the Directory appeared to share in the public joy; I had every reason to congratulate myself on the reception I experienced on all sides. The nature of past events sufficiently instructed me as to the situation of France; and the information I had procured on my journey had made me acquainted with all that was going on. My resolution was taken. What I had been unwilling to attempt on my return from Italy, I was now determined to do immediately. I held the government of the Directory and the leaders of the councils in supreme contempt. Resolved to possess myself of authority, and to restore France to her former glory, by giving a powerful impulse to public affairs, I had left Egypt to execute this project; and all that I had just seen in the interior of France had confirmed my sentiments and strengthened my resolution.

Of the old Directory only Barras remained. The other members were Roger Ducos, Moulins, Gohier, and Sieyès.

Ducos was a man of narrow mind and easy disposition.

Moulins, a general of division, had never served in war; he was originally in the French guards, and had been advanced in the Army of the Interior. He was a worthy man, and a warm and upright patriot.

Gohier was an advocate of considerable reputation and exalted patriotism; an eminent lawyer, he was a man of great integrity and candour.

Sieyès had long been known to me. He was born at Fréjus, in Provence. His reputation began with the Revolution. He had been called to the Constituent Assembly by the electors of the third estate, at Paris, after having been rejected by the assembly of the clergy at Chartres. He was the author of a pamphlet entitled *What is the Third Estate?* which made so much noise. He was not a man of business: knowing but little of men, he knew not how they might be made to act. All his studies having been directed to metaphysics, he had the fault of metaphysicians, of too often despising positive notions; but he was capable of giving useful and luminous advice on matters of importance, or at any momentous crisis. To him France is indebted for the division into departments, which destroyed all provincial prejudices: and though he was never distinguished as an orator, he greatly contributed to the success of the revolution by his advice in the committees. He was nominated as director, when the Directory was first established; but he refused the distinction at that time, and Lareveillere was appointed instead of him. He was afterwards sent as ambassador to Berlin, and imbibed a great mistrust of the politics of Prussia in the course of his mission. He had taken a seat in the Directory not long before this time; but he had already been of great service in checking the progress of the Société du Manège, which he saw was ready to seize the helm of the state. He was abhorred by that faction; and, fearless of bringing upon himself the enmity of so powerful a party, he courageously resisted the machinations of these men of blood, in order to avert from the Republic the evil with which it was threatened.

At the period of 13 Vendémiaire, the following occurrence had enabled me to form a correct judgement of him. At the most critical moment of that day, when the Committee of the Forty seemed quite distracted, Sieyès came to me, and took me into the recess of a window, while the committee was deliberating upon the answer to be given to the summons of the Sections. 'You hear them, General,' said he; 'they talk while they should be acting. Bodies of men are wholly unfit to direct armies, for they know not the value of time or opportunity. You have nothing to do here: go, General, consult your genius and the situation of the country: the hope of the Republic rests on you alone.'

I accepted an invitation to dine with each of the directors, on condition that it should be merely a family dinner, and that no stranger should be present. A grand entertainment was given to me by the Directory. The Legislative Body wished to follow the example; but when it was proposed to the general committee, a strong opposition arose: the minority refusing to pay any homage to General Moreau, whom it was proposed to include in the entertainment; he was accused of having misconducted himself on 18 Fructidor. The majority, in order to remove every difficulty, had recourse to the expedient of opening a subscription. The festival took place in the church of Saint Sulpice; covers were laid for seven hundred. I remained at table but a short time; I appeared to be uneasy, and much preoccupied. Every one of the ministers wished to give me an entertainment; but I only accepted a dinner with the Minister of Justice, for whom I had a great esteeem: I requested that the principal lawyers of the Republic might be there; I was very cheerful at this dinner, conversed at large on the civil and criminal codes, to the great astonishment of Tronchet, Treilhard, Merlin, and Target, and expressed a desire that the persons and the property of the Republic should be governed by a simple code, adapted to the enlightened state of the age.

Constant to my system, I entered but little into these public entertainments, and pursued the same line of conduct that I had followed on my first return from Italy. Always dressed as a member of the Institute, I showed myself in public only with that society: I received at my house none but men of science, the generals of my suite, and a few friends – such as Regnault-de-Saint-Jean-d'Angely, whom I had employed in Italy in 1797, and subsequently placed at Malta; Volney, the author of the excellent *Travels in Egypt;* Roederer, whom I respected for his probity and noble sentiments; Lucien Bonaparte, one of the most powerful orators of the Council of Five Hundred, who had protected the Republic from the revolutionary regime by opposing the declaration that the country was in danger; and Joseph Bonaparte, who lived in splendour and was highly respected.

I went frequently to the Institute; but never to the theatres, except at times when I was not expected, and then always into the private boxes.

Meanwhile all Europe rang with my arrival; all the troops and friends of the Republic, even the Italians, indulged in the most sanguine hopes: England and Austria were alarmed. The fury of the English was turned against Sir Sidney Smith and Nelson, who commanded the British naval force in the Mediterranean. A variety of caricatures on this subject were seen in the streets of London.

General Jean Victor Moreau, victor of the battle of Hohenlinden, December 1800. A staunch republican, he lived in exile in New Jersey from 1804–13. He then returned to serve the Tsar, and was mortally wounded.

Lucien Bonaparte, brother of Napoleon.

In one of these, Nelson was represented amusing himself with dressing Lady Hamilton while the frigate *La Muiron* was passing between his legs.

Talleyrand was fearful of being ill-received by me. It had been agreed by the Directory and Talleyrand that, immediately after the departure of the expedition for Egypt, negotiations respecting its object should be opened with the Porte. Talleyrand was even to have been the negotiator, and to have set out for Constantinople twenty-four hours after the sailing of the expedition for Egypt from Toulon. This engagement, which had been formally insisted on and positively consented to, had been immediately consigned to oblivion; not only had Talleyrand remained at Paris, but no sort of negotiation had taken place. Talleyrand did not suppose that I had forgotten this, but because the influence of the Société du Manège had procured his dismissal his situation was itself a guarantee that I would not repulse him. Talleyrand, moreover, availed himself of all the resources of a supple and insinuating address, to conciliate a person whose suffrage it was important to him to secure.

Fouché had been for several months Minister of Police; he had, after 13 Vendémiaire, some transactions with me; I was aware of his immoral and versatile disposition. Sieyès had closed the Manège without his participation. I effected 18 Brumaire without admitting Fouché into the secret.

Réal, commissioner of the Directory in the department of Paris, gained more of my confidence. Zealous for the Revolution, he had been deputy for the attorney of the commune of Paris, at a time of storm and troubles. His disposition was ardent, but he was full of noble and generous sentiments.

All classes of citizens and all the provinces of France were impatient to see what I would do. From all sides came offers of support, and of entire submission to my will.

I employed myself in listening to the proposals submitted to me; in observing all parties; and, in short, in making myself thoroughly master of the true state of affairs. All parties desired a change, and all desired to effect it in concert with me, even the leaders of the Manège.

Bernadotte, Augereau, Jourdan, Marbot, etc., who were at the head of the plotters of this society, offered a military dictatorship to me, and proposed to

Charles, Duke of Talleyrand-Perigord, Europe's premier diplomat and master of the art of self-preservation. He served the republic, empire and monarchy, and was trusted by none.

acknowledge me as chief, and to confide the fortunes of the Republic to me, if I would but second the principles of the Sociètè du Manège.

Sieyès, who commanded the vote of Roger Ducos in the Directory, swayed the majority of the Council of Ancients, and influenced only a small minority in the Council of Five Hundred, proposed to place me at the head of the government, changing the constitution of the year III, which he deemed defective, and that I should adopt the institutions and the constitution which he had projected, and which he had by him in manuscript.

Regnier, Boulay, a numerous party of the Council of Ancients, and many of the members of that of Five Hundred, were also desirous to place the fate of the Republic in my hands.

This party was composed of the most moderate and wisest men of the legislature: it was the same that joined Lucien Bonaparte in opposing the declaration that the country was in danger.

The directors Barras, Moulins, and Gohier, hinted at my resuming command of the Army of Italy and re-establishing the Cisalpine Republic and the glory of the French arms. Moulins and Gohier had no secret plan in reserve. They were sincere in the scheme they proposed; they trusted that all would go well from the moment that I should lead our armies to new successes. Barras was far from sharing this confidence; he knew that everything had gone wrong and that the Republic was sinking. But whether he had made engagements with the pretender to the throne, as was asserted at the time, or whether he deceived himself as to his personal situation – for what errors, may not spring from the vanity and self-love of an ignorant man? – he imagined he could keep himself at the head of affairs. Barras made the same proposals as were made by Moulins and Gohier.

However, all the factions were in motion. That of the Fructidorists (who supported the decree of 1795, which had provided for the re-election of two-thirds of the Convention to the new legislature) seemed persuaded of its own influence; but it had no partisans among the existing authorities. I now had the choice of several measures.

I could consolidate the existing constitution and support the Directory by becoming myself a director. But the constitution had fallen into contempt, and a magistracy in several hands could not lead to any satisfactory result: it would, in fact, have been associating myself with revolutionary prejudices and with the passions of Barras and Sieyès.

I could change the constitution and step into power by means of the Sociètè du Manège. This society contained a great number of the rankest Jacobins, they commanded the majority in the Council of Five Hundred and a spirited minority in that of the Ancient. By making use of these men the victory was certain, no resistance would be offered. It was the most certain way to overthrow the existing state of things; but Jacobins do not attach themselves to any leader; they are unbending, and violent in the extreme. It would, therefore, have been necessary, after succeeding by their aid, to get rid of them, and to persecute them. Such treachery would have been unworthy of a noble-minded man.

Barras tendered the support of his friends, but they were men of suspicious morals, and publicly accused of wasting the national wealth. How would it have been possible to govern with such people? For without strict probity it would have been impracticable to restore the finances, or to do any real good.

To Sieyès were attached many well-informed men, persons of integrity and republicans of principle, possessing in general little energy, much intimidated by the faction du Manège, and fearful of popular uprisings but who might be retained after the victory and be employed with success in an orderly government. No objection could be taken to the character of Sieyès: he could not, in any case, be a dangerous rival. But to side with this party was to declare against Barras and the Manège, who hated Sieyès.

On 8 Brumaire (30 October) I dined with Barras; only a few persons were there. A conversation took place after dinner: 'The Republic is falling,' said the director, 'things can go no further; the government is powerless; a change must take place, and Hedouville must be named President of the Republic. As to you, General, you intend to rejoin the army; and for my part, ill as I am, unpopular, and worn out, I am fit only to return to private life.'

I looked steadfastly at him without replying a word. Barras cast down his eyes and remained silent. Thus the conversation ended. General Hedouville was a man of the most ordinary character. Barras did not give utterance to his thoughts; but his countenance betrayed his secret.

This conversation was decisive. A few minutes afterwards I called upon Sieyès: I gave him to understand that for ten days all parties had addressed themselves to me, that I was resolved to act with him and the majority of the Council of Ancients, and that I came to give him an assurance of this. It was agreed that the change might be effected between 15 and 20 Brumaire.

On my return to my own house, I found there Talleyrand, Fouché, Roederer, and Réal. I related to them unaffectedly, plainly, and simply, without any indication of countenance which could betray my opinion, what Barras had just said to me. Réal and Fouché, who had a regard for the director, were sensible how ill-timed his dissimulation was. They went to him on purpose to upbraid him with it. The following day, at 8 o'clock, Barras came to me. I had not risen: he insisted on seeing me, entered, and told me he feared he had explained himself very imperfectly the preceding evening; that I alone could save the Republic; that he came to place himself at my disposal, to do whatever I wished, and to act whatever part I chose to assign him. He entreated me to give him an assurance that, if I had any project under way, I would rely upon him.

But I had already made up my mind. I replied that I had nothing in view; that I was fatigued and indisposed; that I could not accustom myself to the moisture of the atmosphere of the capital, just arrived, as I was, from the dry climate of the sands of Arabia; and I put an end to the interview by similar commonplace observations.

Meanwhile Moulins went daily between 8 o'clock and 9 o'clock to my house, to request my advice on the business of the day. He always had military intelligence, or civil matters, on which he wished for instructions. On what related to military affairs, I replied as I felt; but with respect of civil concerns, thinking that I ought not to disclose my private opinions to him, I answered only in a vague manner.

Gohier came also occasionally to visit me, to make proposals to me and ask my advice.

The officers of the garrison, headed by General Moreau, commanding the citadel of Paris, demanded to be presented to me; they could not succeed in their object, and, being put off day to day, they began to complain of my manifesting so little desire to see my old comrades again.

The forty adjutants of the National Guard of Paris, who had been appointed by me when I commanded the Army of the Interior, had sought as a favour to see me. I knew almost all of them; but, in order to conceal my designs, I put off the time for receiving them.

The 8th and 9th Regiments of dragoons, which were stationed in Paris, were old regiments of the Army of Italy; they longed to muster before their former general. I accepted the offer, and informed them that I would fix the day.

The 21st Light Horse, which had contributed to the success of the day of 13 Vendémiaire was likewise in Paris. Murat came from this corps, and all the officers went daily to him, to ask him on what day I would review it. They were as unsuccessful as the rest.

The citizens of Paris complained of my keeping so close; they went to the theatres, and to the reviews, where it was announced I would be present, but I came not. Nobody could account for this conduct; all were becoming impatient. People began to murmur against me: 'It is now,' they observed, 'a fortnight since his arrival, and he has as yet done nothing. Does he mean to behave as he did on his return from Italy, and suffer the Republic to be torn to pieces by these contending factions?'

But the decisive hour approached.

On 15 Brumaire, Sieyès and I had an interview, during which we resolved on the measures for the 18th. It was agreed that the Council of Ancients, availing itself of the 102nd article of the Constitution, should decree the removal of the Legislative Body to Saint Cloud, and should appoint me commander-in-chief of the guard belonging to the Legislative Body, of the troops of the military division of Paris, and of the National Guard.

This decree was to be passed on 18 Brumaire, at 7 o'clock in the morning, at 8 o'clock I was to go to the Tuileries, where the troops were to be assembled, and there assume the command of the capital.

On 17 Brumaire I informed the officers that I would receive them next day at 6 o'clock in the morning. As that hour might appear to be unseasonable, I feigned being about to set off on a journey: I gave the same invitation to the forty adjutants of the National Guard; and I informed the three regiments of cavalry that I would review them in the Champs-Elysées, on the same day at 7 o'clock in

Marie-Annunciade-Caroline Bonaparte, wife of Joachim Murat, and her children.

the morning. I also intimated to the generals who had returned from Egypt with me, and to all those with whose sentiments I was acquainted, that I should be glad to see them at that hour. Each thought that the invitation was confined to himself alone, and supposed that I had some orders to give him; for it was known that Dubois-Crancé, the Minister at War, had taken the reports of the state of the army to me, and had adopted my advice on all that was to be done, on the Rhine and in Italy.

Moreau, who had been at the dinner of the Legislative Body, and whom I had there, for the first time, become acquainted with, having learned from public report that a change was in preparation, assured me that he placed himself at my disposal, that he had no wish to be admitted into any secret, and that he required but one hour's notice to prepare himself. Macdonald, who happened then to be in Paris, had made the same tenders of service. At 2 o'clock in the morning, I let them know that I wished to see them at my house at 7 o'clock, and on horseback. I did not apply to Augereau, Bernadotte, etc., however Joseph brought the latter.

General Lefebvre commanded the military division; he was wholly devoted to the Directory. I sent an aide-de-camp to him, at midnight, desiring he would come to me at 6 o'clock.

Everything took place as had been agreed. At about 7 o'clock in the morning, the Council of Ancients assembled under the presidency of Lemercier. Cornudet. Lebrun, and Farges depicted in lively colours the miseries of the Republic, the dangers with which it was surrounded, and the obstinate conspiracy of the leaders du Manège for the restoration of the Reign of Terror. Regnier, deputy for La Meurthe, moved that, in pursuance of the 102nd article of the Constitution, the sittings of the Legislative Body should be transferred to Saint Cloud; and that I should be invested with the chief command of the troops of the 17th military division, and charged with the execution of this measure. He then spoke in support of his motion. 'The Republic,' said he, 'is threatened by anarchists and by the foreign party: measures for the public safety must be taken; we are certain of the support of General Bonaparte: under the shelter of his protecting arm the Councils may discuss the changes the public interest renders necessary.' As soon as the majority of the Council was satisfied that I agreed with the motion, the decree passed; but not without strong opposition. It was couched in these terms:

The Council of Ancients, by virtue of articles 102, 103, and 104, of the Constitution, decrees as follows:

Article 1. The Legislative Body is transferred to Saint Cloud; the two Councils shall there sit in the two wings of the palace.

2. They shall assemble there tomorrow, 19 Brumaire, at noon; all exercise of their functions and all discussions, elsewhere and before that time, is prohibited.

3. General Bonaparte is charged with the execution of the present decree. He will adopt all measures necessary for the safety of the national representation. The general commanding the 17th military division, the guards of the Legislative Body, the National Guard, the regular troops in the commune of Paris and throughout the whole extent of the 17th military division, are placed immediately under his command, and enjoined to recognize him in that capacity; all the citizens are to aid and assist him on his first requisition.

4. General Bonaparte is summoned to the council table to receive a copy of the present decree, and to take the oath; he will act in concert with the committees of inspectors of the two Councils.

5. The present decree shall be immediately transmitted by messengers to the Council of Five Hundred, and to the Executive Directory; it shall be printed, posted, proclaimed, and sent to all the communes of the Republic by special couriers.

This decree was made at 8 o'clock. Half an hour later the state messenger who was the bearer of it arrived at my house. He found the avenues filled with officers of the garrison, adjutants of the National Guard, generals, and the three regiments of cavalry. I had the folding doors opened; and, my house being too small to contain so many persons, I came forward to the steps in front of it, received the compliments of the officers, harangued them, and told them that I relied upon them all for the salvation of France. At the same time I gave them to understand that the Council of Ancients, under the authority of the Constitution, had just conferred on me the command of all the troops; that important measures were under way, designed to rescue the country from its alarming situation; that I relied upon their support and good will; and that I was at that moment going to mount my horse to ride to the Tuileries.

Enthusiasm was at its height: all the officers drew their swords and promised their service and fidelity. I then turned towards Lefebvre, demanding whether he would remain with me or return to the Directory. Lefebvre, powerfully affected, did not hesitate. I instantly mounted, and placed myself at the head of the generals and officers, and of 1,500 horse whom I had halted upon the boulevard, at the corner of the Rue Mont-Blanc. I gave orders to the adjutants of the National Guard to return to their quarters, and beat the call to arms, to communicate the decree that they had just heard, and to announce that no orders were to be observed but such as should emanate from me.

I presented myself at the bar of the Council of Ancients, attended by this brilliant escort. 'You are the wisdom of the nation', said I: 'At this crisis it behoves you to point out the measures which may save the country: I come, surrounded by all the generals, to promise you their support. I appoint General Lefebvre my lieutenant; I will faithfully fulfil the task with which you have entrusted me: let us not look into the past for examples of what is now going on. Nothing in history resembles the end of the 18th century; nothing in the 18th century resembles the present moment.'

All the troops were mustered at the Tuileries; I reviewed them, amid the unanimous acclamations of both citizens and soldiers. I gave command of the troops entrusted with the protection of the Legislative Body to General Lannes; and to General Murat the command of those sent to Saint Cloud.

I deputed General Moreau to guard the Luxembourg; and, for this purpose, I placed under his orders 500 men of the 86th Regiment. But, at the moment of setting off, these troops refused to obey: they had no confidence in Moreau, who was not, they said, a patriot. I was obliged to harangue them, assuring them that Moreau would act uprightly. Moreau had become suspected through his conduct in Fructidor.

The intelligence that I was at the Tuileries, and that I alone was to be obeyed, quickly spread throughout the capital. The people flew to the Tuileries in crowds: some led by mere curiosity to behold so renowned a general, others by patriotic enthusiasm to offer him their support. The following proclamation was everywhere posted:

Citizens, the Council of Ancients, the depository of the national wisdom, has just pronounced a decree; for this it has authority from articles 102 and 103 of the Act of the Constitution: it imposes upon me the duty of taking measures for the safety of the national representation. The immediate removal of the representation is necessary; the Legislative Body will then find itself in a condition to rescue the Republic from the imminent danger into which the disorganization of all branches of the administration is conducting us. At this important crisis it requires union and confidence. Rally round it: there is no other method of fixing the Republic upon the basis of civil liberty, internal happiness, victory, and peace.

To the soldiers I said:

Soldiers, the special decree of the Council of Ancients is conformable to articles 102 and 103 of the Constitutional Act. It has confided to me the command of the city and of the army. I have accepted that command, in order to support the measures it is about to adopt, which are all in favour of the people. Two years has the Republic been ill-governed; you have indulged in the hope that a period would be put to so many evils by my return. This event you have celebrated with an unanimity which imposes obligations upon me that I am about to discharge; you will also discharge yours, and you will support your general with the energy, firmness, and loyalty that I have always found in you. Liberty, victory, and peace will reinstate the French Republic in the rank which she held in Europe, and from which imbecility and treachery were alone capable of removing her.

I now sent an aide-de-camp to the guards of the Directory to communicate the decree to them and to enjoin them to accept no order except from me. The guard sounded 'To horse!' The commanding officer consulted his soldiers and they answered with shouts of joy. At this very moment an order from the Directory, contrary to that of my own, arrived; but the soldiers, obeying only my commands, marched to join me. Sieyès and Roger Ducos had been ever since the morning at the Tuileries. It is said that Barras, on seeing Sieyès mount his horse, ridiculed the awkwardness of the unpractised equestrian – he little suspected where they were going. Being shortly after apprised of the decree, he joined Gohier and Moulins: they then learnt that the troops followed me; they saw that even their own guard forsook them. Upon that Moulins went to the Tuileries, and gave in his resignation, as Sieyès and Roger Ducos had already done. Boutot, the secretary of Barras, came to me; I warmly expressed my indignation at the peculations that had ruined the Republic and insisted that Barras should resign. Talleyrand hastened to tell the Director this. Barras removed to Gros-Bois, accompanied by a guard of honour of dragoons. From that moment the Directory was dissolved, and I alone was invested with the executive power of the Republic.

In the mean while the Council of Five Hundred had met, under the presidency of Lucien. The constitution was explicit; the decree of the Council of Ancients was consistent with its privilege: there was no ground for objection. The members of the council in passing through the streets of Paris, and through the Tuileries, had learnt of the occurrences that were taking place and witnessed the enthusiasm of the public. They were astonished and confounded at the ferment around them. They submitted to necessity, and adjourned their sitting to the next day, the 19th, at Saint Cloud.

Bernadotte had married the sister-in-law of Joseph Bonaparte. He had been two months in the war department of the administration, and was afterwards removed by Sieyès: all he did in office was wrong. He was one of the most extreme members of the Société du Manège. His political opinions were then very violent and were censured by all respectable people. Joseph had taken him in the morning to my house, but when he saw what was happening he stole away and went to inform his friends of the Manège of the state of affairs. Jourdan and Augereau came to me at the Tuileries, while the troops were passing in review. I recommended them not to return to Saint Cloud to the sitting of the next day, but to remain quiet, and not to obliterate the memory of the services they had rendered the country; for no effort could extinguish the flame that had been kindled. Augereau assured me of his devotion, and of his desire to march under my command. He even added, 'What! General, do you not still rely upon your little Augereau?'

Cambacérès, Minister of Justice, Fouché, Minister of Police, and all the other ministers went to the Tuileries and acknowledged the new authority. Fouché made great professions of attachment and devotion: being in direct opposition to Sieyès he had not been admitted into the secret of the day. He had given directions for closing the barriers and preventing the departure of couriers and coaches. 'Why, good God!' I said to him, 'why all these precautions? We go with the nation, and by its strength alone: let no citizen be disturbed, and let the triumph of opinion have nothing in common with the transactions of days in which a factious minority prevailed.'

The members of the majority of the Five Hundred, of the minority of the Ancients, and the leaders of the Manège, spent the whole night in factious consultations.

At 7 o'clock in the evening I held a council at the Tuileries. Sieyès proposed that the forty principal leaders of the opposite parties should be arrested. The recommendation was a wise one; but I believed I was too strong to need any such precautions. 'I swore in the morning,' said I, 'to protect the national representation, I will not this evening violate my oath: I fear no such weak enemies.' Everybody agreed with Sieyès, but nothing could overcome this delicacy on my part. It will soon appear that I was wrong.

It was at this meeting that the establishment of three Provisional Consuls was agreed on; and Roger Ducos and I were appointed; the adjournment of the councils for three months was also resolved on. The leading members of the two councils came to an understanding on the manner in which they should act at the sitting of Saint Cloud. Lucien, Boulay, Emile Gaudin, Chazal, and Cabanis, were the leaders of the Council of Five Hundred; Regnier, Lemercier, Cornudet and Fargues, were those of the Ancients.

General Murat, as has been observed, commanded the public force at Saint Cloud; Pansard commanded the battalion of the guard of the Legislative Body; General Serrurier had under his orders a reserve stationed at Point-du-Jour.

Workmen were getting ready the halls of the palace of Saint Cloud. The Orangery was allotted to the Council of Five Hundred and the Gallery of Mars to the Ancients. The apartments since designated the Saloon of Princes and the Emperor's Cabinet were prepared for me and my staff. The inspectors of the hall occupied the apartments of the Empress. So late as 2 o'clock in the afternoon, the place assigned to the Council of Five Hundred was not ready. This delay of a few hours was very unfortunate. The deputies, who had been on the spot since noon, formed groups in the garden, their minds grew heated; they sounded one another out, exchanged views about their feelings, and organized their opposition. They demanded of the Council of Ancients, what was its object? Why had it brought them to Saint Cloud? Was it to change the Directory? They agreed that Barras was corrupt and Moulins entitled to no respect; they would name, they said, without hesitation, me and two other citizens to form the government. The small number of individuals who were in the secret then explained that the object was to regenerate the state, by ameliorating the Constitution, and to adjourn the councils. These hints not being successful, a degree of hesitation showed itself, even among the members most to be relied on.

At length the sitting opened. Emile Gaudin ascended the tribune, painted in lively colours the dangers facing the country, and proposed thanks to the Council of Ancients for the measures of public safety which it had set in motion. He proposed that it should be invited to explain its intentions fully. At the same time, he proposed to appoint a committee of seven persons, to make a report upon the state of the Republic.

The furious rushing forth of the winds imprisoned in the caverns of Aeolus never raised a more raging storm. The speaker was violently hurled to the bottom of the tribune. The ferment became excessive.

Delbrel desired that the members should swear anew to the Constitution of the year III. Chenier, Lucien, and Boulay, trembled. The chamber proceeded to the roll call.

During the roll call, which lasted more than two hours, reports of what was happening circulated through the capital. The leaders of the assembly du Manège, the Tricoteuses, etc., hurried to the Orangery. Jourdan and Augereau had kept out of the way; believing me lost, they made all haste to Saint Cloud. Augereau drew near to me, and said, 'Well! here you are, in a pretty situation!'

'Augereau,' I replied, 'remember Arcole: matters appeared much more desperate there. Take my advice, and remain quiet, if you would not fall a victim to this confusion. In half an hour you will see what a turn affairs will have taken.'

The assembly declared itself with such unanimity that no deputy dared refuse to swear to the Constitution – even Lucien was compelled to swear. Shouts and cries of 'bravo' were heard throughout the chamber. The moment was critical. Many members, on taking the oath, added their own observations and such speeches might influence the troops. All minds were in a state of suspense; the zealous became neuter; the timid deserted their standard. Not an instant was to be lost. I crossed the Gallery of Mars, entered the Council of Ancients, and placed myself opposite the president.

'You stand,' I said, 'upon a volcano; the Republic no longer possesses a government; the Directory is dissolved; factions are at work; the hour of decision is come. You have called in my arm, and the arms of my comrades, to the support of your wisdom. But the moments are precious and I must now play a conspicuous part. I know that Caesar and Cromwell have been talked of – as if this day could be conquered with past times. No, I desire nothing but the safety of the Republic and to maintain the resolutions you are about to make. And you, grenadiers, whose caps I perceive at the doors of this hall, speak! Have I ever deceived you? Did I ever let you down when, in camp, in the midst of privations, I promised you victory and plenty; and when, at your head, I led you from conquest to conquest? Now, say, was it for my own aggrandisement or in the interests of the Republic?'

I spoke with energy. The grenadiers were electrified; waving their caps and arms in the air, they all seemed to say, 'Yes, true, true! He always kept his word!'

Upon this a member (Lingley) rose and shouted, 'General, we applaud what you say; swear then, with us, obedience to the Constitution of the year III which alone can save the Republic.'

The astonishment caused by these words produced a most profound silence.

I gathered myself for a moment and then continued emphatically: 'The Consitution of the year III! You have it no longer! You violated it on 18 Fructidor, when the government infringed upon the independence of the Legislative Body; you violated it on 30 Prairial, in the year VII, when the Legislative Body struck at the independence of the government; you violated it on 22 Floréal, when, by a sacrilegious decree, the government and the Legislative Body invaded the sovereignty of the people, by annulling the elections made by them. The Constitution being violated, there must be a new compact, new guarantees.'

The force of this speech, and my energy, brought over three-fourths of the members of Council, who rose to indicate their approval. Cornudet and Regnier spoke powerfully to the same effect. A member rose in opposition; he denounced me as the only conspirator against public liberty. I interrupted the orator, and declared that I knew the secrets of every party and that all despised the Constitution of the year III; that the only difference between them was that some desired to have a moderate Republic, in which all the national interests and all property should be guaranteed, while others wished for a revolutionary government, as warranted by the dangers of the country. At this moment I was informed that the roll call had ended in the Council of Five Hundred, and that they were endeavouring to force the president, Lucien, to put the outlawry of his brother to the vote. I immediately hastened to the Five Hundred, entered the chamber with my hat off, and ordered the officers and soldiers who accompanied me to remain at the doors. I wanted to present myself at the bar, to rally my party, which was numerous, but which had lost all unity and resolution. But to get to the bar, it was necessary to cross half the chamber, because the president had his seat on one of the wings. When I had advanced alone across one-third of the Orangery, two or three hundred suddenly rose, crying, 'Death to the tyrant! down with the dictator!'

Two grenadiers, who, by my order, had remained at the door, and who had reluctantly obeyed, saying to me, 'You do not know them, they are capable of anything!' rushed in, sabre in hand, overthrowing all who opposed their passage, to join me and protect me with their bodies. All the other grenadiers followed this example, and forced me out of the chamber. In the confusion one of them, named Thomé, was slightly wounded by the thrust of a dagger, and the clothes of another were cut through.

I descended into the courtyard, called the troops into a circle by beat of drum, got on horseback, and harangued them: 'I was about,' said I, 'to point out to them the means of saving the Republic, and restoring our glory. They answered me with their daggers. It was thus they would have accomplished the wishes of the allied kings. What more could England have done? Soldiers, may I rely upon you?'

Unanimous acclamations formed the reply to this speech, I instantly ordered a captain to go with ten men into the chamber of the Five Hundred, and to liberate the president.

Lucien had just thrown off his robe. 'Wretches!' exclaimed he, 'you insist that I should put out of the protection of the laws my brother, the saviour of the country, he whose very name causes kings to tremble! I lay aside the insignia of the popular magistracy; I offer myself in the tribune as the defender of him whom you command me to immolate unheard.'

Thus saying, he quitted the chair, and darted into the tribune. The officer of grenadiers then presented himself at the door of the chamber, crying, '*Vive la République.*' It was supposed that the troops were sending a deputation to express their devotion to the councils. The captain was received with a joyful expression of feeling. He availed himself of the misapprehension, approached the tribune, and secured the president, saying to him in a low voice, 'It is your brother's order.' The grenadiers at the same time shouted, 'Down with the assassins!'

Upon these exclamations, the joy of the members was converted into sadness; a gloomy silence testified to the dejection of the whole assembly. No opposition was offered to the departure of the president, who left the chamber, rushed into the courtyard, mounted a horse, and cried out in his stentorian voice, 'General – and you, soldiers – the President of the Council of Five Hundred proclaims to you that factious men, with drawn daggers, have interrupted the deliberations of that assembly. He calls upon you to employ force against these disturbers. The

Council of Five Hundred is dissolved.'

'President,' I replied, 'it shall be done.'

I then ordered Murat into the chamber, at the head of a detachment in close column. At this crisis General B – ventured to ask me for fifty men, in order to place himself in ambuscade upon the way and to fire upon the fugitives. I replied only by enjoining the grenadiers to commit no excesses. 'It is my wish,' said I, 'that not one drop of blood may be shed.'

Murat presented himself at the door and summoned the Council to disperse. The shouts and vociferations continued. Colonel Moulins, aide-de-camp of Brune, who had just arrived from Holland, ordered the charge to be beaten. The drum put an end to the clamour. The soldiers charged into the chamber with their bayonets. The deputies leaped out at the windows and dispersed, leaving behind their gowns, caps, etc. In one moment the chamber was empty. Those members of the Council who had shown most pertinacity fled with the utmost precipitation to Paris.

About one hundred deputies of the Five Hundred rallied at the office and round the inspectors of the hall. They presented themselves in a body to the Council of the Ancients. Lucien represented that the Five Hundred had been dissolved at his instance; that, in the exercise of his functions as President of the Assembly, he had been surrounded by daggers; that he had sent attendants to summon the Council again; that nothing had been done contrary to form, and that the troops had but obeyed his mandate. The Council of the Ancients, which had witnessed with some uneasiness this exercise of military power, was satisfied with the explanation. At 11 o'clock at night the two Councils re-assembled; they formed large majorities. Two committees were appointed to report upon the state of the Republic. On the motion of Beranger, thanks to me and the troops were carried. Boulay de la Meurthe in the Five Hundred, and Villetard in the Ancients, detailed the situation of the Republic and the measures that needed to be taken. The law of 19 Brumaire was passed; it adjourned the Councils to 1 Ventôse following; it created two committees of twenty-five members each, to represent the Councils provisionally. These committees were also to prepare a civil code. A Provisional Consular Commission, consisting of Sieyès, Roger Ducos, and myself was charged with the executive power.

This law put an end to the Consitution of the year III.

The Provisional Consuls repaired on the 20th, at 2 o'clock in the morning, to the chamber of the Orangery, where the two Councils were assembled. Lucien, the president, addressed them in these words:

> Citizen consuls, the greatest people on earth entrusts its fate to you. Three months hence, your measures must pass the ordeal of public opinion. The welfare of thirty millions of men, internal quiet, the wants of the armies, peace – these are the objects of your cares. Doubtless you will need courage and devotion to your duties in undertaking functions so important, but the confidence of our people and warriors is with you, and the Legislative Body

knows that your hearts are wholly with the country. Citizen Consuls, we have, before adjourning, taken the oath which you will now repeat in the presence of us all – the sacred oath of inviolable fidelity to the sovereignty of the people, to the French Republic, one and indivisible, to liberty, to equality, and to the representative system.

The assembly dispersed and the Consuls returned to Paris, to the palace of the Luxembourg.

Thus was the Revolution of 18 Brumaire crowned with success.

Sieyès, during the most critical moments, had remained in his carriage at the gate of Saint Cloud, ready to follow the march of the troops. His conduct during the danger period was becoming: he evinced coolness, resolution, and intrepidity.

It would be difficulty to describe the anxious suspense of the capital during the Revolution of 18 Brumaire; the most alarming reports were universally circulated; it was said that I was overthrown; the renewal of the Reign of Terror was expected. It was not so much the danger of the Republic that was apprehended, as that which every private family dreaded.

About 9 o'clock in the evening, the news from Saint Cloud spread throughout Paris: the public was informed of the events which had taken place; and the liveliest joy succeeded the most agonizing fears. The following proclamation was read by torchlight:

Citizens!

On my return to Paris I found discord pervading every department of government, and only this single truth unanimously agreed on, *that the constitution was half destroyed and no longer capable of maintaining our liberty.* Every party applied to me, confided to me its designs, disclosed its secrets, and solicited my support. I refused to become the head of any faction. The Council of Ancients called on me. I answered the appeal. A plan for a general reform had been devised by men in whom the nation is accustomed to behold defenders of liberty, of equality, and of property: this plan demanded calm, free, and impartial examination, unfettered by influence or fear. The Council of Ancients, therefore, determined upon the removal of the Legislative Body to Saint Cloud. It entrusted me with the disposal of the force necessary for the maintenance of its independence. I deemed it due from me to our fellow-citizens, to the soldiers who are laying down their lives in our ranks, to the glory purchased by their blood, to accept the command. The Councils met at Saint Cloud: the troops of the Republic guaranteed safety without; but assassins spread terror within. Several deputies of the Council of Five Hundred, armed with daggers and firearms, dealt threats of death around them. The plans that were to have been brought forward were withheld, the majority of the assembly was disorganized, the most intrepid orators were disconcerted, and the futility of any sober proposition became only too evident. Indignant and grieved, I hastened to the Council of Ancients: I entreated it to allow me to put my designs for the public good into execution. I urged the misfortunes of the country which had suggested them. The Council seconded my views, by new testimonies of its unaltered confidence. I offered myself to the Chamber of Five Hundred, alone, unarmed, my head uncovered, exactly as I had been received by the Ancients with so much approbation. I went to remind the majority of their designs, and to satisfy them of their power. Instantly the daggers that menaced the deputies were raised against their defender. Twenty assassins rushed upon me, aiming at my breast. The grenadiers of the Legislative Body, whom I had left at the door of the chamber, hastily interposed between the assassins and myself. One of these brave grenadiers received a thrust from a dagger, which pierced his clothes. They carried me off, and at the instant they were doing so, cries were heard to outlaw him who was at that very time the defender of the law. It was the savage yell of murderers against the power destined to crush them. They crowded round the president, threatening him, with arms in their hands; they ordered him to pronounce the outlawry of his brother. Apprised of this, I gave orders to rescue him from their fury, and ten grenadiers of the Legislative Body charged into the chamber and cleared it. The factious parties, intimidated, dispersed and fled. The majority, relieved from their violence, returned freely and peaceably into the chamber, listened to the proposals made to them for the public safety, and on due deliberation, framed the wholesome resolutions which are about to become the new and provisional law of the Republic. Frenchmen! you will, doubtless, recognize in my conduct the zeal of a soldier of liberty, of a citizen devoted to the Republic. The principles of preservation, protection, and liberality, are restored to their due preponderance by the dispersion of those factious men who tyrannized over the Councils, and who, though they have been prevented from becoming the most hateful of mankind, are nevertheless the most wretched.

On the morning of 11 November, the Consuls held their first sitting. It opened with a discussion about the election of a president. The decision depended on the vote of Roger Ducos, whose opinion, in the Directory, had always been governed by that of Sieyès; the latter, therefore, relied upon his observing the same line of conduct in the Consulate. The event proved otherwise. The Consul, Roger Ducos, had scarcely entered the cabinet, when, turning towards me, he said, 'It is useless to go to the vote on the presidency; it belongs to you of right.' I then took the chair; and Roger Ducos continued to vote with me. He had some warm discussions with Sieyès on this subject; but he remained firm to his system. This conduct was the result of conviction that I alone was capable of re-establishing and maintaining order. Roger Ducos was not a man of great talent; but he possessed sound common sense and his intentions were good.

Lagarde, the Secretary of the Directory, did not enjoy an unblemished reputation. Maret, afterwards Duke of Bassano, was appointed to that office. He was born at Dijon. He was attached to the principles of the Revolution of 1798, and was engaged in the negotiations with England before 10 August; he afterwards treated with Lord Malmesbury at Lille. Maret is a man of great abilities, of a mild temper, and of great propriety of manners; his probity and delicacy are proof against every temptation. He had escaped the Reign of Terror, having been arrested with Semonville as he crossed Lombardy on his way to Venice, intending to go from there to Naples in the character of ambassador. After 9 Thermidor he was exchanged for Madame the daughter of Louis XVI, then a prisoner in the Temple.

The first sitting of the Consuls lasted several hours. Sieyès had hoped that I would interfere only in military matters, and would leave the regulation of civil affairs to him; but he was much surprised when he observed that I had formed settled opinions on policy, finance, and justice, even on jurisprudence – in a word, on all branches of administration; that I supported my ideas with arguments at once forcible and concise and that I was not easily convinced. In the evening, on his return home, Sieyès said in the presence of Chazal, Talleyrand, Boulay, Roederer, Cabanis, etc., 'Gentlemen, you have a master; Napoleon *will* do all, and *can* do all. In our deplorable situation, it is better to submit, than to excite dissensions which would draw down certain ruin.'

Napoleon in his uniform as First Consul.

X

THE ARREST AND EXECUTION OF THE DUKE D'ENGHIEN [1]

LETTER from the First Consul to the Minister at War
Paris, 19 Ventôse, Year XII [10 March 1804]

You will please, Citizen General, order General Ordener, whom I place at your disposal for this purpose, to proceed post to Strasbourg by night, travelling under an assumed name, and to see the general of the division.

The object of his mission is to advance on Ettenheim, surround that town, and bring off from thence the Duke d'Enghien, Dumouriez, an English colonel, and all other persons in their suites. The general of the division and the quartermaster of gendarmerie, who has been to Ettenheim to reconnoitre the place, will give him all necessary information.

You will direct General Ordener to send from Schelestadt 300 men of the 26th Dragoons, who will repair to Rheinau, where they will arrive at 8 o'clock in the evening.

The commandant of the division will send to Rheinau fifteen pontooners who will set out post, or on the horses of the light artillery, so that they reach Rheinau by 8 o'clock in the evening. He must previously have arranged for four or five large boats, in addition to the ferry-boat, to be in readiness, so that 300 horses may be carried over in a single trip.

[1] The Duke d'Enghien, a scion of the royal house of Bourbon, was suspected of heading a royalist conspiracy against Napoleon that was discovered in January 1804. Napoleon, in one of the most controversial episodes in his career, had Enghien kidnapped from the neutral territory of Baden, tried, and, in the early hours of 21 March, shot. Here we have Napoleon's detailed personal instructions for the kidnapping.

157

Grandson of the Prince of Condé, son of the Duke of Bourbon, 32-year-old Louis-Antoine-Henri, Duke d'Enghien, was kidnapped, taken to Paris and executed in March 1804. Napoleon was inconsistent in his response to the execution; he denied responsibility, but declared himself willing to repeat the action if necessary.

The troops will take enough bread for four days, and provide themselves with cartridges. The general of division will add to them a captain or officer, and a lieutenant, with three or four brigades (thirty men) of gendarmes.

As soon as General Ordener has passed the Rhine, he will proceed straight to Ettenheim, and march directly up to the houses of the Duke and Dumouriez; after completing this expedition, he will return to Strasbourg.

In passing Luneville, General Ordener will order the officer of carabineers, who commanded the depot at Ettenheim, to repair to Strasbourg, there to wait for orders.

General Ordener, on reaching Strasbourg, will very secretly despatch two agents, either civil or military, and will make arrangements with them to come and meet him.

You will give orders that on the same day and at the same hour, 200 men of the 26th Dragoons, under the command of General Caulaincourt (to whom you are consequently to give the necessary orders) shall proceed to Offenburg to surround that town and arrest the Baroness de Reich, if she has not been taken at Strasbourg, and other agents of the English government, respecting whom the prefect, and citizen Mehee, now at Strasbourg, will give him information.

From Offenburg, General Caulaincourt will direct patrols on Ettenheim, until he learns that General Ordener has succeeded. They will afford each other mutual assistance.

At the same time the general of the division will send 300 cavalry to Kelh, with four pieces of light artillery, and send a post of light cavalry to Willstadt, the intermediate point between the two routes.

The two generals will take care that the greatest discipline prevails, and that the troops require nothing from the inhabitants; for this purpose you will cause 12,000 francs to be paid them.

If it should happen that they cannot accomplish their mission, but should expect to fulfil it by remaining three or four days and sending out patrols, they are authorized to do so.

They will inform the bailiffs of the two towns that if they continue to afford asylum to the enemies of France they will draw heavy retribution upon themselves.

You will order the commandant of Neuf Brisac to send 100 men and two pieces of cannon to the right bank. The post of Kelh, as well as those of the right bank, will be evacuated the moment the two detachments have effected their return.

General Caulaincourt will have thirty gendarmes with him, and will, with General Ordener and the general of division, hold a council and make such alterations in the present arrangements as may be deemed advisable.

Should it happen that neither Dumouriez nor the Duke d'Enghien remains at Ettenheim, a special courier is to be despatched with an account of the state of affairs.

You will give orders to arrest the postmaster of Kelh and other individuals capable of giving information on the subject.

(Signed) BONAPARTE

Napoleon's signature as General Napoleon.

Copy of the Report made by Citizen Charlot, Chief of the 38th squadron of National Gendarmerie, to General Moncey, first Inspector-General of the Gendarmerie, 24 Ventôse, year XII [15 March 1804]

General,

It is now two hours since I returned into this town from the expedition to Ettenheim in the Electorate of Baden, whence, with a detachment of gendarmerie and a party of the 22nd Dragoons, I have, by the orders of Generals Ordener and Fririon, brought off the persons whose names follow:

Louis Antoine Henri de Bourbon, Duke d'Enghien

General the Marquis de Thumery

Colonel the Baron Grunstein

Lieutenant Schmidt

The Abbé Wemborn, formerly proctor of the bishopric of Strasbourg

The Abbé Michel, secretary to the bishopric of Strasbourg and Secretary to the Abbé Wemborn (both Michel and Wemborn are French)

The Duke d'Enghien's secretary, named Jacques

Feraud (Simon), valet de chambre to the Duke

Poulain (Pierre), servant to the Duke

Joseph Cannon, do.

The General Domouriez, who was said to reside with Colonel Grunstein, is no other than the Marquis de Thumery above mentioned, who occupied an apartment on the ground floor, in the house inhabited by Colonel Grunstein, whom I arrested at the Duke's house, where he had slept. I am indebted to the colonel for the honour of writing to you at this moment. The Duke, being informed that his lodgings were surrounded, seized a double-barrelled gun and levelled it at me as I was desiring several persons who were at the Duke's windows to open the door to me, and threatening that, if they did not, I would carry off the Duke by force. Colonel Grunstein prevented him from firing, by saying, 'My Lord, have you involved yourself?' The latter having answered in the negative, 'Well,' said Grunstein, 'all resistance is useless, for we are surrounded, and I perceive a great number of bayonets; it appears that this is the commanding officer. Recollect that by killing him you would ensure your own destruction and ours.' I well remember hearing the words 'This is the commanding officer,' but I was far from supposing my life in imminent danger, as the Duke has since repeatedly declared to me it was. At the moment of the Duke's apprehension, I heard a cry of fire! I immediately went to the house in which I expected to arrest Dumouriez; and on my way I heard the cry of fire! repeated in several directions. I stopped a person who was going towards the church, probably to sound the tocsin; and at the same time I satisfied the inhabitants of the place, who were running out of their houses in consternation, by saying, 'It is all by your sovereign's consent,' an assurance which I had already given to the Duke's Master of the Hunt, who had hastened to the Duke's lodgings on hearing the first cries. On reaching the house in which I expected to seize Dumouriez, I arrested the Marquis de Thumery. I found this house in a state of tranquillity, which removed my anxiety, and invested as I had left it before I proceeded to the Duke's.

The other arrests were effected without noise. I made enquiries to ascertain whether Dumouriez had appeared at Ettenheim, and was assured that he had not. I presume the idea of his having been there must have arisen from confounding his name with that of General Thumery.

Tomorrow I shall look into the papers I have hastily brought away from the prisoners' houses, and shall then have the honour to make my report thereon to you. I cannot too highly applaud the firm and distinguished conduct of Quartermaster Pfersdorff in this affair. He is the person whom I sent the day before to Ettenheim, and who pointed out to me the lodgings of our prisoners: he stationed all the vedettes, in my presence, at the exits to the houses they occupied, which he had reconnoitred the preceding day. At the moment when I was summoning the Duke to yield himself prisoner to me, Pfersdorff, at the head of several gendarmes and dragoons of the 22nd regiment, penetrated into the house from the rear, by getting over the walls of the courtyard: these were the men perceived by Colonel Grunstein, at sight of whom he prevented the Duke from firing at me. I solicit, General, the brevet of a lieutenant for Quartermaster Pfersdorff, for which place he was proposed at the last review of the Inspector-General Wyrion. He is in all respects fit to be promoted to that rank. Generals Ordener and Caulaincourt will mention this sub-officer to you, and what they will say to you about him leads me to hope that you will take into serious consideration the favour I ask of you for him. I have to add that this sub-officer has informed me that he was particularly seconded by the gendarme Henne, of the brigade of Barr. As Pfersdorff speaks several languages, I should hope his promotion would not remove him from the squadron.

The Duke d'Enghien has assured me that Dumouriez has not been at Ettenheim; that he might possibly, nevertheless have been charged to bring him instructions from England; but that he would not have received him, because his rank did not allow his holding communication with such people; that he esteemed Bonaparte as a great man, but that, being a prince of the house of Bourbon, he had vowed an implacable hatred against him, as well as against the French, with whom he would wage war on all occasions.

He is extremely fearful of being taken to Paris; and I believe that, in order to carry him thither, he must be very viligantly guarded. He expects that the First Consul will confine him, and says he repents his not having fired on me, as that would have decided his fate by arms.

The Chief of the 38th squadron of National Gendarmerie,

(Signed) CHARLOT

The death of the Duke d'Enghien was long imputed, and is still ascribed by people unacquainted with the truth, to M. de Caulaincourt.

Caulaincourt, my aide-de-camp, was bound to obey the instructions for the mission that Berthier and Talleyrand, the Minister of Exterior Relations, were ordered to give him.

First, to frustrate the intrigues of the English ministry on the right bank of the Rhine.

Secondly, to secure the persons and papers of the Baroness Reich and her accomplices, who were at Offenburg plotting the overthrow of the consular government and the death of the First Consul.

Thirdly, to inspect and expedite the armament of the flotilla.

Fourthly, to cause explanations to be transmitted to the Court of Baden respecting the violation of its territory, as soon as Ordener had seized the Duke d'Enghien.

It was Ordener's duty to obey the order to pass the Rhine with 300 dragoons and to carry off the prince.

It was the duty of the military commission to condemn him, if found guilty. Innocent or guilty, it was the duty of Ordener and Caulaincourt to obey: if guilty, the military commission ought to have condemned him; if innocent it ought to have acquitted him, for no order can justify the conscience of a judge. There is no doubt but that if Caulaincourt had been appointed the Duke d'Enghien's judge, he would have refused the office; but being charged with a diplomatic commission, he had only to obey; the whole affair is so simple, that only folly, or the delirium of the spirit of party, can object to it.

This party madness, however, eager to assail an ancient name distinguished by new and honourable services, furiously attacked Caulaincourt on this occasion. The hatred and injustice thus manifested were among the causes of his favour. Before the Imperial reign, Caulaincourt was entrusted with one department of the duty of the palace, and received at a subsequent period only the title appertaining to functions which he already fulfilled.

The death of the Duke d'Enghien ought to be attributed to those persons at London who directed and ordered my assassination and who intended the Duke de Berri to enter France by Beville-cliffs and the Duke d'Enghien by Strasbourg; it ought also to be ascribed to those who eagerly sought, by reports and conjectures, to represent the Duke as the head of the conspiracy; it ought to form an eternal reproach against those who, driven by a criminal zeal, did not wait for the orders of their sovereign to execute the judgment of the military commission. The Duke d'Enghien fell a victim to the intrigues of the time. His death, with which I have been so unjustly reproached, was injurious to me and could not have served any political purpose. Had I been capable of such a crime, Louis XVIII and Ferdinand would not now be reigning: their deaths, as has already been observed, were several times proposed, and even recommended to me.

The Duke d'Enghien suffered because he was one of the principal actors in the conspiracy of Georges, Pichegru, and Moreau.

Pichegru was arrested on 28 February, Georges on 9 March, and the Duke d'Enghien on 18 March 1804.

In March 1803, the speech from the throne to the British parliament announced the commencement of a new war, and the breaking of the peace of Amiens. The French government manifested an intention to carry the war into England. During 1803 and 1804, it covered the cliffs of Boulogne, Dunkirk, and Ostend, with camps; it fitted out formidable squadrons at Brest, Rochefort, and Toulon; it put *praams*, sloops, gunboats and great and small pinnaces on the stocks throughout France; it employed thousands of hands in digging harbours on the Channel for its numerous flotillas. England, on her side, promptly took up arms. Pitt abandoned the peaceful labours of the exchequer, and dreamed only of warlike engines, battalions, forts, and batteries; the good and venerable George III left his royal mansions and daily reviewed troops; camps were pitched on the downs of Kent and Sussex; the two armies were in sight of each other, and nothing but the straits divided them.

England, however, omitted nothing that was adapted to stir up the powers of the Continent; but Austria, Russia, Prussia, and Spain were allies or friends of France, which country commanded all Europe; the attempts made to rekindle the war in the Vendée were equally unsuccessful. The Concordat had rallied the clergy round me, and the disposition of the inhabitants of that province was much improved; they witnessed with gratitude the progress of my administration; the great public works I had ordered occupied thousands of hands; a canal was being dug to join the Vilaine and the Rence, which would enable the French coasters to come from the coast of Poitou to that of Normandy without doubling the cape of Ushant; a new town was rising in the middle of the department of the Vendée, and eight new grand roads were to be made in the west; lastly, considerable sums were distributed to the Vendéans, in the form of premiums for rebuilding their houses, churches, and chapels, burnt or destroyed by the orders of the Committee of Public Safety.

The Cabinet of Saint-James's had often been led into error by the royalists, who, self-deceived, had involved it in disastrous expeditions; but it formed an exaggerated idea of the power and means of the Jacobins; persuaded itself that a great number of them were discontened and disposed to join their efforts to those of the royalists; that they would be seconded by dissatisfied generals; and that, by combining the strength of opposite parties, united by a passion common to them all, a faction might be formed sufficiently powerful to operate an effectual diversion.

As the First Consul I had, for four years, united the various parties which divided France; the list of emigrants had been closed; all who were willing to return to their country had first had their names erased from it, and afterwards received an amnesty; all their existing property, which had not been sold, had been restored to them, except woods, the revenue of which, however, the law secured to them. None now remained on the list except persons attached to the princes, or declared enemies of the Revolution who had not chosen to profit by the amnesty; but thousands of emigrants had returned, and were subject to no conditions but an oath of obedience and fidelity to the Republic. Thus I had the sweetest consolation a man can enjoy, that of reuniting more than thirty thousand families, and restoring to their country all that remained of the descendants of the men who had most contributed to the glory of France at different periods; even those who continued emigrants often obtained passports to visit their families. The altars were again raised up; the deported and exiled priests were replaced over dioceses and parishes, and paid by the Republic. These various laws had produced a great amelioration in public affairs, but yet they had the inevitable disadvantage of emboldening, by this system of extreme indulgence, the enemies of consular government, the royalist party, and the hopes of foreigners.

Between 1803 and 1804, there had been five conspiracies; all the emigrants in the pay of England had received orders to assemble at Brisgaw, and in the duchy of Baden. Mussey, an English agent, the medium of correspondence with the ministers, Drake and Spencer Smith, resided at Offenburg, and profusely supplied the money necessary for all these plots.

The Duke d'Enghien, a young prince of the most distinguished bravery, resided within four leagues of the frontier of France.

'His consular majesty.' Napoleon as First Consul, reproduced from a marble bas-relief, brought to America by Joseph Bonaparte.

XI

POLITICAL CRIMES

I NEVER committed crimes. What could have been more advantageous to me than the murder of the Count de Lille and of the Count d'Artois? This crime was proposed to me several times; and it would not have cost two millions. I rejected it with contempt and indignation. No attempt was ever made, under my reign, against the lives of these two princes.

When the Spaniards were in arms in the name of Ferdinand, that prince and his brother Don Carlos, the only heirs to the throne of Spain, were at Valençay, at the extremity of Berry. Their murder would have settled the affairs of Spain. It would have been useful – nay, necessary. I was advised to do it, but it would have been unjust and criminal. Did Ferdinand and Don Carlos die in France?

Ten other instances might be cited, but these two are sufficient, because they are the most striking. My hands, accustomed to gain victories by the sword, were never stained with guilt, even under the empty pretext of the public good – a dreadful principle that has, in all ages, been the maxim of weak governments, but which the religion, however, and civilization of Europe disclaim.

I reached the summit of human greatness by direct paths, without ever having committed an act that morality could reproach. In that respect my rise is unparalleled in history – in order to reign, David destroyed the house of Saul, his benefactor; Caesar kindled a civil war, and overthrew the government of his country; Cromwell caused his master to perish on the scaffold. I was a stranger to all the crimes of the Revolution. When my political career began, the throne had crumbled to dust, the virtuous Louis XVI had been put to death, and France was torn by contending factions. It was by the conquest of Italy, by the peace of Campo Formio, which secured the greatness and independence of the country, that I began my career; and in 1800, when I attained the supreme power, it was the dethroning of anarchy. My throne was raised by the unanimous wishes of the French people.

Ferdinand VII resided at Valençay, in the château of Prince Talleyrand; this was one of the finest situations in France, in the midst of an extensive forest. His brother and uncle were with him; there was no guard set over him; he had all his officers and servants, and received what visits he pleased; he was at liberty to make excursions of several leagues, either for the purpose of hunting, or in his carriage. Besides the 72,000 francs that the French Treasury annually paid as the rent of Valençay, Ferdinand received for his maintenance 1,500,000 francs per annum. He wrote every month to me, and I answered his letters. On 15 August, and on the Empress's birthday, he always illuminated the château and park of Valençay and distributed alms. He several times asked my leave to go to Paris, which was successively adjourned. He asked me to adopt him as his son and to marry him to a French princess. He had the enjoyment of a very fine library and often received visits from the gentlemen of the neighbourhood and from the merchants of Paris, who were eager to carry novelties to him. For a long time he had a theatre and a company of comedians, but at length his confessors inspired him with scruples and he dismissed the troupe.

King Charles IV, his father, and the queen, his mother, were, for a considerable time, at the palace of Compiègne; thence they went to Marseilles, and afterwards to Rome, where they resided in the palace of the Princess Borghese. They enjoyed an allowance of three millions. The Queen of Etruria, Maria Luisa, sister to Ferdinand, was one of those who had the greatest share in the Spanish Revolution; her correspondence with Murat, then commanding in Spain, is very curious. She was one of her mother's party and took a very active party in the events of Madrid. She resided a long time at Nice, where she opened a secret correspondence with the English commanders in the Mediterranean. Being informed that she was anxious to leave France, I caused it to be signified to her that I should be very glad if she would retire to England, Sicily, or any other country in Europe. In fact, this princess was of no importance and her departure would have saved the treasury 500,000 francs.

Ferdinand always showed the greatest aversion to the Cortes. The Spaniards will long regret the Constitution of Bayonne. Had that Constitution triumphed, they would not now be under an ecclesiastical jurisdiction in secular matters, they would be subject to no feudal services, no interior tolls. Their national domains would not continue uncultivated and useless to the government and the nation. They would have a secular clergy; a nobility without feudal privileges, or exemption from taxes and public burthens; and they would now be quite another people.

Ferdinand often said he would prefer remaining at Valençay to reigning in Spain with the Cortes; nevertheless when in 1813 I proposed that he re-ascend his throne, he did not hesitate. Count Laforest was sent to him to negotiate this business. The treaty was soon drawn up; no condition was imposed on Ferdinand; for the engagement he entered into to ratify the sales of national

Prince Camillo Borghese, second husband of Pauline Bonaparte,
Napoleon's second sister.

domains made during his absence, and not to prosecute any of those who had filled offices, can scarcely be called conditions. Ferdinand then earnestly declared his determination to take matters in Spain as he should find them and to reign as a consitutional king. As soon as the treaty was concluded, he again proposed to contract a closer alliance with me, by marriage. This proposal was neither rejected nor accepted. I answered that the moment for consenting to it had not yet come, but that if Ferdinand renewed the request from Madrid, when he was re-established on his throne, it would be received with the attention due to it.

The treaty of Valençay had been negotiated with the greatest secrecy. It was important that the English should not be acquainted with it; they would have endeavoured to thwart an operation in Spain, the result of which was to render the army disposable, so that it might reach the plains of Champagne in time for the campaign of 1814. The plans then in progress at Paris produced a different result. The party which was exerting itself to overthrow me succeeded in discovering this negotiation, and attempted to persuade me that my glory would be implicated in renouncing Spain and to induce me not to sign the treaty of Valençay. Failing in this attempt, this party promulgated the existence of the treaty, and employed all the resources of intrigue to delay Ferdinand's departure, in order to delay the return of the army from Spain into France. Ferdinand was to quit Valençay in the course of November 1813, yet he did not cross the Pyrenees until March 1814.

XII

BERNADOTTE

THE King of Sweden[1] wanted a French prince from me. The viceroy[2] was his first choice, but that he would have to change his religion was an insuperable obstacle. There remained only the Prince of Pontecorvo, and he was conceded, after long negotiations carried on in Paris by the Swedish general Count de Wrede.

Bernadotte was destitute of military reputation. There were in France twenty generals who had commanded in chief and were more celebrated than he. Besides, he was very unpopular, from having been attached to the Société du Manège. He had received no education whatever.

In 1798, while I was in Egypt, Joseph married his sister-in-law, Désirée, to Bernadotte. Her father was one of the principal merchants of Marseilles, and not of Avignon. I had intended her for General Duphot, who was murdered in Rome in 1797. That Bernadotte became a Marshal of France, Prince of Pontecorvo, and at length a king, it is to this marriage that he is indebted. Désirée, the reigning Queen of Sweden[3], was the object of my earliest attachment – I was to have married her. When I became Emperor, I took pleasure in making my sister-in-law, actually Joseph's sister-in-law, first the wife of a marshal, then a princess, and finally a queen. Her son, Oscar, Prince of Södermanland, is my godson, his baptism was delayed until I returned from Egypt. I named him Oscar, because I

[1] Charles XIII (1748–1818).

[2] Napoleon's stepson, Eugène de Beauharnais (1781–1824), Viceroy of Italy.

[3] Although Désirée formally became queen in 1818, she did not reside in Sweden until 1823, after Napoleon's death.

Jean-Baptiste-Jules Bernadotte started life as a sergeant-major in the pre-Revolutionary army, became one of Napoleon's marshals and ended life as Charles XIV of Sweden.

was then reading with much interest the poems of Ossian, in the excellent translation of a professor at Padua.[1] All Bernadotte's errors and foolish actions during the Imperial reign were constantly pardoned on account of this marriage.

If this election had been disagreeable to me, it would not have taken place; for it was to obtain my protection and the goodwill of France that the Swedes made it.

I was seduced by the glory of seeing a Marshal of France become a king: a woman in whom I was interested, a queen, and my godson, a prince royal. I gave

[1] Napoleon is, of course, unaware that these '3rd-century' poems were mainly the work of the 18th-century poet and forger, James Macpherson.

Bernadotte, on his departure from Paris, several million francs, to enable him to appear in Sweden with suitable splendour.

Bernadotte was born in the apostolic Roman Catholic faith; this he abjured for the Reformed Religion. Many would have done as much, but it was this circumstance that prevented Prince Eugène from being sent to reign over Sweden. His wife, a princess of Bavaria, would have been inconsolable. Désirée, the reigning Queen of Sweden, refused to change her religion and still professes the Roman Catholic faith in which she was born.

Bernadotte was for two months Minister of War; his administration was marked only by folly, and by the protection he afforded to the vulgar declaimers of the Société du Manège. He effected nothing in the way of organization, and the Directory was obliged to dismiss him from office because of his seditious intrigues. He had ceased to be minister when Massena decided the campaign by the victory of Zurich, towards the end of September 1799. He was completely ignorant of these combinations, and his causing a diversion to be made on Philipsburg with 25,000 men was an operation contrary to all rules.

On 18 Brumaire, Bernadotte joined the Société du Manège in opposing the successful transactions of that day. I pardoned him for his wife's sake.

In Hanover, he protected and participated in the peculations of the Intendant Michaux.

The destruction of eleven ships of war, of which three was unserviceable, did not in any respect alter the situation of the Republic, which was in 1800 quite as inferior by sea as in 1798. Had she been mistress of the sea, her forces would at once have marched against London, Dublin, and Calcutta: it was to obtain that superiority that the Republic sought the possession of Egypt. It still retained, however, sufficient vessels to send reinforcements to Egypt whenever it should be necessary to do so. Admiral Brueys, with forty-six men of war, was master of the Mediterranean: he would have sent reinforcements to the Army of the East, had not the troops been wanted in Italy, in Switzerland, and on the Rhine.

Three months after 18 Brumaire, I marched 160,000 men into Germany, the finest army France ever had, and an army of reserve into the plains of Marengo! Is it imagined that all the men in these armies were recruits? If this were true, a standing army might be dispensed with; the National Guard would be more than sufficient. Brune's victories rendered the Army of Holland disposable; the pacification of the Vendée, the respect and popularity the government enjoyed, and the love of France by which it was surrounded, placed at its disposal the Army of the West and all the battalions the Directory maintained in the interior to uphold it authority and overawe the various parties. All these troops were united; they were better managed and paid, and the cavalry was remounted; the levies of conscripts, in these three months, amounted only to 80,000 men. As First Consul I did several excellent things – I gave a judicious direction to everything – but I performed no miracles; the heroes of Hohenlinden and Marengo were not recruits, but good veteran soldiers. Of the army of reserve, a third consisted of conscripts but it contained a great number of veterans who had not served in the previous campaign and who decided the victory in the fields of Montebello and Marengo.

At the time of the passage of St Bernard, in May and June 1800, I had won twenty pitched battles, conquered Italy, dictated peace to the King of Sardinia, the King of Naples, the Pope, and the Emperor of Germany, within twenty leagues of Vienna; negotiated at Radstadt with Count Cobentzel for, and obtained the surrender of, the fortress of Mentz to France; created several republics; raised two hundred millions in contributions, which I employed in the subsistence, clothing, and maintenance of my army for two years, and in paying the Army of the Rhine, and the squadrons of Toulon and Brest. I had enriched the national museum with four hundred masterpieces of the arts of ancient Greece and the age of the Medicis; conquered Egypt, and established the French sway there upon solid foundations, having overcome what, in Volney's opinion, was the greatest difficulty, by conciliating the principles of the Koran and Mohammedan religion with the presence of an army from the West. I had been for six months at the head of the Republic, which elevation I owed to the spontaneous choice of three millions of citizens; I had restored the finances, appeased factions, and ended the war in the Vendée.

Dessaix formed his column in front of Saint-Giuliano: he was killed a league and a half from the village of Marengo.

Between the battle of Marengo and the affair of the infernal machine, that is to say, during the last six months of 1800, the factions were more active than ever. I had certainly nothing to fear from the chiefs of the Revolution, or from those of the Vendée, but the Brutus-Septembrizers and Chouans talked of nothing but assassinating me.

XIII

OVERTURES FOR PEACE IN 1800

COULD the English minister[1] reject the overtures made to him by me in 1800 without rendering himself responsible for the disasters of the war? Was his rejection politic and conformable to the interests of the English nation? Was war at that time desirable for France? What was, under these circumstances, my interest?

Pitt refused to enter into negotiation, hoping that by continuing the war he would compel the French to recall the princes of the House of Bourbon and to restore Belgium to the House of Austria. If these were just and legitimate objects, then he could, with justice, refuse to treat for peace; but if they were both illegitimate and unjust, he rendered his country responsible for all the miseries of the war. Now the Republic had been acknowledged by all Europe; England herself had recognized it in 1796 by empowering Lord Malmesbury to treat with the Directory. This plenipotentiary had successively attended at Paris and at Lille and had negotiated with Charles Lacroix, Letourneur, and Maret, ministers of the Directory. Besides, the object of the war was not the restoration of the Bourbons. As to Belgium it had been ceded by the Emperor of Austria at the treaty of Campo Formio, in 1797, and England had recognized its union with France by the negotiations of Lord Malmesbury at Lille. It constituted, by the law of nations, a part of the Republic. To separate them could only be to usurp, to tear to pieces, to dismember, an established state. These two objects were therefore unjust and unlawful.

Was this policy of the minister, Pitt, truly conformable to the interests of England? Could he reasonably flatter himself with the hopes of obtaining

---

[1] William Pitt the Younger (1759–1806).

172

Belgium by continuing the war? Would it not have been more prudent to have given peace to the world, and at the same time to have secured the real, solid advantages that he might have obtained? The Kings of Sardinia and Naples, the Grand Duke of Tuscany, and the Pope, would have been restored and established on their thrones; the Milanese would have been secured to the House of Austria; the French troops would have evacuated Holland, Switzerland, and Genoa; the influence of England might have been established in those countries; Egypt would have been restored to the Grand-Seignior; the Isle of Malta to the Grand-Master; Ceylon and the Cape of Good Hope would have strengthened English power in the two Indies. What splendid results from the campaign of 1799! These advantages were certain; but as to the hopes to which they were sacrificed, was there even a probability of their accomplishment? In 1799, the coalition had been victorious in Italy, but it had been vanquished in Switzerland, in Holland, and in the East. France had just changed her government. Five persons, disunited, and of no great abilities, were succeeded by a man whose military knowledge and talents were unquestionable; he had been elevated by the consent of the nation: at his name alone the Vendée had already submitted: the Russian armies had commenced their march to recross the Vistula. Lord Grenville himself admitted that even if the First Consul were willing to cede Belgium, the French nation, *en masse*, would oppose the measure. The object of the war was, then, popular in France. The Courts of Berlin, of Vienna, and of London, were deceived in 1792; *the circumstances were so novel!* But could anything excuse the statesmen of England for falling into the same error in 1800? It was then probable that the campaign of 1800 would be favourable to France; that she would reconquer Italy; and, in short, even supposing the success of the campaign to be doubtful, contrary to all probability, it was at least not likely to fulfil the end the English ministry proposed to themselves. They would, therefore, have to continue to pay immense subsidies for several years; for they could not expect to wrest Belgium from France without the adhesion of Russia and Prussia, or at least one of these powers, to the coalition. Now, this political result could not be attained by the campaign of 1800. It was therefore impolitic to risk the chances of that campaign.

The interest of the Republic was the reverse of that of England; if France had made peace at that time under existing circumstances, she would have made it after a campaign of disasters; she would have drawn back in consequence of a single campaign: this would have been dishonourable and would only have encouraged princes to form new coalitions against her. All the chances of the campaign of 1800 were in her favour: the Russian armies were leaving the theatre of war; the pacification of the Vendée placed a new army at the disposal of the Republic; in the interior, factions were overruled, and the chief magistrate possessed the entire confidence of the nation. It behoved the Republic not to make peace until after restoring the equilibrium of Italy; she could not, without abandoning her destiny, consent to a peace less advantageous than the treaty of Campo Formio.

At this period peace would have ruined the Republic; war was necessary to it for the maintenance of energy and union in the state, which was ill-organized; the people would have demanded a great reduction in taxes, and the disbanding of the army; so that, after a peace of two years, France would have taken the field again under great disadvantages.

War was necessary to me myself. The campaigns of Italy, the peace of Campo Formio, the campaigns of Egypt, the transactions of 18 Brumaire, the unanimous voices of the people for raising me to the supreme magistracy, had, undoubtedly, placed me very high: but a treaty of peace derogatory to that of Campo Formio, annulling all that I had done in Italy, would have destroyed my influence over the imaginations of the people, and deprived me of the means of putting to an end the anarchy of the Revolution, by establishing a definitive and permanent system. I felt this: I awaited with impatience the answer of the Cabinet of London. This answer filled me with secret satisfaction – the more the Grenvilles and Chathams indulged themselves in railing against the Revolution and in showing the contemptuous attitude that seems to be the patrimony of all oligarchies, the more they favoured my private interests. I said to my minister: 'This answer could not have been more favourable to us.' I then foresaw that from such impassioned policy I should meet with no obstacles to the fulfilment of my high destinies. Pitt, distinguished as he was by his parliamentary talents and his knowledge of the internal administration, was completely ignorant of what is called policy. *The English in general know nothing of the affairs of the Continent, particularly of those of France.*

The glory of France was afterwards carried to the highest pitch; all Europe was subjected to her sway; and the English ministry, a few months after indulging in such outrageous declamations against the French people and state, was obliged to sign the treaty of Amiens. France, now acknowleged mistress of all Italy, made a more favourable peace than that of Campo Formio, because she gained Piedmont and Tuscany by it: and nothing but the poniard of a fanatic,[1] which caused the command of the Army of the East to devolve upon a man[2] who, though eminent in some respects, was entirely destitute of military talents and genius, could have prevented Egypt from being for ever united to France.

There is no military man, English, Turkish, or French, who will deny that the army of Abercromby must have been defeated and destroyed if Kléber had lived. The Porte had already evinced a disposition to make peace, independently of Egypt. How material was the weight of a young fanatic of twenty-four, acting on the faith of a doubtful passage of the Koran, in the general balance of the world!

[1] General Kléber, who was left in command of the French Army in Egypt when Napoleon returned to France, was assassinated, by an Egyptian patriot, after he had recaptured Cairo from the Turks.

[2] General Menou.

XIV

THE REBELLION OF TOUSSAINT⸱ LOUVERTURE

THE narrative of the events that took place on Santo Domingo, after 18 Brumaire commences in this chapter. The general of division Toussaint-Louverture, Commander-in-Chief of the northern part of Santo Domingo, had disregarded the authority of General Hedouville, commissioner of the executive directory. He had negotiated with the English, both directly and secretly, while the general was on the island, treating this representative of the mother country in such an insulting manner that he had obliged him to return to France. But General Hedouville, before he left the colony, distrusting the intentions of Toussaint-Louverture, gave powers to General Rigaud, chief of the men of colour, confiding to him, independenly of Toussaint, the command of all the southern part of Santo Domingo. The island thus became severed into two divisions – the North, under Toussaint, which was under the dominion of the blacks, and the South, under Rigaud, in which the men of colour were the prevailing faction. A terrible civil war soon broke out between these two parties. The Directory seemed to look on this contest with pleasure, thinking the rights of the mother country secured by its duration. This war was raging at its utmost height at the beginning of 1800.

The first question I had to consider on coming to the head of affairs was whether it would be in the best interest of the mother country to foment and encourage this civil war or to put an end to it. After mature reflection, but without any hesitation, I decided on the latter course.

First, because a fallacious policy, calculated to keep up internecine war, was unworthy of the greatness and generosity of the nation, and was likely in the end to render both parties equally hostile to the mother country. Secondly, because domestic hostilities, instead of weakening a nation, recharge its energies and inure it to war, and therefore whenever the time should come for restoring the authority of the mother country, she would have had to deal with a more formidable people. Thirdly, because if this civil war continued, the inhabitants would lose all industrious habits, and the colony be deprived of what little remained of its ancient prosperity. Thus morality and policy equally dictated the propriety of stopping the effusion of French blood without delay. But how?

The Directory had tried to restore the status quo between the two parties, but the passions that drove the blacks and the men of colour were too violent to be restrained, while the mother country had no means of repressing them. The men of colour were, undoubtedly, braver and more warlike than the blacks; but they were so much inferior in numbers that it was easy to anticipate the moment of their defeat. The triumph of the blacks would have been marked by the total massacre and destruction of the men of colour – an irreparable loss to the mother country, which could only hope to re-establish its authority by making use of the influence of the latter against the blacks. I therefore resolved to support the stronger party; to withdraw the powers held by General Rigaud, to recall him to France, to disarm the men of colour, to extend Toussaint's authority over the whole colony, to appoint him Commander-in-Chief of Santo Domingo, and to give all his confidence to the blacks.

Colonel Vincent, director of the fortifications of Santo Domingo, possessed in a high degree the confidence of Toussaint, whose chargé d'affaires he was. This officer was then at Paris. I sent for him, informed him of his partiality for the blacks, and his perfect confidence in the character of Toussaint, and sent him back to the colony, carrying, first, the decree by which Toussaint was appointed Commander-in-Chief of Santo Domingo; secondly, the constitution of the year VIII; thirdly a proclamation to the blacks, in which he said to them: 'Brave blacks, remember that France alone acknowledges your liberty!' I added two other commissioners who, with Colonel Vincent, were ordered to take all necessary measures to restore tranquillity and put an end to hostilities. This well-advised policy had the happiest effects. Regaud returned to France; the men of colour laid down their arms; the authority of the blacks was peaceably acknowledged throughout the colony: they applied themselves to agriculture; the colony seemed for a moment to revive from its ashes: the whites were protected; even the men of colour, secured by the moral influence of the mother country, breathed again, and began to repair their losses. The years 1800 and 1801 were two prosperous years for the colony; agriculture, laws, and commerce flourished once more under the government of Toussaint; the authority of the mother country was acknowledged and respected (at least in appearance); Toussaint regularly made a monthly report to the Minister of Marine.

The real views of the chiefs of the blacks could not, however, long remain concealed from the French government. Toussaint kept up a secret intelligence both with Jamaica and London; he was guilty of irregularities in his administration which could not be attributed to ignorance. He constantly evaded my reiterated order that he have inscribed in gold letters on the standards the words from my proclamation: 'Brave blacks, remember that France alone acknowledges your liberty.'

When Admiral Gantheaume sailed from Brest at the beginning of 1801, with a division of troops under the command of General Sahuguet, he took on board a great number of blacks and men of colour, bound for Santo Domingo. Toussaint appeared extremely uneasy about this. From that time he resolved to allow no more than 2,000 French troops to enter the colony, and to burn Cape Town if the army of Sahuguet had been too strong for him to defend the town against it. But Admiral Gantheaume steered towards the Mediterranean – he was bound for Egypt.

The prosperity which the Republic enjoyed in the course of 1801, after the peace of Luneville, made it easy to foresee that England would soon be compelled to lay down arms, when decisive measures might be adopted with regard to Santo Domingo. Two alternatives then claimed my consideration: the first was to invest General Toussaint-Louverture with the whole civil and military authority, under the title of governor-general of the colony; to entrust the command to the black generals; to consolidate and legalize the regulations respecting labour established by Toussaint, which had already been crowned with the most brilliant success; to oblige the black farmers to pay a rent or acknowledgement to the ancient French proprietors; and to preserve to the mother country the exclusive commerce of the whole colony, by employing numerous cruisers to guard the coasts. The second scheme consisted in reconquering the colony by force of arms; in removing to France all the blacks who had held commands superior to that of a chief of battalion; in disarming the blacks, securing their civil liberties, and in restoring the property to the colonists.

Each of these projects had its advantages and disadvantages. The benefits of the first were palpable. The Republic would have an army of from 25,000 to 30,000 blacks, which would make all America tremble: this would be a new element of power which would cost her no sacrifice, either of men or money. The old proprietors would, no doubt, lose three-fourths of their fortunes; but the commerce of France would lose nothing, as it would still enjoy the exclusive privilege. The second project was more advantageous to the colonial proprietors; it was more conformable to justice: but it required a war which could not but produce the destruction of a great number of men and the loss of a considerable sum of money: the opposite pretensions of the blacks, the men of colour and the white proprietors, would always be an object of discord and embarrassment for the mother country; Santo Domingo would always be in jeopardy. Accordingly I inclined to the former scheme, because it appeared to be most consistent with true policy, and most conducive to the influence of his flag in America. With an army of from 25,000 to 30,000 blacks, what might I not undertake against Jamaica, the Antilles, Canada, the United States themselves, or the Spanish colonies? With such important political interests, could the difference of a few millions more or less of revenue to France be placed in competition? But such a project required the concurrence of the blacks; it was necessary that they should show their loyalty to the mother country, and to the Republic which had conferred such benefits upon them. The children of the black chiefs educated in France, in the colonial schools instituted for this purpose, daily strengthened the ties which connected these islanders with the mother country. Such was the state of Santo Domingo and the policy adopted by the French government towards it, when Colonel Vincent arrived at Paris.

He was the bearer of the constitution which Toussaint-Louverture had adopted of his own mere authority, which he had caused to be printed and put in execution, and which he now notified to France. Not only the authority, but even the honour and dignity of the Republic were outraged by these proceedings: of all possible ways of proclaiming his independence, and unfurling the flag of rebellion, Toussaint-Louverture had chosen the most insulting, and that which the Republic could least tolerate. From that moment there was no longer room for deliberation: the black chiefs were ungrateful and rebellious Africans with whom it was impossible to establish any system. Both the honour and the interest of France required that they should be effectually humbled. Thus the ruin of Toussaint-Louverture, and the misfortunes that afflicted the blacks, were the effects of that rash step, which was doubtless prompted by the English, who had already foreseen all the reverses which they must experience if the blacks should contain themselves within the bounds of moderation and submission and attach themselves to the mother country. To give an idea of the indignation I felt, it may suffice to mention that Toussaint not only assumed authority over the colony during his life, but invested himself with the right of naming his successor; and pretended to hold his authority, not from the mother country but from a soi-disant colonial assembly which he had created: and as Toussaint-Louverture was the most moderate of all the black generals; as Dessalines, Christophe, Clervaux, etc. were more violent, disaffected, and hostile to the authority of the mother country, there was no longer room for deliberation. The former scheme was now impracticable: it was inevitably necesaary to adopt the latter, and to make the sacrifice which it required.

Colonel Vincent's connections with the blacks, and the confidence that Toussaint-Louverture reposed in him, had long excited the suspicion of government, although it continued to employ this officer for the purpose of influencing the blacks, and convincing them, as far as possible, of its good intentions towards them. But when he presented himself as bearer of the declaration of independence published by the blacks, and even seemed inclined to defend it, he excited a sentiment of disgust, which was, however, dissembled, in order to avoid alarming Toussaint, and to collect the valuable information which this colonel possessed, respecting the military position of the blacks and the fortifications they had constructed in the hills. As soon as this was effected, Colonel Vincent was ordered to keep himself, for the future, a stranger to the affairs of Santo Domingo: he was placed at the disposal of the minister of war, to be employed in his military duties; and as he wished to be sent to a warm country, he obtained the direction of the fortifications of Tuscany. He afterwards attended as director of fortifications, for several years successively, at the January council of works which was held in my presence: he there got his plans adopted for the châteaux Despresides, of Florence, Leghorn, and Porto-Ferrajo. He was partial to Florence, where one of his daughters was married. All this ought not to have given rise to libellous assertions. I could not possibly have communicated my projects respecting Santo Domingo, which required profound secrecy, and were to be executed in a few months, to a person who was the agent of Toussaint and whose secret machinations were no longer a mystery. No notes passed between us and no conferences or negotiations with England about the expedition to Santo Domingo ever took place.

Throughout this business I acted only through the medium of my ministers. Had I not placed confidence in Decres, the Minister of Marine, what could have prevented me from dismissing that minister and selecting another? Was it the influence he possessed over the constituted authorities or the nation; the naval victories he had gained; or the great affection which the navy had for him? Absurd. This minister drew up all the naval instructions. If he judged it necessary to appoint three rallying points for the squadrons of Brest, L'Orient, and Rochefort – the first at Cape Finisterre, the second at the Canaries, the third at Cape Samana – it was because such was the usage in his time and particularly in the war of 1778. Were a minister to sign instructions contrary to his opinion and experience, he would be the most base and infamous of men. Why slander an old minister and general officer by attempting to justify him? *An injudicious friend is often more dangerous than an enemy.*

Admiral Villaret-Joyeuse was forty-six days on his passage from Brest to the Cape, that is to say, four or five days more than the average passage of a convoy; but this circumstance is of no importance with respect to the burning of the Cape and the fate of Santo Domingo. It was impossible to surprise Toussaint-Louverture: the armaments that had been assembled in the ports of France had attracted the attention of the whole world, and the blacks had agents and friends at Paris, Nantes, Bordeaux, Rochefort, Antwerp, Amsterdam, and London. The American ships covered the ocean; not a day passed but several of them arrived in the ports of the colony. The American ships are fast sailers: besides, a vessel sailing alone is faster than a convoy. The armament of Admiral Gantheume at Brest, in January 1801, had put the blacks on their guard; from that time they had begun to erect fortifications in the interior, and to collect magazines of powder and provisions; they had also come to a resolution to burn the Cape and the towns, if they should be unable to defend them, and to retire to the hills. Their works had been designed and directed by white officers and engineers. All the admirals and generals commanding troops or squadrons, whether of Brest, L'Orient, Rochefort, Cadiz, or Toulon, had orders from the minister of marine. For the execution of these orders it was necessary that the general of the land forces and the admiral should concert their measures together; besides, Admiral Villaret-Joyeuse, commanding all the squadrons in chief, had general orders for the sea-service, as the Captain-General Le Clerc had for the land-service. These orders were not intended to be published; but nevertheless they were not what are called secret orders. The squadron and divisions intended to take possession of Port-au-Prince were next in importance to those of the Cape. Admiral Villaret-Joyeuse and Captain-General Le Clerc were instructed to land at the Cape. Latouche Treville, commander of the Rochefort squadron, and general of division Boudet, were intended to land at Port-au-Prince. Admiral Latouche Treville was the ablest officer of our navy, and except the admiral of the fleet, the eldest. General Boudet had served in the war of the colonies; he was esteemed by the men of colour, who are numerous in the southern part of the island. The Rochefort squadron destined for Port-au-Prince was to take on board the men and stores requisite for this operation.

From these orders no deviation could be made, except pursuant to an agreement between the captain-general and the admiral. It appears that the captain-general entertained a momentary intention of landing Boudet's division to take possession of the Cape, and mentioned it to the admiral, who convinced him of the disadvantages of this plan. 'Admiral Latouche and General Boudet,'

Victor-Emmanuel Le Clerc, husband of Marie-Pauline Bonaparte.

Marie-Pauline Bonaparte, Madame Le Clerc, Princess Borghese.

said he, 'having understood, when they left France, that they were going to Port-au-Prince, have made their arrangements accordingly. If we alter these dispositions of government arbitrarily, and the expedition to Port-au-Prince should happen to fail, you and I will be responsible for it.' Captain-General Le Clerc immediately yielded to these prudent considerations, not being able to allege any necessity or urgent occasion for changing the original destination of the troops of General Boudet. Had the admiral complied with the first wishes of the captain-general, General Boudet would not have reached the Cape an hour sooner; Cape town would still have been burnt, and it is probable that the expedition to Port-au-Prince would have failed, and that this town would have shared the fate of the capital. It was the want of pilots which caused the delay in the occupation of the Cape; and it was an unpardonable piece of negligence in the marine department not to provide them before leaving Brest. But, even had Admiral Villaret-Joyeuse been provided with pilots, he would on his arrival have instantly entered the Cape roads under a press of sail; and had he immediately landed his troops, Cape town would nevertheless have been burnt, because five or six hours were sufficient for the blacks to accomplish its destruction, as they had long before irrevocably determined on this measure, and made all their preparations accordingly.

I hesitated for a moment whether I ought to order the captain-general not to effect his landing or commence hostilities, until his letter to Toussaint-Louverture, which the children of that general carried with them, should be sent back to me; but this would have been productive of great inconveniences – Toussaint would have kept the children and the letter following him from place to place as long as it suited him to do so. There were many examples of this species of cunning. This, then, would have exposed the army to the loss of a most precious opportunity and would have given the blacks time to recover from their first surprise. It was unlucky that Toussaint's children were for several days prevented from landing; but this circumstance was ultimately of no importance. In reflecting on the conduct of Toussaint-Louverture with General Hedouville during the whole reign of the Directory, and that which he pursued in 1800 and 1801, it is evident that he had resolved to perish or attain independence; that is to say, not to permit the presence of any white force of more than 2,000 men in the colony. Toussaint well knew that in proclaiming his constitution he had unmasked himself, drawn the sword, and thrown away the scabbard.

Captain-General Le Clerc was an officer of the first merit, equally skilful in the labours of the Cabinet and in the manoeuvres of the field of battle: he had served in the campaigns of 1796 and 1797 as adjutant-general to me; and in that of 1799 as a general of division under Moreau. He commanded at the battle of Freisingen, where he defeated the Archduke Ferdinand; he led into Spain an army of observation of 20,000 men intended to act against Portugal; finally, in this expedition of Santo Domingo, he displayed great talent and activity. In less than three months he vanquished and reduced to submission that black army which had signalized itself by the defeat of an English force.

At the time of his departure from France, Captain-General Le Clerc had, in fact, received from my own hands secret instructions with respect to the political line of conduct he was to pursue in the government of the colony. These instructions remained unknown until the death of General Le Clerc: they were delivered, sealed up, to his successor. The general officer who wrote the *History of the Revolutions of Santo Domingo* knew of their existence but was never able to discover their contents. Captain-General Le Clerc would have prevented many disasters, and spared himself much vexation, had he scrupulously adhered to the spirit of his secret instructions. By these he was ordered to place the greatest confidence in the men of colour, to treat them as the equals of the whites, to promote the marriages of men of colour to white women, and of women of colour to white men; but to pursue a system directly the reverse with the blacks. Within the first week after the pacification of the colony, he was to order all the black generals, adjutant-generals, colonels, and chiefs of battalions on service in their respective ranks in the continental divisions of France. He was to put them on board eight or ten ships in the different parts of the colony, and despatch them to Brest, Rochefort, and Toulon; he was to disarm all the blacks, excepting ten battalions of 6,000 men each, commanded by one-third of black officers and non-commissioned officers, one-third of officers and non-commissioned officers of colour, and one-third of white. Lastly, he was to take all necessary measures for securing the enjoyment of civil liberty to the blacks, and to confirm the orders of classification and labour that Toussaint-Louverture had established.

But Le Clerc suffered himself to be prejudiced against the mulattoes: he participated in the antipathy of the creoles against them, who hate them worse than even the blacks: he sent Rigaud, their chief, out of the colony. The mulattoes were alienated, and they now joined the blacks: Le Clerc placed his confidence in the black generals, such as Dessalines, Christophe, Clervaux, and not only retained them in the colony but gave them important commands. He consented to allow Toussaint-Louverture to reside in the colony: nevertheless, having afterwards detected a secret and culpable correspondence of this general, he had him arrested and conveyed to France: but the black staff, generals, adjutant-generals, colonels, and chiefs of battalions retained their situations. When I was informed of this conduct, I was exceedingly concerned: the authority of the mother country in the colony could only be established through the influence of the men of colour: it was to be feared that by the delay in removing the black chiefs from the colony, the opportunity had been lost. It was impossible for persons who had governed as sovereigns, whose vanity was equal to their ignorance, to live quietly and submit to the rule of the mother country; the first thing necessary for the security of Santo Domingo was, therefore, to remove from 150 to 2,000 of the chiefs. In this proceeding no moral principle would have been violated, since all generals and officers are bound to serve in any part of the state in which it may be thought proper to employ them. As all these black chiefs were in correspondence with Jamaica, and with the English cruisers, this measure would at once have deprived the whole population of its military leaders and cut off every channel of communication with foreigners. Finally, it would have been much more proper for Toussaint to have returned to France as a general of division, than as a criminal answerable to the mother country not only for old offences which had once been pardoned but for other crimes of subsequent date.

The decree of 28 Floréal 1801, which ordained the continued slavery of the blacks in Martinique and the Isle of France, and their liberty in Santo Domingo, Guadaloupe, and Cayenne, was just, politic, and expedient. It was necessary to secure the tranquillity of Martinique, which had just been surrendered by the English. The general law of the Republic was the liberty of the blacks: if this particular law had not been made for this colony and the Isle of France, the blacks of those colonies would have demanded the benefit of the general law: the consequent reaction would have fallen much more heavily on the blacks of Santo Domingo. Had the government remained silent, and the blacks continued slaves at Martinique, they would naturally have asked why, notwithstanding the law, persons of their colour were kept in a state of slavery at Martinique? It was, therefore, incumbent on the government to say: 'The blacks shall be slaves at Martinique, and at the Isles of France and Bourbon; and they shall be free at Santo Domingo, Guadaloupe and Cayenne,' and to proclaim the status quo as a principle.

It cannot be supposed that there are men extravagant enough, after the experience of past events, to insist that I ought abruptly to have given liberty to the blacks of Martinique and of the Isles of France and Bourbon: the consequence of this would have been insurrections in both these islands, and the continuance of their separation from the mother country; as well as the destruction of the colony of Martinique, which had just been restored by the English to a quiet and prosperous state. Many thousands of the white French inhabitants would have become the prey of the ferocious African population.

The question of the liberty of the blacks is very complicated and difficult. In Africa and in Asia it has been resolved; but it has been so by means of polygamy. The whites and the blacks there form parts of the same family. The head of the family having white and black wives, and wives of colour, the white and mulatto children are brothers, are bred in the same cradle, bear the same name, and eat at the same table. Would it then be impossible to authorize polygamy in our islands, restricting the number of wives to two, a white one and a black one? I had several conferences with theologians to prepare this grand measure. The patriarchs had several wives in the first ages of Christianity: the Church permitted and tolerated a species of concubinage, the effect of which was to allow one man to have several wives. The Pope and the Councils have the authority and the means to authorize such an institution, because the object of it is the conciliation and harmony of society, and not the increasing of carnal pleasures. The effect of these marriages would be confined to the colonies; proper measures would be taken to prevent them from spreading disorder in the bosom of European society.

The fact is, that the decree of May, relative to the blacks, was but a pretext. Their insurrection was the effect of the intrigues of the English in that month, and of the cruel disease which swept off the best of our troops. It was then that the captain-general repented his imprudent indulgence in neglecting my orders during the first week of May. Everything would have turned out very differently if he had then freed the colony of two or three hundred of the black chiefs. *In politics, as in war, the lost moment never returns.*

XV

RELATIONS WITH THE POPE

I N Italy, in 1796 and 1797, I had paid particular attention to religious affairs – this kind of knowledge was necessary for the conqueror and legislator of the Transpadane and Cispadane Republics, etc. In 1798 and 1799 I had occasion to study the Koran, and to acquire a knowledge of the principles of Islam, the government and the tenets of its four sects, and their relations with Constantinople and Mecca. I must have become well acquainted with both religions, for my knowledge contributed to my gaining the affections both of the Italian clergy and of the ulemas of Egypt.

I never regretted making the Concordat of 1801. The sentiments on this subject that have been put into my mouth are false – I have never said that the Concordat was the greatest error of my reign. The discussion I afterwards had with Rome arose out of the abuse that that Court made of the mixture of spiritual and temporal affairs. This may sometimes have produced in me a momentary fit of impatience, like that of the lion who feels himself stung by flies, but it never changed my views, whether with respect to the principles of my religion, or to that great work which had such important results. All my laws were liberal, even those of conscription and of the state prisons – the people were never my enemies, in any country. Only oligarchies were hostile to me, for my government was eminently popular.

The Concordat of 1801 was necessary to religion, to the Republic, to government. The temples were shut up, the priests were persecuted. They were divided into three sects, that of the Constitutionals, that of the Vicars Apostolic, and that of the emigrant bishops in the pay of England. The Concordat terminated these divisions, and raised up the catholic apostolic Roman Church from the ruins. It rebuilt the altars, put an end to disorders, commanded the faithful to pray for the Republic, dissipated all the scruples of the purchasers of national domains, broke the last thread by which the ancient dynasty was still connected with the country, by depriving the bishops who had remained faithful to them, and by pointing at them as rebels who had preferred the things of this world and their temporal interests to the affairs of heaven, and the cause of God.

It has been said, 'Napoleon ought not to have meddled with religious affairs, but should have tolerated religion by practising its rites and restoring its temples.' Practising its rites! What rites? Restoring its temples! To what guardians – the Constitutionals, the Anglicized clergy, or the Papist vicars in the pay of England?

The question of suspending for a time the exercise of the Pope's right of instituting bishops was discussed in several conferences during the negotiation of the Concordat. But the Pope had already made great concessions; he consented to the suppression of sixty dioceses, which were almost as old as Christianity; he deprived, by his own authority, a great number of ancient bishops, and consummated the sale of the property of the clergy to the amount of 400 millions, without any indemnity. It was even thought that the interest of the Republic required that no new stipulations favourable to the Ultras ought to be demanded. It was in one of these conferences that I said, 'If the Pope had not existed, it

Pope Pius VII, with whom Napoleon made the Concordat of 1801.

would have been necessary to create one for this occasion; as the Roman Consuls, in circumstances of emergency, elected a dictator.' The Concordat allowed, it is true, a foreign jurisdiction in the state, which might disturb it; but this power was not intoduced by the Concordat. It existed from time immemorial. Being master of Italy, I considered myself master of Rome, and this Italian influence helped me to destroy the influence of the English.

The pamphlets printed in London on the discussions between the Courts of the Tuileries and of Rome are apocryphal: they have never been acknowledged. They were published in the hope of kindling the enthusiasm of the Spaniards, and of all the bigots in Christendom: the inferior clergy hawked them about most industriously. Some of these pieces are wholly false: all the others are more or less falsified. First, the Court of the Tuileries never promised legations, directly or indirectly, and the Pope never required this as the condition of his journey to Paris; perhaps it may be true that he flattered himself with the hope of obtaining from my gratitude, Romania, in which country Cesena, his native place, is situated; and even that during his stay at Paris, he signified a wish on the subject directly to me, but very slightly, and with scarce a hope of success. Secondly, how can it be supposed that the institution of a patriarch was requested of the Court of Rome? A patriarch would have had no influence except in France: the influence of the Pope, who was the patriarch of the grand empire, extended all over the world: France would, therefore, have lost by the change. Thirdly, why should I demand the acceptance of my civil code? Did not the Code Napoleon then govern France and Italy? Did I need the aid of the Court of Rome to make laws in my own dominions? Fourthly, why should I require the freedom of worship? Was not freedom of worship a fundamental law of the French constitution? Did it then require the sanction of the Pope, any more than that of the minister Marron and the consistories of Geneva? Fifthly, why should I demand the reform of the bishoprics, which were too numerous in Italy? Had not the Concordat of Italy provided a remedy for this? Some negotiations, indeed, took place, with respect to the bishoprics of Tuscany and Genoa; but they were transacted in the forms established for matters of this kind. Sixthly, for what purpose could the abolition of pontifical bulls for the Italian bishoprics and cures be required? Were not all these matters settled by the Concordat of Italy? Seventhly, why should I demand the abolition of the religious orders? Were they not already abolished in France and Italy? Had not the sale of their property been consummated and ratified by the Concordat? Eighthly, how can it be supposed, embroiled as I was with the Court of Rome, that I should stipulate for the marriages of the priests; which would have been wantonly giving an advantage to my enemies? What was the celibacy of the clergy to me? Had I any time to waste in theological disputes? Ninthly, what interest could I have in getting Joseph Bonaparte consecrated King of Naples by the Pope? Had the Pope been willing to perform this ceremony, I would have opposed it; lest it should be relied on as an act of sovereignty over Naples.

My direct correspondence with the Pope from 1805 to 1809 has remained

Jean-Jacques-Régis de Cambacérès, Duke of Parma. Organizer of the Code Napoleon – *the Emperor's most lasting achievement.*

secret only as regards to temporal matters, on which I did not need the consent or advice of his bishops; but in 1809, when the Pope, relying on a passage of the Council of Lyons, attemped, by the brief of Savona addressed to the Chapters of Florence and Paris, to obstruct the exercise of the functions of capitular vicars during the vacancies of sees, the discussions between the Pope and me were extended to spiritual matters. I then felt the necessity of the advice and intervention of the clergy: I established a council of theologians. My choice was fortunate: the Bishop of Nantes, who had been for half a century one of the oracles of Christianity, was the soul of this council: from that period, all the discussions became public.

Fox, conversing with me, after the treaty of Amiens, blamed me for not having stipulated for the marriage of the clergy. I replied, 'I wanted, and still want, to pacify: theological volcanoes are to be quenched with water, not with oil: I should have found it less difficult to introduce the Confession of Augsburg into my Empire.'

After the coronation, discussions took place respecting cardinals' hats, and about the Pope's having thought proper to suppress certain points in his allocutions on the organic laws, and respecting penitentiary briefs; also relating to some circumscriptions of the dioceses of Tuscany and Genoa, and some secret affairs relative to the Kingdom of Italy: but the two sovereigns were not directly engaged in any of these discussions; they were always left to the care of the proper chancellors, who treated all these matters with moderation and prudence.

The quarrel between me and the Pope, which lasted five years, and terminated in 1810 in the annexation of the temporal estates of the Holy See to the Empire, originated in 1805. The Courts of Vienna, Russia, and England had just concluded the third coalition against France: an Austrian army occupied Munich, put the King of Bavaria to flight, and took up a position on the Iller, there awaiting the junction of two Russian armies. The Archduke John, at the head of the principal army of the House of Austria, advanced, to the Adige, threatening the conquest of all Italy. A French corps of observation, from 15,000 to 20,000 strong, under the command of Marshal Saint Cyr, occupied the peninsula of Otranto: he was separated from the army of the Adige by the states of the Pope. An English squadron appeared in the Mediterranean, and had cruisers in the Adriatic; an Anglo-Russian army was expected at Naples. The corps of observation at Otranto was compromised; the citadel of Ancona belonged to the Pope; being on the line of communication with the French Army of Italy, it was not in a state of defence; had 1,200 men been landed, they might have seized this important post. I requested the Pope, in a direct communication, to put Ancona in a state of defence; to garrison it with 3,000 men; and to entrust the command to a man who could be depended on; to allow me to send a French garrison there. This being refused, I then required and insisted on fresh guarantees. I demanded, categorically, first that the Pope should conclude an offensive treaty with the Kings of Italy and Naples for the defence of Italy: the Court of Naples, which was dissembling, had consented to this. Secondly, that the ports of the Roman states should be closed against the English. Thirdly, that a French garrison of 3,000 men should be received into the citadel of Ancona. To these demands the Pope answered that, as father of the faithful, he could enter into no league against his children; that it would, besides, be compromising the Roman Catholic subjects of the powers against which he should declare; that he had no reason to complain of any one, and that he neither would nor could make war against any power whatever. I answered that when Charlemagne invested the Pope with a temporal sovereignty it was for the benefit of Italy and Europe, and not for the purpose of introducing infidels and heretics into them; that the history of the Popes was full of leagues and alliances with the Emperors and the Kings of Spain and France; that Julius II had commanded armies; that in 1797 my headquarters were in the episcopal palace of Bishop Chiaramonti, when I was marching against the army of Cardinal Busca, which Pius VI had raised to make a diversion in favour of the Austrians – a war which was terminated by the treaty of Tolentino; therefore that, as in our own times the banner of Saint Peter had marched against France, by the side of the Austrian eagle, it might now march with the French eagle; that nevertheless, to testify my deference to the Holy

189

Father, I would consent that this treaty should not extend to Austria or Spain, but should only be applicable to infidels and heretics. On these conditions I would undertake to protect the coasts and the flag of the Church against the Barbary powers. The correspondence on these subjects was kept up during 1805 and 1806. The letters of the Pope were written with the pen of Gregory VII: they formed a striking contrast to the mildness and amenity of his character – he was merely their signatory. He perpetually spoke of his jurisdiction, of his supremacy over terrestrial powers; 'Because,' he said, 'Heaven is above earth, spirit superior to matter.'

After the peace of Presburg, however, a French army had entered Naples; King Ferdinand had taken refuge in Sicily; the whole kingdom had been conquered; a French prince had ascended the throne, who found himself separated by the states of the Pope from the army of upper Italy. The agents of the Courts of Palermo and Cagliari, and the intriguers in the pay of England, whom that power always maintains on the Continent, had made Rome the centre of their operations: soldiers were frequently assassinated in traversing the part of the route which crosses the dominions of the Church between Milan and Naples. This state of affairs was intolerable: I informed the Pope that it could not be endured; and gave him to understand that, according to the nature of things, it was indispensable that the Court of Rome should make an offensive and defensive alliance with France; and it should close its ports against England; that it should drive from Rome all foreign incendiaries, or that it must expect to lose that part of its territory situate between the Apennines and the Adriatic – that is to say, the Marches of Ancona, which when united to the Kingdom of Italy would secure the communication between Naples and Milan. The answer of the Holy See consisted of impotent menaces: it was evident that my forbearance, which was somewhat inconsistent with my character, had given rise to an opinion, at Rome that I dreaded the thunders of the Church. To dissipate this foolish notion I ordered a corps of 6,000 men to enter Rome, under pretext of intending to proceed to Naples, but to remain at Rome. I gave particular instructions to the general who commanded that expedition to show the greatest respect for the Court of the Vatican, and not to interfere on any occasion: at the same time I caused it to be insinuated, that, having ventured to occupy Rome I was determined to proceed to all extremities; that I would not be impeded in temporal affairs by spiritual menaces; and that the weak must resort to the strong for protection.

The Court of Rome was thrown into an absolute delirium: monitory letter, prayers, sermons, circular notes to the diplomatic body, were all employed to increase the mischief; all the spiritual arms of the Papal See were brandished in support of its temporal processions; but the amount of their efficacy had been well calculated by the Cabinet of St Cloud. At length, early in 1808, I wrote to the Pope, that it was time to put an end to all this trifling; and that unless his Holiness should adhere to the federative treaty of the powers of Italy within two months, I would consider Charlemagne's grant as null, and would confiscate the patrimony of Saint Peter; without intending thereby to infringe on the respect due to the sacred person of the Pope, or on his freedom as chief of the Catholic Church. It was impossible for any notice to be more explicit; yet no regard was paid to it. Thus braved and driven to extremities, I decreed in 1808 the annexation of the Marches to the Kingdom of Italy, leaving to the Pope the city of Rome and all his dominions between the Apennines and the Mediterranean. The French agents declared at the same time that the troops of France would quit Rome and the states of the Church as soon as the Roman Court would acquiesce in the separation of the Marches; but, on receiving this news, it sent orders to its minister at Paris to demand his passports and to return without taking leave: the passports were instantly granted and war was declared. Thus a feeble power, incapable of resistance, defied and declared war against the strongest and most victorious power in the world; but it was the system of the Court of Rome to rush into extremes and to oppose spiritual to temporal arms. It still cherished a hope of witnessing the return of those ages when the world fell prostrate before the thunders of the Church. These have few terrors for me; but I was fettered by my sentiments towards the Pope; and I left everything still *in statu quo.*

But in the beginning of 1809 the fourth Coalition was declared. The Court of Vienna announced hostilities: the general commanding in Rome asked for reinforcements to enable him to keep in awe the population of that great city and the neighbouring country; and if this could not be granted, he desired that an end might be put to the anarchy of the pontifical government. He received orders to assume the government, to incorporate the Papal troops in the French Army, to maintain a good police, and to take care that the Pope should continue to receive the sums that had customarily been paid out of the treasury for the maintenance of his household.

The war, in which France was engaged with Austria and Spain, appeared a favourable opportunity to the Holy See, which at length issued its bull of excommunication. The occupation of the states of the Pope was the consequence of the war which he had declared against France; but he had in no respect been disturbed in the direction of spiritual affairs, and he had received assurances that his person should not be the less sacred, provided he did not disturb the government established at Rome in the exercise of its functions. He would not take advantage of this proposal, considering that his quality as sovereign of Rome was blended with and inherent in his spiritual character. The French troops in his states were not numerous, and the battle of Essling having rendered the issue of the war in some degree doubtful, the populace was in a state of agitation: the Holy Father, shut up in his palace, had caused it to be surrounded by barricades; these were guarded by several hundred armed men with the strictest vigilance. The French troops which occupied the outposts picked a quarrel with these guards; who, they thought, set them at defiance, which excited their sarcasms. The situation of the Pope was dangerous: every moment it was feared that they would come to blows: bullets respect nobody. The general commanding at Rome made the strongest remonstrances: he could not make those around the Pope understand that his Holiness would be much more secure if guarded only by the sanctity of his character; and that the opposition of force to force might produce the most fatal consequences. Finding his advice neglected, he resolved to act accordingly to the exigencies of the case, and to remove the Pope to Florence. His duty to the Holy Father, to the troops under his command, to the French nation, and to Europe, all dictated this step. What would Catholic Christendom have said, had a life so precious been lost in a fray? Was it not the French general's office to watch over the preservation of public tranquillity? And tranquillity was instantly restored. But the Grand Duchess of Tuscany, astonished that the Pope had been sent to Florence without my order, caused him to proceed in the direction of Turin. The same motive induced the governor-general of Piedmont to compel him to proceed to Grenoble. I learned what had taken place, at Schoenbrunn, by a Roman courier: I instantly sent orders to Florence, that if the Pope had arrived there he should be placed in a country house of the Grand Duchy and treated with all the honours and attention due to his sacred character; to Turin, that if the Pope had arrived there, he should be conducted to Savona; and to Paris, to go to meet his Holiness, in order to take him to Florence, if he should not have crossed the Apennines, and to Savona, if he should have passed those mountains. However dissatisfied with what had happened, I could not discountenance my general at Rome, whose conduct had been prescribed by necessity. It was impossible to send the Pope back to Rome without incurring the risk of occurrences still more vexacious than those that had already taken place. The battle of Wagram was impending, which would in all probability determine the question of peace, and it would afterwards be a proper time to negotiate with the Holy See, and to bring these troublesome affairs to a close.

The whole of the Imperial mansion at Turin was placed at the Pope's disposal; at Savona he was lodged at the archiepiscopal palace, where he was suitably accommodated. The intendant of the civil list, Count Sulmatori, provided him with all his needs. He remained thus several months, during which he was offered liberty to return to Rome, provided he would consent not to disturb the public peace, but to acknowledge the government established in that capital, and to interfere only in spiritual matters; but he, perceiving that there was a disposition to weary him out, and that the world went on as usual without him, addressed briefs to the Metropolitan chapters of Florence and Paris, to disturb the administration of the dioceses, during the vacancies of sees, at the same time that Cardinal Pietro was sending Vicars Apostolic into the vacant dioceses. It was then that the discussion which had been carried on for five years first ceased to be temporal, and assumed a spiritual character; which produced the first and second assemblies of the bishops at the Council of Paris, the Bull of 1811, and finally the Concordat of Fontainebleau in 1812. Nothing was yet determined with respect to the temporal state of Rome; this uncertainty encouraged the Pope in his resistance. I, who had now been trifled with for five years, by the most contemptible arguments, originating in this mixture of temporal and spiritual

Napoleon, Emperor of France, at his coronation. Painting by Ingres.
Musée de l'Armée, Paris (Bridgeman Art Library).

OPPOSITE ABOVE *The Empress Josephine at Malmaison. Painting by François Gerard. Château de Malmaison, Paris (Bridgeman Art Library).*

OPPOSITE BELOW *Napoleon's finest victory – the battle of Austerlitz, 2 December 1804. Painting by Claude-Joseph Vernet. Château de Versailles, France (Bridgeman Art Library).*

ABOVE *The Master of Europe. Painting by Appiani the Elder. Kunsthistorisches Museum, Vienna (Bridgeman Art Library).*

OPPOSITE ABOVE *The battle of Eylau against the Russians, February 1807.*
Although technically a French victory, the battle cost Napoleon dearly.
Painting by Baron Gros. Louvre, Paris (Giraudon/Bridgeman Art Library).

OPPOSITE BELOW *Napoleon and Marie-Louise enter the Tuileries in Paris*
on the day of their wedding, 1 April 1810. Painting by Etienne-Barthelemy
Garnier. Château de Versailles, France (Bridgeman Art Library).

ABOVE *The battle for Moscow, 7 September 1812. Painting by Louis Lejeune.*
Château de Versailles, France (Bridgeman Art Library).

The Modern HANNIBAL alias The King of ROME, swearing Eternal Enmity to ENGLAND.

OPPOSITE ABOVE *The Empress Marie-Louise with her son, the King of Rome, born 20 March 1811. Painting by François Gerard. Château de Versailles (Giraudon/Bridgeman Art Library).*

OPPOSITE BELOW *The King of Rome, 1814. Cartoon by George Cruikshank. Victoria and Albert Museum, London (Bridgeman Art Library).*

ABOVE *Distribution of the eagles on the 'Field of May,' in 1815. Painting by Louis David. Château de Versailles, France (Bridgeman Art Library).*

TOP *Supper at Beaucaire, from a painting by Lecomte-du-Nouy.*

ABOVE *The arrest of Toussaint-Louverture by Chole Obin.*
Reproduced by courtesy of Mr Mark Laracy, Anguilla.

power, at length resolved to separate those attributes for ever, and no longer to permit the Pope to be temporal sovereign. Jesus Christ said: 'My kingdom is not of this world.' Although heir to the throne of David, he desired to be a high priest – not a king. The Senatus-Consultum of 17 February 1810 annexed the states of Rome to the Empire, and settled all that related to the temporal concerns of the Pope. Throughout these negotiations, the deputations of bishops always had instructions to offer the Pope liberty to return to Rome, on condition of his acknowledging the temporal government which had been established there, and concerning himself in spiritual affairs exclusively; but he constantly rejected these proposals. When removed to the palace of Fontainebleau, to place him in security from an attempt which it was intended to make by sea, he occupied the apartments in which he had formerly resided: he had always about him seven or eight French bishops to do the honours of the palace; several cardinals, amongst whom were Doria and Ruffo, his medical and ecclesiastical establishments, his almoner, chaplain, etc.; he regulated his expenses at his own discretion. A great number of carriages belonging to the Court were at his command: the guards waited on him for the password every morning, and the Grand Marshal Duroc superintended the supply of everything necessary for him and his court, with the greatest attention. Pius VII had few wants: the table of the refectory of a convent would have satisfied him. The Grand Marshal of the Palace, therefore, had only one point to attend to; not to reduce the expense, but to increase it, and to take care that it should be suitable, and on the same footing as that of the Tuileries; in short, his court there was equal to the Vatican. I only saw him in January 1813, in company with the Empress: we paid him the first visit; he returned it immediately, as is usual. During the three days we passed in the palace, all communications were in an amicable and gracious form. The Concordat was signed before several cardinals, a great number of French and Italian bishops, and part of the Imperial Court.

I evinced, on this occasion, more patience than was consistent with my character and the situation in which I stood; and if I sometimes used sarcasms in my correspondence with the Pope, I was always provoked to them by the style of the Roman chancellor, which resembled that of the times of Louis le Debonnaire, or the Emperors of the House of Suabia: a style the more ill-judged, because it was addressed to a man exceedingly well acquainted with the wars and affairs of Italy, who knew by heart all the campaigns, leagues, and temporal intrigues of the Popes. The Court of Rome might have avoided all this by frankly embracing the French system, closing its ports against the English, voluntarily requesting the assistance of a few French battalions for the defence of Ancona, and, in short, by preserving tranquillity in Italy.

As to spiritual questions, I never discussed with the Pope any others than those comprehended in the procès-verbaux of the two ecclesiastical commissions and of the Council of Paris: the only one of importance is that relating to the bishops.

It was my desire to raise the Italian nation from its ruins: to unite once more the Venetians, Piedmontese, Genoese, Milanese, Tuscans, Parmesans, Modenese, Romans, Neapolitans, Sicilians, and Sardinians in one independent nation, bounded by the Alps and the Adriatic, Ionian, and Mediterranean seas: such was the immortal trophy which I was raising to my glory. This great and powerful kingdom would have been, by land, a check to the House of Austria, while by sea its fleets, combined with those of Toulon, would have ruled the Mediterranean and protected the ancient road of Indian commerce by the Red Sea and Suez. Rome, the capital of this state, was the eternal city; covered by the three barriers, the Alps, the Po, and the Apennines; nearer than any other to the three great islands. But I had many obstacles to surmount. I said at the Council of Lyons: 'It will take me twenty years to re-establish the Italian nation.'

The geographical configuration of Italy has greatly influenced its fate. If the Ionian Sea had washed the foot of Monte Velino; if all the countries that form the Kingdoms of Naples, Sicily, and Sardinia had been placed between Corsica, Leghorn, and Genoa, how materially would events have been affected by these circumstances! Before the Romans, the Gauls took possession of all the north of Italy, from the Alps to the Magra westward and the Rubicon eastward; while the nations of Greece occupied Tarentum, Reggio, and all the south of the peninsula: the Italians were confined within the limits of Tuscany and Latium.

But the public spirit of the Italians, an ardent and enlightened people, would have overcome these local difficulties, had it not been baffled by Papal politics; the Vatican however, although too weak to unite all Italy under its dominion, has nevertheless always possessed sufficient power to prevent any republic or prince from conquering all the neighbouring states. There were three impediments to this grand design: the possessions of foreign powers in Italy, the influence of localities, and the residence of the Popes at Rome.

Ten years had scarcely elapsed, from the date of the Consultum of Lyons, before the first obstacle was entirely removed: foreign powers no longer possessed any part of Italy, which was entirely under the immediate influence of the French Emperor. The abrogation of the Republic of Venice, the deposition of the King of Sardinia and the Grand Duchess of Tuscany, the annexation of Saint Peter's patrimony to the Empire, had set aside the second impediment. As those skilful founders who have to transform seversl guns of small calibre into one 48-pounder, first throw them all into the furnace, in order to decompose them, and to reduce them to a state of fusion; so the small states had been united to Austria or France in order to reduce them to an elementary state, to get rid of their recollections and pretensions, that they might be prepared for the moment of casting. The Venetians, having been annexed to the Austrian monarchy for several years, had experienced all the bitterness of a subjection to the Germans: when these people were restored to an Italian government, they cared little whether their city was to be the capital, or whether their government was to be more or less aristocratic. A similar change took place in Piedmont, Genoa and Rome, disorganized by the grand movements of the French Empire. There were now no Venetians, Piedmontese, or Tuscans: the inhabitants of the whole peninsula were no longer anything but Italians: all was ready to form the great

Napoleon-François-Charles-Joseph, Prince Imperial, King of Rome, Duke of Reichstadt, later died in 1832, an officer in the Austrian army. It was said of Napoleon, 'His patience and kindness for the child was inexhaustible.'

Italian nation. The Grand Duchy of Berg was vacant for the dynasty which for the time occupied the throne of Naples: I impatiently awaited the birth of my second son,[1] to take him to Rome, to crown him King of Italy, and to proclaim the independence of the beautiful peninsula, under the regency of Prince Eugène. Italiam! Italiam! The third obstacle, the residence of the Popes, had vanished; the Holy Father was at Fontainebleau: the Sacred College, the Datarium, the Archives, the Propaganda, all the papers of the Missions were at Paris. Several millions had been expended on the episcopal palace: the pharmacy of the Hotel Dieu had been removed, and its site had been given to the Datarium: the Hotel Dieu itself had been transferred to the four new hospitals, and its place had been wholly given up to the establishments of the Court of Rome. The quarter of Notre-Dame and the Isle of Saint Louis were to become the central seat of Christianity. The Grand Empire comprised five-sixths of Christian Europe – France, Italy, Spain, the Confederation of the Rhine, and Poland. It was therefore proper, for the interests of religion, that the Pope should establish his residence at Paris and unite the See of Notre-Dame with that of the Lateran.

[1] The first being, presumably, his stepson, Eugène de Beauharnais.

XVI

THE NOBILITY

THE institution of a national nobility is not contrary to equality, and is necessary to the maintenance of social order. No social order can be founded on agrarian laws. The principle of property, and its transmission by sale or donation between the living, or by testamentary devise, is a fundamental principle that does not militate against equality. From this principle is derived the usage of transmitting from father to son the remembrance of services rendered to the state. Fortune may sometimes be acquired by shameful and criminal means. Titles gained by services to the state always spring from a pure and honourable source; their transmission to posterity is but an act of justice. When I put to a great number of partisans of the Revolution, most tenaciously attached to the principle of equality, the question whether the establishment of these hereditary titles would be contrary to the principles of equality, they all answered in the negative.

I had three objects in view in establishing an hereditary national nobility. First, to reconcile France to the rest of Europe; secondly, to reconcile ancient with modern France; thirdly, to banish the remains of the feudal system from Europe by attaching the idea of nobility to services rendered to the state and detaching it from every feudal association.

All Europe was governed by nobles who had strenuously opposed the progress of the French Revolution. This was an obstacle which on all sides counteracted the influence of the French; it was necessary to remove it, and for that purpose to invest the principal personages of the Empire with titles equal to theirs. This plan was completely successful. The nobility of Europe ceased to oppose France and saw with secret joy a new nobility, which, by the very circumstance of being new, appeared inferior to the old. They did not foresee the consequence of the

French system, which tended to uproot and depreciate the feudal nobility, or at least to compel it to renew its constitution on a new foundation.

The old French nobles, on recovering their country and part of their wealth, had resumed their titles, not legally, but actually; they more than ever regarded themselves as a privileged race; all blending and amalgamation with the leaders of the Revolution was difficult; the creation of new titles wholly annihilated these difficulties; there was not an ancient family that did not readily form alliances with the new dukes; in fact, the Noailles, the Colberts, the Louvois, and Fleurys were new houses; from their origin, the most ancient families in France had sought their alliance; thus the families which had arisen through the Revolution were strengthened, while ancient and modern France were united. It was not without design that I bestowed the first title I gave on Marshal Lefebvre, who had been a private soldier, and whom everybody at Paris remembered as a sergeant in the Guards.

My project was to reconstitute the ancient nobility of France. Every family that counted among its ancestors a cardinal, a great crown officer, a marshal of Europe, or a minister, etc. would on that account have been entitled to seek from the Council of the Seals the title of duke; every family that had an archbishop, ambassador, first president, lieutenant-general, or vice-admiral, the title of count; every family that could number among its members a bishop, brigadier, rear-admiral, counsellor of state, or judge-president, the title of baron. These titles would only have been granted on condition of the applicants settling a revenue of 100,000 francs for each duke; 30,000 francs for each count; and 10,000 francs for each baron. This rule was to apply to the past, the present, and the future. Hence arose a historical nobility connecting the past, present, and future and constituted, not on distinctions of blood, which are an imaginary nobility, since there is but one race of men, but on services rendered to the state. As the son of an agriculturist might say, I shall some day be a cardinal, marshal of France, or minister; he might also say, I shall some day be a duke, count, or baron: just as he might say, I will engage in commerce, and accumulate so many millions which I will leave to my children. A Montmorency would have been a duke, not because he was a Montmorency, but because one of his ancestors had been constable and done the state service. This vast idea altered the plan of the nobility, which was merely feudal, and erected on its ruins an historical nobility, founded on the interests of the country and on services rendered to the people and their sovereigns. This idea, like those of the Legion of Honour and of the university was eminently liberal; it was calculated at once to confirm social order, and to annihilate the empty pride of the nobility; it destroyed the pretensions of the oligarchy and maintained the dignity and equality of man inviolate. It was an idea fertile in important results, and highly liberal: it would have become a distinguishing feature of the new age. I did not hurry the execution of my schemes; I thought I had sufficient time. I often said to the Council of State, 'I want twenty years to accomplish my plans.' Of this number five were denied me.

*Marshal Joachim Murat, created King of Naples in 1808. He led the
cavalry charge at Jena armed only with his riding whip. Liked by his subjects,
he died in 1815 attempting to reclaim his throne.*

THE LEGION OF HONOUR

No comedian ever received the decoration of the Legion of Honour. Are Gretry,
Paesiello, Mehul, and Lesueur, our most celebrated composers, to be compared
to singers? Must the proscription be extended to David, Gros, Vernet, Renaud,
and Robert Lefebre, our most eminent painters; and even to Lagrange, La Place,
Berthollet, Monge, Vauquelin, Chaptal, Guyton de Morveau, Jouy, Baour
Lormian, Fontanes, Sismondi, and Guinguene? The French soldier must
entertain sentiments highly unworthy of him before a decoration worn by such

men can, on that account, lose any part of its value in his eyes. If the Legion of Honour were not the recompense of civil as well as military services, it would cease to be the Legion of Honour. It would be a strange piece of presumption indeed, in the military, to pretend that honours should be paid to them only. Soldiers who knew not how to read or write, were proud of bearing, in recompense for the blood they had shed, the same decoration as was given to distinguished talents in civil life; and, on the other hand, the latter attached a greater value to this regard of their labours because it was the decoration of the brave. But then, Crescentini? It is true that, in a moment of enthusiasm, just after hearing the fine scenes of Romeo and Juliet, I gave him the cross of the iron crown. Crescentini, however, was of good birth; he belonged to the worthy citizens of Bologna, a city so dear to my heart. I thought it would please the Italians; I was mistaken; ridicule attacked the transaction; had it been approved by public opinion, I would have given the cross of the Legion of Honour to Talma, Saint-Prix, Fleury, Grandmenil, Lais, Gardel, and Ellevious: I refrained from so doing, out of consideration for the weakness and prejudices of the age; and I was in the wrong. The Legion of Honour was the property of everyone who was an honour to his country, stood at the head of his profession, and contributed to the national prosperity and glory. Some officers were dissatisfied because the decoration of the Legion of Honour was alike for officers and soldiers. But if ever it ceased to be the recompense of the lowest class of the military, and a medal be instituted, through aristocratical feelings, to reward the soldier, or if ever the civil order be deprived of it, it will be the Legion of Honour no longer.

XVII

PRISON REFORM

THERE were never more than fifty-three priests detained in consequence of the discussions with Rome, and all were lawfully confined. Among them were Cardinal Pietro, for being at the head of the correspondence with the inferior clergy about appointing Vicars Apostolic, which was contrary to the principles of the Gallican Church and the safety of the state; Cardinal Pacca, for having signed the bull of excommunication (no resentment was felt towards the Pope, but the minister who had signed the bull was held responsible – it was intended, if any individual had been assassinated at Rome in consequence of the bull, to have made this cardinal answerable for it; in fact the excommunication excited only the most profound contempt on all sides, which was a most fortunate circumstance for all the cardinals and prelates of the Court of Rome); and D'Astros, the Vicar of Paris, who was in correspondence with Cardinal Pietro – he had clandestinely received and distributed bulls which were not known or admitted in France, an act contrary to the principles of the Gallican Church and designated as a crime by the penal code.

But how could 500 priests, as has been suggested, be in confinement on account of the affairs of the Church, when in the six state prisons there were at this time only 243 individuals altogether. There were four groups of prisoners. First, there were the priests mentioned above, together with emigrants black-listed as having borne arms against the nation, or as being agents of England or other foreign powers, who had returned from exile contrary to law; had these been delivered up to the tribunals, they would have been immediately condemned to death – a severity it was not wished to exercise. Secondly, there were the chiefs of the Chouans, or agents in the civil war, who had been condemned to death but reprieved because their knowledge might be useful, to confront them with other Vendéans who had been taken, to obtain local information, or gain from them intelligence about such past events as it was thought expedient to sift to the bottom. Thirdly, there were emigrants who had availed themselves of the amnesty but had been kept under observation by the police and found to have planned conspiracies against the state and government. Had these been delivered up to the tribunals they must have been condemned to death, but the judicial proceedings would have kept the public in continual anxiety about the risk the nation ran of losing its chief. Besides, some of these plots, although criminal, were so contemptibly foolish (such as that of the Baron de la Rochefoucauld and of Vaudricourt, the quartermaster of Condé's army), that it was sufficient to hold these individuals in the state prisons until peace. Fourthly, there were men of the lowest classes, guilty of numerous crimes that came within the jurisdiction of the provosts' courts, but whom the juries had not dared to condemn, though well convinced of their guilt, for fear of their accomplices. These facts were established by a procès-verbal signed by the judges who had presided at the trial; another procès-verbal of the prefect and council of the prefecture supported the first and demanded that these persons would not be set free on the grounds that their liberation would be dangerous to public tranquillity. These were the 243 prisoners out of the 40,000,000 population of an empire just emerging from a terrible revolution which had shaken all the foundations of society – an empire which had long been agitated by internal discord and was still harassed by foreign wars. Such a state of things is unparalleled in the history of nations; for in the ordinary course of affairs every country in Europe keeps a greater number of state prisoners in confinement by means of various authorities, under forms sanctioned by the laws. These 243 individuals, a number which from that time forward was gradually reduced, were confined in six prisons (Vincennes was one), each of which, therefore, contained from thirty to forty individuals.

Under the convention, the laws relating to suspected persons and emigrants had given rise to a great number of state prisons. There were more than 2,000, containing no less than 60,000 persons, during the early part of the government of the Directory. This number had greatly diminished. All these prisons were successively abolished; the number of state prisoners was reduced to little more than 3,000; they were confined in the ordinary prisons; the inspection of them was left to the administration, particularly the police. The commissioners and the minister of police were magistrates of public safety; they had authority to imprison: a special article of the constitutions of that period gave this right to the minister of police, or to the administration, in case of any plot against the state. This number of prisoners increased, in 1799, after the revolution of Prairal, through the execution of the law of hostages. There were 9,000 persons imprisoned at the period of 18 Brumaire: these were mostly set at liberty. At the commencement of the Imperial reign, there remained scarcely 1,200 belonging to one or other of the foregoing classes.

The police exercised the most arbitrary tyranny. The necessity of investing the courts with the superintendence of the prisons, and of authorizing the Imperial attorneys to visit them, and to liberate all persons not confined by lawful process, was generally felt. The regulation of the prisons was restored to the courts, the police were no longer suffered to retain prisoners in the usual places of confinement; the state prisoners above-mentioned were placed under the immediate administration of the minister of police, with power reserved for the Imperial attorneys to visit and to examine the warrants of these state prisoners and to set at liberty every individual not arrested by virtue of a decision of the Privy Council ordering a detention of less than one year and countersigned by the Grand Judge. From that moment liberty was secured in France: every prisoner was enabled to address himself to the magistrates; the minister of police and his agents were thus stripped of that terrible power of committing any individual at their own pleasure, and of keeping him in their own hands, without the tribunals taking any cognizance of the case. Thus, instead of a warrant issued by a mere commissary of police, a deliberation of the Privy Council was necessary to retain a prisoner in the hands of justice. This Privy Council consisted of myself, the five grand dignitaries, two ministers, besides the minister of police and the Grand Judge, two senators, two counsellors of state, the first president, and the Imperial attorney of the Court of Cassation. Sixteen persons, including the head of the state, decided on the imprisonment of the individuals included in the provision of exception. Were there ever more guarantees given to citizens? This decree declared that a prisoner of state must be set at liberty after one year unless the Privy Council should prolong his captivity by a new deliberation. For this purpose, two counsellors of state yearly visited the prison, examined the records of his charge and defence, and made their report to the Grand Judge, who, in the Privy Council, in the presence of the two counsellors of state who there took their seats, proposed the liberation of the prisoner or his confinement for another year. The Privy Council then voted thereon, beginning with the vote of the first President of the Court of Cassation.

This decree, therefore, was a benefit; it was a liberal law, a diapason to establish the harmony of society; it left no arbitrary power, either in the magistrate, the administration, or the police; it guaranteed security to the citizens. There was not a counsellor of state who inspected the prisons who did not take pride in releasing the greatest possible number of captives. All those who have assisted in the Privy Councils can bear witness that these counsellors of state acted as the advocates of the prisoners. These prisons would in time have disappeared, with the circumstances that had created them; with that race of brigands nourished in civil war; those intriguing petty priests of the inferior clergy; those persons exasperated by the Revolution, and the losses they had sustained in its progress, who were always hatching plots for subverting the government. There were in France 2,000,000 individuals who had emigrated, suffered deportation, or figured in the civil war, and to whom I had restored their country of subjection to a special superintendence. It was from this class of men that the state prisoners were taken; it was this right of superintendence, alienated from arbitrary power, and legalized conformably to a liberal spirit and to the principles of justice, which animated all the acts of the Privy Council.

Whenever a fourth of the members of the Privy Council were of opinion that the prisoner ought to be released, his discharge was instantly ordered. Besides, these prisoners had, independently of this recourse to the council of state and Privy Council, a constitutional protection in the committee of the senate for individual liberty; they never failed to apply to it; the committee deliberated, demanded explanations from the Minister of Police, and caused a great number of prisoners to be released. It was necessary to attend to the demands of this committee, because when once it had pronounced its opinion, if the administration had not listened to it, it would have reported the affair to the senate. But it must not be supposed, because this committee of individual liberty made no noise, never vented pompous harangues, or was desirous to be talked of, that it was not of great utility. If the state prisons had contained, like the Bastille, prisoners who were the victims of various intrigues, or of the prince's displeasure, this intervention alone would have sufficed to put an end to the abuse. It is equally erroneous to suppose that the legislative body had no hand in the making of the laws; the legislative committee discussed projected laws with the counsellors of state, and deliberated thereon; their influence was not tumultuous, but it was not on that account the less effectual.

A circumstance which happened at Danzig induced me to frame the decree on the state prisons. An old man had been detained fifty years in a tower at Weiselmunde; he had lost his memory; it was impossible to find out whom he belonged to or why he was detained in prison.

I wished to enforce the strict execution of the law which ordained that in all ordinary cases prisoners should be placed in the hands of the magistrates within twenty-four hours after their arrest; and that in extraordinary cases there should be no exception for more than one year, and that in this case the detention should be authorized by the decree of a Privy Council of sixteen persons.

No people ever enjoyed more extensive civil liberty than the French nation under myself; there is no state in Europe which has not a greater number of prisoners committed to prisons, under different warrants or forms, without being necessarily subjected to a regular trial by the courts. A country where the arbitrary violence of the press gangs, on the quays and in the public streets, is authorized by the laws ought not to boast of enjoying true civil liberty; no such thing exists for the lower classes in England, although it is certainly enjoyed by gentlemen. If the criminal legislation of England be compared with that of France, the abuses and imperfection of the former, compared to the latter, will be easily seen. As to the criminal legislation of Austria, Russia, Prussia, and the other states of Europe, it is sufficient to say that there is no publicity either in the informations, the debates, or the examinations of the parties, and witnesses. My laws are accordingly very dear to the Italians, and to every nation in which they have been put in force: the inhabitants have obtained as a favour that they should continue to be the law of the land.

XVIII

AUSTERLITZ

IN 1805, after having taken 80,000 prisoners and all the equipment of the Austrian army, I thought it expedient to march on Vienna. First, to clear Italy, and fall on the rear of the army of the Archduke Charles, who had beaten the Prince of Essling and had already arrived on the Adige. Secondly, to prevent the Austrian army from joining that of the Emperor Alexander. Thirdly, to break, defeat, and intercept the army of Kutuzov. Having entered Vienna, I heard that the Archduke Charles was in full retreat from Italy, followed by the garrisons he had thrown into Venice and Palmanuova and by the corps of observation left in Carniola; that he was returning to Hungary with only 35,000 men; and that the Emperor Alexander was at Olmütz. I resolved to cross the Danube at Vienna to cut off Kutuzov at Hollabrunn – he had crossed the Danube at Krems, after having been defeated at Amstetten. This movement had succeeded, when Prince Murat allowed himself to be deceived by Prince Bagration, who diverted him with talk of peace and in the mean time escaped from him. I hastened to the spot by night and commanded an attack at break of day, but Bagration had extricated himself during the eighteen hours of the armistice. On 2 December I defeated the combined Russian and Austrian armies, commanded by the Emperors of Austria and Russia, at Austerlitz. I had left the Duke of Treviso at Vienna, with 15,000 men; the Duke of Ragusa, with 20,000 men, was on the Simmering, watching the movements of Prince Charles; the Prince of Eckmühl, with 30,000 men, was on the borders of Hungary. The Duke of Treviso's 15,000 men, the Duke of Ragusa's 20,000, the Prince of Eckmühl's 30,000, and the 40,000 of the Prince of Essling, who had already reached Klagenfurt, thus formed a mass of upwards of 100,000 men opposed to the 35,000 of the Archduke Charles.

Marshal Édouard-Adolphe-Casimir Joseph Mortier, Duke of Treviso,
was the son of a cloth merchant and half-English. One of the few marshals
to be brought back into favour by the Bourbons, he ended his life as
Minister of War.

The manoeuvre of Austerlitz, to engage the Russian army and prevent its junction with the Army of Italy, was conformable to all the rules of the art – it succeeded, and deserved to have succeeded. The Prince of the Moskowa, with the 6th Corps, was in the Tyrol; the Duke of Castiglione, with the 7th Corps, was in reserve in Swabia; Marshal Saint-Cyr was before Venice; the King of Bavaria had a reserve at Munich. As to Prussia, we were not at war with that power. The convention of Potsdam was contingent; it was conditional only on my refusal of the proposals that Count Haugwitz was charged to make. I was at headquarters;

and had I been defeated at Austerlitz, those proposals would have been accepted; and the effect of the loss of that battle would instantly have excited the jealousy of the Court of Berlin against Austria and Russia. Besides, the Prussian army could not have been mobilized in less than six weeks.

If the Emperor of Russia had evacuated Olmütz, plunged into Hungary, and joined the Archduke Charles without giving battle, the army that fought at Austerlitz would then have been reinforced by two divisions of the Prince of Eckmühl's, which did not engage at Austerlitz, by the corps of the Dukes of Ragusa and Treviso, and the Prince of Essling. The advantage would have been wholly on the side of the French, whose army would have been superior in number to the two Allied armies together.

In this campaign the army had three lines of operations: one in Italy, by the Simmering and Klagenfurt; another, also in Italy, by the Simmering, Cratz, and Palma-nuova; and a third on the Rhine, by Saint-Polten, Ens, Brauman, Munich, and Augsburg. Ens was fortified and contained great magazines of provisions and military stores. Braunau, a bridgehead on the Inn, was a fortified place in a condition to withstand fifteen days' open trenches; General Lauriston commanded there, and had magazines, hospitals, and ammunition. Passau, a fortress on the Inn at its junction with the Danube, contained great magazines. General Moulins commanded at Augsburg, a storehouse and magazine on the left bank of the Lech, which he had fortfified and put in a state of defence against any sudden attack.

During the campaigns of Austerlitz, Jena, Friedland, and Moscow, not a single courier was intercepted, not one convoy of sick was taken, and there was no day on which news from Paris did not reach headquarters. An erroneous idea prevails with respect to Moravia and Russia; provisions are plentiful there.

The invasion of England was always regarded as practicable. Once the descent had been effected, London must infallibly have been taken. The French king being in possession of that capital, a very powerful party would have arisen against the oligarchy. Did Hannibal look behind him when he passed the Alps? Or Caesar, when he landed in Epirus or Africa? London is only a few marches from Calais, and the English army, scattered to defend the coasts, could not have united in time to have covered that capital once the descent had been made. Certainly this invasion could not have been effected by an army corps, but it would certainly have succeeded with 160,000 men, provided that they could have presented themselves before London five days after their landing. The flotillas were the only means of landing these 160,000 men in a few hours, and of occupying all the shallows. The passage would have been effected under the protection of a squadron assembled at Martinique and then sailing to Boulogne. If this plan failed in one year, it might succeed in the next. Fifty ships, sailing from Toulon, Brest, Rochefort, L'Orient, and Cadiz and assembled at Martinique, would have arrived before Boulogne and secured the landing in England while the English squadrons were still crossing the seas to protect the Indies.

XIX

WAYS OF WAR

Is cowardice innate? The question is theological – at the sound of the trumpet the horse neighs, draws himself up, and paws the ground in ardour.

Discipline fixes the troops to their colours. They are not to be rendered brave by harangues when the firing begins – the old soldiers scarcely listen to them, the young ones forget them on the first discharge of cannon. Not one of the harangues in Livy was ever really delivered by a general to an army, for not one of them has a striking or impromptu character. A gesture by a beloved general, esteemed by his troops, is as good as the finest harangue in the world. If declamations and arguments are of any use, it is in the course of the campaign, to remove the effects of rumour and false reports, to keep up confidence in the camp, and to furnish materials for the conversation of the bivouacs. The printed order of the day is much more effectual than the harangues of the ancients.

When I used to say, as I rode through the ranks amidst the fire, '*Unfurl those colours? The moment has at last arrived!*', my gesture and manner filled the French soldiers with ardour and impatience.

The Greeks, in the service of the Great King, were not passionately attached to his cause! The Swiss, in the service of France, Spain, and the Italian princes, were not enthusiastic in the cause of their employers! It was not passion that inspired the troops of Frederick the Great, which were in great measure composed of foreigners. A good general, good officers, a judicious organization, able instructions, good and severe discipline – these make good troops, independently of the cause for which they fight. It is, however, true that fanaticism, love of their country, and national glory are useful to animate young troops.

Every offensive war is a war of invasion; every war conducted according to the rules of the art is a methodical war. Plans of campaign may be infinitely modified,

'Perhaps an angel, perhaps a devil – certainly not a man.' Napoleon I,
Emperor of the French.

according to circumstances, the genius of the commander, the nature of the troops, and the topography. There are two sorts of plans of campaign – the good and the bad. The good sometimes fail through fortuitous circumstances, and the bad occasionally succeed through the caprice of fortune.

Were Russia and Spain republican states? Were the governments of Holland and Switzerland despotic?

The wars of Genghis-Khan and Tamerlane were methodical, because they were carried on according to rule, and rational, because their enterprises were proportioned to the strength of their army – the coat of a giant is not that of a pigmy.

Every war ought to be methodical, because every war ought to be conducted in conformity with the principles and rules of the art and with an object. It should be carried on with forces proportioned to the obstacles that are foreseen. There are therefore two sorts of offensive war – one that is well understood and conformable to the principles of the science and one that is ill understood and which violates those principles. Charles XII was beaten by the Tsar, the most despotic of men, because he conducted the war in an ill-considered manner; Tamerlane would have been defeated by Bajazet, if his plan of war had resembled that of the Swedish monarch.

There should be only one army, for unity of command is of the first necessity in war. The army must be kept united. The greatest possible number of forces must be concentrated on the field of battle. *The favourable opportunity must be seized, for fortune is female – if you balk her today, you must not expect to meet with her again tomorrow.*

Make offensive war like Alexander, Hannibal, Gustavus Adolphus, Turenne, Prince Eugène, and Frederick. Read again and again the history of their eighty-eight campaigns and model yourself upon them – that is the only way to become a great commander and to attain the secrets of the art. Your genius, when thus enlightened, will lead you to reject maxims contrary to the principles of those great men.

This was the system of the Hanoverian war from 1758 to 1763. Mixed fortificiations of earth, raised in a fortnight or three weeks, are not secure against assault. How much time is needed to build vaults, to place the army's magazines out of danger from howitzers and bombs?

After the battles of Thrasymene and Cannae, the Romans lost their armies, which could not rally – only a small number of fugitives reached Rome. Yet these battles were fought in the midst of Roman fortresses, only a few days' march from their capital itself. Had Hannibal suffered the same fate, it would have been said that it was because he had advanced too far from Carthage, from his magazines and fortresses. But when routed at Zama, at the very gates of Carthage, he lost his army, as the Romans had lost theirs at Cannae and Thrasymene. After the battle of Marengo, General Melas lost his army. But he did not lack fortresses, he had them everywhere – at Alessandria, Tortona, Genoa, Turin, Fenestrella, and Coni. Mack's army on the Iller was in the midst of its own country, yet it was compelled to lay down arms. And Frederick's veteran army, led by so many heroes – Brunswick, Müllendorf, Russel, Blücher – when defeated at Jena could effect no retreat. In the course of a few days 250,000 men laid down their arms. Yet they did not want for armies of reserve – they had one at Halle and one on the Elbe – or for fortresses. And they were in the centre of their country, not far from their capital! If you are fighting a great battle, seize every possible chance of success, especially if you have to contend with a great commander, for if you are defeated, even if you are surrounded by your magazines and are close to your fortresses, woe to the vanquished!

Unless there is shelter for the magazines, the howitzers will destroy everything and the necessary fieldworks, unless they are covered by inundations, require enormous garrisons. It is much better to fortify the towns.

Fortresses are useful in defensive as well as in offensive war. Certainly a fortress is by itself no substitute for an army, but it may be the only means of delaying, encumbering, weakening, and harassing a victorious enemy.

XX

DIVORCE FROM JOSEPHINE

THE divorce of the Empress Josephine is an event unparalleled in history. It did not, in any respect, alter the union of the two families. It was a painful sacrifice, equally distressing to both consorts, but endured for the interest of the state. Marriage is considered in France as a civil act and a religious sacrament; to effect its dissolution the double intervention of the civil authority and of the Church is requisite. The Senate was the civil authority competent to pronounce the dissolution of my marriage. We two consorts declared our consent to the divorce in a family assembly. This ceremony took place in the grand apartments of the Tuileries. It was extremely interesting – all the spectators were in tears. The consent being certified by the Arch-Chancellor, the dissolution of the marriage was pronounced by the Senate. The Empress left the Tuileries and proceeded to Malmaison. All the furniture of my apartments, in that small but delightful country seat, remained in place. She had, besides, the estate of Navarre, a revenue of two millions per annum, the greater part of which she employed in encouraging the arts and relieving the unfortunate. Malmaison is three leagues from Paris and one from Saint-Cloud. She constantly resided there. In the course of five years, she received three or four visits from me. The whole Court regularly went there. When the Allies entered Paris, the Emperor Francis, the Emperor of Russia, and the King of Prussia paid her frequent visits.

The prince[1] who had been adopted by me to succeed to the crown of Italy after me, in default of legitimate children of my own, was considered as an Italian prince of the blood. He enjoyed a landed property in Italy valued at twenty-five millions. In 1806 he married the eldest daughter of the King of Bavaria, a

---

[1] Josephine's son, Eugène de Beauharnais.

210

*Josephine, six years Napoleon's senior, was the great and abiding passion
of his life. His marriage to her was annulled in 1808 but Napoleon wished her
to retain the title Empress, and keep her own court at Malmaison.
She subsequently died in 1814.*

beautiful and accomplished princess. A cousin of the Empress Josephine,
Stephanie Beauharnais, was married, in 1806, to the Grand Duke of Baden and is
now reigning at Karlsruhe. She has several children, is handsome and intelligent,
and possessses all the various graces of her sex.

Another cousin of the Empress Josephine married the Prince of Aremburg, one
of the first houses in Belgium, enjoying a sovereign principality. This marriage
was not as fortunate as that of the grand duchess, but that was not the fault of the
princess. The prince, who commanded a regiment of chasseurs, distinguished
himself in the war in Spain, where he was made prisoner by the English Army. I
attached some importance to this marriage. I intend to make the prince Governor-

General of the Netherlands and to establish his court at Brussels, in order to give Brussels a new proof of my solicitude. Because of this plan I bought with my own money from the Prince of Saxe-Teschen the château of Lacken and had it magnificently furnished.

Another cousin of Josephine was sought in marriage by Ferdinand VII, to reign over the Spaniards.

My civil marriage was annulled by the decision of the Senate and officials in Paris made the enquiries usual in the Catholic Church and pronounced the dissolution of the marriage. The Court of Rome claimed jurisdiction in the matter but the French clergy declared the claim to be contrary to the privileges of the Gallican Church because a sovereign was only a man in the sight of God, and so should be subject to the jurisdiction of his parish and of his bishop. The archiepiscopal authorities at Vienna had to examine this question before my marriage with the Archduchess of Austria was solemnized. The judgement of the authorities in Paris was communicated to the ecclesiastical court at Vienna, which acquiesced therein.

My divorce excited great attention. My throne, the most elevated in Europe, was the object of the ambition of every reigning family. Three princesses, in particular, seemed to be called to it by political considerations – one from the house of Russia, another from that of Austria, and a third from that of Saxony.

Negotiations on the subject were immediately opened with Russia. Something of the kind had already been hinted at by the Emperor Alexander at Erfurt.

The Count de Narbonne wrote to Fouché, the Minister of the Police, that when he had passed through Vienna he had heard about my proposed marriage and it had been suggested to him that I thought an alliance with an archduchess might suit the views of Austria. I could take no direct step without knowing how the Emperor Alexander stood disposed. I had Prince Schwarzenberg, the Austrian ambassador at Paris, sounded out. This private negotiation was conducted in such a manner that I was not involved, in case any difficulties should arise respecting my marriage with the sister of the Emperor Alexander. These difficulties did, in fact, arise; there were differences of opinion about the marriage in the Russian imperial family. The Emperor Alexander himself did not hesitate, but it was required that the princess who was to become my bride should have a Russian chapel in the palace of the Tuileries, with her own priests, and the free exercise of her religion. Negotiations had taken place on this subject and answers from St Petersburg were expected, on receipt of which a decision was to be made. (It had been ascertained that the Austrian ambassador would, at a proper time, whether he had received instructions or not, give consent to the projected alliance.) The answers arrived. Prince Schwarzenberg was absent on a hunting-party, but a courier was sent to him and he hurried back to Paris.

An extraordinary Privy Council was summoned for 4 o'clock in the afternoon. The despatches from St Petersburg were read and the choice put before it. Opinions were divided between a Saxon, Russian, and Austrian princess. The Austrian option was favoured by the majority and was dictated by the weighty consideration of the maintenance of general peace. It was remarked that of all the powers in Europe, Austria was the one that would most fear the intentions of France towards her. The proposed alliance would disperse all those jealousies, furnish an indisputable ground for confidence, and be the pledge of a permanent peace. These considerations were decisive, and the marriage with the archduchess was preferred. At 6 o'clock in the evening I instructed Prince Eugène to make a formal request to Prince Schwarzenberg. At the same time I gave my Minister for Foreign Affairs powers to sign, with that ambassador, my marriage contract with the Archduchess Marie-Louise using that between Louis XVI and Marie Antoinette as a precedent. At 7 o'clock, Prince Eugène reported the success of his mission and in the course of the evening the marriage contract was signed. The Prince of Neufchatel was sent to Vienna to ask for the archduchess's hand in the solemn accustomed forms. Then the Archduke Charles, as my authorized proxy, married the Archduchess Marie-Louise. Archduke the Grand Duke of Würzburg, now Grand Duke of Tuscany, represented the Emperor of Austria on the occasion of the marriage at Paris.

Prince Clemens Wenzel Nepomuk Lothar von Metternich-Winneburg, Foreign Minister of Austria. He initially supported Napoleon, and arranged the marriage of Napoleon with Marie-Louise, the Emperor's daughter. But in 1812 he took Austria into the war against France.

'The art of war is to gain time . . .', but Napoleon also needed an heir. The marriage of Napoleon and the 18-year old Marie-Louise of Austria produced the infant King of Rome.

I went to receive the archduchess at Compiègne. The civil marriage was celebrated at Saint-Cloud, the religious marriage in the grand saloon of the Musée Napoleon. Five or six cardinals, after having assisted at the civil marriage at Saint-Cloud, declared that they could not assist in the religious marriage, from respect for the Holy See, which ought to be concerned in the marriages of sovereigns. The French bishops, and the majority of the cardinals, rejected this claim with indignation; the Pope himself censured these cardinals, who were exiled from Paris, and called the Black Cardinals, because they were, for a certain period, prohibited by the Holy See from wearing red.

Splendid fêtes were given on this occasion. Prince Schwarzenberg, the Austrian ambassador, gave one in the name of his master. For this purpose he had a ballroom erected in the garden of his hotel. In the midst of the ball, some gauze draperies caught fire and the apartment was instantly ablaze. I retired leisurely, holding the Empress by the arm. Prince Schwarzenberg remained near her. She set out for Saint-Cloud. I remained in the garden until the morning. Nothing could stop the progress of the conflagration, in which several people died. The Princess Schwarzenberg, of the family of Aremberg, wife to the ambassador's brother, escaped from the ballroom, but fearing for the safety of one of her children she returned and was stifled while trying to escape through a door leading into the hotel. In the morning, the remains of this unfortunate lady were found consumed to ashes. Prince Kurakin, the Russian ambassador, was severely hurt.

In 1770, at the fête given by the city of Paris in celebration of the marriage of Louis XVI to Marie Antoinette, 2,000 people were precipitated into the ditches of the Champs Elysées, where they perished. When Louis XVI and Marie Antoinette afterwards suffered death on the scaffold, this terrible accident was remembered and people looked upon it as an omen of what afterwards took place – for it is chiefly to the insurrection of that great capital that the Revolution is to be attributed. The unfortunate result of the entertainment given by the Austrian ambassador, on a similar occasion, in honour of the alliance of two houses in the persons of myself and Maria-Louise, seemed a sinister omen. The misfortunes of France are wholly to be attributed to the change of policy in the Austrian Cabinet. Although I was not superstitious, I myself experienced a painful presentiment on this occasion. The day after the battle of Dresden, when we were pursuing the Austrian army, a prisoner told me that he had heard that Prince Schwarzenberg had been killed. I replied, 'He was a brave man, but there is this consolation for his death, that it is now evident that the threatening omen of his ball pointed at him and not at me.' Two hours later it was learned at headquarters that it was Moreau, and not Prince Schwarzenberg, who had been killed the day before.

XXI

WAR IN SPAIN AND RUSSIA

THE Spanish war ended in 1809. In three months I had beaten and dispersed the four Spanish armies of 160,000 men, taken Madrid and Saragossa, and forced General Moore to re-embark, after losing half his army, his stores, and military chests. Spain was conquered. When the war of Vienna obliged me to return to France, the war of Spain recommenced. King Joseph was not competent to direct it. England made unheard of efforts and her armies obtained some success in Portugal. Spain was surrounded by sea on three sides and English fleets unexpectedly carried new forces into Catalonia, Biscay, Portugal, the Kingdom of Valencia, and Cadiz.

The error committed in Spain was not that of proceeding too rapidly, but that of proceeding too slowly after my departure. Had I remained there a few months, I would have taken Lisbon and Cadiz, united all parties, and pacified the country. My armies never lacked military stores, clothing, or provisions. The Duke of Dalmatia's army in Andalusia, the Duke of Albufera's in the east, and that of the north, were very fine, of great strength, and abundantly supplied. The guerillas were not formed until two years after, when they arose in consequence of the disorders and abuses which had crept into the whole army, except the corps of Marshal Suchet, which occupied the Kingdom of Valencia. The Anglo-Portuguese army became as skilful in manoeuvres as the French army; the latter was afterwards defeated through the accidents of war, manoeuvres, and strategical errors, at Talavera, Salamanca, and Vitoria. Spain was lost after a struggle of five years. The argument on the want of fortresses is extremely mis-placed – the French Army had taken them all. The Spaniards formerly offered the same resistance to the Romans. The people of conquered nations become the subjects of the victor only through a mixture of policy and severity and by being

---

amalgamated with the army. These points were not successfully managed in Spain. If the French had amused themselves, as the author of 'Considerations on the Art of War' says they ought to have done, with forming establishments on the Ebro, instead of marching on the Somosierra and on Madrid, Burgos, and Benavente to drive out the English, after the victories of Vitoria, Espinose, Tudela, and Burgos, they would within two months have had 200,000 English, Portuguese, and Spaniards in line against them, and would have been driven before them beyond the Pyrenees.

After the re-embarkation of the English army, the King of Spain remained inactive, wasting four months. He should have marched on Cadiz, Valencia, and Lisbon – political means would then have done the rest. No-one can deny that had the Court of Austria not declared war and had allowed me to remain four months longer in Spain, all would have been over. *The presence of a general is indispensable – he is the head, the whole of an army.* It was not the Roman army that subdued Gaul, but Caesar himself: nor was it the Carthaginian army that made the Republic tremble at the gates of Rome, but Hannibal himself; neither was it the Macedonian army which reached the Indus, but Alexander; it was not the French army which carried the war to the Weser and the Inn, but Turenne; nor was it the Prussian army which, for seven years, defended Prussia against the three greatest powers of Europe, it was Frederick the Great.

Joseph Bonaparte, eldest brother of Napoleon was trained as a barrister. As King of Naples before Murat he made a number of necessary reforms and it was with great reluctance he gave up Naples to become King of Spain. He retired in exile to America, then returned to Florence where he died.

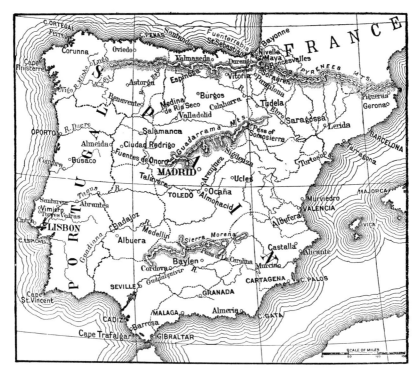

Map of the Spanish Campaign.

THE WAR IN RUSSIA

The Russians lost the battle and Moscow was taken; but had they won the battle, Moscow would have been saved! Then 100,000 Russians – men, women, and children – would not have perished in the snow in the neighbouring woods. Russia would not have seen its proud capital, the work of centuries, annihilated in a single week and property to the value of hundreds of millions buried under its ruins. Had it not been for the burning of Moscow, an event unprecedented in history, Alexander would have been compelled to make peace. The results of the battle of the Moskva[1] were of immense importance. Never was it more expedient to risk a battle than on this occasion – it was demanded by the court, in despair at the ravaging and burning of the provinces; by the nobility; and by the army, which was fatigued, weakened, and disheartened by so many retreats.

It is not true that the Russians voluntarily retreated as far as Moscow in order to draw the French army into the interior of their country. They abandoned Vilna because it was impossible for them to effect the junction of their armies

---

[1] More familiar to British historians as the battle of Borodino.

before that place. They wanted to rally on the entrenched camp they had constructed on both banks of the Dvina, but Bagration, with half the army, could not reach it. The Prince of Eckmühl's march on Minsk, Borisov, and Mohilov separated Barclay de Tolly's army from that of Bagration, which obliged de Tolly to march on Vitebsk and thence on Smolensk to join Bagration. After effecting this junction, he marched with 180,000 men on Vitebsk, to give battle to the French army. It was then that I executed the fine manoeuvre which was the counterpart of one I directed at Landshut in 1809 – using the forest of Babinoritski as a shield, I turned the left of the Russian army, crossed the Dnieper, and advanced on Smolensk. I reached the city twenty-four hours before the Russian army, which retreated precipitately, but a division of 15,000 Russians, who happened to be in Smolensk, succeeded in defending it for one day, which gave Barclay de Tolly time to reach it.

Had the French army succeeded in surprising Smolensk, it would have crossed the Dnieper there and attacked the Russian army in the rear, while it was in disorder and not united. This grand stroke was missed, but I still gained great advantage from my manoeuvre, which led to the battle of Smolensk, in which Poniatowski and the Poles covered themselves with glory. Barclay de Tolly, driven back beyond the Dnieper, came to a determination to give battle.

The history of the campaign of Russia will never be well known, because the Russians either do not write at all or write without the slightest regard to truth, while the French are seized with a strange mania for dishonouring and decrying their own glory. The Russian war became a necessary consequence of the Continental system the moment the Emperor Alexander violated the conventions of Tilsit and Erfurt, but a consideration of much greater importance determined me to begin it. I thought that the French Empire, which I had created by so many victories, would be dismembered at my death and the sceptre of Europe would pass into the hands of a tsar, unless I drove back the Russians beyond the Dnieper and raised up the throne of Poland, the natural barrier of the empire. In 1812 Austria, Prussia, Germany, Switzerland, and Italy, marched under the French eagles. Was it not natural that I should think the moment had come to consolidate the immense edifice I had raised, but on which Russia would lean with all her weight as long as she could send her numerous armies, at pleasure, to the Oder? Alexander was young and vigorous, like his empire; it was to be presumed that he would survive me. This is the whole secret of that war. No personal feeling was ever concerned in it, as pamphleteers have pretended. The campaign of Russia was the most glorious, the most difficult, and the most honourable to the Gauls of all that are recorded in ancient and modern history. The Russians are very brave troops and their whole army was united. At the battle of Moskva they had 170,000 men, including the Moscow troops. Kutosov had taken up a fine position, and occupied it judiciously. All advantages were on his side – superiority in infantry, cavalry, and artillery, an excellent position, and a great number of redoubts. Nonetheless he was vanquished. Intrepid heroes – Murat, Ney, Poniatowski – it is to you that the glory of the victory is due! What

Marshal Jozef Anton, Prince Poniatowski, drowned trying to swim a river after protecting the French rear during the evacuation of Leipzig in 1813. He was Napoleon's only Polish marshal.

great, what brilliant actions might history cull from these events! She might tell how those dauntless cuirassiers forced the redoubts and sabred the cannoneers at their guns; she might relate the heroic devotion of Montbrun and Caulaincourt, who met their death in the midst of glory; she might say what our exposed artillerymen achieved in the open field against more numerous batteries protected by good breastworks; and she might record how the intrepid infantry, at the most critical moment, needed no encouragemernt from their general, but exclaimed 'Be not alarmed; your soldiers have sworn to conquer this day, and they will conquer!' Will some few particles of so much glory reach posterity? Or will falsehood and calumny prevail?

The idea of burning a city almost as extensive as Paris, containing 300,000 souls, was not regarded as a possibility. In fact it would have been more reasonable to make peace than to be guilty of such a piece of barbarity. The Russian army gave battle three days' march in advance of Moscow and was defeated. The French army entered the town and was master of all its riches for eight and forty hours. The resources it found there were immense – the inhabitants had remained, the five hundred palaces of the nobles were still furnished, the household officers and servants stayed on, not even the diamonds and trinkets of the ladies had been removed. Most of the rich proprietors who had fled the city had left letters addressed to the general who should occupy their house, declaring that in a few days, when the first moments of disturbance should be over, they would return home. It was then that eight or nine hundred police, entrusted with the watch and fire-engines, took advantage of a violent wind that arose and set fire to every quarter of the town. A great part of it, built of wood, contained warehouses of brandy, oil and other combustible materials. All the fire-engines had been carried off – the city kept several hundred, the service being very carefully organized, but only one could be found. For some days the army struggled in vain against the fire but everything was burnt. The inhabitants who had remained in the town escaped to the woods or to their country houses; none remained but the lowest rabble, who stayed for the sake of pillage. This great and superb city became a desert and a sink of desolation and crime. The French might have adopted the plan of marching on St Petersburg. The Russian court heard this and had sent its archives and most valuable treasures to London. It had also directed Admiral Tchitchagov's army to cover that capital. Considering that it is as far from Moscow to St Petersburg as from Smolensk to St Petersburg, I preferred going to pass the winter at Smolensk on the borders of Lithuania, reserving my march on St Petersburg to the spring. I began my march on Smolensk by again attacking and defeating Kutusov's army at Maloyaroslavets. I continued the march, unimpeded, until the ice, the snow, and the cold killed 30,000 horses in one night, and obliged the army to abandon the waggons. It was

A wounded cuirassier quitting the field. The Empire fed upon such images of high romance.

221

this that caused the disasters on that march, for it ought not to be called a retreat, since the army was victorious and could equally well have marched on St Petersburg, Kaluga, or Tula, which Kutusov would in vain have attempted to cover. The army would have wintered at Smolensk had not Prince Schwarzenberg abandoned it and marched on Warsaw, which allowed Admiral Tchitchagov to proceed to the Berezina, and to menace the grand magazines and depots of Vilna, where there were provisions for the army for four months, clothing for 50,000 men, horses, ammunition, and a division of 10,000 men to guard them. General Dabrowski, who occupied the fort of Borisov and the bridge of the Berezina, could not defend them – he had only 9,000 men, and was dislodged. Admiral Tchitchagov crossed the Berezina to march to the Dvina, but attempted no attack on Vilna. He was met by the Duke of Reggio, who defeated him, and drove him back on the Berezina, after having taken all his baggage. In his consternation the Admiral burnt the bridge of Borisov.

Had it been August and not November the army would have marched on St Petersburg. It was retiring to Smolensk not because it was beaten but so that it could winter in Poland. Had it been summer, neither Admiral Tchitchagov's nor Kutusov's army would have dared to approach within ten days' march of the French army, on pain of immediate destruction.

Originally a sergeant in the royal army, Marshal Nicolas-Charles Oudinot, Duke of Reggio, rose rapidly during the Revolution. He was wounded in battle at least twenty-two times! A soldier for nearly sixty years, he transferred his allegiance to the Bourbons and ended his career as a governor of the Invalides.

XXII

THE RETURN
FROM MOSCOW

IN the Russian campaign, the army's magazines were not on the Vistula, fifty days' march from Moscow. Those of the first line were at Smolensk, ten days' march from Moscow; those of the second line at Minsk and Vilna, eight marches from Smolensk; those of the third line at Kovno, Grodno, and Bialystok; those of the fourth line at Elblag, Marienwerder, Thorn, Plock, Modlin, and Warsaw; those of the fifth line at Danzig, Bamberg, and Posen; those of the sixth line at Stettin, Cüstrin, and Glogow. Out of 400,000 men who crossed the Niemen, 240,000 remained in reserve between that river and the Dnieper; 160,000 passed Smolensk and marched on Moscow; out of these 160,000 men, 40,000 remained in echelon between Smolensk and Mozhaisk. It was therefore the natual course to retreat on Poland. No general ever represented to me the necessity of halting on the Berezina; they all felt that when once I was master of Moscow I would put an end to the war. As far as Smolensk, I was manoeuvring in a country which was as well disposed towards me as France itself; the population and authorities were on my side; I was able to obtain men, horses, provisions; and Smolensk is a fortified town. In my march on Moscow, I never had an enemy in my rear. During the twenty days that I remained in that capital, not one of my couriers or convoys of artillery was intercepted; not one of my entrenched positions, of which there was one at every station, was attacked; the convoys of artillery and military equipage arrived without any accident. If Moscow had not been burnt, the Emperor Alexander would have been compelled to make peace. After the conflagration of Moscow, if the severe cold had not set in fifteen days earlier than usual, the army would have returned to Smolensk without loss and there it would have had nothing to fear from the Russian armies beaten at the Moskva and at Maloyaroslavets, which had great need of rest. It was well known that it would be

Alexander I, Tsar of Russia.

cold in December and January, but there was reason to think, from the rise in temperature that had occurred in the twenty preceding years, that the thermometer would not fall six degrees below freezing point during November. The premature cold affected both armies equally. The French army needed only three days more to have accomplished its retreat in good order, but in those three days it lost 30,000 horses. The event might justify the censure of myself for having remained four days too long at Moscow, but I was induced to do so by political reasons and I thought I should have time to return into Poland – the autumns are very late in the North.

When the army left Moscow, it carried with it provisions sufficient for twenty days, which was more than enough to enable it to reach Smolensk, where it could have obtained abundant supplies to subsist on until its arrival at Minsk or Vilna. But all the teams of the convoys, and most of the artillery and cavalry horses perished, every department of the army became disorganized; it was an army no longer. It became impossible to take up a position nearer than Vilna. Prince Schwarzenberg's and General Reynier's corps, which were on the Vistula, instead of resting on Minsk as they ought to have done, retired on Warsaw, thus abandoning the army. Had they proceeded to Minsk, they would have been joined by Dabrowski's division, which, being unable to defend Borisov alone, could not prevent Admiral Tchitchagov from occupying that place. It was the admiral's plan not to take possession of the Berezina but to proceed to the Dvina to cover St Petersburg. It was through this fortuitous circumstance that the Duke of Reggio met with him, beat him, and drove him back to the right bank of the Berezina. Tchitchagov was again defeated after the crossing of the Berezina – Doumerc's cuirassiers took 1,800 of his men in a charge.

When the army was within two days' march of Vilna, and no further dangers threatened it, I conceived that the urgency of affairs required my presence in Paris – only there could I dictate to Prussia and Austria. Had I delayed, the passage might have been closed against me. I left the King of Naples and the Prince of Neuchâtel in command of the army. The Guard was then entire and the army contained more than 80,000 combatants, not counting the Duke of Tarento's corps, which was on the Dvina. The Russian army, at the utmost, did not now exceed 50,000 men. Flour, biscuits, wine, meat, dried pulse, and forage abounded at Vilna. According to the report of the stores of provisions, presented

Marshal Étienne-Jacques-Joseph-Alexandre Macdonald, Duke of Tarento.

225

to me on my passage through that city, there then remained 4,000,000 rations of flour, 3,600,000 rations of meat, and 9,000,000 rations of wine or brandy. Considerable stores of clothing and other articles, as well as of ammunition, had likewise been established. Had I remained with the army, or delegated the command to Prince Eugène, it would never have retreated beyond Vilna – there was a corps of reserve at Warsaw and another at Königsberg. In the event a few Cossacks intimidated the French commanders and Vilna was evacuated by night in a disorderly manner. It is from this period in particular that the great losses of this campaign may be dated. It was a misfortune that at that time I was, in all the highly critical circumstances, required to be with the army and at Paris at the same time. Nothing was, or could have been more totally unforeseen by me than the senseless conduct that was adopted at Vilna.

The four hundred leagues between the Rhine and the Dnieper were occupied by friends and allies – from the Rhine to the Elbe, by the Saxons; thence to the Niemen by the Poles; thence to the Dnieper by the Lithuanians. The army had four lines of fortresses – those of the Rhine, the Elbe, and the Vistula, and Pillau, Vilna, Grodno, and Minsk on the Niemen. Until it crossed the Dnieper at Smolensk it was in friendly country. Between Smolensk and Moscow were a hundred leagues of hostile country – Muscovy. Smolensk had been captured and fortified and had been the pivot of the march on Moscow. Hospitals for 3,000 men were established there, with magazines of military stores, which contained more than 250,000 cartridges for cannon and considerable supplies of clothing and provisions. Between the Vistula and the Dnieper 240,000 men were left; only 160,000 crossed the bridge at Smolensk to march on Moscow. Of these, 40,000 remained to guard the magazines, hospitals, and depots of Dorogholowy, Vyazma, Chjot, and Mozhaisk; 100,000 entered Moscow; and 20,000 had been killed in the march and in the great battle of the Moskva, in which 50,000 Russians perished.

Not one sick soldier or straggler, not a single courier or convoy, was lost in this campaign from Mentz to Moscow. Not a day passed without intelligence from France, nor was Paris a single day without receiving letters from the army. At the battle of Smolensk more than 60,000 cannon shots were fired, double that number were fired at Moskva, and the consumption in minor actions was considerable, and yet, on leaving Moscow, every piece was provided with 350 rounds. There was such a superabundance of aummunition and cartridge boxes that 500 were burnt in the Kremlin, where several hundred thousands pounds of powder and 60,000 muskets were also destroyed. There never was a lack of ammunition, which is highly creditable to Generals Lariboissière and Eblé, who commanded the artillery. Never did the officers of that corps serve with more honour or show greater talent than in this campaign.

It reveals little knowledge of Russia to imagine that the inhabitants took part in war. The peasants are slaves and the lords, dreading their revolt, removed them to lands in the interior of the empire, much as horses or herds of oxens are driven.

The slaves were very friendly to the French, from whom they expected their liberty. The burghers, or slaves who had been enfranchised and inhabited the little towns, were much disposed to put themselves at the head of an insurrection against the nobility. Because of this threat the Russians set fire to all the towns along the army's routes, causing immense loss, independently of that of Moscow. I always preserved my line of operations. I received intelligence and convoys from France daily. I placed three-fourths of my army in reserve, between the Vistula and the camp of Moscow. I acted with 400,000 men.

The march from Smolensk to Moscow was made in the belief that to save that capital the enemy would fight a battle, that he would be defeated, that Moscow would be taken, and that Alexander, to preserve or deliver his capital, would make peace. I wanted to restore the Kingdom of Poland, because it was the only way to erect a barrier against that formidable empire which threatened sooner or later to subjugate Europe. If Alexander does not, like Paul, turn his attention to India, to acquire wealth and furnish employment for his numerous nations of Cossacks, Calmucks, and other barbarians, who have acquired a taste for luxury in France and Germany, he will be obliged, in order to prevent a revolution in Russia, to make an irruption into the south of Europe. Should he succeed in merging Poland with Russia, and in reconciling the Poles to the Russian government, all must bend beneath his yoke. Every country in Europe, and England in particular, will then regret their having neglected to re-establish the Kingdom of Poland independently of Russia, and their having made it a Russian province at the Congress of Vienna; but the English ministers were then blinded by their hatred of men. All they did was impolitic. Had the Congress of Vienna made peace with me, Europe would now have been in a state of tranquillity, and the revolutionary spirit would not be undermining every throne. In France, it would have been repressed and satisfied by new institutions.

Almost all historians have treated the Russian campaign as an unmitigated and unnecessary disaster. Here Napoleon sets the record straight. These pages, lost in the Notes of the 1823 edition, are of great significance. Had Napoleon after invading Russia, defeating its army at Borodino and occupying its capital for five weeks, then razed it to the ground, as Hitler had intended to do, this would have been regarded as a successful if ruthless conquest. The fact is that it was abandoned by the government and aristocracy, then burnt to the ground by some of the remaining inhabitants. Napoleon withdrew, and devastating weather conditions were experienced during his withdrawal. This does not alter Napoleon's claim to have achieved what he set out to do. This was to teach Russia a lesson not to interfere in French affairs in future when his son should become Emperor and to punish the Tsar for opening his ports to Britain. His view that he left a defeated and humiliated Russia with its capital in ruins is hard to ignore. It is the word 'retreat' which has given the impression of defeat. It was admittedly a harrassed return, beginning with the withdrawal onto Smolensk. It was not as if the French had ever intended to occupy Russia and administer it from Moscow. They were a successful invading army, not an army of occupation. If Hitler had succeeded, where Napoleon did not ever intend to remain, it would have been a very different story. (S. de C.)

XXIII

THE BATTLE OF LEIPZIG

O F the 250,000 men composing my army in this campaign, 50,000 were Saxons, Westphalians, Bavarians, Württembergers, Badenese, Hessians, or troops of the Grand Duchy of Berg who were very ill disposed and proved rather detrimental than useful. The remaining 200,000 were young troops, particularly the horse, except for the Guard, the Poles, two or three regiments of light cavalry, and four or five of heavy cavalry. The want of light cavalry prevented our gaining intelligence of the enemy's movements.

We had a bridge over the Elbe at Dresden, one at Meissen, one at Torgau, one at Wittenberg, one at Magdeburg, and one at Hamburg. The movements on Dresden were foreseen; everything was done to draw the enemy there. I had caused works to be raised, roads opened, and bridges constructed on the Elbe before Königstein, to facilitate the communication between that place and Stolpen.

The victories of Lützen and Wurzen, on 2 and 21 May, had re-established the reputation of the French arms. The King of Saxony had been brought back in triumph to his capital; the enemy had been driven from Hamburg; one of the corps of the Grand Army was at the gates of Berlin; and the Imperial headquarters was at Breslau. The Russian and Prussian armies, greatly discouraged, had no choice but to go back across the Vistula, when Austria, interfering, advised France to sign an armistice. I returned to Dresden. The Emperor of Austria left Vienna and proceeded into Bohemia; the Emperor of Russia and the King of Prussia stationed themselves at Schweidnitz. The conferences began. Prince Metternich proposed the Congress of Prague; it was accepted, but it was only a pretext – the Court of Vienna had already entered into engagements with Russia and Prussia. Austria was to have declared herself in May, but the unexpected successes of the French army compelled her to proceed more circumspectly. Notwithstanding all the efforts she had made, her army was deficient in numbers, ill-organized, and in no condition to take the field. Prince Metternich demanded the Illyrian Provinces, a frontier with the Kingdom of Italy, and the Grand Duchy of Warsaw; he wanted me to give up the Protectorate of the Confederation of the Rhine, the mediation of the Swiss Confederacy, the population of the 32nd military division, and the departments of Holland. These extravagant conditions were evidently brought forward in expectation that they would be rejected. The Duke of Vicenza, however, proceeded to the Congress of Prague and the negotiations began. All efforts to induce the powers to abandon some part of their pretensions resulted only in some insignificant modifications. I resolved to make important concessions, and to send them to the Emperor of Austria by Count Bubna, who resided at Dresden. I agreed to relinquish the Illyrian Provinces (divided from the Kingdom of Italy by the Isonzo), the Grand Duchy of Warsaw, and the titles of Protector of the Confederation of the Rhine and Mediator of the Swiss Confederacy. As to Holland and the Hanseatic towns, I engaged only to retain these possessions until peace, and as means of compensation to obtain from England the restoration of the French colonies.

Frederich William III, King of Prussia.

'The only man in Prussia' was Napoleon's description of Queen Louisa, wife of Frederich William.

When Count Bubna arrived at Prague, the term for the duration of the armistice had expired several hours before; on this ground Austria declared her adhesion to the coalition and the war recommenced.

The striking victory gained at Dresden by the French army on 27 August, over the army commanded by the three sovereigns, was followed by the disasters of Marshal Macdonald's corps in Lusatia, and of that of General Vandamme in Bohemia. The superiority, however, was always on the side of the French army, which was supported on the fortresses of Torgau, Wittenberg and Magdeburg.

Denmark had just concluded, at Dresden, a treaty of offensive and defensive alliance with France; and the Prince of Eckmühl's army at Hamburg was reinforced by a contingent of Danish troops. In October I left Dresden, and proceeded towards Magdeburg by the left bank of the Elbe, in order to deceive the enemy. My plan was to recross the Elbe at Wittenberg and to march on Berlin. Several corps had already arrived at Wittenberg and the enemy-held bridges at Dessau which had been destroyed, when a letter from the King of Württemberg confirmed doubts about the loyalty of the Court of Munich. The King of Bavaria had suddenly changed sides and, without any declaration of war, or any previous notice, and in consequence of the treaty of Reid, the two armies, Austrian and Bavarian, cantoned on the banks of the Inn, had joined into a single camp. These 80,000 men, under the command of Genereal Wrede, were marching on the Rhine; that Württemberg, compelled by the force of this army, was obliged to add its contingent; and that it must be expected that 100,000 men would shortly surround Mentz.

On receiving this unexpected intelligence I thought it necessary to change the plan of campaign that I had been meditating for two months, and according to which my fortresses and magazines were arranged. This plan was to throw the Allies between the Elbe and the Saale, and, by manoeuvring under the protection of the fortresses and magazines of Torgau, Wittenberg, Magdeburg, and Hamburg, to contain the war between the Elbe and the Oder (the French army possessing the fortresses of Glogau, Custrin and Stettin on the Oder), and, according to circumstances, to relieve Danzig, Thorn, and Modlin on the Vistula. Such success was to be expected from this vast plan as would have dissolved the coalition and confirmed all the princes of Germany in fidelity to their alliance with France. If Bavaria had, as was with reason expected, delayed changing sides only by a fortnight, she would not have changed at all.

The armies met on the field of Leipzig, on 16 October. The French army was victorious, and would still have been so on the 18th, notwithstanding the check sustained on the 16th by the Duke of Ragusa, had it not been for the defection of the Saxon army which, occupying one of the most important positions of the line, crossed over to the enemy with a battery of sixty guns, which it turned against the French army. Such an unheard-of piece of treachery might have been expected to produce the destruction of the army and secure the Allies all the honours of the day. I hastened up with half my Guards, repulsed the Saxons and Swedes, and drove them from their positions. The battle of the 18th terminated; I fixed my bivouacs beyond the field of battle, which remained in the possession of the French.

At Leipzig the Young Guard was engaged, under the Dukes of Reggio and Treviso. The Middle Guard, commanded by General Curial, attacked and routed the Austrian corps under General Merfield, who was made prisoner. The cavalry of the Guard, with General Nansouty at its head, went to the right, repulsed the Austrian cavalry, and took a great number of prisoners. The artillery of the Guard, directed by Count Drouot, was engaged throughout the day. Of all the Guards, the old infantry alone remained constantly drawn up in line, posted on an eminence where their presence was necessary, but there they never had to form the square.

In the course of the night the French army began its movement to place itself behind the Elster, in direct communication with Erfurt, whence it expected the convoys of ammunition of which it stood in need. It had fired more than 150,000 cannon-shot in the battles of the 16th and 18th. Owing to the treachery of several German corps belonging to the Confederation of the Rhine, misled by the example set the day before by the Saxons, and to the accident of the bridge at Leipzig, which a sergeant blew up before he had received orders from his commanding officer, the army, although victorious, suffered through these fatal occurrences the losses commonly resulting from the most disastrous actions. It recrossed the Saale by the bridge at Weissenfels. There it was to have rallied and waited for ammunition from Erfurt, which was abundantly supplied, but intelligence being received that the Austro-Bavarian army had, by forced marches, reached the Maine, it became necessary to meet it.

On 30 October, the French army came up with the enemy drawn up in line of battle before Hanau, intercepting the road to Frankfurt. Although his force was strong and occupied fine positions, it was overthrown, completly routed, and driven from Hanau. The French army continued its retreat behind the Rhine, which it recrossed on the 2nd of November.

Marshal August-Frédéric-Louis Viesse de Marmont, created Duke of Ragusa, secretly surrended his corps to the Allies in 1814. From this action came the verb raguser – *to betray.*

Conferences took place at Frankfurt, between Baron Saint-Aignan, Prince Metternich, Count Nesselrode, and Lord Aberdeen. The Allies laid down as the primary basis of peace that I should renounce the protectorate of the Confederation of the Rhine and to give up Poland and the departments of the Elbe; that France should remain entire within her natural limits of the Elbe and the Rhine, and that a frontier in Italy should be determined on to separate France from the states of the House of Austria. I agreed to this. The Duke of Vicenza set out for Frankfurt, but the Congress of Frankfurt was merely a stratagem brought forward, like the Congress of Prague, in hopes that France would refuse. A new text was wanted for a manifesto to work upon the public mind; for at the very moment when these conciliatory proposals were being made, the Allies violated the neutrality of the cantons, entered Switzerland, refused to receive the French plenipotentiary at Frankfurt, and pointed out Châtillon-sur-Seine as the place for the early meeting of the Congress. They gave it to be understood that the basis of negotiation must be the surrender of all Italy, of Holland, Belgium, the departments of the Rhine, and Savoy – which would put France back within her boundaries of before 1792. A draft treaty handed in on 15 February further required the fortresses of Huninguen, Befort, and Besançon to be immediately surrendered to them. Such demands were certainly not of a nature to be admitted without discussion. The negotiations were still proceeding when the Allies declared the Congress dissolved.

I wished for peace, but I would never have consented to conditions derogatory to the national honour, and it was only in this sense that I could have said I would sooner have cut off my hand. I must have wished for peace; for immediately after the battle of Brienne, when the conferences were about to open, I wrote from Troyes to my plenipotentiary at Châtillon, giving him all necessary powers and authorities, in short *carte blanche*, to conclude peace, in order to stop the progress of the enemy, so fatal to our provinces, to save the capital, and to avoid a great battle, the loss of which would ruin all the hopes of the nation. These absolute full powers, this blank signature, I gave on 4 or 5 February; I did not revoke them until after my victories; thus, during upwards of a fortnight, peace might have been concluded and signed at Châtillon, if the Allies had wished it, without any necessity for the French plenipotentiary to take new instructions from me. I would not then have been strong enough to refuse to ratify a treaty already signed. But peace was not the object of the Allies; they wanted to wreak their revenge for the triumphs of France; they remembered those days of mourning when they had beheld the French eagle hovering over the capitals. The propositions of Châtillon, like those of Dresden and Frankfurt, were a mere bait held out to delude their own people, and to sow division in France.

The French plenipotentiary required precise instructions respecting the sacrifices to which I might consent. I was at Nogent-sur-Seine. The Grand Marshal Bertrand, and the Duke of Bassano, who were near me, pressed me to accede to the request of the Duke of Vicenza, still leaving me at liberty to depart from those instructions, and to use the *carte blanche* which had been given him. I had a long conference, which lasted during a great part of the night, with this minister in my closet. It was decided that we ought not to hesitate to abandon Belgium and even the left bank of the Rhine, if peace could only be obtained at this price; but if a treaty could be entered into by means of one of these concessions only, Belgium was to be abandoned first, however desirous I was to preserve that fine province, because the English ministry, whose principal object would have been attained, would have feared to risk such a national advantage by supporting the demand of other concessions; and besides, Belgium might again be conquered at a more prosperous period, at the expense of a maritime war only, which would not compromise the safety of the empire, whilst no attempt could be made to reconquer the left bank of the Rhine, if declared indispensable. Italy, Piedmont, Genoa, and the state of possession to be established in Germany, were sacrifices made in advance.

I was to have signed this despatch at 7 o'clock in the morning; but at 5 o'clock I received a report on the movements of the Russian and Prussian army, which induced me to think that the face of affairs would shortly be changed by glorious events; I deferred my answer to the Duke of Vicenza, and set out for Champ

Hugues-Bernard Maret, Duke of Bassano.

Henri-Gratien, Count Bertrand.

Albert. A series of unexpected triumphs raised my hopes: instead of the great battle I had wished to avoid, I gained five memorable victories; the enemy's army lost upwards of 90,000 men in ten days. Instead of having to save my capital by peace, I thought I had saved it by arms. The state of affairs was altered, and I changed my determination. I wrote to Nangis to my plenipotentiary to withdraw his absolute powers, and desired him to take his orders in future respecting every point of the negotiation, which thenceforth proceeded in the usual forms. I no longer had to anticipate the demands of the Allies by concessions, but to ascertain, by means of the negotiations proceeding at Châtillon, what were the real intentions of the Allies, and the sacrifices which might be avoided, by means of the advantages which had recently been obtained.

Towards the end of February, I received the minutes of a preliminary treaty given in by the Allies at Châtillon. No ultimatum could be discerned in this assemblage of revolting proposals. I thought I had a right to sacrifice all that I had conquered, but, as to abandoning all that republican France had conquered, I did not think I had a right to do it; nevertheless I would have done it, for the safety of the state imposes duties paramount to all other considerations, if a definitive treaty of peace would have been the immediate result of so many painful sacrifices; but it was not a definitive treaty that was proposed to me, but merely preliminaries of peace, and armistice sword in hand; or rather an armistice by which France would have laid down arms, while her enemies would have occupied the part of her territories which they had invaded, and the fortresses of Huninguen, Befort, and Besançon, the surrender of which they required. Such a treaty appeared to me nothing but a dishonourable capitulation. I wrote to my plenipotentiary. 'Why do not the Allies require us to give up our muskets and cannon to them? Come and take them, would be the only answer to make to such proposals of peace.' At the end of the third Punic war, the Romans had at first required the Carthaginians to surrender their ships, and destroy their military engines; Carthage obeyed, and the Roman Senate soon afterwards ordered the inhabitants to abandon the city, because they had been pleased to decide that it should be reduced to ashes.

Instructions were despatched to the Duke of Vicenza for drawing up a counter-proposal. That of the Allies was sent to the Empress, with directions to submit it to an extraordinary council, summoned for the purpose, and chiefly composed of the men who had exercised influence at the different periods of the Revolution, and been raised to the high functions of the empire. One alone rejected the proposal with indignation, as the most insulting of all that are mentioned in the history of France, and as a disgraceful law to which honour itself would not allow the French to remain subject; the others were of opinion that it was proper to submit to necessity.

I, who had never yet been able to discover the true ultimatum of the Allies, sent from Rheims, a few days after the battle of Craonne, new powers to my plenipotentiary, to conclude peace, with this single restriction, that I would sign no treaty of which the evacuation of the territory, and the return of the prisoners made on both sides, should not be the immediate result. This courier met the Duke of Vicenza a few leagues from Châtillon. The Allies had assigned, as at Prague, an absolute limit to the continuance of the negotiations, and they were broken off accordingly.

XXIV

ABDICATION 1814

AT Fontainebleau I still had 25,000 of my Guards with me. There was nothing to stop me rallying the 25,000 men of the army of Lyons, the 18,000 whom Lieutenant-General Grenier was bringing back from Italy, Marshal Suchet's 15,000, and Marshal Soult's 40,000 and thus taking the field once more at the head of upwards of 100,000 combatants. I was master of all the fortresses of France and Italy. I could still have maintained the war for a long time and reckoned on many chances of success, but my enemies declared to Europe that I was the only obstacle to peace, and I unhesitatingly made the sacrifice that the interest of France seemed to me to demand. After labouring for twenty years to promote the happiness and glory of the French people, I voluntarily yielded myself up, and restored to the nation the crown it had bestowed upon me.

When I afterwards learned, in my retreat on the island of Elba, that factions were busy in France, that parties were forming, and that all the horrors of civil war were once more about to burst upon our beloved country, I felt that my hopes had been disappointed. Faithful to my motto, *Everything for the French people*, I resolved to return to France, not for the ambitious purpose of regaining my throne, but to place myself between the factions. I had always thought that France wished only for equality, and I had given her perfect equality. I had now learned from events that she was likewise desirous of liberty, and I resolved to make France the freest nation in the world.

At the end of February 1815 the Congress of Vienna determined to transfer me to St Helena and to violate all the stipulations of the Treaty of Fontainebleau. The Cabinet of the Tuileries had already proved that it did not intend to fulfil any of the engagements it had contracted by that treaty, but these circumstances had no influence on my resolutions. It was not to forward my own interest that I resolved upon the measures that I did. There was a conspiracy, but my return was not its object. I was not recalled by any conspiracy – it was with the imagination and the convictions of great masses that I constantly acted. I reckoned on the love of the French people and of the French army – my march, and the acclamations that attended me from Golfe Juan to Paris, surprised every one but myself.

Marshal Soult served the king loyally. He was at the time accused of treason, by a party that has always been extreme, but the troop movements and dispositions for which he was censured, because they turned out so favourably for my march, had been executed by the king's particular order and upon the repeated solicitations of the French plenipotentiaries at the Congress of Vienna. When he heard of my landing at Cannes, he thought that the men at arms would settle the affair, unless my object was Italy. Duke Cambacérès, the Duke of Rovigo, the Duke of Otranto, and Count Carnot often confessed to me during the Hundred Days that that had also been their opinion. They never imagined I

Anne-Jean-Marie-René Savary, Duke of Rovigo.

Joseph Fouché, Duke of Otranto.

would reach Paris but the events that had just taken place had revealed to them the secret sentiments of the people and army.

During these three months I constantly worked fifteen or sixteen hours every day; no one can say that I was asleep. Never, at any period of history, were more things done in three months. I armed and provisioned a hundred fortresses, repressed the civil war in Marseilles, Bordeaux, and the Vendée, recruited an army, and caused arms to be manufactured, clothes made, and horses commandeered.

XXV

THE RETURN FROM ELBA

THERE was an English sloop cruising between Genoa, Leghorn, Civitayecchia, and Elba. It carried out the commissions of the agent Campbell[1] and often afforded a passage to English travellers from Leghorn or Genoa to Elba. It had no responsibility to me other than that of suitable behaviour, but it afforded all the little services in its power to the French on Elba. The idea that entered into my mind of landing in France and making war against the French king had not been foreseen by any of the powers, thanks to the lampoonists.

I formed the resolution of re-entering France as soon as it was proved to me that the Royal government wished to evade the execution of the treaty of Fontainebleau and to continue the third dynasty and that it was declaring the governments of the Republic and Empire illegitimate and usurped. The consequences of this were, strictly that the ancient bishops could reclaim their sees, suppressed by the Concordat of 1801; that the clergy could require the restoration of their effects and the Catholic Church become once more predominant in the state; that the ancient lords and privileged persons could protest against Republican spoliations and demand the restitution of their privileges and of the property they had lost, in the cause of legitimacy; and that all acts against the Republic and Empire, all the treasonable plots to deliver Toulon and Brest to the English, deserved rewards.

I had thought that such pretensions would be inadmissible – that the Restoration, powerful as it was, would start back with horror from them; that it would be impossible to satisfy all the false hopes of the clergy; the emigrants, the old privileged classes, and the Vendéans. They would all, necessarily, be

---

[1] Sir Neil Campbell, the English commissioner on Elba.

---

discontented, but the nation would be roused against them and would seek guarantees against their vain pretensions.

The national energy was not extinct but I needed the months of January, February, and March to repel the aggression of 800,000 men and to complete the grand means of defence I had organized. Had the Allies not crossed our frontiers, until April, they would have been driven back beyond the Rhine.

If France, in 1792, repulsed the aggression of the first coalition, it was because she had had three years to prepare herself and to raise 200 battalions of national Guards and because she was attacked by armies that did not exceed at most, 100,000 men. Had 800,000 men marched under the command of the Duke of Brunswick, Paris would have been taken, in spite of the energy and enthusiasm of the nation.

How can it be said that I could make neither war nor peace? With 50,000 men I fought 300,000, who would not have entered Paris, or at least would have been driven from it twenty-four hours after entering it, but for the aid of treason. I always had it in my power to make peace on the basis of the ancient limits of France, and I would have obtained a peace honourable to myself and the nation but for the defection of the senate and of part of the army.

The French Revolution was a general movement of the nation against the privileged classes. Its principal objects were to destroy all privileges, abolish signorial jurisdictions, suppress feudal rights (remnants of the ancient slavery of the people), and proclaim equality in taxation and in rights. The kingdom was composed of successive additions made to the domain of the crown through inheritance or conquest. The provinces had no natural boundaries between them, but were unequal in extent, population, and privileges; they were governed by local laws and customs, in civil and administrative affairs. France was not so much a state as an union of several states, adjacent to each other but amalgamated. The Revolution, essentially guided by the principle of equality, destroyed all the remains of feudal times and created a new France, with a homogenous division of territory, consistent with local circumstances; a uniform judicial and executive organization; universal civil and criminal laws; and a uniform system of taxation. The convulsion produced by the effects of the Revolution, both on persons and property, was as great as that immediately resulting from the principles of the Revolution itself. Everything that had resulted from past developments since the establishment of the monarchy ceased to exist. Regenerated France presented the spectacle of 25,000,000 souls forming a single class of citizens governed by one law, one regulation, and one system of order. All the alterations were conformable to the good of the nation, its rights, and the progress of civilization.

The whole population of France was attached to the interests acquired during twenty-five years of sacrifices and of triumph. If the nation calmly beheld the throne of the third dynasty restored, it was because peace was felt to be necessary, and the presumptive heir to the crown declared that *'nothing was changed in France, except that there was one Frenchman more.'* This conduct was not new; Henry IV, after conquering his subjects, had given them guarantees, abjured his religion, surrounded himself with members of the league, and carried the wish to inspire confidence so far as to remove from about him the very men who had conquered for him at Coutras, Argues, and Ivry. He knew that the love of mankind cannot be extorted by the bayonet, and that a king who does not reign over the hearts of his subjects is nothing; yet Henry IV had not to respect the rights acquired by a Revolution attended by victories which had enforced its acknowledgement throughout Europe. There can be no doubt but that if Cardinal Richelieu had held the reins of the state in 1814, his vast genius would, at a single glance, have comprehended the situation of his king, reigning, by right of birth and the rules of the feudal hierarchy, over a nation proud of so many victories, and happy in the laws it has established for itself since 1789. He would have said to himself that the counter-revolution, if effected, could only be operated through the constant will of the coalition, and the presence and employmernt of hostile armies in France; that the moment the foreign bayonets should quit the country, the nation would resume the enjoyment of its independence, the sentiment of its true interests and rights would revive with new strength, the desire of equality and liberty would be stronger than ever, and then none but a national throne, that is to say, a throne really constitutional, would be compatible with the interests of the king and the people.

I left the island of Elba on 26 February 1815, at 9 o'clock in the evening. I boarded the brig *Inconstant*, which flew the white flag studded with bees throughout the journey. On 1 March, at 5 o'clock in the afternoon, I landed on the beach of the Golfe Juan near Cannes.

My little army put on the tricolour cockade. It consisted of 1,100 men, most of them soldiers of the Old Guard. I passed through Grasse on the 2nd at 9 o'clock in the morning and slept at Sermon, having covered twenty leagues during this first day. On the 3rd I slept at Barrème. On the 4th my advance guard, commanded by General Cambronne, seized the fortress of Sisteron. On the 5th I entered Gap. On the 7th, at 2 o'clock in the afternoon, I came face to face, on the heights before Vizille, with the advance guard of the Grenoble garrison, which was marching against me.

I approached it alone, harangued it, made it fly the tricolour, put myself at its head, and at 11 o'clock in the evening, entered Grenoble, having covered eighty leagues in six days across very mountainous country. This is the most prodigious march of which history has any record.

I spent the 8th at Grenoble and left it on the 9th at the head of 8,000 troops, with thirty guns. At 10 o'clock that evening I entered Lyons, the second city of France. The Count de Fargues, mayor of the city, presented me with the keys. The Count d'Artois, the Duke d'Orléans, and Marshal the Duke of Tarante escaped from it on the 10th. Their arrival unattended at the Tuileries struck stupefaction into the court. At length, on 20 March, at 8 o'clock in the evening, on my son's birthday, I entered Paris. Forty thousand soldiers of all arms had successively ranged themselves under my flag. The little army of the Island of Elba arrived the following day, having covered two hundred and forty leagues in twenty days.

Louis XVIII left Paris during the night of 19/20 March and France on the 23rd. At his departure from Lille all the fortresses in Flanders were flying the tricolour flag. At the first rumour of my disembarkation the Duke of Bourbon had been sent to Nantes to put himself at the head of the Vendée. The Duke d'Angoulême had been entrusted by the government with the provinces on the left bank of the Loire. All attempts to raise the West were futile – the people of this part of the country remembered all they owed to me. The Duke of Bourbon embarked at Paimboeuf on 1 April in an English ship. The Duke d'Angoulême sent Baron de Vitrolles, minister of state, from Bordeaux to set up the headquarters of his government at Toulouse and left the duchess, his wife, at Bordeaux in the hope of keeping this important city on his side and of rallying the Spanish army to it. For his own part, at the head of the 10th Regiment of the Infantry of the Line, the 14th Mounted Chasseurs, and some battalions of Royal Volunteers from Languedoc, he conceived the audacious enterprise of marching on Lyons while the men of Marseilles were marching on Grenoble. He crossed the Rhône by the Saint-Esprit bridge, carried the bridge of Drôme, which the National Guards of Montelimart were defending, entered Valence on 3 April, and established his advance posts along the left bank of the Isère. At the same time the men of Marseilles, to the number of 2,500, supported by the 83rd and 58th of the line under the orders of Lieutenant-General Ernouf, entered Gap and marched on Grenoble.

These successes only lasted one day. The Duchess d'Angoulême on 2 April was obliged to leave Bordeaux on the arrival of Lieutenant-General Clausel; she embarked in an English cutter. Vitrolles was arrested on 4 April by Lieutenant-General Laborde and transferred to prison in Paris. General Gilly, profiting by the enthusiasm of the people of Languedoc, put himself at their head, his advance guard, composed of the 10th Mounted Chasseurs and the 6th Light Infantry, gained possession of the Saint-Esprit bridge and drove the Royalists off it.

At the rumour of the dangers which were threatening Lyons, the people of Burgundy and Auvergne rose en masse and rushed to Lyons demanding arms in order to march against the princes. In all the communes of Dauphiné the tricolour flag was hoisted, and the tocsin announced the march of the Royalists. The troops, at the sight of the imperial eagle that Lieutenant-General Chabert displayed to them at the head of a detachment of the National Guard of Grenoble, deserted the Royalist party. The men of Marseilles, hemmed in on all sides, broke ranks in disorder and were glad to return home. At this the Duke d'Angoulême, in deep dismay, realized the foolhardiness of his enterprise. He evacuated Valence in all haste, hoping to reach the Saint-Esprit bridge. General Gilly took him prisoner. I gave him back his liberty, and had him embarked on 16 April at Cette in a Swedish ship. Marshal Massena, by flying the tricolour flag in

Provence, put an end to the civil war. On 20 April, a hundred guns from the Invalides announced to the capital, and salvoes from the coast batteries and frontier fortifications announced to foreign nations, that the French people had come into their own again.

History will record with admiration the generosity of the victor in these circumstances. Baron Vitrolles, who had been excluded by a decree of Lyons from the general amnesty, the Duke d'Angoulême, whose sentence was pronounced by the law demanding an eye for an eye and a tooth for a tooth, were alike saved by my clemency. 'I want,' I said, 'to be able to pride myself on reconquering my throne without a single drop of blood having been spilt either on the battlefield or the scaffold.'

At the end of 1814 and at the beginning of 1815 discord prevailed at the Congress of Vienna. Austria, France, and England were bound by a secret convention against Russia and Prussia, who appeared not to want to set any limit to their claims. Prussia wanted to incorporate Dresden within its dominion, which was against the interests of Austria; but France, supported by Spain, demanded that the Court of Vienna, in return for the support she gave it, should agree to the Bourbons of Sicily ascending the throne of Naples again. Austria refused this, as much out of jealousy of the House of Bourbon as in order not to betray King Joachim, who had contributed so much to the success of the Allies in 1814 by making common cause with the enemies of his country against the head of his family and his benefactor.

It was Murat who was the decisive factor. If, with his army of 60,000 men, he had joined the Franco-Italian army which the viceroy commanded, he would have forced the Austrian army to remain on the defensive in Carinthia and the Tyrol. The viceroy's army was superior to that of Field-Marshal Bellegarde, but it was nevertheless held by the Neapolitan army. Thus, the weight which he put in the balance on this occasion was 120,000 men. With 100,000 men less, the Allies could not have undertaken the invasion of France before the spring. In 1814, the Neapolitan army was good, because at this period it counted among its ranks 2,000 French officers and NCOs, Corsicans or Italians of the Kingdom of Italy, who left it as soon as they received the circular by which Count Molé, the High-Judge, recalled the Frenchmen from the service of Naples.

The Austrian ministers at the Congress of Vienna often made it obvious how little importance they attached to the intervention of the Court of the Tuileries. Louis XVIII, they said, is not in a position to collect 10,000 men together without fear of seeing the soldiers turn against him. The Prince of Benevento[1] advised the Cabinet of the Tuileries to assemble three camps, one in Franche-Comté, the other in front of Lyons, and the third in the South. These three camps could be expanded to 36,000 or 40,000 men without involving any increase in the military establishment and without being subject to excessive expenditure. They

---

[1] Talleyrand.

244

'Inspiration is nothing but a calculation made with rapidity.' Marshal Nicholas-Jean-De Dieu Soult, created Duke of Dalmatia in 1808, was born the son of a notary. Following his father's death, he enlisted in 1785 and was commissioned in 1792. He served Napoleon well but transferred his allegiance to the Bourbons in 1814, only to return it to Napoleon in 1815. Despite this, he was later reinstated as a Bourbon Marshal.

would, however, raise the credit of France abroad. This plan was adopted.

During the course of February 1815, the troops were mobilized. Ricard, the divisional general, repaired to Vienna and boasted during several conferences of the excellent state of the French army, of its keenness, and of its attachment to the king. He announced pompously that three camps containing 80,000 men were being formed in the neighbourhood of the Alps. The French plenipotentiaries demanded that this army, supported by a Spanish division, should be allowed to proceed either by land, by way of Genoa, Florence, and Rome, or else by sea, to southern Italy. The King of Naples[1], for his part, was not asleep. He

[1] Murat.

assembled his army in the Marches. It consisted of 60,000 men. To counter-balance the effect of the negotiations by the Tuileries, he demanded of Austria passage for the troops he wanted to take over the Alps to enter France, giving as much support thereby as he could to the opinion already widespread that French soldiers were not Bourbon soldiers.

It was at this juncture that I landed. The French regiments, destined to form the three camps in the south, were on the move and were just in the right position to act as my escort from Golfe Juan to Paris. Marshal Soult, the minister of war, was at that time accused of treason; but appearances were deceptive. These troop movements and their disposition, which proved, in the event, to fit in so well with my march, had been carried out by the express order of the king and on the demand of the French plenipotentiaries at Vienna. The foreigners showed that they knew what the secret inclinations of the French army were, better than the princes and ministers of the House of Bourbon.

On 16 February 1815, a few days before leaving Elba, I sent one of my chamberlains to Naples. He told the Court there of my intentions. I was leaving, to re-enter my capital and ascend my throne again; I was resolved to uphold the treaty of Paris, which made me hope that the Allied powers would take no part in this civil war – in any case, the Russian troops were beyond the Niemen, some of the Austrians beyond the Inn, most of the Prussians beyond the Oder, and half the English army in America, the Congress of Vienna had concluded its operations, and the Tsar had left for St Petersburg; my chamberlain said also that I wanted Murat to send a courier to Vienna so that his ambassador could notify this Court that France would continue to carry out the treaty of Paris, and in particular renounce all claims on Italy. Finally he told the Neapolitan Court that in any case hostilities could not begin before the end of July; that France and Naples would have time to act together; that as a preliminary he should reinforce his army, in a good position in front of Ancona, and in all unforeseen circumstances be guided by the principle that it was better to retreat than to advance, and to give battle behind the Garigliano rather than on the Po; that he could achieve a great deal by way of diversion and when supported by a French army; that he could do nothing without that.

My envoy arrived at Naples on 4 March. The brig *Inconstant*, returning from Golfe Juan, arrived on the 12th. A few days afterwards a courier from Genoa brought the news of my triumphal entry into Grenoble and Lyons. The king did not disguise his feelings. He announced loudly his determination to raise Italy. 'The Emperor,' he said, 'will not encounter any obstacle. The whole French nation will fly to his standard. If I delay marching on the Po, if I wait for the month of July, the French armies will have re-established the Kingdom of Italy, and seized the Iron Crown again; it is for me to proclaim the independence of Italy.' My envoy and the queen[1] threw themselves in vain at the king's feet in

---

[1] Napoleon's sister, Caroline.

---

an effort to make him realize the danger and rashness of this enterprise. Nothing could open his eyes. He left for Ancona and arrived at the head of his army on 22 March, but did not even give himself time to wait for news of my entry into Paris. He crossed the Rubicon, traversed the Romagna, and poured his troops into the territory of the Holy See and Tuscany. The Pope retired to Genoa, the Grand-Duke to Leghorn. When he arrived at Bologna, the King of Naples called upon the people of the Kingdom of Italy to rise in revolt. He was asked why he said nothing to them about Napoleon, their legitimate king; and told that without my orders they could not make any move; that it seemed to them, moreover, imprudent to act before the French troops had arrived across the Alps; and that in any case they needed rifles. The province of Bologna alone asked for 40,000. The Neapolitan artillery had not a single one. A few days afterwards the Austrian army, which was concentrated on the left bank of the Po, crossed this river, defeated the Neapolitan army, and entered Naples on 12 May. The king, unable to throw himself into the fortress of Gaeta, embarked in a merchant ship and landed in Provence, where he stayed to await his family and gather his supporters together. For her part, the queen had capitulated to an English commodore, who, following the usual practice of the Allies during the war, as at Danzig and at Dresden, trampled the capitulation underfoot. Instead of transporting this princess to France, he took her to Trieste. During the first days of April Prince Lucien, with one of the Pope's chargé d'affairs in his coach, arrived incognito at Fontainebleau. It was from him that the first news was received in Paris of the King of Naples' invasion. The Pope wrote from Genoa to me that, if I did not guarantee him the possession of Rome, he would go and take refuge in Spain. The chargé d'affairs of the Holy See was received at the Tuileries: he left, taking with him the most favourable assurances to the Holy Father. I guaranteed him all that he was assured by the Treaty of Paris, and let him know that I censured the conduct of the King of Naples as contrary to my policy.

The news of my landing in France was received at Vienna on 8 March. The Congress had not broken up. On 13 and 25 March the ministers of the powers signed acts without parallel in history. They thought I was doomed. 'He will,' they said, 'be immediately repulsed and defeated by the faithful subjects of Louis XVIII.' When they learnt later that the Bourbons, without putting up any resistance, had been unable to hold the north, the south, the west, or the east, and that the whole of France had declared for its former sovereign, the amour-propre of the Allies was compromised. Yet, in spite of that, they hesitated! But, when the Court of Vienna was informed of the opinions of the King of Naples and afterwards of his hostile march, they were no longer in any doubt that he was acting by my orders and that, firm and unswerving in my political methods, I was still the same as I had been at Châtillon, and did not want the crown of France except in conjunction with Belgium, the Rhine, and perhaps even the Iron Crown.

The conference did not hesitate any longer. The ministers signed a treaty against France by which the four principal powers each undertook to furnish 150,000 men. The ratifications were exchanged on 25 April and it was calculated that 1,000,000 men of all the nations in Europe would be assembled at the end of July on the French frontiers. Sweden and Portugal alone refused to supply their contingent. Peace between England and the United States of America had been concluded at Ghent and ratified at the end of February. The English troops, now of no further use in Canada, embarked to return to Europe. The Duke of Wellington had his headquarters at Brussels on 15 April, and Prince Blucher at Liège. On the Thames, the Danube, the Spree, the Neva, and the Tagus, everything resounded of war. The French frigate *Melpomène*, being on the Neopolitan coast, was seized by the English ship *Rivoli*; but a few days afterwards, orders arrived from London to the Commodore in the Mediterranean to respect the French flag, war not having been declared. Thereafter French ships sailed freely. A French frigate brought Madame[1] back from Naples to France.

These orders of the English government were due to the indecision of the sovereigns at Vienna, and to the interest which the Court of London had in gaining time. Its armies in Belgium were in no state to defend that country; and even the admiralty, experiencing great difficulties in arming its ships, feared that the French squadron at Toulon might be equipped and put to sea before its own. Twice a prey to the most extraordinary aberration, the King of Naples was twice a cause of our misfortune, in 1814 by declaring himself against France, and in 1815 by declaring himself against Austria.

On the very night I arrived in Paris, I ordered General Excelmans at the head of 3,000 cavalry to follow the king's military retinue, seize it, break it up, or throw it quickly over the frontier. But this military retinue, composed of such heterogenous elements, had already broken up of its own accord. The remnants were in part surrounded and disarmed at Béthune, the rest got as far as Neuve-Eglise, where Count d'Artois gave it the order to disband. General Excelmans seized all the horses, magazines, and baggage of this corps; the officers and guards, hunted down by the peasants, threw away their clothes and disguised themselves in every variety of costume, in order to elude the popular indignation.

A few days later Count Reille made his way to Flanders with 12,000 men to reinforce the troops of Count d'Erlon, who was garrisoning this frontier. I deliberated then whether, with these 35,000 to 36,000 men, I would begin hostilities on 1 April, by marching on Brussels and rallying the Belgian army to my standard. The English and Prussian armies were weak, scattered, without orders, without leaders, and without a plan; some of the officers were away on leave; the Duke of Wellington was in Vienna; Marshal Blücher was in Berlin. The French army could be in Brussels on 2 April.

But, first, hopes of peace were entertained. France wanted it and would severely have blamed a premature offensive movement. Secondly, in order to

---

[1] Napoleon's mother.

Field-Marshal Arthur Wellesey, Duke of Wellington.

bring together the 35,000 to 36,000 men, it would have been necessary to throw the twenty-three fortresses from Calais to Philippeville, forming the Triple North Line, upon their own resources. If the public spirit of this frontier had been as good as that of Alsace, the Vosges, the Ardennes, or the Alps, this would not have involved any inconvience. But sentiments were divided in Flanders; it was impossible to abandon the fortresses to local National Guards; a month was required to raise and bring from the neighbouring departments picked battalions of the National Guard to replace the troops of the line. Thirdly, and finally, the Duke d'Angoulême was marching on Lyons, and the Marseillese on Grenoble. The first news of the commencement of hostilities would have encouraged the malcontents; it was above all essential that the Bourbons should have abandoned the territory, and that all the French should be united; which only came about by 20 April.

During the course of May, when France was pacified and when there was no longer any hope of maintaining peace abroad, and the armies of the different powers were on the march to the French frontiers, I meditated on the plan of campaign I had to follow. Three plans presented themselves:

The first plan was to remain on the defensive, letting the Allies take upon themselves the odium of aggression, attacking our fortresses, penetrating as far as Paris and Lyons, and to begin around these two bases a lively and decisive war. This project had plenty of advantages.

First, the Allies, not being able to start a campaign before 15 July, would not arrive before Paris and Lyons before 15 August. The 1st, 2nd, 3rd, 4th, 5th and 6th Corps, the four corps of heavy cavalry, and the Guard were concentrating about Paris. These corps had, on 15 June, 140,000 men under arms. By 15 August they would have had 240,000. The 1st Reconnaissance, or 'Jura', Corps, and the 7th Corps would concentrate on Lyons. They had, on 15 June, 25,000 men under arms and would have by 15 August, 60,000.

Secondly, the fortifications of Paris and Lyons would be completed and perfected by 15 August.

Thirdly, by this period there would have been time to complete the organization and arming of the forces destined for the defence of Paris and Lyons, to reduce the Paris National Guard to 8,000 men, and to quadruple the sharpshooters of this capital, bringing them up to 60,000 men. These battalions of sharpshooters, under regular officers, would give valuable service; and they, joined with 6,000 gunners of the line, of the navy, and of the National Guard, and to 40,000 men from the depots of seventy infantry regiments and from the non-uniformed guard belonging to the corps of the Paris army, would bring up to 116,000 men the force designed to guard the entrenched encampment of Paris. At Lyons the garrison would be comprised of 4,000 National Guards, 12,000 sharpshooters, 2,000 gunners, and 7,000 men from the depots of the eleven infantry regiments of the army based at Lyons, in all 25,000 men.

Fourthly, the enemy armies, which would penetrate to Paris by the north and east, would be obliged to leave 150,000 men before the forty-two fortresses of these two frontiers. Putting the strength of the enemy armies at 600,000 men, they would be reduced to 450,000 men by the time of their arrival in front of Paris. The Allied armies that would penetrate to Lyons would be obliged to guard the ten strong-points of the frontier of the Jura and the Alps. Reckoning them at 150,000 men, they would scarcely be 100,000 strong on arriving before Lyons.

Fifthly, on the other hand, the national crisis having reached its peak would produce great activity in Normandy, Brittany, Auvergne, Berry, etc. Numerous battalions would be arriving every day at Paris. The process would be one of continuous increase on the French side and of diminution on the Allies' side.

Sixthly, 240,000 men under my command, manoeuvring on the two banks of the Seine and the Marne, protected by the vast entrenched camp of Paris, guarded by 116,000 immobile troops, would emerge victorious in an encounter with 450,000 of the enemy. Sixty-thousand men, commanded by Marshal Suchet, manoeuvring on the two banks of the Rhône and the Saône, under the protection of Lyons, guarded by 25,000 immobile men, would overcome the enemy army. The sacred cause of the country would triumph!

The second plan was to forestall the allies and begin hostilities before they could be ready. Now, the allies could not begin hostilities before 15 July. It was necessary, therefore, to start the campaign on 15 June; beat the Anglo-Dutch army and the Prusso-Saxon army, which were in Belgium, before the Russian, Austrian, Bavarian and Württemburg armies, etc. could reach the Rhine. By 15 June it was possible to assemble an army of 140,000 men in Flanders, while leaving a cordon on all the frontiers and strong garrisons in all the fortresses.

First, if the Anglo-Dutch army and the Prusso-Saxon army were beaten, Belgium would rise and its army would become part of the French army.

Secondly, the defeat of the English army would bring with it the fall of the English government, which would be replaced by the friends of peace, liberty, and the independence of nations. This fact alone would put an end to the war.

Thirdly, if events turned out otherwise, the army, victorious in Belgium reinforced by the 5th Corps, which remained in Alsace, and the reinforcements that depots would provide during June and July, would move on to the Vosges against the Russian and Austrian armies.

Fourthly, the advantages of this project were numerous; it was in keeping with the genius of the nation and the spirit and principles of this war. It would avoid the terrible inconvenience, attached to the first project, of abandoning Flanders, Picardy, Artois, Alsace-Lorraine, Champagne, Burgundy, Franche Comté, and Dauphiné, without firing a single shot.

But was it possible, with an army of 140,000 men, to beat the two armies which were covering Belgium, namely the Anglo-Dutch army comprising 104,000 men under arms, and the Prusso-Saxon army of 120,000 men; that is to say, 224,000 men? It was not right to evaluate the strength of these armies in the ratio of 224,000 to 140,000, because the army of the Allies was composed of troops varying in quality. One Englishman, or two Dutchmen, or two Prussians, or two men of the Confederation could be counted as equivalent to one Frenchmen. The enemy armies were quartered under the command of two different generals and formed from nations divided in interest and opinion.

The month of May was passed in these meditations. The revolt of the Vendée weakened the army of Flanders by 12,000 men, and reduced it to 120,000. This was a dire fact which diminished the chances of success. But the war of the Vendée might spread. The Allies, masters of several provinces, would be able to rally supporters to the Bourbons; the march of the enemy on Paris and Lyons would favour them. On the other hand, Belgium and the four departments of the Rhine were stretching out their hands, calling for their liberator, and we had good sources of information in the Belgian army, all of which prompted me to adopt a third course, which consisted in attacking the Anglo-Dutch and Prusso-Saxon armies on 15 June, in dividing them, beating them, and, if I failed, in withdrawing my army on to Paris and Lyons. Without doubt, after having failed in the attack on Belgium, the army would arrive back on Paris in a weakened condition. The opportunity would be lost of reducing the National Guard of the capital to 8,000 men from the existing 36,000 in order to bring the sharpshooters up to 60,000, because this operation could not be done in my absence and during the war.

It is true to say also that the Allies who, if waited for, would not begin hostilities before 15 July, would be ready by 1 July if challenged as early as 15 June; that their march on Paris would be all the quicker after victory; and that the army of Flanders, reduced to 120,000 men, was smaller by 90,000 than that of Marshal Blücher and the Duke of Wellington. But in 1814, France, with 40,000 men under arms, had confronted the army commanded by Marshal Blücher and that commanded by the Prince of Schwarzenberg, with the two Emperors and the King of Prussia present. These united armies were 250,000 men strong and yet France had beaten them often! At the battle of Montmirail the corps of Sacken, York, and Kleist amounted to 40,000 men; they were attacked, beaten and thrown beyond the Marne by 16,000 Frenchmen, namely, the Foot and Mounted Guard, the Ricard Division of 1,150 men, and a Division of Cuirassiers; while Marshal Blücher, with 20,000 men was held by Marmont's corps of 4,000 men, and the army of Schwarzenberg, 100,000 strong, was held by the corps of Macdonald, Oudinot, and Gérard, comprising, in all, less than 18,000 men.

The Duke of Dalmatia was appointed chief of staff to the army. On 2nd June he gave the following order of the day[1], and immediately afterwards left Paris to inspect the fortresses in Flanders and the army:

> Our Institutions have just been consecrated by the most august ceremony. The Emperor has received from the People's deputies, and from deputations of all the corps in the army, the expression of the goodwill of the whole nation on the Supplementary Act to the constitution of the Empire which had been submitted to him for acceptance, and a new oath unites France and the Emperor. Thus destiny fulfils itself, and all the efforts of an impious league are unable any longer to separate the interest of a great people from the hero whose brilliant triumphs have made him the admiration of the universe.
>
> It is at the moment when the national will expresses itself with so much energy that war cries are heard. It is at the moment when France is at peace with all Europe that foreign armies advance on our frontiers. What is the hope of this new coalition? Does it want to drive France out of the ranks of the nations? Does it want to plunge 28,000,000 Frenchmen into servitude? Has it forgotten that the first league that was formed against our independence contributed to our aggrandisement and our glory? A hundred smashing victories, which momentary reverses and unfortunate circumstances have not been able to efface, remind it that a free nation, led by a great man, is invincible.

[1] *Moniteur* of 4 June, 1815.

Everyone in France is a soldier when the national honour and liberty are at stake; a common interest today unites all Frenchmen. The pledges that were wrung from us by force are cancelled by the flight of the Bourbons from French territory, by the appeal they had made to the foreign armies in order to remount the throne they have abandoned, and by the unanimous wish of the nation which, in resuming the free exercise of its rights, has solemnly disavowed everything that has been done without its participation.

The French cannot accept laws from abroad. Even those who have gone abroad to beg for assistance in killing their own kith and kin, like their predcessors will not be slow to recognize and feel that contempt and infamy follow their footsteps, and that they cannot wash themselves free of the opprobrium with which they are covered except by re-entering our ranks.

But a new career of glory opens up before the army; history will consecrate the memory of the military deeds which will render illustrious the defenders of the country and of the national honour. The enemy is numerous, it is said. What does that matter to us? It will be all the more glorious to defeat them and their defeat will be all the more resounding. The struggle which is about to begin is not beyond the genius of Napoleon, nor above our strength. Can not all the Departments be seen vying with each other in enthusiasm and devotion, forming as if by magic five hundred separate battalions of National Guards, who have already come forward to double our ranks, defend our fortifications, and associate themselves with the glory of the army? It is the enthusiasm of a great-hearted people, which no power can conquer, and which posterity will admire. To arms!

Soon the signal will be given. Let each man do his duty. From the array of the enemies our victorious phalanxes are going to win a new renown. Soldiers! Napoleon guides our steps. We are fighting for the independence of our beautiful country. We are invincible.

XXVI

THE BATTLE OF MONT-ST-JEAN (WATERLOO)

I WAS camped in front of Plancenoit, astride the main Brussels highway, and four and a half leagues from that great city. With me were the 1st, 2nd, and 6th infantry Corps, the Guard, a light cavalry division of Pajol's and the two cuirassier corps of Milhaud and Kellermann – in all 68,900 men and 242 guns. In front of me was the Anglo-Dutch army, 90,000 men strong, with 250 guns, with its headquarters at Waterloo. Marshal Grouchy, with 34,000 men and 108 guns, should have been at Wavre, but he was in fact in front of Gembloux, having lost sight of the Prussian army, whose four corps, 75,000 strong, were in fact at Wavre.

At 10 o'clock in the evening, I sent an officer to Marshal Grouchy, whom I supposed to be at Wavre, to let him know that there would be a big battle next day and that the Anglo-Dutch army was in position in front of the forest of Soignes, with its left resting on the village of La Haye. I ordered him to detach from his camp at Wavre, before daylight, a division of 7,000 men of all arms and 16 guns to go to St Lambert to join the right of the Grand Army and co-operate with it. As soon as he was satisfied that Marshal Blücher had evacuated Wavre, whether to continue his retreat on Brussels or to go in any other direction, he was to march with the bulk of his troops to support the detachment he had sent ahead to St Lambert.

At 11 o'clock in the evening, an hour after this despatch had been sent off, a report came in from Marshal Grouchy, dated from Gembloux at 5 o'clock in the evening. It reported that he was at Gembloux with his army, unaware whether Marshal Blücher had gone towards Brussels or Liège and that he had accordingly established two advance guards, one between Gembloux and Wavre and the other a league from Gembloux in the direction of Liège. Thus Marshal Blücher had given him the slip and was three leagues from him! Marshal Grouchy had only covered two leagues during the day of the 17th.

A second officer was sent to him at 4.00 a.m. to repeat the order that had been sent to him the evening before. An hour later, at 5 o'clock, a new report, came in, dated from Gembloux at 2.00 a.m. In this the Marshal reported that he had learned at 6.00 p.m. that Blücher had moved with all units on Wavre and that he had wanted to follow him immediately, but because the troops had already made camp and prepared their meal, he would start only at daylight. He would thus arrive early in front of Wavre, which would come to the same thing, and when the men would be well rested and full of dash.

During the night, I gave all the orders necessary for the battle next day, although everything seemed to show that it would not take place. During the four days since hostilities had begun, I had, by the most skilful manoeuvres, surprised my enemies, won a smashing victory, and divided the two armies. It added considerably to my glory, but had not yet sufficiently improved my position. The three hours' delay which the left had suffered, during its movements, had

'Marshal Foreward.' Gebhart Leberecht von Blücher, Prince of Wahlstadt,
was over seventy when he helped win the battle of Waterloo.

prevented my attacking the Anglo-Dutch army, as I had intended, during the afternoon of the 17th, which would have crowned the campaign with success! It was, in fact, probable that the Duke of Wellington and Marshal Blücher were taking advantage of this very night to cross the forest of Soignes and join up in front of Brussels. After that junction, which would be effected before 9 o'clock in the morning, the position of the French army would become extremely delicate. The two armies would be reinforced with everything that they had in their rear. Six thousand English had disembarked at Ostend within the last few days – they were troops returing from America. It would be impossible for the French army to risk crossing the forest of Soignes in order to encounter, on emerging, forces more than twice as strong, joined up and in position; and yet, in less than a few weeks, the Russian, Austrian, and Bavarian armies, etc., would cross the Rhine, and move towards the Marne. The 5th Corps, on the look-out in Alsace, was only 20,000 strong.

At 1 o'clock in the morning, much preoccupied with these weighty thoughts, I went out on foot, accompanied only by my Grand Marshal. My intention was to follow the English army in its retreat and to attempt to engage it, in spite of the darkness of the night, as soon as it was on the march. I went along the line of the main defences. The forest of Soignes looked as if it were on fire. The horizon between this forest, Braine-la-Leud, and the farms of La Belle Alliance and La Haye, was aglow with the fires of bivouacs. The most complete silence prevailed. The Anglo-Dutch army was wrapped in a profound slumber, following on the fatigues it had experienced during the preceding days. On arriving near the woods of the Château of Hougoumont, I heard the noise of a column on the march; it was half past two. Now, at this hour, the rearguard would be leaving its position, if the enemy were in retreat; but this illusion was short-lived.

The noise stopped; the rain fell in torrents. Various officers sent out on reconnaisance and some secret agents, returning at half past three, confirmed that the Anglo-Dutch were showing no signs of movement. At 4 o'clock, the despatch riders brought me a peasant who had acted as a guide to an English cavalry brigade which had gone to take up a position on the extreme left at the village of Ohain. Two Belgian deserters, who had just quitted their regiment, told me that their army was preparing for battle, and that no retreating movement had taken place; that Belgium was offering prayers for my success; and that the English and Prussians were both equally hated there.

The enemy general could do nothing more at variance with the interests of his cause and his country, to the whole spirit of his campaign, and even to the most elementary rules of war, than to remain in the position which he occupied. He had behind him the defiles of the forest of Soignes. If he were beaten any retreat was impossible.

The French troops were bivouacked in the middle of the mud. The officers considered it impossible to give battle during the day. The artillery and cavalry could not manoeuvre on the ground, so drenched was it. They calculated that it would require twelve hours of fine weather to dry it up.

The day began to dawn. I returned to my headquarters thoroughly satisfied with the great mistake the enemy general was making and very anxious lest the bad weather should prevent my taking advantage of it. But already the sky was clearing. At 5 o'clock I perceived a few rays of that sun which should, before going down, light up the defeat of the English army: the British oligarchy would be overthrown by it! France was going to rise, that day, more glorious, more powerful, and greater than ever!

The Anglo-Dutch army was in battle position on the road from Charleroi to Brussels, in front of the forest of Soignes, standing on a fairly good plateau. The right, composed of the 1st and 2nd English Divisions and the Brunswick Division, commanded by Generals Cook and Clinton, rested on a ravine beyond the Nivelles road. It occupied the Château of Hougoumont, in advance of its front, with a detachment. The centre, composed of the 3rd English Division and the 1st and 2nd Belgian Divisions, commanded by Generals Alten, Collaerts, and Chasse, were in front of Mont-St-Jean. The left rested on the Charleroi road, and occupied the farm of La Haye and Sainte with one of its brigades. The left, made up of the 5th and 6th English Divisions and the 3rd Belgian Division, under the command of Generals Picton, Lambert, and Perponcher, had its right resting on the Charleroi road and its left behind the village of La Haye, which it occupied with a strong detachment. The reserve was at Mont-St-Jean, at the intersection of the roads from Charleroi and Nivelles to Brussels. The cavalry, drawn up in three rows on the heights of Mont-St-Jean, lined the whole rear of the army's battle front, which covered a distance of 2,500 toises.

The enemy's front was protected by a natural obstacle. The plateau was slightly hollow at its centre and the ground sloped away gently to a deep ravine. The 4th English Division, commanded by General Colville, occupied, as right flank, all the exits from Hal to Braine-la-Leud. An English cavalry brigade occupied, as left flank, all the exits from the village of Ohain. The units which the enemy revealed were of varying strength; but the most experienced officers estimated them at 90,000 men, including the flanking corps, which tallied with the general information received. The French army numbered only 69,000 men, but victory appeared no less certain on that account. These 69,000 men were good troops; and, in the enemy army, only the English, who numbered 40,000 men at most, could be counted as such.

At 8 o'clock breakfast was brought to me, in which I was joined by several generals. I said, 'The enemy army exceeds ours by nearly a quarter; but the odds are nine to one in our favour.'

'No doubt,' said Marshal Ney, who came in at this moment, 'if the Duke of Wellington were simple enough to wait for Your Majesty; but I come to inform you that, already, his columns are in full retreat. They are disappearing into the forest.'

'You have not seen right,' I replied. 'There is no longer time, he will expose himself to a certain defeat. He has thrown the dice, and our number has turned up!'

Sir Thomas Picton kept secret a severe wound so he could lead his troops at Waterloo – where he died. An eccentric officer 'dressed in a shabby old greatcoat', he was nevertheless one of Wellington's most able subordinates.

At this moment some artillery officers, who had been all over the plain, announced that the artillery could manoeuvre, although with some difficulty, which, in an hour's time, would be considerably lessened. I mounted my horse at once and went to the sharpshooters opposite La Haye Saint; reconnoitred the enemy line again; and told the sapper General Haxo, a reliable officer, to get nearer to it, in order to satisfy himself as to whether they had erected some redoubts or entrenchments. This general returned promptly to report that he had seen no trace of fortifications.

I reflected for a quarter of an hour, dictated the battle orders, which two generals, seated on the ground, wrote down. The aides-de-camp carried them to the different army corps, who were standing to arms, full of impatience and ardour. The army moved off and began to march forward in eleven columns.

It had been arranged that, of these eleven columns, four were to form the first line, four the second line, and three the third.

The four columns of the first line were: the first, that on the left, formed by the cavalry of the 2nd Corps; the next, by three infantry divisions of the 2nd Corps; the third, by three infantry divisions of the 1st Corps; and the fourth, by the light cavalry of the 1st Corps.

The four columns of the second line were: the first, that of the left, formed by Kellermann's corps of cuirassiers; the second, by the two infantry divisions of the 6th Corps; the third, by two light cavalry divisions, one of the 6th Corps, commanded by the divisional General Daumont, the other detached from Pajol's corps and commanded by the divisional General Subervic; the fourth, by Milhaud's corps of cuirassiers.

The three columns of the third line were: the first, that of the left, formed by the division of mounted grenadiers and the dragoons of the Guard, commanded by General Guyot; the second, by the three divisions of the Old, Middle, and Young Guard, commanded by Lieutenant-Generals Friant, Morand, and Duhesme; the third, by the mounted chasseurs and the lancers of the Guard, under Lieutenant-General Lefebvre-Desnouettes. The artillery marched on the flanks of the columns; the parks and the ambulances at the tail.

At 9 o'clock, the heads of the four columns forming the first line arrived at the point where they were to deploy. At the same time the other seven columns could be seen not very far off debouching from the heights. They were on the

Marshal Michel Ney, created Duke of Elchingen in 1808 and later Prince of the Moskwa, was born the son of a cooper. He was a staunch republican but under the influence of Napoleon, who called him 'The bravest of the brave', he changed his beliefs. In 1815 he was tried and shot for treason by the Bourbons.

march, the trumpets and drums summoning them to battle. The music resounded with airs which brought back to the soldiers the memories of a hundred victories. The very soil seemed proud to support so many brave men. This was a magnificent spectacle; and the enemy, who were situated in such a way that every man was visible, must have been struck by it. The army must have seemed to them twice as big as it really was.

These eleven columns deployed with such precision that there was no confusion; and each man took up exactly the place which had been planned for him in the mind of his leader. Never had such huge masses moved about with such ease.

The light cavalry of the 2nd Corps, which formed the first column of the left in the front line, deployed in three lines astride the road from Nivelles to Brussels, more or less on a level with the first woods of Hougoumont park, with a view, on the left, of the whole plain with large numbers of Guards at Braine-la-Leud and its light artilley battery on the Nivelles highway.

The 2nd Corps, under the orders of General Reille, occupied the area between the Nivelles and Charleroi roads, a stretch of between 900 and 1,000 toises. Prince Jérôme's division held the left near the Nivelles highway and the Hougoumont wood; General Foy the centre; and General Bachelu the right, which reached the Charleroi road near the farm of La Belle Alliance. Each infantry division was in two lines, the second thirty toises from the first, with its artillery in front and its parks in the rear near the Nivelles road.

The third column, formed by the first corps, and commanded by Lieutenant-General Count d'Erlon, rested its left on La Belle Alliance, on the right of the Charleroi road, and its right opposite the farm of La Haye, where the enemy's left were. Each infantry division was in two lines; the artillery in the gap between the bridges.

Its light cavalry, which formed the fourth column, deployed on its right in three lines, watching La Haye, Frischermont, and throwing out posts at Ohain, in order to observe the enemy's flank. Its light artillery was on its right.

The front line was scarcely formed up before the heads of the four columns of the second line reached the point where they were to deploy. Kellermann's cuirassiers established themselves in two lines thirty toises from each other, resting their left on the Nivelles road, a hundred toises from the 2nd Corps, and their right on the Charleroi road. They covered an area of 1,100 toises. One of their batteries took up position on the left, near the Nivelles road; the other on the right, near the Charleroi road.

The second column, under Lieutenant-General Count de Lobau, moved up to fifty toises behind the second line of the 2nd Corps; it remained in columns, drawn up by divisions, occupying a depth of about a hundred toises, along and on the left of the Charleroi road, with a distance of ten toises between the two divisional columns, and its artillery on its right flank.

The third column, its light cavalry, under the divisional General Daumont, followed by General Subervic's, placed itself in column drawn up by squadrons, with the left resting on the Charleroi road, opposite its infantry, from which it was only separated by the roadway; its light artillery was on its right flank.

The fourth column, Milhaud's corps of cuirassiers, deployed in two lines thirty toises apart and a hundred toises behind the second line of the 1st Corps, the left resting on the Charleroi road, the right in the direction of Frischermont; it covered about nine hundred toises, its batteries were on its left, near the Charleroi road, and in its centre.

Before this second line had formed up, the heads of the three reserve columns arrived at their deploying points. The heavy cavalry of the Guard placed itself a hundred toises behind Kellermann, ready for action in two lines, thirty toises apart, the left on the side of Charleroi, with the artillery in the centre.

The central column, composed of the infantry of the Guard, deployed in six lines, each of four battalions, ten toises from each other, astride the Charleroi road, and a little in front of the farm of Rossomme. The artillery batteries belonging to the different regiments placed themselves on the left and right, those of the reserve, both on foot and mounted, behind the lines.

The third column, the mounted chasseurs and the lancers of the Guard, deployed in two lines thirty toises apart, a hundred toises behind General Milhaud, the left on the Charleroi road, and the right in the Frischermont direction, with its light artillery at its centre. At half past ten, which seemed incredible, the whole manoeuvre was complete, all the troops were in their positions. The most complete silence reigned over the field of battle.

The army was drawn up in six lines, forming the figure of six V's: the first two, of infantry, having the light cavalry on the wings; the third and fourth, cuirassiers; the fifth and sixth, cavalry of the Guard, with six lines of infantry of the Guard, placed at right angles at the head of the six V's, and the 6th Corps, drawn up in columns, at right angles to the lines taken up by the Guard. The infantry was on the left of the road, its cavalry on the right. The Charleroi and Nivelles roads were clear, being the means of communication whereby the artillery of the reserve could reach the different points of the line quickly.

I passed along the ranks; it would be difficult to express the enthusiasm which animated all the soldiers: the infantry raised their shakos on the ends of their bayonets; the cuirassiers, dragoons, and light cavalry, their helmets or shakos on the ends of their sabres. Victory seemed certain; the old soldiers who had been present at so many engagements admired this new order of battle. They sought to divine what aims their general had in mind; they argued about the point at which, and the manner in which, the attack would take place. During this time, I gave my final orders and went at the head of my Guard to the apex of the six V's on the heights of Rossomme, and dismounted; from there I could see both armies; the view extended far into the distance to right and left of the battlefield.

A battle is a dramatic action, which has its beginning, its middle, and its end. The order of battle which the two armies take up, the opening moves to come to grips, are the exposition; the counter-moves, which the attacked army makes, form the crux which imposes new dispositions and brings on the crisis; from which springs the result, or dénouement. As soon as the attack by the centre of the French army was revealed, the enemy general would make counter-moves, either with his wings, or behind his line, in order to provide a diversion, or rush to the support of the point attacked; none of these movements could escape my experienced eye in the central position I had taken up, and I had all my reserves under control to send them according to my will or wherever the pressure of circumstances should demand their presence.

Ten artillery divisions, including three divisions of twelve, came together, the left resting on the Charleroi road on the hillock beyond La Belle Alliance and in front of the left-hand division of the 1st Corps. They were intended to support the attack on La Haye Sainte, which two divisions of the 1st Corps and the two divisions of the 6th were to make, at the same time as the two other divisions of the 1st Corps were moving on La Haye. By this means, the whole left of the enemy would be turned. The light cavalry division of the 6th Corps, drawn up in close formation, and that of the 1st Corps on its wings, were to take part in this attack, which the 2nd and 3rd lines of cavalry would support, as well as the whole Guard, both on foot and mounted. The French army, master of La Haye and Mont-St-Jean, would cut the Brussels road along the whole right of the English army where its principal forces were.

I had preferrerd to turn the enemy's left, rather than his right, first, in order to cut it off from the Prussians who were at Wavre, and to oppose their joining up again, if they had intended doing so; and, even, if they had not intended doing so, if the attack had been made on the right, the English army, on being repulsed, would have fallen back on to the Prussian army; whereas, if made on the left, it would be separated therefrom and thrown back in the direction of the sea; secondly, because the left appeared to be much weaker; thirdly and finally because I was expecting every moment the arrival of a detachment from Marshal Grouchy on my right, and did not want to run the risks of finding myself separated from it.

While everything was going forward for this decisive attack, Prince Jérôme's division, on the left, exchanged shots at the Hougoumont wood. Soon the firing became very brisk. The enemy having unmasked closed on forty guns, General Reille moved forward the artillery battery of his 2nd Division, and I sent orders to General Kellermann to have his twelve light guns moved up. Soon the cannonade became really hot. Prince Jérôme carried the Hougoumont wood several times, and was several times turned out of it. This was defended by an English Guards division, the enemy's best troops, which I was glad to see on his right, which made the attack on the left all the easier. Foy's division supported Prince Jérôme's, and both sides performed prodigies of valour. The English Guards covered the woods and avenues of the château with their dead, but not without selling their lives dearly. After various vicissitudes, which took up several hours of the day, the whole wood remained in French hands; but the château, where several hundred stout fellows were embattled, put up an unbreakable resistance. I gave orders to assemble a battery of eight field howitzers which set fire to the barns and roofs, and made the French masters of this position.

Marshal Ney received the honour of commanding the big attack in the centre. It could not be entrusted to a braver man, nor to one more accustomed to this kind of thing. He sent one of his aides-de-camp to announce that everything was ready and that he waited only for the signal. Before giving it, I wanted to cast a final look over the whole battlefield, and perceived in the direction of St Lambert a cloud which looked to me like troops. I said to my chief of staff, 'Marshal, what do you see towards St Lambert? I think I can see five to six thousand men there; that is probably a detachment of Grouchy's.'

All the glasses of the general staff were fixed on this point. The weather was rather misty. Some maintained, as often happens on such occasions, that they were not troops, but trees; others that they were columns in position; some others that they were troops on the march. In this uncertainty, without further deliberation, I sent for Lieutenant-General Daumont, and ordered him to go with his division of light cavalry and General Subervic's to reconnoitre the right, get into touch speedily with the troops who were arriving at St Lambert, effect a junction with them if they belonged to Marshal Grouchy, hold them if they belonged to the enemy. These 3,000 cavalrymen only had to do a right wheel in fours to get outside the lines of the army; they moved quickly and without confusion for three hundred toises, and there drew themselves up in battle array, as a cross-piece to the whole right of the army.

A quarter of an hour later, a chasseur officer brought in a Prussian Black Hussar who had just been taken prisoner by the despatch riders of a flying column of three hundred chasseurs, who were out scouting between Wavre and Plancenoit. This hussar was the bearer of a letter. He was extremely intelligent and gave by word of mouth all the information that could be desired. The column which was to be seen at St Lambert was the advance-guard of the Prussian General Bülow, who was arriving with 30,000 men; it was the 4th Prussian Corps, which had not been engaged at Ligny.

The letter was in fact the announcement of the arrival of this corps; the general was asking the Duke of Wellington for further orders. The hussar said that he had been at Wavre that morning, but the three other corps of the Prussian army were camped there, that they had spent the night of the 17th to 18th there, that there were no Frenchmen in front of them, that he presumed the French to have marched on Plancenoit, that one patrol of his regiment had been as far as two leagues from Wavre during the night without encountering any French body. The Duke of Dalmatia immediately sent the intercepted letter and the hussar's report to Marshal Grouchy, to whom he repeated the order to march, without halting, on St Lambert, and to take General Bülow's corps in the rear.

It was 11 o'clock; the officer had at most only five leagues to cover, on good roads all the way, to reach Marshal Grouchy; he promised to be there at 1 o'clock. From the recent news received of this marshal, it was known that he was to move, at daylight, on Wavre. Now, from Gembloux to Wavre is only three leagues: whether or not he had received the orders sent from the imperial

Friedrich Wilhelm von Bülow.

headquarters during the night, he must without doubt be engaged at that moment before Wavre. The glasses turned in that direction picked up nothing; no gunfire could be heard. Soon after, General Daumont sent word that some well-mounted despatch riders who were going ahead of him had run into some enemy patrols in the direction of St Lambert; that it could be taken as certain that the troops to be seen there were enemy troops; that he had sent out picked patrols in several directions to communicate with Marshal Grouchy, and take information and orders to him.

I immediately gave orders to Count de Lobau to cross the Charleroi road, by a change of direction to his right by divisions, and to go towards St Lambert to support the light cavalry; to choose a good intermediate position where he could, with 10,000 men, hold up 30,000, if that became necessary; to attack the Prussians vigorously, as soon as he should hear the first cannon shots from the troops that Marshal Grouchy had detached in their rear.

These dispositions were carried out at once. It was of the utmost importance that the Count de Lobau's movement should take place without delay. Marshal Grouchy must have detached fom Wavre 6,000 to 7,000 men to search in the direction of St Lambert, and these would find themselves compromised, since General Bülow's corps amounted to 30,000 men. In exactly the same way General Bülow's corps would be compromised and lost, if, at the moment when he was attacked in the rear by 6,000 to 7,000 men, he were attacked in front by a man of Count de Lobau's calibre.

Seventeen to eighteen thousand Frenchmen, disposed and commanded in this fashion, were worth a great deal more than 30,000 Prussians; but these events involved a change in my original plan. I found myself weakened on the battlefield by 10,000 men, whom I was obliged to send against General Bülow. I only had 59,000 men against 90,000; moreover, the enemy army, which I was to attack, had just been increased by 30,000 men, already on the battlefield. It was 120,000 strong against 69,000 – two to one.

'This morning the odds were nine to one in our favour,' I said to the Duke of Dalmatia. 'Bülow's arrival deprives us of three; but that still leaves us with six to four in our favour, and, if Grouchy retrives the horrible blunder he made yesterday of twiddling this thumbs at Gembloux, and sends his detachment with speed, victory will be all the more decisive, because Bülow's corps will be entirely destroyed.'

No anxieties were felt for Marshal Grouchy's safety. After dispensing with the detachment to St Lambert, he still retained 27,000 to 28,000 men. Now the three corps that Marshal Blücher had at Wavre, and which, prior to Ligny, were 90,000 strong, were reduced to 40,000 not merely by the loss of 30,000, which he had suffered in the battle, but also by that of 20,000 who had fled in disorder and were ravaging the banks of the Meuse, and by that of some detachments, which the marshal had been obliged to use to make good their loss, as well as by that of the baggage trains which were in the Namur and Liège areas. Now 40,000 or 45,000 Prussians, beaten and disheartened, could not impose their will on 28,000 Frenchmen well placed and victorious.

It was noon, and the sharpshooters were engaged all along the line; but the battle had only really begun on the left, in the wood and around the Château of Hougoumont. On the extreme right General Bülow's troops were still stationary. They appeared to be forming up and to be waiting for their artillery to come through the defile.

I sent orders to Marshal Ney to open fire with his batteries, to get possession of the farm of La Haye Sainte and to put an infantry division in position there; also to get hold of the village of La Haye and turn the enemy out of it, in order to cut all communication between the Anglo-Dutch army and General Bülow's corps. Eighty pieces of artillery soon belched forth death upon the whole left of the English line; one of their divisions was entirely wiped out by the cannon-balls and grapeshot.

While this attack was being unmasked, I watched closely to see what would be the movement of the enemy's general. He made none on his right; but I saw that on his left he was preparing for a big cavalry charge; I dashed there at the gallop. The charge had taken place; it had repulsed a column of infantry which was advancing on the plateau, had taken two eagles from it, and put seven guns out of action.

I ordered a brigade of General Milhaud's cuirassieras, of the second line, to charge this cavalry. It went off with shouts of *'Vive l'Empereur';* the English cavalry was broken, most of the men were left behind on the battlefield; the guns were retaken; the infantry protected.

Various infantry and cavalry charges took place; the detailed narration of them belongs rather to the history of each regiment than to the general history of the battle, into which these accounts, if multiplied, would only bring confusion. It is enough to say that, after three hours' fighting, the farm of La Haye Sainte, despite the resistance of the Scots regiments, was occupied by the French infantry; and the objective which I had set myself realized. The 6th and 7th English Divisions were destroyed, and General Picton was left dead on the battlefield.

During this engagement I went along the line of the infantry of the 1st Corps, the cavalry of Milhaud's cuirassiers, and the Guard in the third line, in the midst of the cannon-balls, grapeshot and shells; they ricocheted between the lines. Brave General Devaux, commanding the artillery of the Guard, who was beside me, was killed by a cannon-ball. This loss was keenly felt, especially at that moment, for he knew better than anyone the positions occupied by the artillery reserves of the Guard, ninety-six pieces strong. Brigadier-General Lallemand succeeded him, and was wounded soon afterwards.

Confusion reigned in the English army. The baggage trains, the transport, and the wounded, seeing the French approaching the Brussels highway and the principal exit of the forest, scrambled en masse to effect their retreat. All the English, Belgian, and German fugitives who had received sabre wounds from the cavalry rushed towards Brussels. It was 4 o'clock. Victory ought from then on to have been assured; but General Bülow's corps carried out its powerful diversion at this moment. From 2 o'clock in the afternoon onwards General Daumont had reported that General Bülow was debouching in three columns, and that the French chasseurs were keeping up their fire all the while they were retiring before the enemy, which seemed to him very numerous. He estimated them at more than 40,000 men. He said, moreover, that his despatch riders, well mounted, had gone several leagues in different directions and had not reported any news of Marshal Grouchy; and that, therefore, he could not be counted on.

At this very juncture, I received extremely annoying news from Gembloux. Marshal Grouchy, instead of leaving Gembloux at first light, as he had announced in his despatch of two in the morning, had still not left his camp at 10.00 a.m. The officer attributed this fact to the horrible weather – a ridiculous reason. This inexcusable inertia, in circumstances of such delicacy, on the part of such a zealous officer, was inexplicable.

However, the exchange of artillery fire between General Bülow and Count de Lobau broke out with little delay. The Prussian army was marching in echelons, with the centre in front. Its line of battle was at right angles to the right flank of the army, parallel to the road from La Haye Sainte to Plancenoit. The centre echelon unmasked about thirty pieces of artillery. Our artillery opposed an equal number to it.

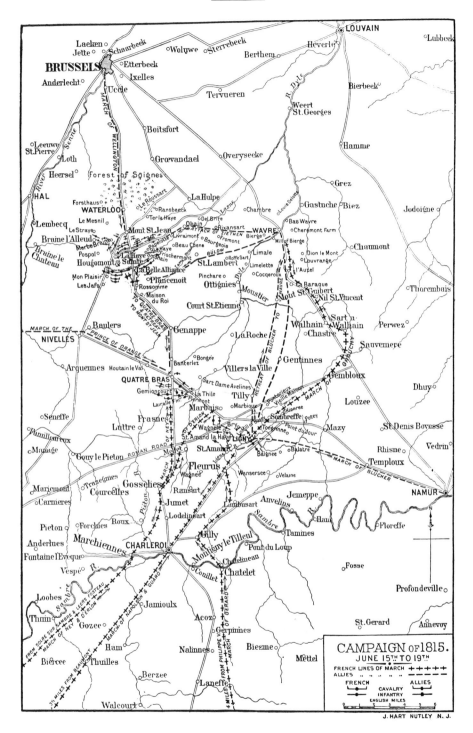

Map of the battle of Waterloo.

After an hour's cannonade, Count de Lobau, seeing that the first echelon was not supported marched up to it, broke into it, and pushed it back a long way; but the other two lines, which appeared to have been delayed by the bad roads, rallied to the first echelon, and, without trying to breach the French line, sought to outflank it by a left wheel in battle. Count de Lobau, fearing that he might be turned, carried out his retreat, chequerwise, approaching the army. The fire of the Prussian batteries redoubled; up to sixty pieces of artillery could be counted. The cannon-balls were falling on the roadway before and behind La Belle Alliance, where I was with my Guard: it was the fighting zone of the army.

At the most critical moment the enemy got so close that his grapeshot raked this road. I thereupon ordered General Duhesme, commanding my Young Guard, to go to the right of the 6th Corps with his two infantry brigades and twenty-four pieces of artillery, belonging to the Guard. A quarter of an hour later, this formidable battery opened up; the French artillery did not take long to gain the advantage: it was better manned and placed. As soon as the Young Guard were in action, the movement of the Prussians seemed to be halted; one could see signs of wavering in their line; however, they still continued to extend it to their left, outflanking the French right and reaching as far as the heights of Plancenoit.

Lieutenant-General Morand thereupon proceeded with four battalions of the Old Guard and sixteen guns to the right of the Young Guard. Two regiments of the Old Guard took up positions in front of Plancenoit. The Prussian line was outflanked, General Bülow was repulsed, his left moved backwards, closed in, and imperceptibly his whole line fell back. Count de Lobau, General Duhesme, and Marshal Morand marched forward; they soon occupied the positions that General Bülow's artillery had held. Not only had this general exhausted his attack, and brought into play all his reserves, but, held at first, he was now in retreat. The Prussian cannon-balls not only fell short of the Charleroi road, but did not even reach the positions that Count de Lobau had occupied; it was 7.00 p.m.

It was two hours since Count d'Erlon had got possession of La Haye and had outflanked the whole English left and General Bülow's right. The light cavalry of the 1st Corps, pursuing the enemy infantry on the plateau of La Haye, had been brought back by a superior force of cavalry. Count Milhaud thereupon climbed the height with his cuirassiers and warned General Lefebvre-Desnouettes, who started at once at the trot to back him up.

It was 5 o'clock, the moment when General Bülow's attack was at its worst, when, far from being held, he kept on throwing in new troops, which extended his line to the right. The new English cavalry was repulsed by the bold cuirassiers and chasseurs of the Guard. The English abandoned all the battlefield between La Haye Sainte and Mont-St-Jean, which their left had occupied, and were brought to bay on their right. At the sight of these brilliant charges, shouts of victory were heard on the battlefield. I said, 'It is an hour too soon; nevertheless what has been done must be followed up.'

I sent an order to Kellermann's cuirassiers, who were still in position on the left, to go at full trot to support the cavalry on the plateau. General Bülow was at this moment threatening the flank and rear of the army; it was important not to fall back at any point, and to hold the present position which the cavalry had taken, although it was premature. This move at full trot by 3,000 cuirassiers who passed by with shouts of *'Vive l'Empereur'*, and under the gunfire of the Prussians, created a fortunate diversion at this critical moment. The cavalry were marching on as if to pursue the English army, and General Bülow's army was still making progress on the flank and in the rear. To know whether we were victorious or in danger the soldiers, even the officers, sought to divine the answer from the expression on my face; but it radiated only confidence. It was the fiftieth pitched battle that I had conducted in twenty years.

However, the heavy cavalry division of the Guard, under the orders of General Guyot, who was in second line behind Kellermann's cuirassiers, followed at full trot and proceeded to the plateau. I noticed this, and sent Count Bertrand to recall it; it was my reserve. When this general got there, it was already committed and any movement of withdrawal would have been dangerous. From 5.00 p.m. onwards, I was thus deprived of my cavalry reserve, which skilfully employed, had so often brought me victory.

However, these 12,000 picked cavalrymen performed miracles; they over-whelmed all the more numerous enemy cavalry which sought to oppose them, drove in several infantry squares, broke them up, seized sixty pieces of artillery and, in the middle of the squares, captured ten standards, which three Chasseurs of the Guard and three cuirassiers presented to me in front of La Belle Alliance. The enemy, for the second time that day, thought the battle lost, and saw with apprehension to what extent the bad battle-site he had selected was going to add to his difficulties in his retreat. Ponsonby's brigade, charged by the red lancers of the Guard under General Colbert, was broken into. Its general was pierced by seven lance thrusts, and fell dead. The Prince of Orange, on the point of being seized, was severely wounded; but, not being backed up by a strong mass of infantry, which was still contained by General Bülow's attack, this gallant cavalry had to confine itself to holding the battlefield which it had conquered.

At length, at 7 o'clock, when General Bülow's attack had been repulsed and the cavalry was still holding its own on the plateau it had carried, the victory was won; 69,000 Frenchmen had beaten 120,000 men. Joy was visible on every face and hearts were lifted high. This feeling followed on the shock that had been experienced during the flank attack, launched by an entire army, which, for an hour, had even threatened to bring about the retreat of the army. At this juncture Marshal Grouchy's gunfire could be heard distinctly. It had passed beyond Wavre at the most distant point and at the nearest point; it was behind St Lambert.

Marshal Grouchy had only left his camp at Gembloux at 10 o'clock in the morning, and was half way to Wavre between noon and 1 o'clock. He heard the dreadful cannonade of Waterloo. No experienced man could have mistaken it: it was the sound of several hundred guns, and from that moment two armies were hurling death at each other. General Excelmans, commanding the cavalry, was profoundly moved by it. He went up to the marshal and said to him, 'The Emperor is at grips with the English army; there can be no doubt about it, such a furious fire can be no skirmish. Monsieur le Maréchal, we must march towards the sound of the guns. I am an old soldier of the Army of Italy; I have heard General Bonaparte preach this principle a hundred times. If we turn to the left we shall be on the battlefield in two hours.'

'I believe,' the marshal said to him, 'that you are right, but if Blücher debouches from Wavre on to me, and takes me in the flank, I shall be compromised for not having obeyed my orders, which are to march against Blücher.'

Count Gerard joined the marshal at this moment, and gave him the same advice as General Excelmans. 'Your orders,' he said to him, 'were to be at Wavre yesterday and not today; the safest thing is to go straight to the battlefield. You cannot conceal from yourself the fact that General Blücher has gained a march on you; he was at Wavre yesterday and you were at Gembloux, and goodness knows where he is now! If he has joined up with Wellington we shall find him on the battlefield, and from then on your orders will have been fulfilled to the letter! If he is not there, your arrival will decide the battle! In two hours we can take part in the firing, and, if we have destroyed the English army, what is it to us that Blücher is as good as beaten!'

The marshal appeared to be convinced; but at this moment he received the report that his light cavalry had arrived at Wavre and was at grips with the Prussians; that all their units were assembled there; and that they amounted to at least 80,000 men. At this news, he continued his move on Wavre: he reached there at 4 o'clock in the afternoon. Believing that he had in front of him the whole Prussian army, he took two hours to take up battle stations and make his dispositions. It was then that he received the officer sent from the battlefield at 10 o'clock in the morning. He detached General Pajol with 12,000 men to go to Limate, a bridge on the Dyle, a league in the rear of St Lambert. This general arrived there at 7.00 p.m. and crossed the river. Meanwhile Grouchy attacked Wavre.

Marshal Blücher had spent the night of the 17th to 18th at Wavre with the four corps of his army, amounting to 75,000 men. Being told that the Duke of Wellington had decided to accept battle in front of the forest of Soignes, if he could count on his cooperation, he detached this 4th Corps during the morning, which crossed the Dyle at Limate, and assembled at St Lambert. This corps was complete – it was the one that had not been engaged at Ligny. Marshal Blücher's light cavalry, which was out scouting two leagues from his camp at Wavre, still had no news of Marshal Grouchy; at 7.00 a.m. it could only see a few pickets of despatch riders. Blücher concluded from this that the whole army was together in front of Mont-St-Jean; he set the 2nd Corps, commanded by General Pirch, in motion. This corps was reduced to 18,000 men. He himself marched with General Zwietten's 1st Corps, reduced to 13,000 men, and left General

Thielman with the 3rd Corps in position at Wavre.

General Pirch's 2nd Corps marched by way of Lasne, and Blücher with the 1st Corps marched on Ohain, where he joined the English cavalry brigade, which was on the flank, at 6 o'clock in the evening. There he received the report that Marshal Grouchy had appeared before Wavre in considerable strength at 4 o'clock, that he was making his dispositions for attack, and that the 3rd Corps was not in a position to resist it.

Marshal Blücher saw that there was only one thing to do. He brought his main strength to the side of General Bülow and the English, and sent orders to General Thielman to hold on as long as possible, and to fall back on him if he was obliged to. Anyhow, he was no longer in a position to turn back towards Wavre; he would only have arrived there after dark, and, if the Anglo-Dutch army was beaten, he would find himself between two fires, whereas, if he continued towards the Anglo-Dutch army and it won the victory, he would still have time to turn round and face Marshal Grouchy.

His progress was extremely slow, his troops were very tired, and the roads completely broken down and full of defiles. These two columns, together 31,000 strong, opened up communications between General Bülow and the English. The former, who was in full retreat, halted. Wellington, who was in despair and had before him only the prospect of certain defeat, saw his salvation. The English cavalry brigade, which was at Ohain, joined him, as well as a part of the 4th Division from the right flank.

If Marshal Grouchy had slept in front of Wavre, as he ought to have done and had orders to do, on the evening of the 17th, Marshal Blücher would have remained in observation there with all his troops, believing himself to be pursued by the whole French army. If Marshal Grouchy, as he had written at 2 o'clock in the morning from his camp at Gembloux, had taken up arms at first light, that is at 4.00 a.m., he would not have arrived at Wavre in time to intercept General Bülow's detachment; but he would have stopped Marshal Blücher's three other corps; and victory would still have been certain. But Marshal Grouchy only arrived in front of Wavre at half past four and did not attack until 6 o'clock; it was no longer the time for it!

The French army, 69,000 strong, which at 7.00 p.m. had gained a victory over an army of 120,000 men, held half the Anglo-Dutch battlefield, and had repulsed General Bülow's corps, saw victory snatched from it by the arrival of General Blücher with 30,000 fresh troops, a reinforcement which brought the Allied army in the line up to nearly 150,000 men, that is two and a half to one.

As soon as General Bülow's attack had been repulsed, I gave orders to General Drouot, who was doing the duties of aide Major-General of the Guard, to rally his whole guard in front of the farm of La Belle Alliance, where I was with eight battalions drawn up in two lines; the other eight had marched on to support the Young Guard and defend Plancenoit. However, the cavalry, which continued to hold the position on the plateau from which it dominated the whole battlefield, saw General Bülow's move but, deriving confidence from the reserves of the

Guard, which it saw there to hold them, did not feel any anxiety as a result, and gave vent to cries of victory when they saw this corps repulsed. They were only waiting for the arrival of the infantry of the Guard to decide the victory; but they were staggered when they perceived the arrival of the numerous columns of Marshal Blücher.

Some regiments drew back. I noticed this. It was of the highest importance to put the cavalry in countenance again; and, realizing that I still needed another quarter of an hour to rally my whole Guard, I put myself at the head of four battalions, and advanced to the left in front of La Haye Sainte, sending aides-de-camp along the line to announce the arrival of Marshal Grouchy, and to say that, with a little determination, the victory was soon to be decided.

General Reille assembled his whole corps on the left, in front of the Château of Hougoumont, and prepared his attack. It was important that the Guard should be in action all at once, but the eight other battalions were still in the rear. Being at the mercy of events, and seeing the cavalry put out of countenance, and realizing that a reserve of infantry was needed to support it, I ordered General Friant to go with these four battalions of the Middle Guard to meet the enemy's attack. The cavalry pulled itself together and marched forward with its accustomed dash. The four battalions of the Guard repulsed everybody that they encountered; cavalry charges struck terror into the English ranks. Ten minutes later, the other battalions of the Guard arrived. I drew them up in brigades, two battalions in battle array and two in columns on the right and the left; the 2nd Brigade in echelons, which combined the advantage of the two types of formation.

The sun had gone down. General Friant, who had been wounded, and was passing by at this moment, said that everything was going well, that the enemy appeared to be forming up his rearguard to support his retreat, but that he would be completely broken, as soon as the rest of the Guard debouched. A quarter of an hour was needed!

It was at this moment that Marshal Blücher arrived at La Haye and overthrew the French unit defending it; this was the 4th Division of the 1st Corps; it fell back, routed, and only offered slight resistance. Although it was attacked by forces four times as strong, if only it had shown a little resolution, or had barricaded itself up in the houses, since night had already fallen, Marshal Blücher would not have had the time to carry the village. It is there that the cry of '*Sauve qui peut*' is said to have been heard.

The breach effected, the line having been broken owing to the lack of vigour of the troops at La Haye, the enemy cavalry swept over the battlefield. General Bülow marched forward; Count de Lobau put on a bold front. The rout became such that it was necessary to give orders to the Guard, which was formed up to go forward, to change direction. This move was carried out in good order; the Guard faced about, with its left on the side of La Haye Sainte and its right on the side of La Belle Alliance, confronting the Prussians and the attack on La Haye. Immediately afterwards, each battalion formed itself into a square. The four squadrons detailed for action charged the Prussians. At this moment the English cavalry brigade, which arrived from Ohain, marched forward. These 2,000 horse got in between General Reille and the Guard.

The disorder became appalling over the whole battlefield; I only just had time to place myself under the protection of one of the squares of the Guard. If General Guyot's cavalry division of the reserve had not committed itself, without orders, to following up Kellermann's cuirassiers, it would have repulsed this charge, prevented the English cavalry from penetrating into the battlefield, and the Foot Guard would then have been able to hold all the enemy's efforts. General Bülow marched on his left, still outflanking the whole battlefield.

Night added to the confusion and obstructed everything. If it had been daylight, and the troops had been able to see me, they would have rallied: nothing was possible in the darkness. The Guard began to retreat, the enemy's fire was already a hundred toises behind and the roads were cut. I remained for a long time, with my general staff, with the regiments of the Guard on a hillock. Four guns that were there fired briskly into the plain; the last charge wounded Lord Paget, the English cavalry general. At last, there was not a moment to lose. I could only effect my retreat across country; cavalry, artillery, infantry, were all mingled pell mell.

The general staff reached the little village of Gennape; it hoped to be able to rally a rearguard corps there; but the disorder was appalling, all efforts were in vain. It was 11.00 p.m. Finding it impossible to organize a defence, I pinned my hope on Girard's division, the 3rd of the 2nd Corps, which I had left on the battlefield at Ligny, and to which I had sent orders to move on to Quatre Bras to support the retreat.

Never had the French army fought better than on this day; it performed prodigies of valour; and the superiority of the French troops over the enemy was such that, but for the arrival of the 1st and 2nd Prussian Corps, victory would have been won, and would have been complete over the Anglo-Dutch army and General Bülow's corps, that is to say one against two (69,000 men against 120,000).

The losses of the Anglo-Dutch army and that of General Bülow during the battle were far higher than those of the French; and the losses the French suffered in the retreat, although considerable, since there were 6,000 prisoners, still do not balance the losses of the allies during those four days. These losses they admit to be 60,000 men; viz.: 11,000 English, 3,500 Hanoverians, and 8,000 Belgian, Nassau, and Brunswick troops; total, 22,800 for the Anglo-Dutch army: Prussians, 38,000; grand total: 60,800 men. The losses of the French army, even including those suffered during the rout and up to the gates of Paris, were 41,000 men.

The Imperial Guard upheld its former reputation; but it was engaged in unfortunate circumstances. It was outflanked on the right and the left, swamped by fugitives and by the enemy, just when it was joining in the fray; for, if this Guard has been able to fight, supported on the flanks, it would have repulsed the efforts of the two enemy armies combined. For more than four hours 12,000

French cavalrymen had been masters of a part of the enemy's side of the battle-field, had fought against the whole infantry and against 18,000 of the Anglo-Dutch cavalry, who were again and again repulsed in all their charges. Lieutenant-General Duhesme, an old soldier covered with wounds and of the utmost bravery, was taken prisoner as he tried to rally a rearguard. Count de Lobau was likewise taken. Cambronne, the General of the Guard, remained on the battlefield, severely wounded. Out of twenty-four English generals, twelve were killed or severely wounded. The Dutch lost three generals. The French General Duhesme was assassinated on the 19th by a Brunswick hussar, in spite of being a prisoner; this crime went unpunished. He was a brave soldier and a consummate general, who was always steadfast and unshakeable in good as in bad fortune.

The Charleroi road is very wide; it was enough for the retreat of the army. The bridge of Gennape is of similar width; five or six files of vehicles can cross abreast there. But from the moment that the first fugitives arrived, the men in the artillery parks there thought it advisable to barricade themselves by placing upturned vehicles on the road in such a way as to leave a passage of only three toises. The confusion was soon appalling. Gennape is, moreover, in a hollow; the first Prussian troops who were pursuing the army, having arrived on the heights that dominate it at 11.00 p.m., easily succeeded in disorganizing a handful of good men whom the brave General Duhesme had rallied, and entered the town. Among the vehicles which they took was my post-chaise, in which I had not ridden since Avesnes. The general practice was that on the battlefield it followed behind the reserves of the Guard. It always carried a dressing-case, a change of clothing, a sword, a greatcoat, and an iron bed.

At 1 o'clock, in the morning I arrived at Quatre Bras, dismounted at a bivouac, and sent several officers to Marshal Grouchy to inform him of the loss of the battle and to order him to retreat to Namur. The officers whom I had sent from the battlefield to take Girard's division to Ligny and place it in position at Quatre Bras, or advance it as far as Gennape, if there were time, reported to me the infuriating news that they had been unable to find this division.

The artillery General Nègre, a most meritorious officer, was at Quatre Bras with the reserve parks, but he only had a weak escort; a few hundred horsemen rallied, Count de Lobau placed himself at their head, and took all possible measures to organize a rearguard. The soldiers of the 1st and 2nd Corps, who had crossed the Sambre by the Marchiennes bridge, went towards this bridge, and left the road at Quatre Bras or at Gosselies to take a short cut. The troops of the Guard and of the 6th Corps withdrew to Charleroi. I sent Prince Jérôme to Marchiennes with orders to rally the army between Avesnes and Maubeuge, and betook myself to Charleroi.

When I arrived, at 6 o'clock in the morning, a large number of men and especially of cavalry had already crossed the Sambre, marching towards Beaumont. I stopped for an hour on the left bank, sent off some orders, and headed for Philippeville in order to be in a better position to communicate with

Marshal Grouchy and to send my orders to the Rhine frontiers. After having stopped for four hours in this town, I took post to get to Laon, where I arrived on the 20th at four in the afternoon. I conferred with the prefect, entrusted my aide-de-camp, Count de Bussy, with the task of seeing to the defence of this important place, and sent Count de Dejean to Guise and Count de Flahaut to Avesnes.

I waited for Prince Jérôme's despatches, which informed me that he had rallied more than 25,000 men behind Avesnes and about fifty guns; that General Morand was commanding the Foot Guard, and General Colbert the cavalry of the Guard; that the army appeared to be increasing visibly; that most of the generals had arrived; that my losses were not as high as might be thought: more than half the artillery equipment had been saved; 170 pieces of artillery were lost, but the men and horses had arrived at Avesnes. I gave orders for them to proceed to La Fère to collect guns there, and entrusted reliable officers with the task of reorganizing a new field force there.

Marshal Soult had orders to place himself at Laon with general headquarters. The prefect took all measures to fill the magazines of the town and to assure supplies for an army of 80,000 to 90,000 men, who would be assembled within a few days around this town. I expected that the enemy generals, profiting by their victory, would push their army forward as far as the Somme. I ordered Prince Jérôme to leave Avesnes on the 22nd with the army and lead it to Laon, the assembly point given to Marshal Grouchy and General Rapp. Not being more than twelve hours' march from Paris, I considered it necessary to go there. There was no need for my presence with the army during the days of the 21st, 22nd, 23rd, and 24th. I counted on being back at Laon on the 25th. I employed these six days in the capital, in organizing the national emergency measures, in completing the preparations for the defence of Paris, and in speeding up the help that the depots and the provinces could provide. It was easy then to judge that, should Marshal Grouchy's corps arrive intact, of which there was little doubt, the losses of the French army would be smaller than those the enemy armies had suffered at the battles of Ligny and Waterloo, and at the engagement of Quatre Bras. It has since been calculated that the Allies' losses amounted to 63,000 men, and that those of the French did not exceed 41,000 men, including the prisoners taken during the retreat.

On the 18th, Marshal Grouchy had attacked Wavre at 6.00 p.m. General Thielman offered a vigorous resistance, but he was beaten. Count Gerard, at the head of the 4th Corps, forced the passage of the Dyle. Lieutenant-General Pajol, with 12,000 men, had been detached to march on Limate. There he repulsed General Bülow's rearguard, crossed the Dyle, and got to the top of the opposing heights; but the night was so dark by 10.00 p.m. that he could not then continue his march; and, moreover, since he could no longer hear the cannonade of Mont-St-Jean, he took up his position. Count Gerard was severely wounded in the attack on Wavre; a bullet passed through his chest, but luckily the wound was not fatal.

On the 19th, at dawn, General Thielman attacked Marshal Grouchy and was vigorously repulsed. The village of Bielau and all the heights beyond Wavre were carried by the French. Brigadier-General Peine, a distinguished officer, was fatally wounded in this engagement. Marshal Grouchy was giving orders to pursue the enemy and to march in the direction of Brussels, when he received the news of the loss of the battle and my order to make his retreat on Namur. He began this at once. The Prussians followed him cautiously; but getting too far ahead, they were repulsed and lost some guns and a few hundred prisoners. General Vandamme took up his position at Namur, Marshal Grouchy at Dinant. General Thielman failed in all the attacks he attempted. On the 24th, the whole of Marshal Grouchy's corps was at Rethel; on the 26th, it joined the army of Laon. It numbered 32,000, among which were 6,500 cavalry and 108 guns, apart from about 1,000 men crippled and little groups of cavalry who were following.

The position of France was critical after the battle of Waterloo, but not desperate. Everything had been prepared on the hypothesis that the attack on Belgium would fail. Seventy thousand men were rallied on the 27th between Paris and Laon; 25,000 to 30,000 men, including those of the Guard who had been left in garrison, were on the march from Paris and the depots. General Rapp, with 25,000 picked troops, was due to arrive on the Marne during the first days of July; all the losses in artillery matériel were made good. Paris alone contained 500 field guns, and only seventy had been lost. Thus, an army of 120,000 men, equal to that which had crossed the Sambre on the 15th, and having an artillery train of 350 pieces of artillery, would cover Paris on 1 July. Apart from this, the capital had, for its defence, 36,000 men of the National Guard, 30,000 sharpshooters, 6,000 gunners, 600 pieces of artillery in batteries, formidable entrenchments on the right bank of the Seine, and, within a few days, those on the left bank would have been completely finished.

However, the Anglo-Dutch and Prusso-Saxon armies, weakened by more than 80,000 men, and now more than 140,000 in number, could not pass beyond the Somme with more than 90,000 men. There they would await the cooperation of the Austrian and Russian armies, which could not be on the Marne before 15th July. Paris thus had twenty-five days to prepare its defence, complete its armament, its supplies, its fortifications, and draw troops from all over France. Even by 15 July, only 30,000 or 40,000 men could have arrived on the Rhine; the bulk of the Russian and Austrian armies could not go into action until later. Neither the arms, not the munitions, nor the officers were lacking in the capital; the sharpshooters could easily be raised to 80,000 men, and the field artillery increased to 600 pieces.

Marshal Suchet, joined up with General Lecourbe, would, by the same period, have more than 30,000 men in front of Lyons independently of the garrison of this town, which would be well armed, well provisioned, and entrenched. The defence of all the fortresses was assured; they were commanded by picked officers, and defended by loyal troops. Everything could be put right; but character, energy, and firmness were needed on the part of the officers, of the government, of the Chambers, and of the whole nation! It was necessary that it should be animated by the feeling of honour, of glory, of national independence, and that it should have in mind the example of Rome after the battle of Cannae, and not of Carthage after Zama! If France attained this level, she was invincible; her people contained more martial elements than any other nation in the world. War material existed in abundance and could meet all requirements.

On 21 June, Marshal Blücher and the Duke of Wellington entered French territory in two columns. On the 22nd, the powder magazines at Avesnes took fire; the place surrendered. On the 24th the Prussians entered Guise and the Duke of Wellington Cambrai; on the 26th, he was at Péronne. During all this time, the fortresses of the 1st, 2nd, and 3rd lines in Flanders were invested. However, these two generals learnt on the 25th day of my abdication, which had taken place on the 22nd, of the revolt of the Chambers, of the despondency into which these circumstances had plunged the army, and of the hopes the enemies in our midst derived from them.

From that moment, their one thought was to march on the capital, under the walls of which they arrived during the last days of June, with less than 90,000 men; a proceeding which would have been disastrous for them, and would have brought about their complete ruin, if they had risked it in opposition to me. But I had abdicated!

Longwood, Napoleon's residence in St Helena after his defeat at Waterloo, where he improved his English by reading Aesop's Fables, was ramshackled, damp and rat-infested. His room contained portraits of the King of Rome, a portrait of Marie-Louise and a miniature of Josephine. His said of his life, 'For the sake of history I should have died at Waterloo . . .'

XXVII

FINAL OBSERVATIONS

FIRST OBSERVATION: I have been reproached on several counts. First, that I gave up the dictatorship at the moment when France needed a dictator most. Secondly, that I changed the constitution of the Empire at a moment when my one concern should have been to preserve it from invasion. Thirdly, that I allowed the Vendéans to be stirred up, when they had first refused to take up arms against the Imperial regime. Fourthly, that I reassembled the Chambers when I should only have assembled the armies. Fifthly, that I abdicated and left France at the mercy of a divided and inexperienced assembly – for, if it is true that it was impossible for me to save the country unless I had the nation's confidence, it was equally impossible, in these critical circumstances, for the country to save either its honour or its independence without me.

I shall express no opinions on these matters, which are dealt with thoroughly and at length in Book X.[1]

SECOND OBSERVATION: The skill with which the movements of the different army corps were concealed from the enemy's knowledge at the beginning of the campaign cannot be too carefully noted. Marshal Blücher and the Duke of Wellington were taken by surprise. They saw nothing and knew nothing of all the moves that were being made close to their advance posts.

To attack the two enemy armies, the French could outflank their right or their left or pierce their centre. In the first case, they would debouch by way of Lille and would meet the Anglo-Dutch army; in the second, they would debouch by Givet and Charlemont and would meet the Prussian army. These two armies remained together since they would be pressed close together, with the left to

---

[1] If so, the book has not so far come to light.

278

the right, and vice versa. I adopted the course of covering my movements by the Sambre and of piercing the line of the two armies at Charleroi, the hinge of their junction, manoeuvring with speed and skill. Thus I found, in the secrets of the art, additional resources which served me in lieu of the 100,000 men of which I was short. This plan was conceived and carried out with boldness and wisdom.

THIRD OBSERVATION: The character of several generals had been softened by the events of 1814. They had lost something of that dash, that resolution, and that self-confidence which had won so much glory for them and had contributed so much to the success of former campaigns.

1. On 15 June, the 3rd Corps was supposed to take up arms at 3.00 a.m. and arrive before Charleroi at 10 o'clock; it only arrived at three in the afternoon.

2. On the same day, the attack on the woods in front of Fleurus, which had been ordered for 4.00 p.m., did not take place until 7 o'clock. Night supervened before Fleurus could be entered, where it had been my intention to place my headquarters that same day. This loss of seven hours was extremely disconcerting at the beginning of a campaign.

3. Ney received the order to get in front of Quatre Bas on the 16th, with 43,000 men who comprised the left which he commanded, to take up position there at first light, and even to dig in there. He wavered and lost eight hours. The Prince of Orange, with only 9,000 men, held on to this important position on the 16th until 3 o'clock in the afterernoon. When finally, at midday, the Marshal received the order dated from Fleurus, and saw that I was going to close with the Prussians, he moved on Quatre Bras, but only with half his force. He left the other half two leagues behind to cover his line of retreat. He forgot it until 6 o'clock in the evening, when he felt the need of it for his own defence. In the other campaigns, this general would have occupied the position before Quatre Bras at 6.00 a.m., would have defeated and taken the whole Belgian division; and would either have turned the Prussian army by sending a detachment by the Namur road which would have fallen upon the rear of the line of battle, or, by moving quickly on the Gennape road, he would have surprised the Brunswick Division and the 5th English Division on the march, as they were coming from Brussels, and from there marched to meet the 1st and 3rd English Divisions, which were coming up by the Nivelles road, both without cavalry or artillery, and worn out with fatigue. Always the first under fire, Ney forgot the troops who were not under his eye. The bravery that a general-in-chief ought to display is different from that which a divisional general must have, just as the latter's ought not to be the same as that of a captain of grenadiers.

4. The advance guard of the French army only arrived in front of Waterloo at 6.00 p.m. But for vexacious hesitations, it would have arrived there at 3.00 p.m. I revealed myself much put out by this. I said, pointing to the sun, 'What would I not give today to have Joshua's power and delay its progress by two hours!'

FOURTH OBSERVATION: Never has the French soldier shown more courage, goodwill, and enthusiasm. He was full of the consciousness of his superiority over all the soldiers of Europe. His confidence in me was complete, and had perhaps grown greater; but he was touchy with his other chiefs and mistrustful of them. The treacheries of 1814 were always present in his mind; every move that he did not understand worried him; he believed himself betrayed. At the moment when the first cannon were being fired near St Amand, an old corporal came up to me and said, 'Sire, don't trust Marshal Soult. You may be certain that he will betray us.'

'You need not worry,' I replied, 'I can answer for him as for myself.'

In the midst of the battle, an officer reported to Marshal Soult that General Vandamme had gone over to the enemy, and that his men were crying out that I should be notified of it. Towards the end of the battle, a dragoon, with his sabre all dripping with blood ran up crying, 'Sire, come quickly to the division. General d'Henin is haranguing the dragoons and telling them to go over to the enemy.'

'Did you hear him?'

'No, Sire; but an officer who is looking for you saw it, and ordered me to tell you about it.'

Meanwhile, the worthy General d'Henin was hit by a cannonball, which shot away one of his thighs, after he had repulsed an enemy charge.

On the 14th, in the evening, Lieutenant-General Bourmont, Colonel Clouet, and the general staff-officer Villontrey had deserted from the 4th Corps and gone over to the enemy. Their names will be held in execration so long as the French people constitute a nation. This desertion had considerably increased the soldiers' uneasiness. It seems to be more or less established that the cry of '*Sauve qui peut*' was raised in the 3rd Division[1] of the 1st Corps, on the evening of the battle of Waterloo, when Marshal Blücher was attacking the village of La Haye. This village was not defended as it ought to have been. It is equally probable that several officers, bearing orders, disappeared. But, if some officers deserted, not a single common soldier was guilty of this crime. Several killed themselves on the battlefield where they had remained wounded, when they learnt of the army's rout.

FIFTH OBSERVATION: During the day of the 17th, the French army was divided into three parts: 69,000 men, under my orders, marched on Brussels by the Charleroi road; 34,000 under the orders of Marshal Grouchy, went towards Brussels by the Wavre road in the wake of the Prussians; 7,000 or 8,000 men remained on the battlefield of Ligny, namely: 3,000 men of Girard's division, to succour the wounded and provide a reserve at Quatre Bras against any unforeseen contingency; 4,000 to 5,000 men forming the reserve artillery parks remained at Fleurus and Charleroi.

Marshal Grouchy's 34,000 men, having 108 guns, were sufficient to overthrow the Prussian rearguard in any position they might take up, press on the retreat of the defeated army, and contain it. It was a splendid result of the battle of Ligny, thus to be able to oppose an army, which had been 120,000 strong, with 34,000

---

[1] Napoleon says earlier (*see* p.272) that it was from the 4th Division that the cry of '*Sauve qui peut*' was heard.

men. The 69,000 men under my orders, were sufficient for defeating the Anglo-Dutch army of 90,000 men. The disproportion which existed on the 15th between the two belligerent masses, which was then in the ratio of one to two, was satisfactorily changed; it was now only in the ratio of three to four.

If the Anglo-Dutch army had defeated the 69,000 men marching against them, I could have been reproached with having miscalculated; but it is established, even by the enemy's own admission, that, but for the arrival of General Blücher, the Anglo-Dutch army would have been driven off the battlefield between 8 o'clock and 9 o'clock in the evening. But for the arrival of Marshal Blücher in the evening with his 1st and 2nd Corps, the march on Brussels, in two columns, during the day of the 13th, had several advantages; the left pressed the Anglo-Dutch army hard, and held it; the right, under the orders of Marshal Grouchy, pursued the Prusso-Saxon army and held it, and by evening the whole French army was to be reunited on a line of under five leagues from Mont-St-Jean to Wavre, with its advance posts at the edge of the forest. But the mistake made by Marshal Grouchy of stopping on the 17th at Gembloux, when he had only covered under two leagues during the day, instead of marching on until he was opposite Wavre, that is, instead of doing another three leagues, was aggravated and rendered irretrievable by the one he made on the following day, the 18th, in wasting twelve hours, and only arriving at 4 o'clock in the afternoon before Wavre, instead of getting there at 6 o'clock in the morning.

1. Though he had been entrusted with the task of pursuing Marshal Blücher, Grouchy lost sight of him for twenty-four hours, from 4.00 p.m. on the 17th to 4.00 p.m. on the 18th.

2. The movement of cavalry on the plateau, while General Bülow's attack was not yet repulsed, was a grievous accident; my intention was to order this move – but an hour later – and to have it backed up by the sixteen infantry battalions of the Guard and a hundred guns.

3. The mounted grenadiers and the dragoons of the Guard, under general Guyot, committed themselves without orders. Thus at 5 o'clock in the afternoon, the army found itself without a cavalry reserve. If, at 8.30 this reserve had existed, the storm which overwhelmed the battlefield would have been averted. With the enemy cavalry charges repulsed, the two armies would have slept on the battlefield, notwithstanding the arrival of General Bülow and Marshal Blücher, one after the other. The balance would still have been in favour of the French army, for Marshal Grouchy's 34,000 men, with eight hundred guns, were fresh and would have bivouacked on the battlefield; the two enemy armies would have taken cover during the night in the Forest of Soignes.

It was the invariable practice, in all battles, that the division of grenadiers and dragoons of the Guard should not lose sight of me, or charge without a verbal order given by me to the general commanding it.

Marshal Mortier, who was Commander-in-Chief of the Guard, gave up this command at Beaumont, on the 15th, just as hostilities were beginning. He was not replaced (an omission) which had several disadvantages.

SIXTH OBSERVATION: 1. The French army manoeuvred on the right of the Sambre on the 13th and 14th. It camped, on the night of the 14th to 15th, half a league from the Prussian advance posts; and, in spite of this, Marshal Blücher was in complete ignorance of it all. When, during the morning of the 15th, he learned at his headquarters in Namur that I was entering Charleroi, the Prusso-Saxon army was still quartered over an area of thirty leagues, and requiring two days to be assembled. He ought, since 15 May, to have moved his headquarters up to Fleurus; to have concentrated his army's billets within a radius of eight leagues, with advance guards watching the crossings of the Meuse and the Sambre. His army could then have assembled at Ligny on the 15th and have awaited there the attack of the French army, or could have marched against it during the evening of the 15th, and thrown it into the Sambre.

2. However, although taken by surprise, Marshal Blücher went on with his plan of assembling his army on the heights of Ligny behind Fleurus, taking the risk of being attacked there before his army had come up. On the morning of the 16th, he had only, so far, got together two army corps, and already the French army was at Fleurus. The 3rd Corps came up during the day, but the 4th, commanded by General Bülow, could not reach the battle. As soon as he knew that the French were at Charleroi, that is to say, during the evening of the 15th, Marshal Blücher ought to have given, as rallying point for his army, not Fleurus, nor Ligny (which was already under his enemy's gunfire) but Wavre, where the French could not arrive until the 17th. He would have had, in addition, the whole day of the 16th and the night of the 16th to 17th to carry out the complete assembly of his army.

3. After having lost the battle of Ligny, the Prussian general, instead of retreating on to Wavre, ought to have manoeuvred back on to the Duke of Wellington's army, either at Quatre Bras, since the latter had held his position there, or else on to Waterloo. The whole of Marshal Blücher's retreat during the morning of the 17th, was in the wrong direction, since the two armies, which were only three thousand toises from each other on the evening of the 16th, with a good road connecting them, so that they could fairly be considered to be together, found themselves, on the evening of the 17th, separated by more than ten thousand toises and divided by defiles and impracticable roads.

The Prussian general violated the three great rules of war: first, to keep one's billets close together; secondly, to give a rallying point which all can reach before the enemy; thirdly, to carry out one's retreat towards reinforcements.

SEVENTH OBSERVATION: 1. The Duke of Wellington was surprised in his quarters. He ought on 15 May to have concentrated them within a radius of eight leagues from Brussels with advance guards watching the exits from Flanders. The French army had been manoeuvring for three days within range of his advance posts; for the last twenty-four hours it had been engaged in hostilities; its headquarters had been at Charleroi for twelve hours; and yet the English general at Brussels still knew nothing about it, and his whole army was still comfortably ensconced in its quarters, extending over an area of more than twenty leagues.

2. The Prince of Saxe-Weimar, who was acting as part of the Anglo-Dutch army, was in position beyond Frasnes at 4.00 p.m. on the 15th and knew that the French army was at Charleroi; if he had sent an aide-de-camp straight to Brussels, he would have arrived there at 6 o'clock in the evening; and yet it was not until 11.00 p.m. that the Duke of Wellington was informed that the French army was at Charleroi. Thus he lost five hours in a situation and against a man where the loss of a single hour was a matter of great importance.

3. The infantry, the cavalry, and the artillery of this army were quartered separately, in such a way that the infantry went into action, at Quatre Bras, without cavalry or artillery; and this caused it to suffer considerable losses, since it was obliged to remain drawn up in columns, in close formation, under a hail of shot from fifty pieces of artillery, in order to face the charges of cuirassiers. These fine men were sacrificed like lambs led to the slaughter, without cavalry to protect them and artillery to avenge them. As the three arms cannot get on for a moment without each other, they ought always to be quartered and placed in such a way as to be able at all times to help one another.

4. The English general, although taken by surprise, gave, as a rallying point to his army, Quatre Bras, which had been in the hands of the French for twenty-four hours. He exposed his troops to being defeated piecemeal as they arrived. The danger to which he exposed them was even greater, since he made them come up without artillery and cavalry. He delivered his infantry into the enemy's hands in small groups, and without the support of the other two arms. His rallying point should have been Waterloo. He would then have had the whole day of the 16th and the night of the 16th to 17th, which was enough to bring the whole of his army, infantry, cavalry, and artillery, together there. The French could not be there before the 17th and would have found the whole of his army in position.

EIGHTH OBSERVATION: The English general gave battle at Waterloo on the 18th. This course was contrary to the interests of his country, and to the general plan of campaign adopted by the Allies; it violated all the rules of the war. It was not in the interests of England, who needs so many men to recruit her armies for India, her American colonies, and her vast establishments to expose herself, wantonly, to a murderous struggle, which could lose her the only army she had, and, at the least, cost her the flower of her manhood. The Allies' plan of campaign consisted in acting en masse and in not getting engaged in detail. Nothing was more contrary to their interests and their plan than to risk the success of their cause in a hazardous battle, with more or less equal forces, where the odds were against them. If the Anglo-Dutch army had been destroyed at Waterloo, of what avail would have been the large number of armies that were preparing the cross the Rhine, the Alps, and the Pyrenees?

The English general, in deciding to accept battle at Waterloo, only based his decision on the cooperation of the Prussians; but this cooperation could not come about until the afternoon; he therefore remained exposed and alone, from 4 o'clock in the morning until 5 o'clock in the afternoon, that is to say, for thirteen hours. Ordinarily a battle only lasts six hours. So this cooperation was illusory.

But, in relying on the cooperation of the Prussians, he assumed that the whole French army was facing him; and, if that were so, he was counting on defending his ground, for thirteen hours, with 90,000 troops of diverse nationality against an army of 104,000 Frenchmen. This calculation was manifestly unsound; he could not have maintained his position for three hours; everything would have been over by 8 o'clock in the morning, and the Prussians would have arrived only to be taken in the rear. Within a single day both the armies would have been destroyed. If he relied on the fact that part of the French army would follow up the Prussian army, in accordance with the rules of war, it must then have been evident to him that he could expect no assistance from it, and that the Prussians, defeated at Ligny, having lost between 25,000 and 30,000 men on the battlefield, and having had 20,000 scattered, pursued by 35,000 to 40,000 victorious Frenchmen, would not have parted with a man, and would have considered themselves scarcely strong enough to hold their own. In that case, the Anglo-Dutch army would have had to bear alone the impact of 69,000 Frenchmen throughout the day of the 18th, and there is not an Englishman who would not concede that the outcome of such a struggle could be in no doubt – their army was not constituted to withstand the shock of the imperial army for four hours.

Throughout the night of 17th to 18th, the weather was horrible, which rendered the ground impassable until 9 o'clock in the morning. The loss of these six hours, since dawn, was all to the enemy's advantage, but could its general let the issue of such a conflict depend upon the probable state of the weather during the night of the 17th to 18th? Marshal Grouchy, with 34,000 men and 108 guns, accomplished the impossible by being, neither on the field of battle at Mont-St-Jean nor at Wavre during the day of the 18th. But had the English general the personal assurance of this Marshal that he would blunder about in such a peculiar manner? Marshal Grouchy's conduct was just as unpredictable as if his army had experienced an earthquake on the way which had swallowed it up.

To sum up, if Marshal Grouchy had been on the battlefield of Mont-St-Jean, as the English general and the Prussian general expected, throughout the night of the 17th to 18th, and if the weather had allowed the French army to get into position for battle at 4 o'clock in the morning, the Anglo-Dutch army would have been cut up and scattered before 7 o'clock; it would have been totally defeated. And, if the weather had not allowed the French army to take up its battle stations until 10 o'clock, by 1 o'clock in the afternoon the Anglo-Dutch army would have met its fate; the remnants of it would have been hurled beyond the forest or in the direction of Hal, and there would have been plenty of time, in the evening, to march on to meet Marshal Blücher, and make him suffer a similar fate. If Marshal Grouchy had camped before Wavre on the night of the 17th to 18th, the Prussian army would not have been able to detach any force to save the English army, and the latter would have been completely defeated by the 69,000 Frenchmen opposing it.

The Mont-St-Jean position was ill chosen. The first essential of a battlefield is not to have any defiles in its rear. During the battle, the English general did not know how to use his numerous cavalry to advantage; he did not judge that he should and would be attacked on his left; he believed that it would come on his right. In spite of the diversion effected in his favour by General Bülow's 30,000 Prussians, he would twice during the day have carried out his retreat, if he had been able to do so. So, in the event – oh, strange irony of human affairs! – the bad choice of his battlefield, which made all retreat impossible, was the cause of his success!

NINTH OBSERVATION. It will be asked: what ought the English general to have done after the Battle of Ligny and the engagement at Quatre Bras? Posterity will not be in any doubt. He ought to have crossed the forest of Soignes on the night of the 17th to 18th, by the Charleroi road; the Prussian army ought similarly to have crossed it by the Wavre road; the two armies ought to have effected their junction on Brussels at first light and have left rearguards to defend the forest. He should have gained a few days to give time to the Prussians, dispersed by the battle of Ligny, to rejoin their army; reinforced himself by fourteen English regiments, which were in garrison in the fortresses of Belgium or had just disembarked at Ostend on returning from America, and have let me manoeuvre as I liked.

Would I, with an army of 100,000 men, have crossed the forest of Soignes, in order to attack, on issuing from it, the two armies joined together, more than 200,000 strong and in position? That would certainly have been the most advantageous thing that could have happened to the Allies. Would I have been content to take up a position myself? My inaction could not have lasted long, for 300,000 Russians, Austrians, and Bavarians, etc., had arrived on the Rhine. They would be on the Marne within a few weeks, which would force me to hasten to the rescue of my capital.

It was then that the Anglo-Prussian army should have marched and joined up with the Allies before Paris. It would have been running no risk, would have suffered no losses, would have acted in conformity with the interest of the English nation, the general war plans adopted by the Allies, and the rules of the art of war. From the 15th to the 18th the Duke of Wellington manoeuvred continuously as I wanted him to; he did nothing that I feared he might. The English infantry was firm and sound. The cavalry could have done better. The Anglo-Dutch army was saved twice during the day by the Prussians; the first time, before 3 o'clock, by the arrival of General Bülow, with 30,000 men, and the second time by the arrival of Marshal Blücher, with 31,000 men. During that day, 69,000 Frenchmen defeated 120,000 men. Victory was snatched from them between 8 o'clock and 9 o'clock, by 150,000 men.

One can imagine the reaction of the people of London at the moment when they heard of the catastrophe that had befallen their army and learned that their best blood had been shed in the cause of kings against peoples, of privilege against equality, of oligarchs against liberals, of the principles of the Holy Alliance against the Soveignty of the People!

INDEX

Aboukir, battle of *110, 113–26*
Acre, siege of *110, 127, 130–4*
Albania *117*
Albitte, Antoine *63, 64, 70, 74*
Aleppo *127, 128*
Alexander I, Tsar of Russia *204, 212, 218, 219, 224, 227*
Alexander the Great *22–5, 123–4, 209, 217*
Alexandria *23, 29, 32–3, 107, 109, 114–20, 128*
Alvinzi, Marshal *94, 95–6, 97, 98, 99, 101, 102, 103, 104–5, 106*
Ambiorix *27*
Angoulême, Duke d' *243, 244, 249*
Antommarchio, Francesco *18*
Antony, Mark *28*
Arcole, battle of *94–106*
Arçon, General d' *75*
Aremburg, Prince of *211*
Austerlitz, battle of *34, 204–6*
Austria
 and Russia *20–1*
Avignon *59–60, 64, 68, 74*

Barbaroux, Charles *64, 66*
Barras, Paul *37, 38, 74, 78, 87, 88, 137, 142, 143, 148*
Barré, Captain *115*
Bathurst, Lord *17*
Beauharnais, Madame de *see* Josephine, Empress
Beauharnais, Prince Eugène de *91–2, 93, 168, 170, 195, 213, 226*
Beauharnais, Stephanie *210–11*
Belgium *172–3, 234, 248, 251–2, 285*
Bellegarde, Field-Marshal *244*
Belliard, General *112*
Bernadotte, Jean (later Charles XIV of Sweden) *34, 141, 149, 168–71*
Berruyer, General *89*
Berthier, Alexandre *136, 162*
Bertrand, Henri-Gratien, Count *17, 18, 233, 235, 269*
Bertrand, Madame *17–18*
Berwick, James Fitzjames, Duke of *31*
Bessus (Artaxerxes IV) *23*
Blücher, Marshal (Prince of

Wahlstadt) *34, 248, 252, 254–5, 256, 265, 270, 271–3, 277, 278, 280, 281, 282, 284, 285*
Boghese, Princess (Pauline Bonaparte) *166, 167*
Bonaparte, Abbé Gregorio *48*
Bonaparte, Carlo *48–9, 52*
Bonaparte, Guiseppe *47*
Bonaparte, Jérôme, King of Westphalia *36, 274, 275*
Bonaparte, Joseph *139, 149, 168, 187, 216, 217*
Bonaparte, Lucien *139, 140, 142, 150, 151, 152–4, 247*
Bonaparte, Marie-Anne-Elisa *51*
Bonaparte, Marie-Annunciade-Caroline *145, 246–7*
Bonaparte, Marie-Laetitia Ramolino *48, 49, 50*
Bonaparte family *47–9, 58*
Borghese, Prince Camillo *167*
Borodino, battle of (Moskva) *218, 219*
Boudet, General *180, 181*
Boulay *142, 150*
Bourbon, Constable de *47*
Bourmont, Lieutenant-General *280*
Boutot *148*
Brissot, Jacques *64, 66–7*
Brueys, Admiral *107, 117, 118, 120, 122, 170*
Bubna, Count *229, 230*
Bülow, General Friedrich Wilhelm von *263, 264–5, 266, 268, 269, 271, 272, 273, 275, 281, 282, 285*
Bussy, Count de *275*
Buzot, François *66*

Caesar, Julius *26–9, 44, 206*
Cairo *109, 118, 119*
Caldiero *99, 100, 101, 103, 104, 106*
Cambacérès, Jean-Jacques-Regis de, Duke of Parma *188, 238*
Cambronne, General *242*
Campbell, Sir Neil *240*
Campo Formio *172, 173, 174*
Carnot, Count *238*
Carteaux, General Jean *58, 60, 61, 63, 64, 74, 77, 89*
Carthage *25–6*

Castiglione, Pierre Augerau, Duc de *34, 205*
Catinat, Nicolas *30*
Cato *29*
Cervoni, Colonel *80*
Chabert, Lieutenant-General *243*
Chambon, Aubin *38*
Charlemagne *189, 190*
Charles, Archduke of Austria *40, 204, 206, 213*
Charles V, Emperor *78*
Charles XII, King of Sweden *42–3*
Chazal *150*
Cherkaoui, Sheik *109*
Chichagov, Pavel *35*
Choiseul, Etienne, Duc de *58*
Cicero, Quintus *27*
Cleitus *23*
Clouet, Colonel *280*
Colbert, General *269, 275*
Concordat of 1801 *185–7, 240*
Condé, Louis, Prince de *123–4*
Condorcet, Marquis de *64, 66*
Constant (Napoleon's valet) *18*
Constaninople *20, 129–30*
Constituent Assembly *55, 71–2, 85*
Constitution of 1791 *71, 85–6*
Convention, the *68, 84–7*
Corfu *116, 117, 119*
Corsica *50–8, 136*
Council of Ancients *142, 144, 146, 147, 148, 149, 153, 154, 155*
Council of the Five Hundred *142, 149, 150, 151–3, 154*
Crancé, Edmond Dubois de *63, 64*
Crusades *108, 127*
Cyrus the Great *23*

Dabrowski, General *22*
Dalmatia, Duke of (Marshal Soult) *34, 216, 237, 238, 245, 246, 252, 263, 265, 275, 280*
Danton, Georges Jacques *84*
Darius III *23*
Daumont, General *259, 260, 263, 264, 266*
Davidowich *96, 97, 104, 105, 106*
Davout, Louis, Prince of Eckmühl *34, 204, 219*

Debon, General *134*
Decius, Emperor of Rome *66*
Demasis *52, 53*
Denmark *230*
Desaix, General Louis *33*
Desirée, Queen of Sweden *168–70*
Devaux, General *266*
Directory, the *137–8, 140, 142, 148, 172, 175, 176, 201*
Doppet, General *77*
Drouot, General *248, 271*
Ducos, Roger *137, 142, 148, 153, 155*
Dugear, General *58*
Dugommier *77, 78–9, 81, 83*
Duhesme, General *268, 274*
Dumouriez, General Charles François *160–1*
Dundas, Sir David *56*
Duphot, General *168*
Duroc, Gérard-Christophe-Michel, Duke of Friuli *111*
Duvos, Roger *149*
Dyrrachium *128*

Egypt *45, 107–12, 114–20, 171, 174*
  and Syria *126, 128, 129*
Elba *237, 240, 242*
Elliott, Sir Gilbert (Baron Minto) *57*
Enghein, Louis-Antoine-Henri, Duke d' *158–64*
England
  and Corsica *56–8*
  troop losses *46*
Essling, battle of *191*
Eugène, Prince of Savoy *22, 30–1, 209*
Excelmans, General *270*

Ferdinand, King of Naples *39, 190*
Ferdinand and Isabella of Spain *20*
Ferdinand VII, King of Spain *162, 165, 166–7, 212*
Fontainebleau, treaty of *237, 240*
Fouché, Joseph, Duke of Otranto *141, 143, 149, 238, 239*
France
  troop losses *45–6*
Francis I, King of France *78*
Frederick the Great, King of Prussia *22, 31, 207, 209, 217*
Frederick William II, King of Prussia *34*
Frederick William III, King of Prussia *229*
Fréron *78, 90*
Friant, General *272*

Gantheaume, Admiral *177*
Gasparin *37–8, 74, 75*
Gassendi, Colonel *74–5*
Gaudin, Emile *150*
Gaul *27–8*
Germany, campaign of 1796 *40–1*
Gilly, General *243*
Girondins *67, 72*
Gohier *137, 142, 148*
Gourgaud, General Gaspard *17, 18*
Gregory VII, Pope *190*
Grenier, Lieutenant-General *237*
Grouchy, Marshal *254, 255, 262, 263–4, 265, 266, 269–70, 271, 272, 274, 275–6, 280, 281, 284*
Grunstein, Colonel *161*
Guieux, General *103*
Gustavus Adolphus, King of Sweden *22, 30, 209*
Guyot, General *259, 269, 273, 281*

Hannibal *25–6, 43, 206, 209, 217*
Hatry, General *93*
Haugwitz, Count *205*
Hedouville, General *175, 182*
Henin, General d' *280*
Henry IV, King of France *242*
Hercule, Major *105*
Hood, Rear-Admiral Samuel *55, 79, 82*
Hougoumont, Château of *256, 257, 265, 272*

Italian campaigns *31–2, 39–40, 174*
Italian nation *193–5*

Jabobins *86, 142*
John, Archduke of Austria *189*
Josephine, Empress (Madame de Beauharnais) *91–2, 210–215*
Julius II, Pope *189*

Kellerman, General *38, 259, 260, 262, 269*
Kléber, General Jean-Baptiste *107, 112, 174*
Kurakin, Prince *215*

Labienus *29*
Laborde, Lieutenant-General *243*
Lacroix, Charles *172*
Lafond *89, 90, 91*
Lagarde *155*
Lallemand, Brigadier-General *266*
Laplace, Pierre de *52, 55*
Lapoype, General *74*
Laraveillière-Lepeaux, Louis-Marie de *85*

Las Cases, Emmanuel de *17, 18*
Latouche Treville, Admiral *180, 181*
Launay, Brigadier-General *98–9*
Le Clerc, Victor-Emmanuel *179–80, 181, 182–3*
Lebanon, Mount *126, 127, 128*
Lecourbe, General *276*
Lefebvre, General *146, 147, 197*
Legion of Honour *198–9*
Legislative Assembly *71, 72*
Leipzig, battle of *228–36*
Levenhaupt, General *42, 43*
Ligny, battle of *280–2, 284*
Little Gibraltar (Fort Mulgrave) *76, 77, 78*
Lobau, Count de *264–5, 266, 272, 274*
Longwood *18, 277*
Louis XVI *55, 71*
Louis XVIII *162, 243, 244, 247*
Louisa, Queen of Prussia *230*
Lyons *60, 74, 136–7, 242, 243, 250, 251, 252*

Macdonald, Jacques-Etienne-Joseph-Alexandre, Duke of Tarente *225*
Mailly, Staff-Officer *131–2*
Malbosquet, Fort *76, 78, 80*
Mantua *99, 100, 104*
Marengo, battle of *171, 209*
Maret, Hughes-Bernard, Duke of Bassano *155–6, 172, 233, 234*
Marie-Louise, Empress *212–15*
Maria Luisa, Queen of Eturia *166*
Maria Theresa, Empress of Austria *20*
Marseilles *58, 59, 63, 64, 65, 67–70, 74, 112, 136*
Martinique *183–4*
Masséna, André *41, 42, 95–6, 98, 105, 106, 170, 204, 206, 243–4*
Mazepa, Ivan *42*
Melas, Michael von *33*
Menou, Jacques François de *87, 88, 90, 107, 110, 112, 174*
Metternich, Prince *213, 228, 229, 233*
Milhaud, General *261, 265–6, 266, 268*
Montebello, Jean Lannes, Duc de *34*
Montholon, General Charles-Tristan de *17*
Montholon, Madame de *18*
Morand, Lieutenant-General *268, 275*
Moreau, General Jean Victor *40, 138, 139, 144, 145, 147, 182, 215*
Moscow
  burning of *218, 220–1, 223–7*

retreat from *223–7*
Moulins *137, 142, 143–4, 148, 150*
Mountain party *66, 67, 69, 72*
Muiron, Captain *79*
Murat, Joachim *39, 87–8, 145, 147, 150, 166, 198, 219, 244, 245–7, 248*

Naples *39*
Nearchus *25*
Nègre, General *274*
Nelson, Horatio, Lord *38, 114, 115, 120, 122, 123, 139, 140*
Ney, Marshal, Prince of the Moskowa *34–5, 219, 257, 259, 263, 265, 279*

O'Hara, General *76, 77*
O'Meara, Barry *18*
Orléans, Philippe, Duc d' *30*

Pacca, Cardinal *200*
Paget, Lord *273*
Pajol, General *270*
Paoli, Pascal *49, 53, 54, 55, 56, 57, 65, 73*
Paris *36, 250, 252*
Parmenio *23*
Pedaduc *52, 53*
Peine, Brigadier-General *276*
Percymont, General *136*
Perré, Rear-Admiral *132, 133, 134*
Persian Empire *22–3*
Peter I of Russia (the Great) *42, 43*
Phelippeaux *52–3*
Picton, Sir Thomas *258, 266*
Pietro, Cardinal *200*
Pirch, General *270, 271*
Pitt, William, the Younger *172–3, 174*
Pius VI, Pope *189*
Pius VII, Pope *186, 193*
Poland *42, 223, 224, 227*
Pompey *28, 29*
Poniatowski, Marshal Jozef Anton, Prince *219, 220*
Portuguese campaign *41–2*
Porus *23–5*
Prison reform *200–3*
Privy Council *202–3*

Ragusa, Duke of *36, 204, 206, 231, 232*
Rapp, General *275, 276*
Réal *141, 143*
Reggio, Duke of *222, 231*
Regnier *142*
Reille, Count *248, 260*
Reynier, General *224–5*
Richelieu, Cardinal *242*
Rigaud, General *175, 176, 183*
Robert, General *102–3*
Robespierre, Maximilien *66, 69, 84*
Roederer *139, 143*
Rogers, Admiral *113*
Rome *26, 28*
Rome, King of (Napoleon-François-Charles-Joseph) *195*
Rovigo, Anne-Marie-Jean-René, Duke of, *17, 238*
Russia *42–3, 45–6*
war in *218–22*

Sahuguet, General *177*
Saicetti *74*
Saint-Etienne, Jean Rabaut *67*
Saint-Vincent, Admiral Lord *113–14*
Santo Domingo *175–84*
Sardinia *54, 65, 73, 114*
Scherer *92–3*
Schwarzenberg, Prince *212, 213, 215, 222, 224–5, 252*
Schwarzenberg, Princess *215*
Scipio *29*
Sieyès, Abbé *90, 137–8, 141, 142, 143, 144, 148, 149, 153, 154, 155, 156*
Smith, Sir Sidney *81, 130, 139*
Smolensk *219, 221–2, 223, 224, 226*
Södermanland, Oscar, Prince of *168–9*
Soignes, forest of *256, 257, 270, 281, 285*
Spain, war in *216–18*
Stanislaus I, King of Poland *42*
Stateira *25*
Subervie, General *263*
Suchet, Marshal *237, 251, 276*
Syria *126–34*

Talleyrand-Périgord, Charles,

Duke of *116, 140, 141, 143, 156, 162, 244*
Tchitchagov, Admiral *221, 222, 225*
Terror, the *67*
Thielman, General *270–1, 275–6*
Thumery, Marquis de *161*
Tolly, Barclay de *219*
Toulon *36–8, 55, 63, 112, 115, 116*
siege of *47, 58, 74–83*
Toussaint-Louverture, rebellion of *175–84*
Treviso, Edouard-Adolphe-Casimir, Duke of *204, 205, 206, 231, 281*
Truguet, Admiral *54, 73*
Turenne, Henri de la Tour d'Auvergne, Vicomte de *30, 209*

Valençay, treaty of *167*
Vandamme, General *230*
Vaublanc *86, 90–1*
Vaubois *99*
Vendôme, Louis Joseph, Duc de *30*
Vergniaud, Pierre *66*
Verona *97–8, 99, 100, 101, 106*
Vicenza *97, 106*
Vicenza, Duke of *229, 233, 234, 236*
Victor Amadeus II, King of Italy *31*
Vienna, Congress of *237, 238, 247*
Villaret-Joyeuse, Admiral *125, 179–82*
Villars, Claude, Duc de *31*
Villeneuve, Rear-Admiral *122, 125*
Villeroi, François, Duc de *30*
Vincent, Colonel *176, 178–9*
Vitrolles, Baron de *243, 244*
Volney *139*

Wagram, battle of *192*
Waterloo, battle of (Mont St Jean) *254–77*
Weimar, Charles Augustus, Duke of *34*
Wellington, Arthur Wellesley, Duke of *41, 248, 249, 252, 256, 257, 263, 270, 277, 278, 282, 285*
Wrede, General *231*
Wurmser, Marshall Dagobert Siegmond von *94, 95, 99, 100*